BACK IN THE HIGH LIFE

Also by Alan Clayson:

Call up the Groups:
The Golden Age of British Beat, 1962–67

BACK IN THE HIGH LIFE

A Biography of Steve Winwood

Alan Clayson

SIDGWICK & JACKSON
LONDON

To A.B., C.C., M.D. and R.F of Turnpike, runners–up in the
Battle of the Bands tournament at the University of Reading,
Rag Week 1973

First published in Great Britain in 1988 by Sidgwick & Jackson Limited

Copyright © 1988 by Alan Clayson

ISBN 0-283-99640-4

Typeset by Hewer Text Composition Services, Edinburgh
*Printed in Great Britain by Butler & Tanner Limited, Frome and London
for Sidgwick & Jackson Limited
1 Tavistock Chambers, Bloomsbury Way
London WC1A 2SG*

'I walked along the river. I thought it would be better to be a bit of driftwood, no decisions, no nothing. I got back on the path again, before I started to take myself seriously.'

Hunter Davies, *Here We Go Round the Mulberry Bush*

CONTENTS

Acknowledgements
Somebody Helped Me

I wish to express my deepest gratitude to John Tobler for his encouragement and practical help with this project – and, indeed, with other ventures, quixotic and otherwise, over the years.

I am also grateful to Susan Hill for patience and understanding that went beyond her duties as commissioning editor during the writing of this book.

Let's have a special round of applause too for Jim Simpson, not only for his splendid photographic archives but also for his insight into the Birmingham pop scene. Let's hear it too for Steve Maggs and Paul Tucker, who were always on hand at a moment's notice.

I owe a particular debt to the following for their assistance and for trusting me with archive material: John and Penny Baldwin, Colin Baylis, Birmingham Central Library Local Studies Department, Stuart and Kathryn Booth, Rob Bradford, Trevor Dann, Peter Doggett, Ian Drummond, Ross Fergusson, Pete Frame, Anne Freer, Allan Jones, Garry Jones, Graham Larkbey, Colin Miles, Darrell Paddick, Sarah Parish and Michael Towers.

I have also drawn from conversations with Phil Capaldi, Rees Davies, Spencer Davis, Rob Evans, Tom Knowles, Judith Maycock, Jessica Palin, Eric Roberts, Vivian Stanshall and Pete York – and thank them for their candour.

Thanks is also due in varying degrees to B & T Typewriters, Maurice Bacon, Roger Barnes, Dave Berry, Angela Bettis, Clive Chandler, Terry Clarke, Liz Coley, Mike Cooper, Ron Cooper, Greg and Debi Daniels, Kevin Delaney, Mark Ellen, Tim Fagan, Eric Goulden, Paul Hearne, Debbie Hodder, Matt Holland, Marsha Hunt, Sandra Hunt, Brian Leafe, Yvonne Lambourne, Mark Lewisohn, Kenny Lynch, Jim McCarty, Tom McGuinness, Sandy Newman, Russell Newmark, Martin Nichols, Andy Pegg,

Ray Phillips, Angela Pickard, Ray Pinfold, Reg Presley, Gail Richards, Steve Rowley, Charles and Deborah Salt, Paul Samwell-Smith, Lord David Sutch, John Townsend and Ron Watts. It may be obvious to the reader that I have also received much information from sources that prefer not to be mentioned. Nevertheless, I want to thank them.

I also offer sincere thanks to my mother, who gave me her typewriter, and my father, who proferred a matching swivel chair. There are, too, Jack and Harry, whose dreams were disturbed by the clacking of the typewriter into the graveyard hours – and Inese who bore with unbearable sorrow.

Prologue

'Back in the High Life Again'

In the early spring of 1986, sessions for what I hoped would become my second LP were taking place in a Chatham attic. Assisting me were two members of the Len Bright Combo – drummer Bruce Brand and, on guitar and bass, Eric Goulden. Scorning a proper studio with pound signs hanging over every note, Eric as producer was aiming for the home-made mono passion of the Combo's debut album, which had cost next to nothing to record using anachronistic electronic paraphernalia.

On paper, our project looked interesting. The younger Bruce had been a cult celebrity with the Milkshakes while Eric and I – both thirty-four – had nearly Hit the Big Time as pop stars in the late seventies. To an extent, Eric had actually Made It when signed to Stiff Records as Wreckless Eric. Over at Virgin with Clayson and the Argonauts, I hadn't been quite so lucky.

While we were grappling with the Combo's Heath Robinson equipment, the number one single in the United States was 'Higher Love' by Steve Winwood who wasn't that much older than Goulden and I. When we were sitting our eleven plus at junior school, he'd been in the third year at his Birmingham comprehensive. However, rather than being steered towards university, his already recognizable talent was seized and exploited almost as soon as his million-dollar voice broke. No cute showbusiness brat with top hat and cane, he was a pop scene fixture with the Spencer Davis Group while envious shorter-haired boys of the same age – Peter Gabriel, Mark Knopfler and Robert Palmer among them – pored over logarithms and the Hanoverian claim to the English throne. Furthermore, at a pace which seemed to involve vanishing from pop for years on end, Winwood ended 1986 nominated for six Grammy awards – the music industry equivalent of Oscars – and a

ix

Virgin recording contract of considerably more import than the Argonauts' one-shot single deal eight years earlier.

For ten pence at a car boot sale I'd brought an ex-jukebox copy of 'Higher Love' – almost for old times' sake. Like most other British rock 'n' rollers, I hadn't listened to much of Steve's music since Traffic, the group he formed after leaving Spencer Davis. His first solo album, released in 1977, had been at odds with punk – a sub-cultural explosion which never caught on in North America as it did in Great Britain. Overshadowed by the Sex Pistols' headline-hogging outrage, Winwood's effort was categorized by many as another bland exercise in treated sound for the upwardly mobile. In 1967, a twenty-year-old Steve had protested: 'There are a lot of things that hang me up about the pop scene, including the idea that you are only catering for people between the ages of fourteen and twenty-one. There are a lot of people outside that age limit and I hope we are reaching some of them.'[1] In the United Kingdom ten years later 'people outside that age limit' – the older end – were virtually the only ones he was reaching. Certainly by comparison with the ongoing 'teenage anarchy' he was more a country squire – albeit one who would more likely be engrossed in sequencer programming and digital mixing in his private studio than in tractors or combined harvesters. While embracing aspects of the smoothest modern soul music, Winwood also planted a foot in the 'adult-orientated rock' camp along with Dire Straits, Phil Collins, and, an old friend, Eric Clapton. Cultivated, polished, pleasant – Steve's self-produced and infrequent records were never expected to be astounding by those who had not heard them.

During the four-year silence preceding the award-winning *Back in the High Life* – from which 'Higher Love' was lifted – 'it had been rather a difficult time for me in one way or another. I've been through lots of changes. This new record is a departure for me . . . in as much as I've made a conscious effort to get involved with different musicians, engineers and producers. I'm just really a very slow worker. I thought, mistakenly, that working with other people might've sped the process up. It didn't.'[2] Though some drum machine and sequencer dabbling plus other preliminaries were undertaken on his Cotswolds farm, these were copied on to floppy disc for demonstration purposes when, following a hunch, he decided to cut the bulk of *Back in the High Life* in New York which, he enthused, was 'a fantastic place to work. There's a lot of energy, a lot of music there, a lot of great players. There's a great drive to get things done which I find very attractive . . . maybe "attractive" isn't the right word.'[2]

He laid out a six-figure sum and chose the then unfashionable Unique Recording Studio off Times Square for most of the LP, whose inner sleeve credits read – in pop terms – as voluminously as the cast for *Ben Hur*. Co-directing operations was Russ Titelman, who – as a humble session guitarist – had first met Winwood in 1977. Two years later, Titelman had worked with George Harrison on the ex-Beatle's eponymous album on which Steve had also played. Other landmarks in Titelman's career included producing records by his brother-in-law Ry Cooder, Christine McVie – former girlfriend of Spencer Davis – Miriam Makeba and Rufus, a US band whose singer, Chaka Khan, he called on for the quasi-gospel harmonies on 'Higher Love'.

As well as the cream of New York's session musicians and technicians, more notable bit-part players were, on rhythm guitar, Nile Rodgers from Chic who'd supervised David Bowie's 1984 album *Let's Dance*, and Arif Mardin who'd produced the Bee Gees' first ventures into the disco idiom in 1975. Four years earlier, he'd done likewise for soul star Aretha Franklin, using the Muscle Shoals studio rhythm section who were to tour the world later as part of Traffic. Among representatives of white America on *Back in the High Life* were disco singer Dan Hartman and, from the Eagles, guitarist Joe Walsh. As a nod to Steve's increasingly more distant English roots appeared the names of lyricist Vivian Stanshall and engineer John Clarke, who had been Winwood's Sancho Panza since adolescence.

Buried among the miscellaneous fourteen singled out for 'special thanks' was Steve's ex-manager Chris Blackwell, whose Island record company was on the verge of losing Winwood who'd been on the label for over twenty years. From my outsider's perspective I could see why. Aged sixteen in 1967, I'd half expected anyway not to receive a reply when I applied for the post that had arisen in Traffic when guitarist and songwriter Dave Mason first left. They were looking, apparently, for someone with imagination rather than ability. Two decades on, my next letter to Island – typewritten this time – was to the press department requesting help with Winwood's discography. Having had no acknowledgement of this after a fortnight, I telephoned someone of high office there who, I'd been told, was a 'good bloke'. My own dealings with him tended to contradict this impression. As he was busy, he asked me to call again 'anytime on Monday'. I did – only to be told that he was 'on the other line' and, finally, 'Ring again tomorrow.' Perhaps it was journalistic instinct that caused this reluctance to answer my letter or return my calls. All the same, it saddened me – particularly as

I'd been an admirer and consumer of much of Island's output since it was able to break from its lease agreement with Fontana in 1967.

With Winwood, gone, a vista might have opened for repackagings of every Island recording on which he'd ever breathed. However, as complaints in *Record Collector* magazine in 1987 testified, not only compact discs but even Traffic vinyl was unobtainable except on import, while the pressing quality of available Island reissues was unsatisfactory. Pre-recorded cassettes also left much to be desired – one Traffic album, for instance, began with an unscripted computer blipping. Naturally the firm refuted this sullying of its good name, but still *Record Collector* readers such as Mrs Brenda Cooper of Huntingdon stayed 'disillusioned with Island, a label I used to class as one of the best'.[3]

Perhaps in accord with her opinion, and also with those of Steve Winwood and me, further Island artists fled, including John Cale, Tom Waits and Robert Palmer. A greater blow than these three put together would have been, but for his death in 1981, reggae apostle Bob Marley's transfer to Polygram. Referring to Blackwell as 'Chris Whitehell'[4] behind his back, Marley and his Wailers backing group questioned Island's competence in channelling their music back to the black market for which it was intended.

Yet it wasn't a case of rats leaving a sinking ship, for Island continues to thrive. Big names signed in 1987 were the Christians, who immediately justified the 'Artist and Repertoire' section's faith with a hit record; Aswad, reggae methuselahs, who topped the charts in March 1988; and Andy Gibb, younger brother of the negotiable Bee Gees, who, but for a fatal heart attack, might have filled the marketing gap left by that schoolgirls' heart-throb of the seventies, David Cassidy.

Branching out, there is talk of book publishing – maybe Steve Winwood's biography is on the cards. Already Island Films have presented a self-congratulatory television special – with a large helping of Winwood footage – as well as works by the Comic Strip and, Chris Blackwell's own baby, 'Good to Go', which, as he'd done with Marley, brought new black pop to the wider world. Though periodically glutted with white 'rock', Island, probably more than any other independent label, had always championed 'ethnic' sounds; its most prestigious coup in the eighties was Nigerian 'High Life' grandee King Sunny Ade. The label's Mango subsidiary was also revitalized specifically for less universally accessible African music and hard reggae. However, the ace in the pack in Island mainstream pop was Irish quartet U2, the toast of

North America, whose vocalist – for want of anyone better – had been proclaimed a New Rock Messiah.

In 1981, Blackwell had discovered U2 in a small club as he had young Steve Winwood seventeen years earlier. Evolving into an international star, Steve had outgrown Island well before his contract had expired. Time was when deals between entrepreneurs and artists could be mapped out on a serviette over lunch, as was Brian Epstein's with Billy J. Kramer. Now the legal profession had insinuated its complex mumbo-jumbo into pop – so much so that acting for Steve in Europe in Blackwell's stead was hot-shot lawyer Paul Rodwell, who had defended Innervision Records against Wham! and, later, ZTT against Frankie Goes to Holly-wood's Holly Johnson. Relinquishing the reins of Winwood's management, it must have felt strange for Chris – so long Aaron to Steve's Moses – to discuss business complications pertaining to *Back in the High Life*, the last new Winwood album for Island, with his boy's new Californian representative, Nu-Visions Management Ltd.

A more absolute estrangement from Steve's old life was his divorce in December 1986 after ten years with his first American wife, Nicole: 'the less said about that marriage the better'.[5] Needless to say, the tabloid press made a meal of this not uncommon middle-aged mishap – the most pungent whiff of public scandal ever to involve publicity-shy Winwood. To Fleet Street's disappointment, Steve didn't swap thirty-eight-year-old Nicole for two nineteens. Instead, on 19 January 1987, in a New York church, he married Eugenia 'Gina' Crafton, the twenty-four-year-old 'scarlet woman' cited as co-respondent by Nicole's brief. A respectable business administration graduate from Tennessee, Gina 'isn't really interested in my concerts at all but she is really great at checking my accounts'.[5] The couple's daughter and Winwood's first child, Marie Clair, was born in June – yes, I can count too – in the Barbara Mandrell suite in a Nashville hospital, her father witnessing the delivery.

When pestered by the paparazzi, he'd overcome earlier inhibitions born of 'an inbred hatred of being interviewed',[6] and refined an unblinking self-assurance as nicotine-stained fingers scribbled down quotable jocularities. They could write what they liked about him, Gina and Nicole. He'd been overlooked for Live Aid, but nothing could take from him the two Grammies he'd won at the Hollywood Palladium from the six possibilities judged by the National Academy of Recording Arts and Sciences. Yet, even with *Back in the High Life* as Album of the *Decade*, Winwood had kept a grip on the reality of the rich. No more a Gloucestershire gentleman-farmer, he'd allocated a cool half-million pounds for a ranch in his new wife's home state while keeping his eyes peeled for places of comparable investment in the Big Apple – as well as back in the old country because, said Vivian Stanshall, 'he really likes England. He must be crazy for God knows what it's cost him.' Though he'd insisted that he was 'not that flush',[7] his pragmatic 1987 Christmas present to himself was, rather than risk reassembling the components of his English studio in the States, a spanking new Mitsubishi thirty-two track system. Like George Harrison, Winwood now owned one of the world's most sophisticated personal recording studios.

He was now on a plateau of wealth where hit singles are mere sideshows, and the Winwood name cropped up more often in high society gossip columns than in *Melody Maker*. In October 1987 at a £100-a-head charity party for the rehabilitation of heroin addicts, Steve and 'young Nashville socialite' Gina were spotted among the two hundred other big-names-in-good-cause in the plush London hotel. Conspicuously, they were keeping a wide berth of the first Mrs Winwood, despite her anxiety to forgive and forget. Three weeks later, at another upper-crust party, Nicole posed for a piquant *Daily Express* photograph with Patti Boyd, former spouse of both George Harrison and Eric Clapton, and – looking rather down-in-the-mouth – philandering Rolling Stone Bill Wyman's ex-girlfriend, Astrid.

Nevertheless, for all this 'Hollywood wives' *vita nuova* and his altered commitments, the changeless and the changed Steve Winwood still maintained many contacts with his past. Shortly after the heroin do, he was sighted thumbing through a vintage record stall's dog-eared wares at folk-rock godfathers Fairport Convention's annual reunion jig-and-reel at the Oxfordshire village of Cropredy, not far from his old farm. Out of the blue he'd also rolled up with an acoustic guitar for a floor spot, to the disbelief of a Birmingham folk club audience, reinforcing a statement that 'you can't really say that you have to play one thousand times better in front of twenty thousand than you do in front of twenty'.[7] At such lowly functions, though he was willing to talk about himself in modest understatement, he seemed quite accustomed to those making a fuss of him suddenly falling silent in that old manner that every survivor of the sixties' beat boom had come to identify – a certain awe mingled with a hint of scepticism, as though you weren't quite real.

In Britain, where 'Higher Love' had meant hardly a light,

Winwood was never as good as he'd been in the sixties. 'I had a long conversation with Van Morrison the other day,' he grumbled, 'and we found that we have that in common. He's always been told that *Astral Weeks*, which he'd made a dozen years ago, is his best record. How's he going to beat that? I have the same problem with what the Spencer Davis Group achieved.'[8] All it took, it seemed, was for a swarthy youth to take his jeans off in a launderette in a television commercial, and Britain in the mid-eighties was awash with nostalgia for the sixties. Soon one in every four records in the charts would be either a reissue or a revival of an old song. Resulting directly from snippet advertisement coverage were UK second comings for records by Ben E. King, Percy Sledge, Nina Simone and, from even further back, Eddie Cochran. Both Rufus Thomas' 'Walkin' the Dog' and the Dave Clark Five's 'Catch Us if You Can' were used to sell shoes. In 1987 Clark's old flame, Cathy McGowan – excitable compère of the mid-sixties' TV pop programme *Ready Steady Go* – arrived from her exile of Twickenham motherhood to present an afternoon chat show.

Many pop stars in middle life re-entered the Top Fifty arena with their latest releases. As well as perennials like professional family man Paul McCartney, the eternal Cliff Richard and former *Ready Steady Go* floor manager Paul Gadd as 'Gary Glitter', there were *Top of the Pops* visitations on video or in the chicken-necked flesh by, among many others, George Harrison, Tom Jones, the Beach Boys, Righteous Brother Bill Medley, the Kinks and, making their umpteenth comeback, the Bee Gees. As young a hopeful as the Brothers Gibb in their late thirties, Steve Winwood had his moment too.

For much of autumn 1987 it seemed like he was never off the television, flogging 'Valerie' which, when first issued as a UK single in 1982, had stopped short of the Top Fifty. No more ploughing energy into keeping out of the public gaze, there he was in person, miming on *Top of the Pops, Wogan* and, sponsored by Nescafé, a new ITV pop series, *The Roxy*, where he was introduced as 'one of the truly nice guys in the music biz'. Endearingly, Steve seemed at a loss when the record stopped but, with his schoolboy grin and freckles, he held his own amid Me-generation acts such as the Christians, whose bald-headed singer was derivative of Ray Charles; Level 42 – current favourites of Winwood's – with their whizz-kid bass guitarist-vocalist's Georgie Fame huskiness; and serious Lloyd Cole, four-eyed and wordy.

Largely through this solitary Top Twenty excursion, at the British record industry's Royal Albert Hall award ceremonies,

Winwood was only just pipped at the post as Best Male Artist of 1987 by George Michael, whose biggest seller had been a duet with plump Aretha Franklin, aged forty-six. For all their lined foreheads, grey hair, galloping alopecia and double chins, the exhumed suzerains of the singles charts fascinated those envious of their unquiet past. In the States too it was standing room only for trans-continental tours by Bob Dylan, Tina Turner and – good grief! – the Grateful Dead. The big new releases were by Paul Simon, Fleetwood Mac and, in his fifties, Leonard Cohen.

That these relics were cleaning up was partly a symptom of artistic bankruptcy among the young, content to imitate or eulogize old heroes. Witness Billy Bragg's 'Levi Stubbs' Tears' or 'Wood Beez (Pray Like Aretha Franklin)' from Scritti Politti. For years the Kinks – whose 'Tired of Waiting for You' of 1965 plugged a brand of shower gel in 1988 – were the source of hits for many groups, including the Jam, Pretenders and Fall. Saddest of all was *Sergeant Pepper Knew My Father*, a charity LP on which several new bands depped for the Lonely Hearts Club Band for a remake of the Beatles's most famous record.

Furthermore, teenagers were no longer pop's largest consumer group. No matter how it was tarted up – twelve-inch club mix on tartan vinyl or whatever – the pop single was a loss leader, an incentive to buy an album, preferably on compact disc. Teenagers had been financially outmanoeuvred by their Swinging Sixties parents and young marrieds who had sated their appetites for novelty. As in the pre-rock 'n' roll years, the young had to put up with pretty much the same music that their elders liked.

Since punk's last great gesture of defiance, nearly all pop was acceptable to your Mum and Dad. Academia had ceased distancing itself from pop, which now had infiltrated school curricula. Postgraduate research had been encouraged to the extent that the University of Liverpool had founded Britain's first Institute of Popular Music. An unsolicited letter in 1986 inquiring whether I'd be interested in running a course entitled 'Sounds of the Sixties' at a Watford adult education centre spurred me to seek similar work, and I rapidly amassed an impressive itinerary stretching into 1988. Those enrolling included both pensioners and those for whom the sixties predated consciousness. I invited some bona fide icons of the era as guest speakers, among them my sometime employer Dave Berry and veteran pop chronicler John Tobler. A bizarre repercussion of Reg Presley of the Troggs' thought-provoking stint at Swindon College occurred when a female student wanted to retrieve the cigarette ends that had graced his lips during the lecture. Unhappily, these artefacts had been cast out by one ignorant of their value. However, the girl was satisfied with the butts from my car ashtray which her idol had filled as I drove him from his Andover home.

If you were unemployed, as British school leavers were more often than not in the austere eighties, your UB40 would have guaranteed you free admission to some of my courses, as it would for ones about Etruscan vases or the inner waterways of Latvia. You could even con money out of government aid to form a band – even if, in the same defeated climate, record companies were no longer chucking blank cheques about. At every turn you'd missed the boat. Rehashes of Mod, psychedelia and other sixties' movements inevitably ended up punier than how they'd been portrayed in Channel Four's *Ready Steady Go* re-runs, *Quadrophenia* and your father's fond recollections of the Fourteen-Hour Technicolour Dream. The sap of young adulthood was rising, yet AIDS and further sexual ailments of the eighties restricted the pursuit of romance, and the state of those blokes screened in another government health warning rather put you off heroin as well. Soon it wouldn't be safe to masturbate.

There was always beer. Yet even up the pub there were reminders of all you'd missed. As well as the oldies on the jukebox, disco turntable and bar band repertoire, their original perpetrators would sometimes still be labouring to set up their equipment at opening time, as was fifty-three-year-old John Mayall at London's Town and Country where, though his name had been mis-spelt on the ticket, he was as ecstatic as his cramped devotees that he was so rabidly remembered.

Mayall's distinguished past was his bread and butter yet, with his lifelong dedication to the blues, he'd never been one to milk the audience. At venues where attractive personality mattered more than cult status, a sixties night was a reliable crowd-puller. Uncomfortable in ties at Blazer's of Royal Windsor, citadel of quality entertainment, you'd punish pricey liquor while a discreet sunken orchestra sight-reads musak as showtime creeps closer. After regaling you with gags that would shock a drunken marine, the Master of Ceremonies in his custard-yellow suit introduces the vivacious Marmalade who showcase excerpts from their four-year chart run. Less peculiar to this cabaret netherworld, the Merseybeats bounce on next with a Beatles medley and their own more modest cache of hits as old as the hills. Another crass build-up and the curtains part again as an unseen mournful baritone breaks into 'Memphis Tennessee'. The well-spring of his penetration is located when a spotlight homes in on fingers curling round a flat where Dave Berry, clothed in black, is making his suspensory Grand Entrance. He's looking as lean and outrageous as on *Ready Steady Go*, with all the essential elements intact – the hand ballets, the microphone glissados, the kismet supercool.

Searching for surviving units from the Golden Age of British Beat could be both intriguing and depressing. With solo stars like Mayall, Berry, Wayne Fontana or Screaming Lord Sutch, who cared about their rather too youthful accompanists? However, where there was no such demarcation line between singer and backing group, it was often not quite the full shilling – Herman's Hermits minus Herman; Dozy, Beaky, Mick and Tich with no Dave Dee; Love Affair consisting entirely of slim-hipped young herberts for whom the Big Beat was a playpen memory at most. Sometimes, however, performance would transcend deceit. After a packed Hollies concert in June 1984 at Reading's Hexagon auditorium, a middle-aged housewife remarked: 'I always thought that the Status Quo show was the best thing I'd seen but this was better.' In the hall, three original Hollies augmented with four jobbing musicians had been bemused by standing ovations from a traditionally sticky audience. As well as the old hits, even tracks from their latest album earned wild applause. Most devastating of all was a revival of the Supremes' 'Stop in the Name of Love' which, amazingly, the Hollies had taken into the US *Billboard* Top Twenty the previous year with the minimum of fuss.

Some were susceptible enough to think that a 'Blues Reunion' quartet who played a couple of London bookings in 1985 was a reconstituted Spencer Davis Group. Mounting the stage at Putney's Half-Moon was, yes, Spencer Davis, a bit moth-eaten, perhaps, but . . . and there's Pete York, the Group's original drummer. For most, credulity wouldn't stretch to Steve Winwood and his bass guitarist brother, Muff. Instead you got Rocket 88's bass player and, on synthesized organ, Brian Auger whose presence could be justified, I suppose, because in 1969 he'd beaten Steve in the keyboards section of a *Beat Instrumental* readers' poll.

More permanant fixtures on the nostalgia circuit were, with but one original member apiece, the Rockin' Berries and the Fortunes who, like the Spencer Davis Group, had started in Birmingham. As much comical as musical, the Berries 'undoubtedly stole the show'[9] at an under-forties weekend at a Hopton-on-Sea holiday camp in December 1987, while that summer I'd found myself glowing with patriotic pride when the Fortunes' impressive reading of the Everly

Brothers' 'Let It Be Me' filled a Dutch conference centre dance floor with smoochers.

Not blessed with hit records but better loved locally were Mike Sheridan and the Nightriders who, in May 1988, celebrated thirty years in showbusiness. Though ex-Nightriders such as Roy Wood and Jeff Lynne cracked the Top Forty nut, Sheridan, so he claimed, had 'never harboured any desires about becoming famous although I'd have accepted it had it happened'.[10] A Birmingham rock 'n' roll institution, Sheridan reflected on his fate as a big fish in a small pond: 'I've seen a lot of changes over the years; the most noticeable being the decline in venues. Back in the sixties and seventies, we worked two gigs, four or five nights a week. Now we're working a steady four days, mainly in clubs and cabaret rooms.'[10] In the same parochially esteemed but personally hitless position as Mike was Raymond Froggett who, despite composing Dave Clark's 1968 smash 'Red Balloon', became so despondent that, after his band's residency at a Sutton hotel, he retired temporarily from the music business in 1984 to run a bar in Warwick. Another casualty was Trevor Burton who, after quitting the Move in 1969, was a frequent guest at Traffic's communal cottage on the Berkshire Downs. By 1983, however, he was back in Birmingham, fronting a band every Wednesday in a Harborne pub.

Another famous group as synonymous with Birmingham as the Move were the Moody Blues who, in 1980, were reported to be lining up a tour – a sentimental journey – of Black Country pubs. Albeit with modernized interiors, some familiar haunts still bore their original names such as the Mackadown and, the one where Traffic originated, the Elbow Room. North-west to Wolverhampton was the Blue Flame, the old Mod hangout – now the Lafayette which, in 1977, was included on the Sex Pistols' 'secret tour' date sheet. On the debit side, the Railway Tavern in Curzon Street, another long-established stamping ground, was refurbished in 1988 to reopen as a steakhouse. Sadder still was the demolition of the longer-running Golden Eagle, also in the city centre, where the primal Spencer Davis Group sound was forged. With the passing of the Big Beat it cradled later, less glorious trends; in the late seventies its walls resounded to the likes of Laughing Torso, G.B.H. and Dead Wretched. After punk came the weedy Mod revival and the pub's hosting of the Lambrettas, the Mods and outfits of like persuasion. For its earlier glory, the Golden Eagle was picked by Robert Plant for an unpublicized performance in 1982 to market research new material. Finally a bikers' haven, its doors closed forever in January 1984; the regulars bidding farewell by trashing the place.

No matter how high he'd flown since the Spencer Davis Group's last fling at the Golden Eagle, Steve Winwood was identified – by the British media anyway – with his birthplace. 'Virtually forgotten by the rock world for a decade,' was the maximum impact announcement on BBC breakfast television, 'the Boy from Brum is back!'[11] In the subsequent interview at one of his homes that morning in September 1987, Steve's 'strange, drawling accent'[6] betrayed his upbringing by the soft, flat vowels peculiar to the Midlands, though without that thick intonation that renders the Birmingham drone ugly to many. Courteously, he played up to the prologue with a good-humoured quip about the 'autumn of my career',[11] nonchalantly sipping tea from fine porcelain lifted from a George III silver tray.

Contrary to the notion that he could be as reclusive – if not as cantankerous – as his mate Van Morrison, Steve came across as quite an outgoing chap. Consenting to give a lucid, helpful account of the evolution of *Back in the High Life* for BBC's *Whistle Test*, he and Gina had accompanied presenter Trevor Dann and some of the programme's camera crew to a Goldhawk Road alehouse near the London Television Centre. In a fit of exuberance he'd sat down at the saloon bar piano and, without preamble, given 'em 'Gimme Some Lovin'' – one of his Spencer Davis smashes and, in May 1988, used to advertise P.G. Tips tea – plus an instrumental that fewer of the astonished clientele recognized as 'Glad' from a Traffic LP. Such displays were, apparently, very much the done thing in brash New York.

The following year, when BBC's *Top of the Pops* was – for a fabulous sum – networked at last in North America, Steve, with 'Valerie' to plug, allowed himself to be photographed for a national newspaper with Mick Jagger cutting a cake – 'a slice of the action' – plastered with UK and US flag icing. More than ever now, it wasn't enough for the music press to inform buyers that his latest record was ready for public consumption, as had happened with his first solo album. Far better these days to lash out on a half-page in the *Daily Mirror* than *Sounds*. You had to howl it from the rooftops, despite some who insisted that there was still a vast gap between 'rock' – that only the finest minds could appreciate – and vulgar 'pop'. Merely making the record was the least of your worries. What about the TV commercial to go with it? How about using a clip from the video with one of those adenoidal streets- of-Islington voiceovers that people seem to go for nowadays? It could be scheduled before the last part of the *Chart Show* on Friday between 'Britain's noisiest crisps' and 'how to catch AIDS'.

While actively concerning himself with learning the new marketing methods, Winwood, in a quest for a wider audience, was 'not
keen to do anything that isn't me'. He'd never, for example,
considered extending himself into film acting, as Mick Jagger had.
Concentrating on the possible, Winwood videos did not try to
project him in dramatic situations but adhered to a straightforward
synchronization with a musical performance. Balancing his dislike
of touring with the necessity of in-person appearances to get
'Higher Love' going in Europe, he resolved to cover as many
prestigious venues as possible in one forty-eight-hour jet-propelled
burst. Session percussionist Jessica Palin joined an English guitarist
and Italian rhythm section backing Steve on this jaunt, which
climaxed at some big something-for-everybody pop festival in
Siena with Joan Armatrading and Sigue Sigue Sputnik. Mainly,
however, it was television, and reported Jessica, all that was
required at each stop – including the festival – was to mime to
'Higher Love'. Nevertheless, the day before the entourage set off
by hired aeroplane from Heathrow, a cursory rehearsal with
amplification was held to satisfy the Musicians' Union (motto:
'Keep Music Live').

'Higher Love' was Rick Astley's favourite single of 1987. The
mis-timed opinion of that nondescript young pop starlet matters
only in that it probably echoes the view of his mentors, Stock-
Aitken-Waterman, a production team who throughout that year
had rattled off further pliable chart fodder by other pretty faces like
models Mandy Smith and Samantha Fox, and Australian actress
Kylie Minogue. More than any Stock-Aitken-Waterman product,
'Higher Love' and, indeed, nearly all the remainder of *Back in the
High Life* were guaranteed disco floor-fillers. When I got round to
giving my car boot 'Higher Love' a spin, I wasn't sure, but successive plays disturbed my private Winwood Top Ten which had
remained unaltered since I lost interest in Traffic in the early seventies. Largely because I hadn't expected to like it, 'Higher Love'
muscled in among entrenchments such as 'I Can't Stand It', 'Keep on
Running' and 'Gimme Some Lovin' ' from the Spencer Davis Group,
and 'Paper Sun', 'Coloured Rain', 'No Face, No Name, No number',
'Withering Tree', 'John Barleycorn' and 'Dream Gerrard' from the
constant personnel flux that was Traffic. Later, as I filled the holes in
my understanding between 'When the Eagle Flies' – Traffic's finale –
and 'Higher Love', there were more surprises.

Overall, its renascent flavour invested *Back in the High Life* with
more energy than the other three solo LPs – which, apart from the
first, Winwood produced and performed, even engineered, with

minimal outside help; 'the only way to not compromise is to work on your own. If you work with people – and there's some fantastically talented people around – you get bounce back and influences from people you work with.'[2] Delegating technicalities to Unique's more knowledgeable staff, Steve applied himself to modern American pop with much the same persistence as that incorrigible old rocker Jerry Lee Lewis had to country and western. Unlike, say, Billy J. Kramer whose wan croon of 1963 dropped about an octave over twenty years, Winwood's more versatile tenor was the only consistency in the patchwork of different styles in which he had indulged since singing in his brother's jazz band at the age of twelve.

Of equal longevity, therefore, was a jazzer's rhythmic emphasis. Gone was the frequently one-dimensional jazz-rock blowing that had tainted Traffic, but a polyrhythm of percussion – most effectively employed by Winwood – remained. On most of the album's value-for-money fifty minutes was a solid formation of a standard kit drummer, a second percussionist who might be thumping congas or shaking tambourine, plus a drum machine programme. Though the latter is a labour-saving device, generally I have found it vaguely contemptuous when its misuse forces a Japanese water torture beat on to the listener. However, perfect time notwithstanding, you'd believe it at least half-human on *High Life* until a scan of the copious inner sleeve notes gave the game away.

Via Unique's hi-tech, still more interchangeable were the five-piece brass-and-woodwind section and the synthesized horns – all of which were scored by David Frank of the System who had also worked for Phil Collins. A flesh-and-blood string octet was considered for 'My Love's Leavin' which, had he not settled instead for Arif Mardin's synthesizer arrangement, would have been the first time Winwood had sung to strings since the session for the third Spencer Davis single back in 1965.

Like a Saxon church in Manhattan, Steve's Hammond organ – an instrument he'd always loved – was lugged from its mothballs to show those new-fangled keyboards what it could do on 'Freedom Overspill' and 'Split Decision', on which it was nearly overwhelmed by an antique sound not as appealing. Picking the dirtiest guitar on the record was 'Split Decision' co-writer Joe Walsh in his raucous, clichéd element, giving *High Life* its good-measure heavy metal touch-up. Leaning more on Alice Cooper than on Van Halen, Walsh's was the album's least subtle moment. Of greater intricacy were such fracturing twists and turns as the 'over and over' chorale on 'Wake Me Up on Judgement Day' and the snarling brass crescendos of 'Freedom Overspill' – which, as follow-up single to 'Higher Love', galloped to number twenty in the US Hot Hundred. Ending side one, the melody and sentiment of 'Back in the High Life *Again*' – from a lyrical idea by Winwood – faintly raked up 'Forever Young' by the Comsat Angels, a defunct Yorkshire New Wave combo, once big in Europe. Other memory banks simultaneously opened here were – via Steve's mandolin and pentatonic synthesizer twirling – both Pictish ceilidh celebration and, though not as raggedly carefree, the *joie de vivre* of early seventies' outfits McGuinness-Flint and Mungo Jerry. Perhaps unconscious was a reference to Pete York's 'I Can't Stand It' drumming in the track's kilted snare rolls.

As a production, *Back in the High Life* was Winwood's – and Titelman's – apotheosis. In its confident, clean breadth of expression, it even sounded stratospheric on a shuddering monophonic Dansette. Would the album's five- to six-minute songs have supported such forceful gusto had they been reduced to the acid test of just voice and piano? Rather than separate pieces, it was almost the blinded-by-science music at any given interval that counted – though 'Take It as It Comes' stands out as an untapped rave-up made to be overhauled by a group like Slade. Creatively, Steve was firing on all cylinders as he paraded his quite exceptional skills both vocally and in his instinctive command of a trade fair of instruments, never overdone to the detriment of any of the eight selections. Somehow most of it was a bit too pat, too dovetailed, too American – but that's the feeling of someone who infinitely prefers the Troggs, Slade, the Len Bright Combo – anyone to Bruce Springsteen, without whom Winwood would be the top-selling pop artist in the United States. How could I criticize *Back in the High Life* when it had spent over sixty weeks in *Billboard*'s album chart? Even its video was still in the Top Ten by the start of 1988.

Curt Yank spelling infiltrated the lyric sheet too. However, the lines Steve was now sanctioning were subject to a more stringent quality control than at the time of Traffic. As he himself had aged, so the topics tackled by his wordsmiths – principally Will Jennings – were more adult than those addressed in 'I'm a Man', 'Medicated Goo' and 'The Low Spark of High-heeled Boys'. In a realistic, conversational flow, marital strife, mortality and the passing time went under the hammer without 'poetic' self-consciousness, and, except during rare bouts of Jacques Brel world-weariness, with breezy stoicism; take it as it comes.

Predictably, the most sensitive and personal verses belonged to Steve's longest-standing collaborator, Viv Stanshall, whose premonitory 'My Love's Leavin' ' was the only native English lyric on the LP. Possibly because it didn't reconcile easily with the prevalent Coca-Cola mood of the rest, another Winwood–Stanshall number, though completed, was put aside. 'Crazy Horse' – concerning the visionary war chief of the Sioux who was a leader at Little Big Horn – came, explained Vivian,

> out of my interest in the Zulu War which is, of course, half a world away. [Crazy Horse is] the only mystic I've ever had total admiration for because, being called an 'eccentric' and all other sorts of derogatory versions of that, he stuck out. After every other Indian was on the reservation and Sitting Bull arrived in Canada, Crazy Horse stuck out and they had to kill him – otherwise they couldn't have got the railroad through.

Since Steve's interest in Red Indians in general is a long-term one, dating back at least as far as Traffic's first US trip, perhaps this item will yet become available to consumers in another Winwood contribution to American popular music, although 'I always prefer to write things at that particular time. The sooner I can get it and complete it, the better because it remains fresh.'[7]

In October 1987, the wheels cranked into motion for Winwood's next album. Some loose ends had already been tied the previous summer, when he'd supervised a remix of ten post-Traffic favourites – including 'Valerie' – for an Island compilation entitled *Chronicles*. In Virgin megastores by Christmas, *Chronicles* sold well even in Britain where, short on hits but reinforced by 'Valerie' at number seventeen, it put up a tasteful fight against a plethora of other winter 'best of' brand names like Paul McCartney, Bryan Ferry and the Pretenders – all with stronger nostalgic familiarity.

Steve had taken the *Chronicles* masters to Nashville which, after peaking as the commercial country music capital, now beckoned to purveyors of more generalized pop. Mixing work with pleasure, while Gina showed him a good time in evening honky-tonk bars, he spent his days in the basement studio at Sixteenth Avenue Sound in the city's wooded business district. On the steps of the complex one afternoon, Winwood bumped into Carly Simon's producer, Paul Samwell-Smith. When bass guitarist with the Yardbirds, Samwell Smith had been present at Birmingham Town Hall on Friday, 28 February 1964 when fifteen-year-old Steve, a member of the Spencer Davis Rhythm and Blues Quartet, completed his final musical engagement as an amateur.

1

'Jump Back'

'To be onstage was the most fantastic thing I could dream of. That's all I really wanted to do,'[1] recalled Steve Winwood from Island's air-conditioned New York headquarters. He was conducting one of a chain of media interviews he'd allowed in order to publicize the lately released *Arc of a Diver*, the record that would revive his career. Misplaced but at ease amid the ticking telexes, tubular steel furniture and perspex-covered portraits of the label's main money-spinners in 1981, thus spake a Cotswolds man-of-the-soil, his reddened hands cracked with minor cuts and scratches.

If from British peasant stock, Steve's family had been disting-uished by musical forebears. His maternal grandfather was a church organist while, on his father's side, his grandmother and her seven sons all performed on enough instruments for both solo and ensemble playing during those 'musical evenings' that preceded television. Front parlours tinkled with the strains of Handel, Debussy or Sir Arthur Sullivan, and were set a-tremble to sonorous renderings of 'Excelsior', 'Greensleeves' or an eye-rolling 'Villikins and His Dinah' – a Victorian smash hit. A small boy would be led forth, glistening with embarrassment, to the centre of the room to pipe in an uncertain treble 'Donkey Riding', 'Billy Boy' or, maybe, 'Linden Lea'. After the children had been packed off to the Land of Nod, bawdier songs might ensue, but the entertainment would conclude – as was proper – with the National Anthem.

Probably deriving from the Welsh 'Wynn' meaning 'fair' or 'white' rather than the Anglo-Saxon 'wine' ('friend'), the Winwood name was imprinted mainly in the Midlands where, in 1987, the Birmingham telephone directory contained fifty-three Winwoods, and Worcester forty-two, as opposed to, say, West Berkshire's meagre tally of three. The greater part of the Midlands had come under the jurisdiction of the Anglo-Saxon kings of Mercia, which became Christian on the death of Penda, who was overthrown by Oswy of Northumbria in 655 near Leeds at the battle of Winwidefeld – rendered as 'Winwaed'[2], or 'Winwood'[3] in some chronicles. Born in Aynhoe, Northamptonshire a millenium later was a Sir Ralph Winwood, secretary to the Duke of Suffolk during the reign of James I. He was described as 'well-seen in most matters but most expert in matters of trade and war'.[4]

With Birmingham's stronger affinity to Wales rather than to Northamptonshire, Steve Winwood is more likely to have descended from Daniel Winwood, a Cradley Heath bucklechape maker who, in 1781, invented the 'joint wire' process. He was alleged to have done great injury to his native trade by emigrating with his two sons to Vienna where, before they returned to Birmingham, he opened a buckle and button manufactory.[5]

Of a like mechanical turn was Lawrence Winwood, a motorcycle engine fitter who, at the onset of the Second World War, married Lillian Saunders, spinster of the parish of Handsworth Wood. The couple's first son, Mervyn – named after an uncle – was born in 1943 in an Erdington nursing home. The dark-haired toddler was never to outgrow his cradle articulation of his Christian name. Shortly after 'Muff', brilliantined, gaberdine-raincoated and short-trousered, started at Cranbourne Road Infants School, Lillian presented him with a baby brother, baptised Stephen Lawrence.

By then, Lawrence was working all hours as a commercial traveller in household fittings and small hardware, amassing goodwill as well as commission. Given that he was likely to be absent from his wife's side when labour began, the last weeks of Lillian's pregnancy were spent at a relation's house – 127 Church Lane, Handsworth – where Stephen was prised into the world on 12 May 1948, as an exceptionally warm and sunny post-war spring gave way to a cool, rainy summer.

The two boys grew up in what remains to this day the family semi-detached – dating from the First World War – in Atlantic Road in the Old Oscott area between Erdington and Kingstanding, a few miles north of Birmingham city centre. It was a densely built-up and predominantly working-class area, with new tangles of bright red-brick terraces continuing to encroach on the unofficial countryside that had resurfaced after Goering's Luftwaffe had assisted the urban renewal programme instigated by Joseph Chamberlain after his election to the City Council in 1869. At Kingstanding's refined north end, where Birmingham bleeds into Staffordshire, mock-Tudor colonies, golf courses and the boating lakes, where Mr Winwood enjoyed taking the children, encircled Sutton Park, an oasis of trees and grass covering four square miles. Down in Old Oscott, half a mile from Atlantic Road, was a smaller patch of green – the city cemetery – now slashed along one side by the roaring M6.

Today indistinguishable to the outsider from any other lugubrious Birmingham suburb, both Erdington and Kingstanding had once been villages separate from the larger settlement to the south known in the Domesday Book as 'Bermingeham'. Smack in the middle of the Trent-Avon-Severn triangle and close to iron and coal mines, Birmingham – as far from the sea as anywhere in Britain – wrested from Bristol the title of Second City as the Industrial Revolution, beginning with the gun trade, expanded the city's boundaries in the nineteenth and early twentieth centuries, swallowing surrounding communities in its path. Roads, waterways and rail fanning out in all directions, trains, lorries and barges shunted myriad factory goods – steamship boilers to pen nibs – from the overcrowded city, haphazard and huddled with cavernous warehouses – and slums with outside toilets; front rooms cold and tidy for funerals; children hopscotching and footballing unsupervised in the streets and catcalling in that accent you could slice with a spade. Yet the new city encouraged newcomers to make something of themselves. James Watt, for example, came from Scotland to patent his improved steam engine for driving his Birmingham paymaster's machines. He also gave his name to a unit of electrical power.

Fouling the air and waterways, the thick black clouds and chemical waste percolating from the conurbation's blast furnaces and factories caked employees' poky dwellings with soot and grime as indelibly as Lady Macbeth's damned spot. 'It's called the Black Country,' escapee Steve Winwood informed an American journalist in 1970, 'the West Midland people are the people Tolkien was supposed to have based his Hobbits on. It's really heavily industrial.'[6]

Unprepossessing as it was, Birmingham almost as palpably forged opportunities for artistic development matching those within any English city except London. A mere twenty miles from Stratford-upon-Avon, the city's Repertory Theatre, launched on a subscription scheme, emerged as one of the most admired in the country – while to perform at the Birmingham Hippodrome is a high priority for aspiring ballet dancers throughout the world. In the city, Mendelssohn conducted the world premiere of 'Elijah'. Birmingham also benefits from the private artistic purchases of nineteenth century industrialists, that were subsequently bequeathed to the city. On the campus of the university, incorporated in 1900, is the Barber Institute of Fine Arts; here, too, is the Midlands Arts Centre, aimed mainly at fostering the arts in the young. As well as possessing a symphony orchestra of formidable reputation, Birmingham has a Youth Choir which accepts only the most promising local talent. One year it included the Winwood boys and Moody Blue-in-waiting Ray Thomas.

Far less conscious of being 'arty' than a Londoner, a trombonist in a Dudley brass band, whilst not claiming to be particularly musical, would automatically buy a ticket for the Birmingham Jazz Festival. A precursor of this event was a more parochial show attended by ten thousand at Lightwoods Park in 1964 – Chris Barber's Jazz Band heading a bill shared with a host of home-grown combos. Founded in 1947, the Hot Club which met at the Bell Hotel off Constitution Hill metamorphosed into the Birmingham Jazz Record Society. Aided by crackling 78s, its members would convene to discuss such estoteria as 'small band Ellingtonia'. Not so cerebral was Bromsgrove's Down Town Jazz Club which, rather than intellectualize to the gramophone, was a platform on which local jazzers could blow. Another key venue was Jazz Studio One in Aston, the brainchild of one Gordon Andrews. Numerous city pubs held jazz nights too, among them the Edward VII and the Golden Eagle – both in the city centre and regular bookers of the Second City Jazzmen, the New Magnolia Jazz Band ('dixieland with a sax') and the Johnny Patrick Quintet.

Possessor of an impressive record collection which included much jazz and some blues, Lawrence Winwood, true to his line, also played tenor saxophone in several Erdington dance bands. Considering music as a profession 'a dicey business',[7] sensibly neither he nor his wife goaded the boys to formalize their inherited musical interests. Of the two, little Stephen seemed keenest. From investigative pounding with plump fists on the household upright piano, by the age of five he'd figured out a one-fingered 'God Save the Queen'. Progressing at his own pace, he added to his repertoire, including hymn tunes from cross-legged primary school assemblies and – then quite a new idea – traditional songs from *Singing Together* and other BBC radio broadcasts to schools. Three decades before 'Baa Baa Black Sheep' was banned in a London council nursery school, no one batted an eyelid when the *Singing Together* pupils' handbook required you to sing 'mah' for 'my' and 'wid' for 'with' on the few 'coon songs' included.[8] Neither were token West Indians or Asians present on the cover of the standard *Oxford School Music Book*, common to most Midlands primary schools; preference was given instead to a blazered boy in National Health specs trumping a euphonium, a girl attentive and beribboned on triangle, a choir in kilts, and rows of young violinists and recorder players in pleated skirts or flannel shorts – all under the baton of a bespectacled teacher.

4

More exciting than the Home Service's dashing white sergeants, drunken sailors, Li'l Liza Janes and John Barleycorns was the Light Programme, which interspersed the likes of *Educating Archie* (comic goings-on of a ventriloquist's dummy) and *Workers' Playtime* with approved items from the newly established *New Musical Express* record sales chart. Though Sunday lunch has never been the same since the departure of the *Billy Cotton Band Show*, most of the music heard on the wireless before about 1955 was directed at the over-thirties, often sung by crooners such as Perry Como and Tony Bennett. Otherwise there was *Housewives' Choice* and Saturday morning's *Children's Favourites* – record requests aired by 'Uncle Mac'. In between Lita Roza's 'How Much Is That Doggie in the Window' and Frankie Laine's quasi-religious 'I Believe', there was no middle ground beyond 'Davy Crockett' novelties and lewd outrages like 'Such a Night' by Johnny Ray, 'the Prince of Wails'. As in the forties, you jumped from nursery rhymes to Frank Sinatra as if the connecting years were spent in a coma.

Over five million adult Britons went ballroom dancing every Saturday to shut off – however fleetingly – the staider realities of post-war rationing and having to start married life in their parents' home. In stiff evening dress, Lawrence Winwood with his shiny saxophone would be among those taking his place on the palais bandstand to begin the night's veletas and square tangos. His younger son was a fascinated listener to 'Dad practising about the house when I was about six. It gave me an incentive to learn so I volunteered for piano lessons. I guess I was fortunate because I picked up things very quickly.'[9] Two years later, he'd accumulated enough birthday postal orders to buy a second-hand guitar, whose gut strings he eventually replaced with more resonant wire.

Not far away lived Uncle Mervyn, whose instrumental prowess covered all waterfronts from bagpipes to harmonica. None the less, despite his and Lawrence's specializations, neither Muff nor Stephen ever got the hang of brass or woodwind. From a school recorder group, Muff took up the clarinet briefly. Ditching the liquorice stick at greater speed, Stephen was put off by its unpredictable harmonics which set his teeth on edge – though it was the unevenness of those very molars that precipitated such squeaks.

The mouths of both brothers were better employed in the choir at the Anglican church of St John's in Perry Barr, where they faced each other across the chancel every Sunday, singing the holy sounds that were novel and unintelligible at seven, over-familiar and long rote-learnt by thirteen. A 1957 photograph of the brothers, proud in ruffs, surplices and cassocks on the church steps, implies that

Muff at least became a head boy. As befitted his office, he was privileged to bear the processional cross as priest and choir filed to and from the vestry. He and Stephen might also have taken turns in dousing the altar candles after the General Confession during Matins. Years later the vicar approached them to rearrange some hymns in a more modern style, but this intriguing project was curtailed by professional preoccupations.

From a musical genesis both ecclesiastical and domestic, Steve Winwood's translation to pop stardom was a gradual development of unconscious forces within his background in tandem with a natural aptitude, rather than an oscillating series of lucky breaks, close shaves and chances-in-a-million. His first cash-in-hand secular performance was as a pianist in the church hall with one of his father's bands. As long as they didn't go on too late, Lillian allowed nine-year-old Stephen to go along to further bookings at wedding receptions, street parties and fêtes. Juxtaposing the life of Cranbourne Road Juniors' ink-stained desks and lumpy custard with extra-curricular Te Deums and cha-cha-chas, thus was set the pattern of what remained of his childhood. Inevitably, clashing educational, artistic and vocational priorities became so confused and unhealthy that the only solution was to give up one of them. However, that decision was not to trouble Stephen and his parents until he approached what was then the minimum school-leaving age of sixteen. But before he'd even entered secondary school he'd already encountered the most crucial factor in reaching that decision.

As well as customary requests for 'The Anniversary Waltz' and 'Que Sera Sera', there was always some young smart alec who wanted dance bands to do 'Rock Around the Clock' or 'Blue Suede Shoes' in those days. Even strict tempo supremo Victor Sylvester featured a sanitized 'rock 'n' roll' sequence and, what with Kay Starr's crafty 'Rock and Roll Waltz' topping the hit parade, it was going stronger than previous crazes like the jitterbug or the creep. What were Bill Haley and the Comets after all? They were a dance band like any other middle-aged dance band, except they'd got lucky with this 'Rock Around the Clock' record and would have been daft not to play up to it.

Gordon Andrews, founder of Jazz Studio One, was – as he'd tell you himself – Birmingham's *only* rock and roll singer'.[9] Briefly holding Eldorado in the hollow of his hand at the Casino Ballroom, Andrews gyrated, snarled and rolled on his back like a man possessed, to the accompaniment of the Unsquare Men. Not letting personal dislike of the style stop them either, better-known jazz and dance band musicians also hung on to rock 'n' roll's coat tails.

Drummers Eric Delaney and Tony Crombie both formed contingent rock 'n' roll groups in the Haley image, while the first record of Ronnie Scott's former vocalist, Art Baxter, with the Rockin' Sinners was 'Shortnin' Bread Rock'. As a genuine American rocker, Chuck Berry, was seen derisively duck-walking with his red guitar in *Jazz on a Summer's Day*, a US film documentary. Britain's 'answer' was to engage the Kirchins, whose record debut was 'Rock and Rolling at the Darktown Strutters' Ball', for a jazz extravaganza at Butlin's Clacton holiday camp.

As pathetic in its way were the twirling sticks of American swing band drummer Lionel Hampton, whose raucous nod to rock 'n' roll during a 1956 concert at the Royal Festival Hall prompted jazz purist Johnny Dankworth to voice his disgust from the audience. Dankworth must have felt like King Canute when England's oldest jazz club, Studio 51, closed to reopen as the 51 Club. Its new policy enabled rock 'n' roll groups and traditional jazz bands to share the same bill. Well, you have to move with the times, as did *Housewives' Choice* idol Lee Lawrence, a trained opera tenor, with his spoof 'Rock 'n' Roll Opera' single that same year.

In common with all but the most serious-minded children of the fifties, Stephen Winwood had been superficially excited by Haley's 'Rock Around the Clock' whenever it disturbed Uncle Mac's red-nosed reindeers and Christmas alphabets as 1955 drew to a close. A more profound impression was created by Elvis Presley's 'Hound Dog', with its heart-stopping second guitar break and hillbilly-blues shout-singing that North America only dared televise from the waist up. Wilder still was shrieking black Little Richard in billowing drapes, pencil moustache and precarious pompadour, beating hell out of a concert grand in the movie *The Girl Can't Help It*, which arrived at the Birmingham Odeon in 1957.

Rock 'n' roll, therefore, was here to stay, no matter how abhorrent to those no longer young. They hated its noise, its gibberish and, most of all, its stylized delinquency – the first Teddy Boy murder had taken place in 1954; less overtly violent but more widespread was the secretive penknife-slitting of cinema seats while young women jived in gingham together in the aisles to 'Jailhouse Rock'. Suddenly 'twixt twelve and twenty you were allowed to make up your own mind about whether you wanted to grow up or not. While you decided, you were labelled a 'teenager', and, because of fuller employment and increases in wages since the war, you'd become a separate target for advertising. Yet a girl still wore socks well into her teens, and a sure sign of growing up was when she peeled on nylon stockings, usually held up with a suspender belt.

Thickest in Birmingham city centre but penetrating the furthest-flung suburb, transport cafés transformed themselves within days into expresso coffee bars complete with jukeboxes loaded with the coin-operated sounds of Elvis, Tommy Steele (his British 'answer'), Little Richard and all the others. As instant as a milkshake, these new havens made it possible to sit for hours on end, chatting with other teenagers, for the price of a cup of frothy coffee. Parents had the pubs; children had playgrounds; until now those in between had had nothing. Foreseeable Sunday press disapproval of such houses of ill-repute, where boys smoked and girls got pregnant, left only one alternative: the local youth club.

Often run by church or school, youth club activities were arranged and supervised by grown-ups in cardigans and included wholesome ping-pong, slide shows and a 'Brains Trust' on topical subjects. Bored silly, formerly tractable young men would get themselves barred from such places by blatantly brandishing a cigarette or letting slip a 'bloody' in front of the curate. If not reinstated after scandalized parents forced an apology, they would take to the streets, denouncing the youth club as 'kids' stuff'. Getting bolder, they'd say 'bloody' or even 'bugger' unreproached, and allow self-generated and false rumours to leak back about what exactly they had got up to at Butlin's last August. Gathering dust on coathangers were the sports jackets and cavalry twills. Pedestrians would cross roads to avoid menacing lamp-post clusters of hybrid Edwardian rakes and Mississippi paddlewheel card-sharps, ripe for more than boyish mischief.

More hopefully radical than a Teddy Boy's knuckleduster was the Beatnik set – would-be college intellectuals in black roll-necks, living in the shadow of the Bomb. With 'cool' defined by Jack Kerouac's Dean Moriarty rather than James Dean or Elvis, girls in glasses from Moseley Art School would hide their figures inside big, baggy sweaters borrowed from 'existentialist' boyfriends with bumfluff beards.

Now attending Great Barr Comprehensive, ten minutes' dawdle from home, Muff Winwood, though never snooty about Teddy Boy rock 'n' roll, had been infected with his father's passion for the sort of jazz records found strewn around beatnik 'pads'. 'Muff's musical tastes influenced me a lot when I was a kid,' confessed his admiring little brother, 'not so much his playing but I always got to like what he liked and through him I started digging modern jazz when I was thirteen and good music generally when I was even younger.'[10] 'Modern jazz' in Muff's terms embraced the mainstream orchestral euphoria of Duke Ellington and the white swing of Woody Herman, Buddy Rich and rockin' Lionel Hampton; vocal daredevils like Sinatra, Anita O'Day and Mel Tormé; and blaring be-bop of Charlie Mingus, the harder Jazz Messengers – inherited from Art Blakey by pianist Horace Silver – and Charlie Parker's Re Boppers with Miles Davis; and the differing textural complexities of Ornette Coleman and Roland Kirk – whom he and Steve were to catch on a bad night at Ronnie Scott's in November 1966.

Many modern jazz recordings could only be purchased at import prices from a specialist shop off Gunmakers' Row near a district known as Soho – much like its London counterpart. Money-conscious Muff would, therefore, rig up a reel-to-reel tape recorder to catch jazz off the radio. Under big Muff's feet as he fiddled about with microphone positioning while the valves warmed up, Steve developed his appreciation of jazz largely through keyboard players whose instruments' logical learning process he understood far better than that of the rejected clarinet on which, no matter how many holes you covered, you'd sometimes emit exactly the same note – if you got any note at all.

One of Steve's particular preferences was Canadian pianist–band leader Oscar Peterson – though more immediate was a liking for the fluid organ beneath the hands of 'Brother' Jack McDuff and, later, Jimmy Smith. Light years away from wheezy Magnificats, when electrified, the organ was transported by McDuff and Smith from jazz to the borders of blues and pop.

Steve half-enjoyed the softer fretboard swing of Wes Montgomery because – as Muff had – he was attending Spanish guitar lessons which had been made available when he entered the first form at Great Barr in September 1959: 'I couldn't make up my mind what I wanted to be, a pianist or a guitarist. I'd stick at the piano for a month or two then decide that I really wanted to play guitar, so I'd go back to guitar and then decide piano was the thing for me to play. Eventually, I made up my mind to be good at both.'[11] Also like Muff, Steve was considered a promising enough pianist for a part-time place at the Birmingham and Midland Institute of Music, which meant taking a bus journey to the city centre. But they didn't like his crouched position as he sweated over Chopin. They nagged him about sight-reading. They didn't think much of the guitar because, as Master Winwood hit the strings without a plectrum, it purged his fingertips of the sensitivity necessary to caress the ivories. Moreover, young men's motives for taking up the guitar were suspect these days. With the instrument slung down to their waists, most stood up to play like that Elvis Priestley. Coming to loathe the Institute's carping discipline, 'I soon realised that I wasn't going to be a great pianist in those terms. I was already interested in other kinds of music.'[12] Not surprisingly, he never finished the course.

9

But the dark cloud dissolved and Steve was sufficiently self-contained to disassociate the music from the drudgery: 'music is a science. In many ways, it's mathematical. For instance, a lot of Bach's things were just mathematical exercises, patterns, but in doing that, he turned out some beautiful pieces of music like the Two–Part Inventions'.[13] Nor would Steve lose his love of works by later composers such as Debussy, Ravel and Holst. That his year of intensive formal training wasn't the waste of time he'd once imagined came to light at a technical college dance booking in 1964. In response to a cheeky demand for 'classical music', Steve's digits on auto-pilot sought a jaw-dropping piece by Chopin.

There had been less demand for this sort of feat three years earlier when the thirteen–year–old returned to a school timetable no longer interrupted by trips to the Institute. Instead Steve became as well-known for his 'jazzy' musical skills as hockey captains and class bullies were in their chosen spheres. More meaningful to him than parallel motion exercises using broken triads was what transpired at a lunch-hour guitar club organized by Tom Knowles, Great Barr's head of speech and drama. Mr Knowles, saw rock 'n' roll and its British tangent, skiffle, not as an evil, but rather as a more effective means of arousing adolescent interest in music than could be achieved through the tedium of diminished fifths and Brahms' German Requiem.

Unthinkable before the advent of the teenager, such a forward-thinking innovation was symptomatic of a change in the climate of English education since the early fifties. For a child to pass the eleven plus examination and so gain a place at a grammar school rather than a secondary modern – where the 'failures' went – was a desirable social coup for ambitious parents. When the ITV soap opera *Coronation Street* was young, Ken Barlow – then a schoolmaster – was once depicted refusing a bribe to rig eleven plus results so that a town councillor's son could attend Market Wetherby Grammar. Fairer was the 'education for all' concept of the comprehensive which, combining elements of both grammar and secondary modern, theoretically enabled children to follow what best suited their abilities and inclinations as they developed.

Opened in 1954, Great Barr – one of the first comprehensives – spared Muff and Steve's future being decided at eleven, although its academic streaming and house system were derived from the headmaster, Oswald Beynon M.A.'s previous appointment at a grammar school in his native Wales. Nevertheless, at its progressive zenith by the turn of the decade, Great Barr was favoured by the liberal intelligentsia from all over Birmingham, as well as the working-class families within its catchment area. While the Winwoods were there, it produced from its two thousand pupils Aston Villa footballer Steve Hunt and – a protégé of Tom Knowles – actor Martin Shaw, best known as a television tough guy.

Steve Winwood is remembered as a conscientious student who put homework before most other extra-curricular pursuits. Though an able all-rounder, he was a particularly proficient mathematician who, in the estimation of his teacher, Eric Roberts, would have been a GCE 'A' level possibility. He was, said Mr Roberts, 'a very balanced, happy sort of chap'.

For Steve himself, 'about three of the people I could say I was close to, I used to go to school with'.[14] Of his friends at Great Barr, most were musicians in some way, whether hoping to study music at university or join pop groups – as did one particular chum, Bugsy Eastwood, who became singer with the Exceptions. Having started the Threshers folk club in a city centre pub in 1966, Tom Knowles was touched when Steve – then, unlike Bugsy, a household name – put in one of his habitual and unsolicited solo performances on the opening night.

Teachers with Knowles' open-minded outlook were, however, unpopular with the headmaster, whose unbending attitude towards those of his charges who were gifted but unconventional, blighted Winwood Minor's otherwise pleasant memories of his schooldays: 'there has never been any opposition to me being a musician – only at school'.[15]

Few at Great Barr found Muff an outstanding musician. His main instrument came to be guitar, but he was to end his performing career on bass. Yet if diffident Muff didn't push himself as a show-off onstage, he was solidly at the music's heart, loud enough for vocal harmonies but quietly ministering to overall effect. 'My brother has never been a performer or a writer,' clarified Steve, 'a bass player is a performer, yes, but really a bass player is an accompanist. The art of accompaniment is as big a subject as being a soloist. His greatest strength has always been as an administrator. He would help on the arrangements and also organise things. Because of that, we always complemented each other.'[1]

The enigma of the relationship between sibling musicians cannot be generalized. Almost unceasingly since 1963, onstage and off, there was an open state of spiritually masochistic warfare between Kinks Ray and Dave Davies. Is there a common thread between these two and Spandau Ballet's Gary Kemp with his arm affectionately round the shoulder of his saxophonist brother in the all-star Band Aid group photograph? Who will ever unravel the emotional complexities of the relationship between a blood cousin and three brothers in the Beach Boys? In any family there is always territory forbidden and inexplicable to outsiders. How else can be explained abrupt, tearful reconciliations after venomous days of mutual character assassination; a tacit implication in a seemingly innocuous utterance sparking off hastily packed suitcases and slammed front doors; home truths leading to thoughts of suicide, and jokes side-splitting to nobody else? How often do you say what you really mean about close relatives to strangers – especially journalists. We would like to have the impossible: videos of, for example, domestic scenes from the Atlantic Road living room. Or sampling with our own sensory organs Muff's feelings about his sibling's more evident musical talent. However, we can learn much from verbatim accounts. Unlike people, they are uninfluenced by the fact of being observed. Being Steve's brother was, for instance, both Muff's 'biggest career break' and 'biggest disappointment'.[16] Though he specified Steve as his 'best friend' in an earlier publicity handout,[17] this was not reciprocated. Indeed, Steve made some hurtful remarks about Muff to the music press [18] – though he qualified these with 'obviously we get on each other's nerves sometimes. I suppose its because we don't get much time off and, ever since we were kids, we've been together and playing every night. I've never shared his friends and he's never shared mine.'[10] 'When he was young,' Muff retorted belatedly, 'he didn't know who his friends were,'[19] but, puffing a mature pipe, Muff nodded and twinkled with pride 'just listening' as Steve rehearsed with his new Traffic. Afterwards, however, his curt comment was 'you seem to have lost your clichés'.[20]

At first Steve failed to see similarities between blunt, introverted, cautious Muff and himself, 'so full of life', as a later acquaintance noted, 'full of zest for living'.[21] None the less, Muff had wild moments occasionally. In response to another clever dick call for 'classical music' at a college booking, he shoved his way centre stage to shout, 'Which raving nutter wanted a number by Tchaikovsky?' – only to discover that the 'raving nutter' was the principal.[22] Alternatively, perhaps age and the fragile nature of pop brought to Steve a more reticent nature and a certain disillusioned ruthlessness. 'He's much more guarded now,' agreed Muff, 'and, as a result, he's not as open as he used to be.'[19]

Steve also grew wary of praise for his singing, especially 'when people say I can blow Wilson Pickett off the stage – no matter how hard you try, you can never sing the blues like a coloured person. That's their life they are singing about.'[23] The lyrics of Pickett's biggest hit, 'In the Midnight Hour', describe a situation not exclusive to black experience. Both Pickett and Chris Farlowe, a white Londoner who covered the song, sound equally thrilled about the prospect of a tryst beneath the stars. How then do you make a value judgement like Winwood's? The argument about white incapacity to 'sing the blues like a coloured person' loses ground through Farlowe's version of T-Bone Walker's 'Stormy Monday Blues' which, released under the guise of Little Joe Cook, fooled most people into believing he was an obscure negro soul singer. What, therefore, is 'soul'? Is it someone who sings as if he needs to clear his throat, or is it the West Indian next door lilting a never-ending 'Stand by me' as he creosotes the toolshed on Sunday afternoon?

If you accept, with skiffle scribe Brian Bird, that blues is the main content of jazz,[24] then 'soul' – with 'classical', the most abused expression in music – can be defined roughly as a form of rhythm and blues in which jazz and gospel meet pop, and the artist sounds as if what's being presented is too intense for satisfactory verbal or expected melodic articulation. With gospel fervour, a soul singer capitalizes on, rather than shrinks from, his inability to reach beyond his vocal compass without cracking. Of course, only the best can put on the agony night after night. Usually 'soul' degenerates into hammy exhibitionism, as most of the Stax and Tamla Motown reviews in the mid-sixties demonstrated: let me hear you say 'yeah'!

It helped if you had something the matter with you. Laying it on with a trowel, while Johnny Ray's hearing aid was always visible when, on cue, he collapsed in tears. Little Willie John was an alcoholic who died in jail. There were drug addicts galore but it was enough for hip white record buyers if you were merely black: direct from the ghetto, 'that's their life they are singing about'.

Black, blind and mainlining on heroin, Ray Charles had it worst – or best – of all. He also had a horrible voice. By European bel canto standards, he was devoid of vowel purity, plummy eloquence or nicety of intonation. Instead you got slovenly diction, disjointed range and a strangled vehemence dredged from a throat with vocal chords and muscles beyond remedy after years of singing any old how in night spots across continental America. However inaudible without electronic assistance, Ray's tortuous vocal endowment still conveyed such exquisite brush strokes of enunciation and inflection that a fractional widening of vibrato during a sustained note could be as loaded as his most anguished wail. These battered nuances compared to the buzzings and rattlings of avant-garde composer John Cage's works for pianos 'treated' with objects from household and office. Less obliquely, much the same gravelly piquancy of extra-tonal shading occurred with guitarist Link Wray's preparatory jabbing of pencils into his amplifier speakers to achieve the crunching rowdiness of his fifties instrumental hit, 'Rumble'.

Ray Charles' long catalogue of vocal records was frequently punctuated by an all-instrumental album but, whatever he did, he always sounded like Ray Charles. As a jazz pianist, he was excellent if stylized – recording with Count Basie and, in 1959, with Milt Jackson of the Modern Jazz Quartet an album entitled *Soul Brothers*. He used melody as structural radar, and his vocal phrasing owed much to his scatting on alto saxophone.

Of course he sold records by the ton, gaining four Grammies in 1961. Love to the loveless shown, he was so worshipped that a white girl fan offered him her eyes. In Britain, there were many inhibited onstage emasculations of Ray's US chartbusters by early home-reared rockers. A particular preference was the call-and-response 'What'd I Say' which twenty-nine-year-old Ray had first improvised in 1959 at a Pittsburgh dance, trading 'heys' and 'yeahs' with his female vocal trio, the Raelettes, like a spiritual's exhorter–congregation interplay.

The mild-mannered Marty Wildes and Johnny Gentles gave way to Merseybeat groups toughened by hundreds of hours on stage in Hamburg clubs. Covers of 'What'd I Say' were dared on vinyl by the Searchers and Gerry and the Pacemakers. Once Charles' intermission band at a concert in Frankfurt, the Beatles were joined onstage at the Top Ten by Tony Sheridan's Jets for a 'What'd I Say' lasting ninety minutes. Five years later, John Mayall's Bluesbreakers recorded their version. Though not as obvious an influence on British pop as Chuck Berry, other Ray Charles numbers cropped up at every point of the spectrum – from the Animals, Dave Berry and Georgie Fame to less rhythm and blues-orientated acts like the Zombies and the Dave Clark Five.

Few British group vocalists were capable, however, of taking on Ray Charles without affectation. Eric Burdon, Cliff Bennett, Van Morrison and Joe Cocker all came close but, as Muff Winwood reminds us,

> before that, Steve had already been turned onto Ray Charles who was then his biggest influence. I remember us listening to 'Hit the Road, Jack' [in 1961] and we bought Ray Charles' 'live' album [*At Newport*, 1959]. Around that time, Steve's voice began to break over a six-month period. While his voice was breaking, he was consciously trying to sing like Ray Charles with a child's voice. After six months, it came out like a black voice and it was quite natural.[19]

As Gene Pitney's polished tenor was warped to a dentist's drill whinge, so Steve's chorister soprano had been corrupted for all time by Ray Charles – except that it was a painless, more robust Ray Charles with a wider register.

It was round the house of another Birmingham schoolboy, Andy Dunkley – later a well-known disc jockey – that the Winwood brothers had first heard Charles and other American rhythm and blues artists. They discovered that 'there was something about R. and B. that was quite irresistible. You couldn't help but want to play it.'[12] As sure as the sunrise, it entered the repertoire of a fluctuating eight-piece jazz band that Muff had formed at school in 1960. The Muff Woody Jazz Band had evolved from a skiffle group that had switched its allegiance to rather less-than-pure traditional jazz, which was to undergo such a revival around 1961 that several of its older practitioners made the pop charts.

However, a transition to trad from skiffle was unusual, as most skiffle groups that hadn't fallen by the wayside were more likely to backslide via amplification to rock 'n' roll and an increasingly more American UK Top Twenty. The reason why skiffle was over by 1958 was firstly that most of it was for the benefit of its performers rather than its audience. Like punk after it, anyone with a little imagination who'd mastered basic techniques could do it. Nationwide, they were – thousands of skifflers thrumming tea chest basses, singing through their nostrils, thimbling washboards, rasping comb-and-paper, clanking dustbin lid cymbals and thrashing that E chord on five-quid guitars like Steve Winwood's.

Another death blow to skiffle was the arrival of Dr Vivian Fuchs at Scott Base after his historic trans-Antarctic trek. He and his team were greeted by a hastily assembled skiffle group going to town on 'My Bonnie Lies Over the Ocean'. With this *Boys' Own Paper* episode as the spur, more youth club big shots saw skiffle, rowdy though it was, as more potent than ping-pong for keeping teenagers off the streets and out of the coffee bars. Another nail in the coffin was a Camberwell vicar's 'Skiffle Mass', making a cheerful noise unto the God of Jacob.

On the bedpost overnight, skiffle lost its flavour. Nevertheless, the British beat boom spearheaded by the Beatles had had its roots in skiffle which – though it was derived from the rent parties, speakeasies and dustbowl jug bands of the US Depression – had never gripped the imagination of young America. If Lonnie Donegan's 'Railroad Bill' hadn't much to do with a tanner for a curling British Rail sandwich, at least it had been sufficiently anglicized – with 'new words and music' – from the American not to be sneered at – as was, say, Jim Dale's unspeakable cover of 'All Shook Up'. Donegan, the craze's figurehead, was – more than Tommy Steele – a British equivalent of Elvis in his vivacious processing of black music for a white audience. Though he was criticized for broadening his appeal with 'My Old Man's a Dustman' and other gems from the Golden Days of Empire, if anything he made skiffle more homogeneously British by fusing black rhythms with pub singalong and English folk music. It was easily more credible than a company director with a trimmed beard hollering behind his banjo about dem ole cotton fields back home.

Because Donegan's later selections were reminiscent of school and wedding receptions, Muff and Steve shied away from the 'Dustman' end of skiffle. They edged instead towards 'ethnic' influences closer to Lonnie's 1955 breakthrough, 'Rock Island Line', originally by a twice-reprieved murderer, Huddie Ledbetter – 'Leadbelly' – doing his bird in Texas State Prison in 1934. 'I came through a folk-blues thing on guitar,' recalled Steve, 'like digging Sonny Terry and Brownie McGhee at first and then Buddy Guy and the rest of them.'[25] Thus stimulated, Steve with Muff and a high percentage of other musicians would flock to whatever blues package show reached Birmingham – such as the American Folk, Blues and Gospel Caravan of April 1964 which presented Chicago blues giant Muddy Waters, his Mississippi pianist cousin Otis Spann and testifying Sister Rosetta Tharpe.

Often supporting on these occasions was the local Ian Campbell Folk Group, skiffle survivors and stalwarts of the Midlands folk scene. From Campbell's combo would emerge future Fairport Convention fiddler Dave Swarbrick, who was usually introduced as 'the Black Country Cowboy'. Among the many forums for Birmingham folk artists was the Boggery Club, which convened in a Solihull rugby pavilion. A Robert Davis of Acocks Green learned his comedian's craft there and would later become famous as 'Jasper Carrott', making his first Hollywood film in 1988. Unable to extend beyond parochial popularity, however, was acoustic blues specialist Mike Brown. Despite his extreme youth, a chaperoned Steve Winwood (now thirteen) entered this circuit as an alternative to 'playing jazz in clubs on Sundays'.[13]

The Muff Woody Jazz Band's flirtation with trad on the Kenny Ball–Acker Bilk axis rather than that of the Temperance Seven had been brief. It was intimidating, anyway, on the trad network of parish halls and pub back rooms, where watching enthusiasts were likely to know more about the music's history than did the musicians. The 'jazz' content in some numbers was frequently negligible because, if some black dotard from New Orleans had recorded a particularly definitive solo, it was sometimes thought prudent to learn it note for note for regurgitation at every public performance. It was not unknown for some purists to boo if a trad band deviated from prescribed Louisiana precedent by including saxophonists or committing the more cardinal sin of amplification.

Like the New Magnolia Jazz Band, Muff's octet didn't stick to the rules. As well as feeling no qualms about saxophones, Muff himself ditched his plinking trad banjo for guitar. Into the bargain, he believed, like his brother, that 'the guitar is actually the only instrument that improves its quality by being amplified'.[26] Tagging along with the other personnel – trumpet, trombone, double bass and drums – was young Steve on his Oscar Peterson piano. Although the band found much of its work in colleges and the university, Steve's 'greatest disappointment was going into a pub in my short trousers hidden behind Muff and the publican refused to let me play because I was under age. He sent me home – that was the lowest I've ever felt.'[24]

Searching for a style compatible with such a nebulous line-up, the eight had the rhythmic kick to try 'small band Ellingtonia' and similar arrangements from Atlantic Road's catholic record archives. None the less, Steve and Muff felt most at ease with 'the bluesier side of modern jazz, people like Ray Charles and Charlie Mingus, although I always preferred the jazz people who had an element of pop in their music . . . Louis Jordan, for instance, or Bill Doggett'.[12] With a growing emphasis on vocal items, Steve became less expendable: 'when the group started, we were looking for a coloured singer but we couldn't get one. I started singing because we couldn't get anyone else. I never expected I'd become known as a singer'.[7]

Already, word of mouth about his keyboard skills alone had led to Steve's freelancing in other bands – provided it did not interfere with school or tax his loyalty to Muff. Led by genial trumpeter Jim Simpson, the New Magnolia combo were among the first to request his services – for the princely fee of fifteen shillings (75p) per engagement. Flattered but slightly awed, the boy depped for Jim's West Indian pianist, Ron Daley, who had absorbed much of Count Basie's mainstream virtuosity. As Steve knocked back lemonade during the intervals, Simpson wondered 'how he was old enough to have heard of these guys he played like'.

More in demand than even this erudite youngster was lofty, beetle-browed Peter York – in Jim Simpson's opinion 'the most driving drummer I've ever heard'. Its avant-garde extremes notwithstanding, Pete loved all roots and branches of jazz with a passion more eager than even the Winwoods, father and sons. Unlike most rock 'n' roll drummers, Pete – with cymbals carefully positioned horizontally like Buddy Rich – had long disciplined himself to regular practice, never resting on any laurels. As well as

New Magnolia and his own Excelsior Jazz Band, he also played with Muff Woody and – for the money – what he referred to with a jazzer's amused disdain as 'bloody pop groups'.

Even though he was studying for a business qualification in Birmingham, Pete had acquired the dedication of a professional musician. If Pete York had given his word on a booking, he'd be there – even if, as once happened, he was doubled-up behind the kit with a chronic stomach complaint. No sympathy-seeking martyr when thus afflicted, Pete was well liked for his over-developed sense of humour which then looked towards the Goons, that late fifties' radio precursor of *Monty Python*. A witty writer as well, had his musical interests not impinged so heavily, he might have carried through his vague plans to write comedy scripts for television.

An only child, born in Redcar, Yorkshire in 1942, he'd been a bit of a card too at the fee-paying Nottingham High School. In the school's compulsory army cadet corps, he elected to join the band where he was taught the rudiments of the trumpet and snare drum; progressing faster on the latter. From the rat-a-tat-tat of military marches, he perfected on a full kit at home the necessary hand and foot co- ordination. His mother, Dorothy, was a keen jazz fan, and Pete often accompanied her to concerts – hearing both Ellington and Basie at Leicester's De Montfort Hall. Dorothy didn't mind the din as he strove to emulate the Max Roaches and Gene Krupas whose records he wore away. Lessons from Lionel Rubin – who drummed with Frenchified trad trombonist George Chisholm – were, however, a more direct indoctrination, leaving an ineradic-able impression on York's approach to percussion.

At Trent College he was a prominent member of the jazz club, making an amateur debut with its group in 1957. But as his father was anxious for his son to make a career in the steel industry, as he himself had done, Pete served a commercial apprenticeship at Guest, Keen and Nettlefold, where he acquired knowledge that would have more than an incidental bearing on his future. But his talent as a drummer, even then, was far above the ordinary, and in his Harborne flat, he was provident enough both to keep up with his business studies and not to lose his touch on the drums.

He came to be regarded with some respect by drummers riding the jazz craze who chanced to hear him when they visited Birmingham. Among them were Ron Bowden from Kenny Ball's Jazzmen and Stepney session player Kenny Clare, with whom acquaintance was renewed backstage at a Wembley Pool spectacular in 1966 after Pete and the Winwoods had become famous with one of these 'bloody pop groups'.

2

The Birmingham Backbeat

In 1985, Alan Clayson and the Argonauts celebrated their tenth unsuccessful year in showbusiness. All our records have missed – one deservedly so. After deducting overheads for a fortnight's tour of Ireland, I was uncertain whether to spend my cut of what remained on a box of matches or a pair of shoelaces. At any given booking, I'm never sure that we're not going to end up being lynched. A significant engagement a few years ago was at a charity function in an asylum.

While recognizing faults, I could seek causes to explain my own conduct and battle false accusation. Otherwise I stay convinced that my artistic purpose has been misunderstood and that it is merely a matter of time before I Make It. As Robert Louis Stevenson wrote: 'Our business in life is not to succeed but to continue to fail in good spirits.' Forgetting the 'in good spirits' bit, I've been this way since 1963.

As some withered pedagogue prattled on about geometry, I'd be stealing illicit squints beneath desk-top level at *Record Mirror*, as others would at *War Picture Library*, Roy of the Rovers in *Hotspur* or selected passages from *Lady Chatterley's Lover*. As homework was neglected in the evening, sometimes the records said it for me – a Pretty Things' B-side, 'I Can Never Say', being a particularly articulate speech of the heart as I traced a guitar in the vapour of my bedroom window and wondered why my mother didn't understand. The reason why I won without effort a pop quiz at the Three Horseshoes twenty years later was that the so-called trivialities of the Big Beat were more meaningful to me than anything that a Farnborough Grammar School master could teach. You can hear Phil May drop his maraccas at the end of 'Rosalyn'. Reg Presley was one of the research team that invented the motorway fog warning light. On the French picture sleeve of 'Terry' you can see one of Twinkle's nipples. Steve Winwood's purple and yellow scarf was knitted by a fan. His trousers were made in Kidderminster. The registration number of his Triumph Vitesse ws 8286 HA. Dave Mason used British Music (BT) strings for his sitar. My friend's cousin knew someone whose sister slept with Roy Wood.

Emulation of heroes is a vital part of growing up, affecting the clothes you can't afford, the hairstyle you're forbidden to have, and the manner in which you mouth into your hairbrush-as-microphone in front of the bedroom mirror. Much of my teenage self-image was formed with Dave Berry – 'the Human Sloth', 'the Singing Spider' – lurking in the shadows in much the same way as Ray Charles had influenced an older schoolboy, Steve Winwood.

Transfixed by the Beatles on ITV's *Sunday Night at the London Palladium*, I was disturbed by my father's remarks about how ephemeral and lowbrow it all was. Partly for the sake of domestic harmony, I supposed he was right, but could anyone old enough to have fought Hitler have guessed that the Beatles would be more than 'a passing phase' – as evangelist Billy Graham put it when they conquered America? In 1963, the Fab Four themselves had made contingency plans should their time be up. Pop was harmless enough as long as you didn't start taking it seriously. You were certainly discouraged from thinking of it as a career. You could form a jazz combo provided it didn't interfere with your exams. At Farnborough Grammar there was even a transitory Blues Club which trod warily amidst an official malevolent neutrality until realization that, beyond a sociological study of aspects of black America, members actually enjoyed listening to its 'screaming idiotic words and savage music'.[1]

Even fourteen-year-old Steve Winwood, then about to join what amounted to a semi-professional pop group,

had the mistaken impression that rock and roll was a juvenile thing. In some ways, it probably is but it's also very hard to do well. I've been surprised by it, by how much is still coming out of it from young groups as well as people who have been around a long time. Rock and roll has become acceptable which means it has lost part of its early charm but it's important to make the music to reflect what you are. On the whole, I think it's a pretty honest kind of music . . . the best of it anyway.[2]

In the offices and factories of Britain today, how many middle-aged employees cast aside adolescent folly in the early sixties by quitting pop groups which, in the wake of the Beatles, became famous and sometimes rich? Perhaps kicking themselves now are such as solicitor Jim Spencer, ex-Dave Clark Five saxophonist; guitarist B. D. Smith, who left what was to become the Yardbirds for the civil service; and drummer Tommy Moore, who found his wages at Garston Bottle Works preferable to sticking it out with the Beatles. Gone from Muff Winwood's jazz band by then were personnel lumbered with wives and children who wanted them home in the evenings. Muff himself had just got engaged to his girlfriend, Zena. Gone from his unit too were the students who, having finished their courses, now had to work to keep alive.

1963 was a boom time for pop groups, true enough, but you still had to be obsessed to go the distance. Back from school or work, you'd dive into a bath. Afterwards, with your sister's drier, you'd restyle your hair from the combed-back flatness often required to avoid persecution in daytime surroundings where even Elvis Presley was not yet a yardstick of masculinity. Depending on how long you were able to grow it, you could try a Beatle moptop, a Rolling Stone feather duster or, to emphasize Mod solidarity, a centre parting to the crown and a bouffant pile-up the rest of the way with the sides brushed straight over the ears. Bolting down a meal, you'd wait for an overloaded van one hour late to transport you to some freezing town hall, ballroom, pub or youth club. Architecturally, it was often some late Victorian monstrosity where, through latticed windows dim with grime, you and the others would be perceived setting up puny amplifiers to power voices – many yet to spit out the plums – and never-never guitars. Unaided by microphones, the drummer would position his kit – snare, cymbals (crash, ride and hi-hats), tom-toms and kick-bass with the group name painted on its front skin.

Unless you'd already done so, now was the time to change into stage suits in whatever alcove had been set aside for this – kitchen, toilet, store cupboard, maybe even a dressing room. There'd be rare cranks like the Rolling Stones, who all dressed differently, but few did not adhere to prevalent fashion various steps behind Carnaby Street. In the provinces a male 'Mod' sartorial conformity surfaced, hinging vaguely on Cuban-heeled winkle-pickers, hipster flares, corduroy jacket and either roll-necked nylon pullover or denim shirt with button-down collar and tie. The last of these, being the cheapest garment, was also the most variable, ranging from Op-art slim-jim to eye-torturing kipper.

On the strength of appearance, 'Mods' wouldn't necessarily get turned away from the parish dance. They'd even earn praise from swingin' vicars for their smartness. You could be a bank clerk and, long hair apart, still look the part without inviting the sack. At the same time, you could still be recognized by other initiates by signs as conspiratorial as a freemason's handshake. Some Mods identified themselves by simply leaving all their coat buttons undone except the top one.

Of corresponding uniformity were Rockers – real or imitation black leather windcheaters, blue jeans, motorbike boots and T-shirts. Their greasy ducktailed coiffure was in direct line of descent from that of the Teddy Boys, as was their taste in music. In Birmingham, one of the leading Rocker bands was the Rockin' Berries, who were steeped in the classic rock 'n' roll of the Berry–Vincent–Lewis–Presley genre. A few months before their formation in 1959, their vocalist, Clive Lea, had defied all comers in an 'Elvis of the Midlands' talent contest. The title was next assumed by Tipton pop singer Nicky James who, backed by a group containing various future Moody Blues and Move members, continued defiantly hip-shakin', smirking lopsidedly and oiling his gravity-defying cockade throughout the Mod-dominated Beat Boom – a shower of paternity suits emphasizing his local appeal.

Except at set-piece clashes at seaside resorts during bank holidays, enmity between Rockers and Mods was never as virulent as the newspapers made out. Usually they'd just congregate at opposite ends of a café. However, if delegations of each tribe showed up at a dance there was likely to be at least the threat of a punch-up – hence the hiring by promoters of squads of narrow-eyed bouncers to keep the peace. Brawling outside the premises was a matter for the local constabulary, who these days had taken to paying routine visits towards the close of functions involving beat groups. If this protection was withdrawn, outnumbered Mods or Rockers might resort to escape via the frosted window of a water closet, as I was obliged to myself on mercifully few occasions.

Deliberately providing inadequate seating to maximize audience capacity – often breaking fire regulations – venues booked groups who were expected to deliver energetic, action-packed pop, frequently in exhausting shifts, in order to divert their flirting, trouble-making, sometimes drunken patrons. Generating a happy, fun-loving onstage atmosphere, groups would feel compelled to maintain ghastly, fearful grins as before their eyes their music would accompany beatings-up. The musicians themselves and their equipment would sometimes be smashed up too. The provocation would be either catching the eye of some hard case's girl, or a repertory infraction – such as not responding to a request, or failing to play enough slow numbers (or fast ones) to facilitate the winning of a maiden's heart.

In those days before the birth pill, pre-marital sex was a bigger step to take than it was when the sixties finally started Swinging. Boys were spotty – girls untouchable. None the less in a pop group – always predominantly male – a perk of the job was readier access to female flesh than most of the blokes who'd paid five bob (25p) to shuffle about in the gloom beyond the burning footlights. Now and then the clothes, bone structure and natural slow-and-easy solitary dance movements of an Ace Face would attract notice, but otherwise members of pop groups – no matter how ill-favoured – had more licence to pull the Quant-cropped dolly-birds with sooty eyes who clustered below the central microphone. It was much like the difference between the glamorous 'over-paid, over-sexed and over here' American GIs during the Second World War and the native common-or-garden squaddie with his dung-coloured regimentals, peanut wages and built-in sense of defeat.

Yet those with this bra-strap *droit de seigneur* in the sixties were sons of Britain, where nearly every town and shire now had a 'sound'. This figment of publicists' imaginations had germinated during the summer of 1963 when 'How Do You Do It' by Gerry and the Pacemakers was replaced at number one in the UK charts by the Beatles' 'From Me to You', which in turn was toppled by Gerry's second single. Six weeks later two more Liverpool groups, the Searchers and Billy J. Kramer with the Dakotas, engaged in a like tussle until both were levelled again by the Beatles, who slugged it out with Gerry for chart suzerainty for the rest of the year. This was interrupted only by the usurping Brian Poole and the Tremeloes from Dagenham who, partly through the implications of Brian's surname, were promoted as the London wing of what was now known as 'Merseybeat' or the 'Liver*pool* Sound'. Simple commercial expendiency sent talent scouts from record company offices in the metropolis to plunder the musical gold of Merseyside. Though the region's groups ran a stylistic gauntlet from country and western to rhythm and blues to traditional jazz, preference was given to those with either Beatle connections or a passing resemblance. Gutted of its major talents, Merseybeat was left to rot as the contract-waving host ploughed on next to Manchester, where too were bands who brushed their hair forwards, played 'Money', 'Twist and Shout' and the entire Chuck Berry songbook, and – at the drop of a cheque – could talk Scouse. The biggest fish to be hooked here were the Hollies, whose only deviation from the format was a guitarist whose hair was quaintly dishmopped like Tommy Steele's.

Nevertheless in snaring the frantic Freddie and the Dreamers, who were fronted by a spindly, four-eyed, trouser-dropping singer, the EMI artist-and-repertoire manager rather broke the pattern. Further deviations were discovered and processed for the hit parade in other northern cities. Knocking 'em dead in Newcastle were the motley Animals, eternal Geordies. Hailing from Sheffield, the Cruisers backed spider-fingered Dave Berry glowering furtively behind an upturned collar. Turning south-wards, the 'Tottenham Sound' of the Dave Clark Five, led by an upwardly mobile Mod drummer, ousted the Beatles from number one in January 1964. Virtually every area in the country put forward some local oiks who enjoyed, however modest, a qualified fame. There were St Albans' minor-key Zombies ('Hertsbeat'), Cheshire's Lancastrians (!), the mordant Poets from Glasgow and the Troggs, all-time Unthinking Man's Pop Group, who heralded the non-existent 'Andover Sound'. Horsham's Beat Merchants vanished as mysteriously as they appeared on ITV's *Thank Your Lucky Stars*, frenziedly miming to 'Pretty Face'. Let's also hear it for the 'Trentside Beat' of Jet Wayne and his Cavaliers, and the Wishful Thinking of Aldershot. Beyond geographical identity, the prayers of a Salvation Army 'beat group', the Joystrings, were answered with two Top Fifty ascents in 1964. Not so blessed were Chinese Londoners, the Ying-tongs and the Etceteras. Though they never made a record, Nottingham's Latvian community could also boast a group. The world will never know what it missed. Everywhere, it seemed, could brag of a sixties band that Hit the Big Time – even if to do so required a degree of logical blindness and retiming of the truth.

What then of Birmingham, midway between London and Liverpool? High on every grasping A. and R. representative's hit list, the Second City was, it was forecast by the *TV Times*, the most likely source of the next Titans of Teen. This opinion was based on 'Go Now', the Moody Blues' number one in January 1965. Sounder argument for this judgement was more deeply rooted. In 1962 the Beatles – still with drummer Ringo Starr's predecessor, Pete Best – had partaken in a 'Battle of the Bands' promotion with Gerry Levene and the Avengers, a quintet of comparable popularity in Birmingham. In March that same year, what came to be regarded as the first 'Brumbeat' record – 'Sugar Babe' by Jimmy Powell and the Five Dimensions – was released on Decca.

A Birmingham venture to the Top Ten interior came two years later with 'Tell Me When' by the red-smocked Applejacks who, discovered at their Monday night residency in that suburb's civic hall, were visualized by Decca as harbingers of a 'Solihull Sound'. As well as a female bass guitarist, a further distinction was a thick Brummagem lead vocal. Within eight months the more accomplished Rockin' Berries carried the throbbing sob-story 'He's in Town' – their fourth single – to number three. Both the Berries and Applejacks had notched up two more chart entries apiece when the Moody Blues' turn came.

No less an authority than Cliff Richard's elderly producer Norrie Paramor – after liaising with 'Ma' Regan, a notorious local promoter – had pronounced 'all the Birmingham groups I have signed have a lot of potential. The Beat Boom is subsiding and I think Birmingham will keep it flourishing.' These remarks were quoted in issue number one of *Midland Beat*, launched in October 1963. The newspaper's editor was Dennis Detheridge, who operated from an office overlooking playing fields in Moseley. From the art school here had sprouted the Rockin' Berries and Gerry Levene's Avengers, whose Kitt's Green guitarist, Roy Wood, was to join Mike Sheridan and the Nightriders for six flop singles on EMI.

With its monthly venue information and chronicling of key personalities, *Midland Beat* was modelled on Bill Harry's unprecedented *Merseybeat* of 1962. That such a sixpenny journal had to reprint after selling out within hours demonstrated the strength of demand for its 'complete coverage of the Midlands Beat and jazz scene'.[3] The main feature of the first *Midland Beat*, however, was an interview with John Lennon, 'one of the Beatles, but otherwise the entire content is restricted to Midlands items'[3] for, according to Detheridge, 'Liverpool started the ball rolling. Now the Midlands is ready to take over.'[3] Yet December's frustrated editorial cried: 'why has the Brum Beat failed to gain a place in the Top Twenty?'[4] Perhaps it was because Dennis had overestimated the cohesion and depth of the city's pop scene. His was an easy mistake. After all, dozens of groups – most less than a year old – infested every borough, many bending over backwards in their hyperbole.

The Grasshoppers, for example, were 'Meriden's answer to the Beatles'. Ruling Wednesbury were Sirius and his Planets. Hot on the heels of the Applejacks in Solihull were the Rinki-dinks, while Bloxwich cradled 'the Midlands' youngest group', the Jaguars. Yardley's fave raves were the Chindits, whose singer copied Mick Jagger. Further afield, the Square Ones and the Huskies held sway in Kidderminster. Coventry, birthplace of Frank Ifield, spewed forth Formula One, the Peeps, the Sabres and the Sovereigns plus

Johnny B. Great and the Quotations, who were to back the Walker Brothers; the Brothers' vocalist, John Maus, producing a CBS single by Wolverhampton's Finders Keepers. The winners of a Midland Search for Tomorrow's Stars, Ken Jackson and his Strangers, hailed from olde worlde Henley-in-Arden. North to Rugby the boss groups were the Mighty Avengers, who wooed the Top Fifty with a Rolling Stones' composition, 'So Much in Love', and, bringing greater honour to the town, Pinkerton's (Assorted) Colours, whose debut 45, 'Mirror, Mirror', shimmering with electric autoharp, got a look in at number nine. From Stoke-on-Trent, the Marauders lived up to *Midland Beat*'s 'Pride of the Potteries'[3] citation by harrying the lower reaches of the Top Fifty with their Decca single, 'That's What I Want' in August 1963 – though the Cheetahs from Erdington brought off this feat twice a year later with 'Mecca' and 'Soldier Boy', respectively Gene Pitney and Shirelles' covers.

As the sixth *Midland Beat* pointed out, duplication of names was a source of confusion. Three bands, for instance, called themselves the Brumbeats, while there was also Beat Limited and the Big Beats – whose rhythm guitarist showed greater imagination in his *nom de guerre*, Wimp Feder. The Renegades of Birmingham put Worcester's Renegades' noses out of joint by chalking up a Finnish number one in 1965, while the Mods from Aston made Perkins of a rash of other opportunists by topping a 'Local Group' popularity poll in *Jackie*, a girls' magazine. Among Norrie Paramor's signings, the Beachcombers – whose drummer was Dario Capaldi – have been confused with a Wembley surfing combo of the same name whence came Keith Moon of the Who. Imagine my chagrin, as founder in the seventies of Billy and the Conquerors, at discovering Erdington's William and the Conquerors – thankfully they signed to RCA as the Frame. Of less erudite portent were the familiar-sounding rings to Dave Dee and the Deeman, the Nazz from King's Heath, the Cult, the Cimarrons and the New Wave.

While the rest of Warwickshire slept, these and others of the county's bands would gather at Alex's Pie Stand opposite the central Albany Hotel in Birmingham for a snack after Saturday night performances. As they ambled past the rows of Bedfords, Commers and the occasional new Transit parked along Smallbrook Queensway, rivalry would often dissolve into ribald cameraderie as musicians boasted, spread rumours, small-talked, borrowed equipment, betrayed confidences, schemed and had a laugh – or a cry – depending on how well they'd gone down. 'There was a great atmosphere – sort of all mates together, pursuing the same dreams,' recalled Sparkhill drummer Beverley Ralston of Carl Wayne and the Vikings. 'I think a lot of bands formed, changed line-ups and broke up at Alex's Pie Stand.'[5] They also provided news and false impressions of impending success for *Midland Beat* journalists. Who would admit, for example, that they'd taken the stage that evening before an audience of the hall caretaker and his barking dog plus two Rockers who left after the first number, setting off a fire extinguisher on the way out. All bookings, so it was frequently made out, were triumphs in retrospect. *Midland Beat* missed a lot of great moments, apparently.

The apogee of the first flush of Brum Beat came when both the Rockin' Berries and the chart-topping Moody Blues appeared on the same editon of the epoch-making *Ready Steady Go*. After 'Go Now' fell from the Top Forty in February 1965, no matter how much poetic licence Dennis Detheridge could wring from, say, the Redcaps' more exciting race through the Isley Brothers' 'Shout' than the hit cover by Lulu – or even a Bilston Town Hall encore by Andy's Clappers – the fact was that, though Birmingham's beat boom was as unstoppable as bubonic plague, it had mushroomed on the crest of a craze, growing in impact after rather than with Merseybeat. Because it lacked Liverpool's unique brand of enthusiasm, matured over years of sub-cultural isolation, scavenging London recording managers found precious few hitmakers among the competent but usually derivative outfits within the Second City's environs. Before the Beatles' breakthrough, scanty parochial opportunities had motivated what bands there were to self-imposed exile in West German clubland, where there was continued demand for British talent. Back from the Fatherland in November 1963, Ray Thomas then of the Krew Kats was astonished to find the Birmingham scene 'in total chaos. There were about two hundred and fifty groups, half thought they were Cliff Richard and the Shadows and the other half thought they were the Beatles.'[5]

Ray's Moody Blues were unusual in not pandering to crowd desires to hear current hits, drawing their repertoire instead from the obscurer archives of rhythm and blues. That this daring approach proved popular in the long run won them respect from less sophisticated brethren. As stylistically tenacious, however, were Dave Lacey's Corvettes and Steve Brett and the Mavericks, who each specialized in country and western. Other groups went in for instrumentals, as did the Telstars; the Second City Sound, who reached number twenty-two in 1966 with their execrable mangling of Tchaikovsky's First Piano Concerto; and the Jaguars – not the 'youngest group' – who, adding singer Al Jackson, became the

Applejacks. There were groups with gimmicks such as – also from Solihull – the crass Batman and his Wonderboys, formerly the Crowin' Codas, who, like the Cheetahs, costumed accordingly and thus made the front cover of *Midland Beat*. The Amazons had an amplified squeeze box, but an instrument more peculiar to Brumbeat than any other area's 'sound' was the flute employed by the Moody Blues, the Falling Leaves – Brumbeat finalists in Redifusion's *Ready Steady Win* contest in 1964 – and others.

When Birmingham pop came of age, circa 1967, Traffic and Tea-and-Symphony – Midlanders all – featured flautists too, but by then regional – and national – differences had diminished to such an extent that a world pop scene had started to flower. On the pop front, the United Kingdom's battle for exports had been won in the mid-sixties through the 'British Invasion' of the United States, spearheaded by the Beatles. Many American groups learnt the wild, long-haired Limey idioms so thoroughly that a lot of US and UK sounds were interchangeable – as were, for instance, in their fusion of Merseybeat and contemporary folk, the sounds of the Searchers and, from California, the Byrds. Later, the Searchers would be copying the Byrds copying the Searchers.

Overlooked amid this internationalism, Birmingham had arrived belatedly at a genuine 'sound' – the last British city to do so. More obviously basking in Birmingham Beat's Indian Summer than Traffic were the Move, whose five-year chart run – as creative as it was remunerative – began in 1967 with 'Night of Fear', using a leitmotiv borrowed from the 1812 Overture. Like the Moody Blues, they'd amalgamated from the cream of top Midlands combos – notably Mike Sheridan's Nightriders and, formed in 1958, Carl Wayne and the Vikings. The latter had metamorphosed from boys to men after a season in Hamburg's red-light clubland where, for £30 a week each, 'we started playing each night at 7 p.m. and did seven 45-minute spots, with 15-minute breaks, until two o'clock in the morning. Each weekend there were three-hour matinees too.'[6] Thus spake Bev Bevan, *né* Ralston; who was to beat an increasingly more splendid drum kit with the Move and then the Electric Light Orchestra, hitmakers of the seventies, whom Roy Wood quit in 1972 to try again with Wizzard, who knocked up two quick UK number ones within a year.

Victor of the ELO power struggle was guitarist Jeff Lynne, who previously had filled Wood's shoes in the Nightriders before leading the Idle Race, a group appreciated only in flashback. Among this unit's lesser achievements was a US-only version of the Move B-side, 'Here We Go Round the Lemon Tree', attended by aptly frugivorous publicity photographs. Like Lennon and McCartney in microcosm, members of the Move earned pin money by composing for other artists. Roy Wood – frontpaged by *Midland Beat* in March 1966 gripping a sitar – raked in most cash by far with such items as a Song for Europe entry and, for Amen Corner in 1969, 'Hello Susie' – their final Top Ten strike. Move bass guitarist Ace Kefford was responsible for the best-remembered single by the Lemon Tree, 'William Chalker's Time Machine', cartoon psychedelia which, had it been attributed to the Move, would have been a surefire hit – unlike its lacklustre follow-up, 'It's So Nice to Come Home', which, lacking Kefford and Move guitarist Trevor Burton's input, still benefited from the console skills of Amen Corner's Andy Fairweather-Low. Birmingham presented as incestuous a game of musical chairs as anywhere else. For example, Lemon Tree's drummer, Keith Smart, had served time in Danny King's Mayfair Set with future Lemon Tree producer Burton, while Lemon Tree guitarist Mick Hopkins had shared the stage with Roy Wood in the Avengers before replacing Denny Laine in the Diplomats, whose sticksman had been Bev Bevan.

In its infancy, Birmingham pop had embraced few groups with self-contained songwriting teams. Belatedly, Mike Pinder and Denny Laine of the Moody Blues made a tentative go of it, but, though they managed a couple of A-sides, only a handful of their compositions were included in the quintet's act. There were more isolated instances, such as Nicky James' composing of 'My Colour Is Blue' for his first single. But, with most bands concentrating instead on arrangements of non-originals, the Tin Pan Alley demarcation line between group and writer persisted well into the sixties. After crestfallen headway as performers, Raymond Froggett and Peter Lee Stirling were two from Birmingham who found their feet as jobbing songwriters. Partnered sometimes by his uncle, Stirling wrote hits for the Merseybeats, Kathy Kirby, Tommy Bruce's Bruisers – in which he played guitar – and, the ultimate accolade, Elvis Presley. As a solo singer in the group age, Peter – an embryonic Steve McQueen lookalike run to fat – could not find a niche, despite a most professional projection, flexible vocal command and commercial records. He was condemned to wait until 1971 when, grizzled and renamed Daniel Boone, he realized an easy-listening bonanza in the British Top Thirty.

That same autumn the Fortunes, after a six-year absence, regained a hold on the UK charts – even briefly denting the US Hot Hundred. One of at least three Midlands groups of that name, the Fortunes began as a Birmingham–Welsh vocal trio with the

Cliftones, a band of no great merit who mined a middle-of-the-road seam up to the coming of the Big Beat. Persuaded to broaden their scope by chucking in the Cliftones, investing in electric guitars and adding a rhythm section, the three singers, Glen Dale, Barry Pritchard and Rod Allen – renamed themselves the Fortunes Rhythm Group and were complimented on their neat, besuited turnout as they gained the day at a beat contest at Edgbaston's Gay Tower Ballroom. On the advice of their new manager, Reg Calvert – who also handled Pinkerton's Colours – they retained their wholesome image and 'quality' repertoire taken from the ilk of Dionne Warwick, Gene Pitney and *West Side Story*.

After pirate Radio Caroline had adopted the Fortunes' second Decca 45 as its theme tune, it was merely a matter of fifteen months before a three-record Top Twenty burst starting with 'You've Got Your Troubles' at number two in August 1965. These heavily orchestrated hits left them in a favourable negotiating position for engagements in cabaret and variety and, later, to do advertising jingles. Nevertheless in the interim, before their chart comeback with 'Freedom Come, Freedom Go', they began recording their own material, much of it a radical departure from the sentimental slop that had made them. That these experiments made no chart headway was connected with public memory of revelations that only Rod, Barry and Glen's impeccable harmonies had been heard on their hits; sessionmen attended to all instrumental offices. Though such practices were not uncommon, press coverage of the Fortunes' ill-advised confessions were not welcome publicity.

The Fortunes were as dissimilar from the Moody Blues as the Applejacks were from the Rockin' Berries. Almost all that the four had in common was that they were hit groups from the same part of the country. Furthermore, at a time when pop entertainers were only as good as their last single, each of the four, without exception, faded within a year of making the charts – though the Moody Blues, like the Fortunes, were granted a second bite of the cherry after a decent interval. There had been inevitable differences between all the successful Liverpool outfits too, but these were all variations on a fundamental structure, exemplified by the two-guitars-bass-and-drums beat group archetype, overlapping repertoires and affected common-as-muck Scouseness balanced by executive insistence that they clean up their acts. This regularity was a launch pad for liberal non-conformity within prescribed limits: Billy J. Kramer was the ballad merchant; the Swinging Blue Jeans wore denim; the Beatles combed their hair across their foreheads; the Merseybeats looked like gigolos; the Fourmost yukked it up as comedians; Gerry and the Pacemakers substituted electric piano for lead guitar.

Mike Pinder hammered the eighty-eights too but, to many watching the Moody Blues miming 'Go Now' on television, the group seemed asymmetrical and cluttered, what with Denny Laine monopolizing the lead vocal and guitar spotlight, while general instrumental factotum Ray Thomas merely wailed 'waaaaaah' into a shared microphone and rattled a tambourine – as did Clive Lea on 'He's in Town', taking an atypical back seat to rhythm guitarist Geoff Turton's falsetto. At a time when fans needed to identify clearly with a group before committing themselves, the Fortunes were on a losing wicket too, swamped by massed strings.

Probably because of the city's landlocked position in the centre of Britain, Birmingham pop, though widespread and possessing an eclectic stylistic approach, was devoid of regional identity. The Rockin' Berries on their first two singles, 'Wah Wah Woo' and 'Itty Bitty Pieces', could be mistaken for Dave Dee, Dozy, Beaky, Mick and Tich from the agricultural county of Wiltshire down south. Not only was it twice the size of Liverpool but Birmingham's catchment area, as *Midland Beat*'s widening circulation demonstrated, sprawled into East Anglia, mid-Wales and as far south as Beaconsfield, home of the Beaconsfield R & B Group – namechecked in issue number nine.

Many Welsh pop groups such as the Bystanders, Lot Thirteen, the Human Beans and, later, Love Sculpture – all from Swansea – plus, of course, Cardiff's Amen Corner, regarded Birmingham as a halfway house between valley obscurity and London Big Time – though a proud few wilfully sang exclusively in Welsh, thus setting the ceiling of their ambition on records released on shoestring labels to be plugged on BBC Wales' *Disc a dawn*: the blues in Welsh. Significantly, the final single by the most popular of such outfits, Y Tepot Piws, was titled 'Nid ydym ni mynda'r Birmingham' ('We're Not Going to Birmingham').

This hardly bothered Dennis Detheridge, who had also branched out into theatre, cabaret and selected book reviews as well as pop and jazz in what, by 1966, was subtitled 'the Midlands' leading entertainment monthly'. Right up to the final issue in August 1967 – outliving *Merseybeat* – the *Midland Beat* reader could select a night out from a vast array of parochial jive hives because, for hot Birmingham combos who failed to scale even the commercial heights of the Applejacks, there was consolation in the guarantee of a full workload within easy reach.

Clasping rock 'n' roll to its bosom in 1961 was the Hereford

Lounge in Yardley which opened the Twitch Club, immortalized in a Rockin' Berries flip side, as the Big Three's Cavern Stomp had the more famous Liverpool club. 'Top Local Groups Four Nights a Week' could be heard at the inescapable Brum Beat Cavern in Birmingham city centre. With as much avaricious haste after 'She Loves You' bounced to number one in September 1963, another entrepreneurial cabal – within it Denmark Street tunesmith Barry Mason – jumped in with the Kavern in nearby Small Heath. It was lent an authentic sheen by its dim lighting, low ceiling and the presence of the Searchers at its inauguration, headlining over locals Danny King and the Royals, the Defenders and Ace Kefford's Shantelles 'shortly before disbanding'.[4] The club's half-a-crown per year membership ballooned to five hundred within a fortnight. So much had the beat explosion impinged on the national consciousness by 1964 that the *Birmingham Evening Mail*, as well as *Midland Beat,* were inundated with advertisements for musicians, bands and venues such as 'Twistin' at the Intown Club' at the Crown near New Street railway station. Drumming with the Senators there, Bev Bevan met his future wife, butcher's daughter Valerie Taylor – a Great Barr Comprehensive contemporary of Steve Winwood's.

In Great Barr itself, the Trees was also offering beat sessions in a functions room, as were scores of other suburban public houses around the city; many of these venues assumed a separate life from the main premises, as, for instance, did the Morgue in the basement of Bearwood's Queen's Head. The Moody Blues' name was chosen for its initials, in the hope of sponsorship from the Mitchell and Butler's pub circuit. Some licensed bars, such as that at East Birmingham Working Men's Club, also provided rehearsal facilities.

Soft drinks only, however, was the order of the day for clubs contained within establishments like Hall Green Youth Club in Small Heath to the west, a respectable middle-class area sliding slowly into seediness. Now featuring pop groups once a week were Stourbridge YMCA and, on the south-west outskirts, the Rubery cinema. Catering likewise but with more professional entertainment for older teenagers were the hard-nosed managements of the Carlton Ballroom, the Ritz in King's Heath, the West Bromwich Adelphi and, capitulating to pop in July 1964, the Silver Blades Ice Rink. At Springfield Hall Pye record producer Tony Hatch thought twice about Denny Laine and the Diplomats, who had supported the Beatles at Old Hill Plaza, Wolverhampton as 'Love Me Do' left a tide mark at number eighteen in November 1962. For

Laine, who was to join Paul McCartney's post-Beatle Wings, this encounter was especially auspicious.

One year on, however, the Beatles had no time to chat when, while the last major sixth of 'Twist and Shout' yet reverberated amid incessant screaming, they did a runner from Birmingham Town Hall disguised as policemen from the West Mercian force. A few local musicians – including the Winwood brothers – had been privileged to be granted a backstage audience there with Bob Dylan in 1965, but of lesser hauteur was Jerry Lee Lewis, pictured in *Midland Beat*[7] sharing a joke with his opening act, Carl Wayne's Vikings.

After its unveiling in December 1964, Wayne, Mike Sheridan, Danny King and their groups forsook Alex's Pie Stand for Club Cedar on Constitution Hill, which served drinks until 2 a.m. If the dramatis personae of the Move came together there, Traffic was hatched at the Elbow Room, while also in the city centre stood another musicians' watering hole, the Rum Runner. For more sordid amusement there was the Las Vegas coffee bar, a stone's throw away in Soho and a haven for a midnight demi-monde of prostitutes, their pimps and – then liable to prosecution – practising homosexuals. Even there, the bands played on. 'Birmingham was and still is a place where everybody "gigs",' said Steve Winwood of these night clubs, 'by that, I mean everybody sits in with everybody else. There aren't many rigidly exclusive groups.'[8] From loose, simple patterns, both the nationally famous and those unknown beyond the Black Country would unwind on small stages in often unlikely combinations as an escape valve from the less off-beat presumptions of their selfish public.

Such ad hoc performances were available for those who had to be at work by eight o'clock the next morning too – if you looked hard enough. One foggy October Monday in 1963 in Hill Street, beneath the shadow of the Town Hall, the art deco interior of the Golden Eagle framed 'the unusual sight of prominent modern jazz instrumentalists like Johnny Collins, Harry Wilkes and Tony Peers playing alongside members of the Renegades and other beat exponents'.[3] Rhythm and blues had also come to Birmingham in the form of the Rhythm Unlimited weekly club, which complemented the Golden Eagle's Wednesday jazz sessions. A mainstay of Rhythm Unlimited was a popular singing guitarist from Wales, Spencer Davis, who had 'been wanting to experiment with this type of music for some time. This club has provided me with the opportunity. I think it is a shot in the arm for the music scene in Birmingham'.[3]

These cells of such crazy, far-out music kept middle-class collegiate adherents happy, but where did it get you? Reputations were made playing assembly-line pop in the ballrooms which provided a link from Hall Green Youth Club-type bashes to record contracts and big theatre tours. Furthermore, the BBC Light Programme's two-hour pop show, *Saturday Club*, was recorded in Birmingham and transmitted nationally, as were dozens of Independent Television programmes, via Sutton Coldfield's transmitter, the first to be built outside London. The jewel in ITV's pop crown was *Thank Your Lucky Stars* – hosted by Brian Matthew, pullovered and *sans* tie, as casually dressed as a balding former announcer in his mid-thirties could be without being called to task by his staider superiors. If he introduced the Beatles as he would *Sportsview*, at least he forewent inane yap and got on the job. As well as some elaborate stage sets, local flavour was injected by an elfin Wednesbury teenager with a half-beehive, Janice Nicholls, who passed judgement on the latest discs. Her over-used catch-phrase, 'I wouldn't buy it but I'll give it five' – the maximum score – delivered in a vile Brummie monotone, formed the lyrical bedrock of her 1964 cash-in single on Decca.

Given the advantage of proximity to both the Light Programme and ITV studios, groups with whom Janice and her mates might have fraternized were transformed from boys-next-door to pop sensations. One such nine-day wonder was Brian Hines who, denying his daytime occupation as a Temple Row department store trainee, made his television debut as Denny Laine with his Diplomats on the topical *Midlands at Six*. Because they toed a clean, amiable line, ITV had Denny's group in matching suits and peroxided locks on two sub-*Lucky Stars* weekday pop showcases – *For Teenagers Only* and *Pop Shop* – and, at the bitter end, as intermission music on *Lunch Box*, the lightest of light entertainment shows, built round the personality of Noele Gordon prior to her *grande dame* part in ITV's long-running soap opera *Crossroads*, set in a Midlands motel.

Denny and the Diplomats role model might have been Shane Fenton and the Fentones from glum Mansfield, where the last chip shop closed at 10.30 p.m. Amassing an extensive work schedule beyond Nottinghamshire, this quintet had mailed a tape of one of their recitals to the Light Programme. Unhappily, before receiving a summons to report for a Corporation audition Shane Fenton (alias John Theakston) died of rheumatic fever. Taking stock, the Fentones convinced their road manager and general dogsbody, Bernard Jewry, to front them as the second Shane Fenton. The

34

group were offered a regular spot on *Saturday Club,* and the programme's musical director, Tommy Sanderson, secured them a Parlophone recording contract in 1961. With their *Saturday Club* renown and scrupulous plugs on *Thank Your Lucky Stars*, Shane-Bernard and the Fentones enoyed a modicom of chart success until folding officially after a poignant showdown on *Saturday Club* in July 1964.

Both Fenton and Laine recorded at EMI's Abbey Road – though Laine's efforts were never released. Even after Merseybeat, most provincial groups were still obliged to make their records in London. To tape their first LP, *Birthday Party*, in 1968, the Idle Race would hurtle down the M1 each Sunday morning for off-peak sessions at Advision studios in Bond Street before driving back like Cinderella to twilit Birmingham to replay the results in Jeff Lynne's Shard End front room, an Aladdin's cave of linked-up reel-to-reel tape recorders, editing blocks and jack-to-jack leads. Boffins like Lynne did not need to be told by a recording engineer that, after a song or 'information' has been taped, you have to listen to the 'playback' of the recording, which is referred to as a 'take'. If any part of the performance is not right, you and your group re-record just that section and the recording engineer can then cut out the bad stuff and patch in the new.

Even this simplistic litany was alien to the majority of British groups, who had progressed from rehearsals to performing to The Day We Went To a Recording Studio. With no amplifier or speaker cabinet in sight when bands mimed to their singles on *Thank Your Lucky Stars*, you could almost be forgiven for thinking that you had to plug 'electric' guitars directly into the mains. For years I thought that 'PA' stood for 'personal assistant'.

Outside London itself, Birmingham coped better than most with beat group demand for audible gauges whereby talent could be measured alongside that of rivals only heard on record. Initially, demonstration tapes and even masters went down in single takes without overdubbing or any contrived atmospherics beyond reverberation and echo chambers. Most suburban studios filled customized garages, sheds or living rooms, as did Jeff Lynne's and Domino Sound, which was several miles up the A41 from Wolverhampton. Among those who coughed up £10 for a Domino afternoon were Wolverhampton's Vendors, a group then containing guitarist Dave Hill and drummer Don Powell, later of Slade.

By 1968, some Second City studios had had eight-track desks installed. The most sophisticated complex was that of Hollick and Taylor which, preening itself in a *Beat Instrumental* advertisement, had the 'latest technical facilities and "Know How" to produce, release records and "Demo" discs'. As well as 'release records' by locals like Jimmy Powell's Five Dimensions, Chances Are, the Staggerlees and Locomotive, plus more famous names such as Dave Berry and Wayne Fontana, this Handsworth studio also had space for a Polish community band's version of 'Delilah' and a Dunlop Tyres' safety film soundtrack. Other signs of the times recorded there included an adaptation of George Formby's 'Hindu Meditating Man' by Alan Randall and, arranged by jazzman Ken Rattenby, a hymn of triumph by the West Bromwich Albion team, 1968's FA cup winners.

The Big Beat was also profitable for city centre music shops such as George Clay's in Broad Street and drum specialists Yardley's of Snow Hill. Once selling five hundred guitars in a day, Jones and Crossland, then in Hinckley Street, regularly paid to brag in *Midland Beat* of patronage by 'all the groups that are getting anywhere',[9] but Ringway Music near the bus station was also so favoured. Spencer Davis praised its friendly customer service; and the Moody Blues and later, Traffic spent lavishly on Laney amplification there.

Outlasting nearly all the groups, these emporiums waited to buy back saleable instruments taking up cupboard space and monolithic speaker cabinets serving as room dividers. Yet, as counter assistants came and went, Mike Sheridan – though outstripped by former underlings – went on forever. He belonged to Birmingham and Birmingham looked after him, which is why 'I made a six-week appearance on *Top of the Pops* with Wizzard, but nobody recognized me because the song 'See My Baby Jive' required two Roy Woods – and I was disguised as the other.'[10] Wood's drummer then was Keith Smart, who afterwards returned, like Sheridan, to his Brum Beat womb when he left Wizzard. He joined the Rockin' Berries who, with Mike's Nightriders, found more time for impersonations, random sketches and knockabout clowning within the staple diet of Top Twenty concessions and the sort of stuff they'd always played.

Far further from his roots, Sheridan's old rival bandleader, Carl Wayne, replaced in the Move by Jeff Lynne in 1969, pursued the path of the all-round entertainer, in which capacity his unforced Brummie urbanity was still apparent, at a Brighton Dome summer season in 1976. Here he preceded Essex pianist Mrs Mills, whose beefy mitts pounded out 'Bill Bailey', 'When You're Smiling' and similar singalongs. To a backwash of the house band and Pisces, a winsome boy–girl harmony quartet that I disliked intensely, Carl burbled mush of the 'Help Me Make It Through the Night' calling.

As the grannies clapped his 'Y Viva Espana', I fought a temptation to barrack for 'Night of Fear' or 'I Can Hear the Grass Grow'. Going the whole hog, Wayne not only took on the role of a milkman in *Crossroads*, but also married in real life the actress who played the late Miss Diane.

Other former denizens of Midlands pop deserted too. Seeking his fortune down south, Kenny Pickett, ex-rhythm guitarist with the Boulevards from Sutton Coldfield, landed on his feet as singer in the Creation, perhaps the most striking of later beat groups, who pioneered the sound of a violin bow drawn across an electric guitar on their brace of 1966 chart entries. Ten years later, Euro-disco behemoths Boney M boosted Pickett's bank balance by their exhumation of the second of these, 'Painter Man'. With Herbie Flowers, then of Blue Mink, Kenny's Christmas 1970 had been made when their composition 'Grandad', sung by comic actor Clive Dunn, tottered to number one.

From the ashes of the Yardbirds, guitarist Jimmy Page refined the Creation's violin bow idea with Led Zeppelin, of whom half – vocalist Robert Plant and drummer John Bonham – were from the Black Country's Band of Joy. The Band of Joy's meat was the drug-related 'underground' pop wafting from California in 1967. Though this influence slopped over on to Led Zeppelin too, the feature most associated with these minstrels was a high energy, blues-plagiarized brutality in which Plant's lungpower was on a par with an instrumental sound picture of Genghis Khan carnage. Beneath twelve-winded skyways of the Midlands, other bands, rather than dancing as Roy Wood whistled, found it easier to tear chapters from Led Zeppelin's book. From this lewd publication, heavy metal outfits popped up all over Birmingham with almost the same frequency as the beat groups. Though kitted out in leather, chains and Satanic fetishist gear, many had, in fact, descended directly from the Beat Boom. The doomful Black Sabbath, for instance, originated in Erdington where, managed in 1966 by an A. Capaldi, rehearsed the Rest, a soberly attired four-piece containing Sabbath's future guitarist Tony Iommi and drummer Bill Ward.

With a more impressive beat antecedent, the Steve Gibbons Band, who ticked off a 1977 British hit with Chuck Berry's 'Tulane', can be traced back to the Dominettes – of the same vintage as Wayne's Vikings. In 1962 as the Ugly's (*sic*), after touting for work in *Midland Beat* small ads – 'anything considered'[11] – attempted to push the electric harpsichord to pop prominence. Notable among the quintet's six singles are 'It's All Right', which brought about a spot on *Ready Steady Go*; 'Wake Up My Mind', which topped charts throughout Australasia; and, by Kink composer Ray Davies, the nonchalant 'End of the Season'. The only constant Ugly, singer Gibbons, drew his first Band from ex-members of the Move, Tea-and-Symphony and the Idle Race in 1972. Their aim was to interpret hard rock with a feel gentler than that of Black Sabbath.

Inhabiting a daintier area bordered by 10cc and Steely Dan, Slenderlorrif, a Mosely Art School band with a synthesizer, were wary of engagements in the Black Country where heavy metal fanaticism was such that some children of the grave would insert their heads into yawning speaker bins to receive the full megadecibel blast of bass guitar. In this teenage wasteland – 'Sabbath territory' – the brain-damaging practice of 'headbanging' was born. Through no accident either did the annual festival at Castle Donington, thirty miles north-east of Birmingham, become the most important date in the heavy metal year.

If not to the same heavy-handed degree, Birmingham was, none the less, represented in later pop fads – though only fleeting sparks of any innovation and radical variation of the Moody Blues, Traffic and Move class reared up. Brummies with a morose touch of the Blarney, Dexy's Midnight Runners always pulled a deft stroke with each of their chameleon-like changes of image. When they were a pseudo-soul band, their horn section was coveted by Robert Plant whose request to employ it on a post-Led Zeppelin solo album was denied. A new wave of heavy metal brought forth Judas Priest, who honoured their Black Country birthplace in the title of their biggest-selling UK album, *British Steel*. Not stressing their Midlands genesis so strongly were those from more nebulous fields of eighties' pop – Duran Duran, Swan's Way producer Trevor Horn, Fine Young Cannibals, Toyah, T'pau and others.

Wiping the floor with these striplings, however, were Slade, who were Birmingham's as the Beatles were Liverpool's and the Animals Newcastle's. Better late than never, the Midlands in 1973 finally produced a world-class beat group when Slade's 'Cum on, Feel the Noize' crashed straight in at number one in the UK charts. There'd been three others that, since 1971, had taken longer to reach the top, and there were more number ones to follow. Though their career has had its ups and downs, the four musicians of Slade racked up more chart entries than the Beatles – even if the number of weeks actually spent there were less impressive. Though unable to re-run any of their home walkovers in North America, Quiet Riot's cover of 'Cum on, Feel the Noize' was a US hit by proxy in 1983. This red-letter year saw Slade in the British Christmas Top Twenty with both the nth reissue of the evergreen 'Merry Christmas Everybody' – a number one ten years before – and, at number two, their latest single, 'My Oh My'. As always, Slade's re-emergence as a chart concern – even after disturbing years of flop records in the seventies – was never out of the question.

The group's longevity owed much to the fact that Birmingham inspired in its groups a deep commitment to their craft. Slade are tenacious and unselfconsciously professional. Their hand-clappin', foot-stompin' pacing in concert, while pulling out all the stops on their hefty backlog of hits, is kept from rampant chaos by the instinctive if indelicate crowd control of rhythm guitarist and lead singer, Neville 'Noddy' Holder.

Prior to his Slade eminence, Walsall-born Holder had perfected his stagecraft in a number of outfits adrift in the trivial round of Black Country hops. When he was in the Memphis Cut-outs in the early sixties, for example, Noddy had performed Rodgers and Hammerstein's 'You'll Never Walk Alone' which was resuscitated as a Slade showstopper. With Dave Holland – a bass guitarist destined to play alongside jazz giant Miles Davis – Noddy next joined Steve Brett and the Mavericks, with whom he made several appearances on *For Teenagers Only*. The Mavericks were to release 'Sugar Shack,' a 45 that fared reasonably well but didn't quite reach the charts. A year earlier, fifteen-year-old Holder's eyes had been opened to more attractive musical possibilities when he came across a group led by the fellow who played in the Golden Eagle most Mondays. Noddy's gut reaction to the Spencer Davis Rhythm and Blues Quartet in 1964 is worth quoting at length:

> Of all the bands I saw in those days, they were the ones who impressed me most musically. They had this small public address system, one of the smallest I have seen, and were very unassuming on stage . . . and then this spotty kid on the organ suddenly opened his mouth and screamed 'I love the way she walks . . .' and launched into that old John Lee Hooker number, 'Dimples' . . . gosh, my mouth fell open and I felt a chill down my spine. That was the night I discovered rhythm and blues for the first time.[12]

3

'Night Time Is the Right Time'

The worst aspects of pop idolatry are exemplified by deed-poll Presleys, the lethal antics of Mark David Chapman, and a lady from Sunderland who is clinically mad about the late cowboy singer Jim Reeves. Milder ritualists are represented by a Cambridge fellow whose entire record collection consists of the works of producer Joe Meek. On the other side of the coin, however, are those who, from a more respectable but comparably single-minded root, are motivated by quasi-evangelical zeal to further the cause of one favoured musical form irrespective of personal popularity or financial gain. In the sixties, the most vital of these interests was the blues.

Though elderly Mississippi blues grandee Big Bill Broonzy's Kingsway Hall concert in September 1951 marked British blues' sluggish conception, its growth as a bohemian cult only really gained ground ten years later, partly through scorn for the hit parade toot-tooting of traditional jazz. Epitomizing this was the Dick Lester film *It's Trad, Dad*, in which performances by pop singers Helen Shapiro, Gene Vincent and Chubby Checker were juxtaposed with those by the jazz combos of Acker Bilk, Terry Lightfoot and Bob Wallis. Playing over the closing credits, Chris Barber seemed to have sold out to pop too. Even so, though like Bilk and Kenny Ball he'd had a chart hit, Barber was a major catalyst in the development of British blues.

Unlike others who merely acted as agents for American blues artists, Chris actually financed the conservation of the form. In the face of financial losses such as that sustained on a Muddy Waters concert at St Pancras Town Hall, he had underwritten tours by other leading American bluesmen including Little Walter, Howlin' Wolf, Roosevelt Sykes and the multi-instrumental duo Sonny Terry and Brownie McGhee. Blues and 'rhythm and blues', as it became, infiltrated the Barber band repertoire. Indeed, they were possibly the first British act to try Muddy's 'I Got My Mojo Working,' which became the movement's anthem.

Ironically it was two disgruntled ex-Barber sidemen, Cyril Davies and Alexis Korner, who in 1957 had established the Blues and Barrelhouse Club at the Roundhouse pub in Soho. At its first meeting it drummed up a clientele of three. More encouraging were the attendance figures five years later, at their celebrated Ealing Club, which was patronized immediately by the blues zealots of Middlesex and beyond. Many of them might have arrived after having 'dressed down' for the evening in 'pads' strewn with paperbacks of Kerouac and Hemingway, while *Jimmy Reed at Carnegie Hall* or Bob Dylan's first LP warmed up the Dansette. Alternatively, if in highbrow mood, you'd dry your hair to Mingus, Coltrane or Charlie 'Yardbird' Parker.

These enthusiastic amateurs were responsible for a fair number of well-intentioned musical assassinations, as art students and weekend dropouts queued to thrash guitars and holler Negro blues with the house band, Blues Incorporated, presided over by Korner and Davies. Yet among the beatnik beards, frayed jeans and CND badges were future Kinks, Yardbirds, Manfred Menn, Rolling Stones and Pretty Things – all poised to breach the Top Twenty within eighteen months.

Other venues gradually embraced rhythm and blues. Foremost among them were Richmond's Crawdaddy, Eel Pie Island and the Thursday night residency at the Marquee – which by 1963 had moved from Oxford Street to Wardour Street, and was still hosting 'an evening with the blues' in 1966. By the time Blues Incorporated's debut album was released, Cyril Davies had left, owing to his dislike of saxophones – forever associated with the hated jazz – and his preference for a narrower, Chicago-style interpretation of the music than Korner's 'everything from Louis Jordan to Martha and the Vandellas'. With Long John Baldry, Cyril now formed a splinter group, the All-Stars, and founded a suitably purist club in Harrow-on-the-Hill.

London boasted by far the highest concentration of blues clubs, but there were many isolated provincial strongholds. Off-the-cuff examples in the Home Counties were Saturday night functions held at Reading's Olympia (where the first hundred girls were admitted free), the Wooden Bridge Hotel in Guildford, and, of course, Uncle Bonnie's Chinese Jazz Club down in Brighton. Further afield there was Sheffield's Mojo, the dingy Downbeat in Newcastle's dockland, and the Old Sailors' Maritime Dance Hall in Belfast. Predating all these, at Manchester's Bogeda Jazz Club in 1950, John Mayall, a seventeen-year-old ex-window dresser, having painstakingly taught himself boogie-woogie piano, made his debut with his blues trio.

Moving the clock forward to October 1963 and relocating to Birmingham, the rhythm and blues night at the Golden Eagle was a howling success. Within an hour of its start, at 7.30, over eighty newcomers had been turned away. 'The packed crowd at the opening session and subsequent evenings make it quite clear,' crowed co-promoter Brian Allen, 'that there is a tremendous following for R. and B. in the city.'[1] Of the music, *Midland Beat* commented, 'the most authentic touches of rhythm 'n' blues were provided by Spencer Davis whose singing and twelve-string guitar and harmonica brought roars of appreciation from the fans'.[1]

'Authentic' he may have been, but there was no trace of the black American underdog in the background of Spencer David Nelson Davis. The 'David' was after his father, who'd been a paratrooper when Spencer was born at the family semi-detached on the Bonymaen council estate in Swansea in 1941. From his mother, Mary, he inherited some Danish blood, but from the cradle he caught and held the sounds of Welsh as well as English. As his life moved him further away, he'd become almost maudlin about his Gower Coast origins. An early memory was of flares illuminating the sky as Luftwaffe bombs pounded Swansea's metal works and oil refineries. In later years he would learn to love the country whence those hostile shadows had emerged.

During Spencer's formative years, his father's services posting obliged the family to move briefly to a Derbyshire farm, where the children travelled to school in a hand-drawn cart. Spencer lacked his younger brother Paul's mechanical turn, and learning was always his strongest suit. By three, he could understand the dialogue balloons elucidating the lurid monkey tricks of the *Beano*'s Dennis the Menace. After passing the eleven plus he went to Dynevor Grammar, where his methodical approach to his studies – particularly languages – and a photographic memory enabled him to procure seven 'O' levels. Though the possibility of university beckoned, Spencer, at his father's wish, left school the same year as Paul, who became a tugboat hand. The prospect of the sea flashed across Spencer's mind too, but after a tedious sojourn at a Hammersmith post office he became a Customs and Excise clerk for eighteen soul-destroying months: 'we always wrote in red ink. It was like writing in my own blood. I always admired one man [who] worked away all morning. Then he went out for lunch and never came back.'[2] Spencer's grasp of French, Spanish and German remained intact, thanks to a one-day-a-week secondment to a Victoria adult education centre. Boosted by a back-dated pay award, the frustrated Spencer found the courage to chuck in his rotten job and join the third-year sixth at his old school. His French exam was blighted by a migraine attack, but he sailed through his other two 'A' levels and began a degree course in German at Birmingham University in 1960.

All work and no play may have rewarded Spencer with first- rather than second-class honours. To some he certainly seemed an introverted and self-effacing academic, but a different Spencer had a dry wit and a frequently irritating appetite for airing his knowledge. 'We threatened to beat him up once,' said Steve Winwood, 'it was an argument about which river ran through Bristol. Spencer was right, of course.'[3]

A different Spencer also performed music in public, and had done so for many years. From singing in Eisteddfod choirs back in the Land of Song, at sixteen he had found crooning 'A Pretty Girl Is Like a Melody' in a Boy Scout Gang Show more his forte. Already he'd mastered the harmonica, having been intrigued by Ronald Chesney's incidental music on *Educating Archie*. His Danish Uncle Herman's ability on mandolin and another uncle's on banjo had caused Spencer to pester his parents for what he thought was a kind of guitar. Instead, he was given a sensible piano accordion as a Christmas present one month early so that he could get to grips with the three carols required for his first professional engagement on Boxing Day. From the proceeds came the guitar – a cheap model with a butterfly etched on its table. He got by on three chords but, whilst in London, he sought to add to these by engaging a very eager tutor. It turned out that the teacher had designs on his pupil's attractively bespectacled girlfriend, Pauline Campbell, whom Spencer had bumped into on the dodgems at a Bexleyheath fairground as the sound of the Vipers' 'Don't You Rock Me, Daddy-o', engulfed the arena.

Davis got 'gone' on skiffle earlier than most through his appreciation of Chris Barber's Jazz Band, in which Lonnie Done- gan on banjo, accompanied by Beryl Bryden's washboard and Barber himself on double bass, was allowed to sing a couple of blues-tinged American folk tunes to break the interweaving intensity of the front-line trad horns. With his own group, of course, Lonnie's energetic whine came to boss skiffle in its 1957 prime. Before the craze drowned in the rip-tide of rock 'n' roll, Spencer's skiffle group, the Saints, busked for pennies while on the lookout for prowling peelers at various West End tube stations. At the Gyre and Gimble and Two I's coffee bars in Soho, the Saints played on the same stages as Tommy Hicks, Harry Webb and Terry Nelhams well before these singers changed their respective names to Tommy Steele, Cliff Richard and Adam Faith. The Saints even recorded a privately pressed single of the skiffle standard 'Midnight Special' and Buddy Holly's 'Oh Boy'. With a blander voice and milder stage presence than Godhead Donegan, Spencer proved no natural show-off, preferring to come to the fore only for a prescribed interval, as Lonnie used to with Barber.

His scholarly nature dictated researching beneath skiffle's chewing gum-flavoured veneer to its blues and hillbilly nitty-gritty. Visits to Dobell's, Charing Cross Road's specialist record shop, polarized his tastes in traditional Americana. He was especially taken with the grippingly personal styles of post-war country bluesmen like Snooks Eaglin and the endlessly inventive Lightnin' Hopkins, and with rowdy jug bands such as Gus Cannon's Jug Stompers from Texas. Another favourite Davis area was the Appalachian highlands, where early British settlers had stabilized a conservative repertoire that, with minimum melodic variation – the formal opposite of jazz – had persisted for centuries. Perhaps the best-known item from this source was 'Go and Tell Aunt Nancy', which cropped up in the repertoire of walking archive Leadbelly, who during his eventful life had absorbed folk as well as blues. Like those of one-man band Jesse Fuller and other Davis finds, Leadbelly's vocal lines were fired by the impetus of a twelve-string guitar. Big Bill Broonzy too was thrumming one as he flickered from ITV's earliest pop show, *Six-Five Special*, in 1956.

In place of the butterfly guitar Spencer had now acquired a twelve-string Harmony, on which he tuned the bottom eight in octaves like Leadbelly. Emulating Lightnin' Hopkins, he experimented unsuccessfully with amplification. Nevertheless, though you could buy one from Jones and Crossland for 26 guineas, the instrument was still such a novelty by Spencer's final college year that, as avid listener Steve Winwood observed, 'Spence was a kind of monument in Birmingham. He was the guy everyone went to see because he had a twelve-string guitar'.[4]

A born organizer, Davis had become a power on the university's entertainments committee – so much so that he booked himself for college bar functions, often as part of a duo with Stourbridge blues chanteuse Christine Perfect – with whom he was romantically linked as well. Otherwise he was a member of Pete York's Excelsior Jazz Band, whose clarinettist-trumpeter Don Campbell had converted him to the mainstream flair of Basie and Ellington. However, just like Donegan with Barber, Spencer's four-song intermission with his Harmony and harnessed harmonica became the highlight of the set. This was typified by 'Midnight Special', 'The House of the Rising Sun' – a soaring whorehouse ballad featured by both Broonzy and Josh White – Lonnie Johnson's sweetly sinister 'Careless Love' and, as a grand finale, 'I Got My Mojo Working'. In this last number he could, ideally, take it down easy, work up audience participation and build up the tension to raving panic before sweeping into the wings and leaving 'em wanting more. Minus the rose-tinted spectacles, Spencer in truth wasn't bad. 'He was never exciting,' was Jim Simpson's assessment, 'but he never let me down either.'

No slouch in front of a boozy audience within and without the campus, Davis had honed his art when the honours course required his studying in Berlin, where he developed a liking for Charlotten-burger pilsner beer and the unpolished Dust Bowl ramblings of Woody Guthrie – quaffing the first and performing the second in Teutonic beatnik hangouts. With a fiver in his pocket and clutching his guitar, Spencer would take off in summer for Paris or the Mediterranean coast, earning his bread as a street singer.

Making up for time lost as a civil servant, Spencer was to reminisce wistfully on his three most agreeable years at college. Flattered to be asked, he didn't let the old place down when in autumn 1966 he delivered a lecture on popular culture and entertainment at the University's Centre for Contemporary Studies. 'To me, Spencer was and still is the typical University student,' mused Steve Winwood that same year, 'he still uses long words all the time that nobody understands.'[5]

At a vocational crossroads in 1963, Davis had vacillated between music and the securer anonymity of teaching, favouring the latter more when the faithful Pauline – now his wife – presented him with a daughter, Sarah, at their Sutton Coldfield home on Christmas Eve. 'I never expected him to be a pop star,' pondered the softly spoken Pauline, 'but I always knew he'd be a success in one way or another.'[6]

Still featured singer in the Excelsior mob, he was far from being a pop star then, though he had made an attempt to form an amorphous rhythm and blues-orientated splinter group with, among others, saxophonist Michael Burney and Dave Grounds, a flame-headed pianist who eyed the yellowing keys through thick bi-focals. However, what spurred Davis into more concrete action was the offer of a Golden Eagle residency. The warm, sometimes

45

riotous, reception of his Excelsior solo spot had been noted, but 'I had to take over from an out-and-out rock band with dyed hair and playing their guitars behind their backs' – the Renegades – 'I felt I needed a rock band to compete.'[7]

From a pool of musicians that he knew Davis always managed to sort out some kind of band to back him every week. Since hearing them a few months previously he'd become friendly with the Winwood brothers who, from the differing sophistications of Count Basie and Roland Kirk, had grown more and more attracted to the earthier sounds of the blues. By this time Steve was not only singing and playing piano but, like Roland Kirk, often managed two instruments at once. Pete York remembered him fingering left-handed piano while blowing a solo on melodica with his right. With the Muff Woody Jazz Band on its last legs, Steve was keen to pitch in on Spencer's random Golden Eagle nights. 'I had some of my happiest moments there,' he enthused, 'everything was informal; people would just get up and sing or play. We never used to learn any numbers. Spencer would say "We'd like to play something or other," then we'd vamp like mad while he sang his own words.'[8]

Gradually Steve – alternating between guitar and piano – became the most reliable stand-in whenever Spencer's voice needed a rest. Finding the rapid turnover of personnel prohibitive in his campaign for more bookings, Davis proposed that he and the versatile Steve could form the nucleus of a more fixed set-up. As long as Muff and his driving licence came too, Steve was game. That was OK, agreed Spencer, providing Muff switched to bass. What about a drummer? Years later, Pete York cited meeting Davis in the Excelsior Jazz Band as the most fateful juncture of his career, 'though it didn't seem so at the time.'[9]

As the Rhythm and Blues Quartet, Pete, Spencer and the Old Oscott brothers first cast their net at a students' dance for Oxfam in April 1963. Largely extemporizing from 'Rock Island Line' and further Davis stock-in-trade, the unassuming band also explored obscurer trackways with the likes of John Lee Hooker's 'Louisiana Blues', Little Walter's 'You're So Fine' and the Muddy Waters lament 'I Can't Be Satisfied'. There was even 'Evans' Shuffle', the signature tune of Tennessee violinist John Evans, uncle of Brownie McGhee.

'Birmingham's first authentic R. and B. combo'[1] they were to *Midland Beat* and, as such, were block-booked at the Rhythm Unlimited club. To become as much the hosts of the Hill Street tavern as the Beatles were at Liverpool's Cavern took three weeks.

One Wednesday it was two-thirds full – the next it was packed out. From then on, there would be queues round the block. Rejecting the hit parade detritus that the average pop fan knew and liked to dance to, the Davis group lured instead much the same aficionados who, if visiting London, might frequent Alexis Korner's club in Ealing. Though the group veered further than Korner towards the modern black sounds on the Atlantic and early Motown record labels, they made one irresistible concession to hardline pop – the Coasters' six-year-old 'Searchin', a Merseybeat standard, with which the Hollies had probed the Top Twenty that August. Stripped of the 'gonna find her' backing responses, the Davis retread – sung by Steve – reinvested it with much of the original's intrinsic wit, while remaining danceable. More overt humour was retained likewise in a faster arrangement of Rufus Thomas' self-mocking 'Jump Back'.

Far from the speakeasies and juke joints of black America, the well-intentioned Quartet would try to copy the Hookers, Waterses and Howlin' Wolves of this world but – as similarly motivated units throughout Britain were also discovering – the results (especially vocal) were usually nothing like. Sometimes the Quartet looked and sounded dangerously like a pop group. To blues trainspotters sweltering in the Golden Eagle crush they were almost as superficially exciting as the Yardbirds, the abandoned Pretty Things and, from the Dartford delta, the Rolling Stones who had all sucked Chuck Berry into the vortex of blues. Though the Quartet didn't capitulate to the Brown-Eyed Handsome Man, they were as near the knuckle.

Luckily, there was a saving grace that put them a cut above any also-ran British R and B exponents. In this band, Spencer found he was no longer the drawing card. More Barber than Donegan now, he still clung to his lion's share of lead vocals but, as Jim Spencer quickly noticed, the wildest ovations were saved for 'this pale-faced slip of a kid who had this mountainous roar that didn't look like it came from him at all'. Steve was barely the Mannish Boy that Muddy Waters bragged about being, but if you closed your eyes, with delicate suspension of logic you could believe that he'd truly got the blues from the Chicago ghettos or the chain gang; that he was world-weary, cynical and knowing far beyond his fifteen years. From this compounded passion, however unsubstantiated, Steve slipped comfortably from raucous lust through lazy insinuation to intimate anguish. Twisting the heartstrings tightest was his shivering 'Georgia on My Mind', the Hoagy Carmichael ballad that Ray Charles had made his own in 1960. Tellingly, 'Georgia' had once been in Spencer's Excelsior repertoire. In similar vein but less familiar was, from the *Ray Charles in Person* album, 'Drown in My Own Tears', in which Steve, virtually alone, would silence drinkers like a mass bell in Madrid with his piano continuo and baby cement mixer voice.

With Pete and Muff otherwise carrying the rhythmic momentum, where did that leave Spencer, whose imperceptible demotion from the main spotlight had begun at the Oxfam ball? Could they do without him? Look at the Big Three. They didn't need a second guitarist to be one of the most popular acts on Merseyside. Yet one of the reasons given for the Three's failure to sustain national success was that, lacking the fourth part of the beat group's two-guitars-bass-drums fixation, people thought there was a bit missing from their music too. It was rumoured that the Hollies showed their understanding of this pre-requisite by insisting that, onstage, vocalist Graham Nash should continue hacking an inaudible rhythm guitar unconnected to any power point.

While Spencer's new Stratocaster copy was always loud and clear, his offstage machinations were at least as crucial as his playing. None of the others – with the possible exception of the disinclined Pete – had quite the same silver-tongued guile that Davis brought into play in his negotiation of engagements at the more refined pop venues within Birmingham's semi-professional catchment area – such as that before a seated audience at the Atlas in Stechford, or the Beeches Hotel off Great Barr Park. He also applied his more systematic objectivity and diplomacy to group realpolitik. 'Spence . . . gets on well with everbody,' smiled Steve, 'what usually happens is, we are bombing along in the car and arguing about money or work. Muff has a go, Pete mumbles, then Spencer says "hey fellows – I think . . ." and we all agree.'[5]

Perhaps it was Spencer's neo-managerial capabilities that prompted the band to adopt a more colourful name, giving him prominence. As the Metropolitan Blues Quartet had metamorphosed into the Yardbirds, so the Rhythm and Blues Quartet became the Spencer Davis Rhythm and Blues Quartet before abbreviating by summer 1964 to the less unwieldy Spencer Davis Group – the punchy symmetry of an unusual forename and run-of-the-mill surname having subliminal magnetism as in 'Stirling Moss', 'Thunderclap Newman' or 'Shane Fenton'.

It might not have been wise to draw attention to Steve anyway, owing to English licensing laws forbidding consumption of alcohol in pubs by minors. Technically, Steve wasn't even old enough to drink a cherryade on the premises. If a copper came along, he'd be shepherded into the kitchen or shoved under a grand piano. A law student acquaintance of Tom McGuinness, then bass guitarist in the Oxford-based Roosters, was present at one of many Spencer Davis engagements which, on his mother's instructions, young Stephen left after the first set to get to bed at a reasonable hour for a change.

As well as Wee Willie Winkie's apoplexy, there was also concern as the late nights took their toll on Steve's schoolwork. Hands supporting head, his eyes would glaze over unblinking at the monotony of compound interest in pounds, shillings and pence. Presently, he'd be slumped across the ink-welled desk with even more passive disinterest in the lesson. What did the Diet of Worms matter when a return booking at the Rum Runner tonight would coin more for him than a month of paper rounds? He was famous, wasn't he? He was round here, anyway. At Aston and District Schools Sports Day, Great Barr Comprehensive's head of PE, shirtsleeved in the heat, was distracted from watching the high jump by a crowd movement in the terraces. It was a coterie of girls from another school elbowing towards – yes, you might have guessed – that long-haired Winwood boy from the fourth. No doubt they'd seen him do his Tommy Steele impressions at some Teddy Boys' gala, and were fishing autograph books from their satchels.

To the school authorities, Steve Winwood was clearly creating an unpalatably bad impression of Great Barr that was immediately obvious to outsiders. The deputy head, Walter Legon, was asked by the headmaster to discuss with Lawrence and Lillian Winwood their younger son's academic future. Maybe to beef up a picture of himself as a rebel rocker, Steve would insist later that he was expelled because, 'like, I was a bit more fiery in those days. At the time I got kicked out, I knew exactly what I was going to do and didn't even bother to go back for a leaving certificate.'[10] However there were evidently no hard feelings on either side when Steve left halfway through the fifth form, having reached the school-leaving age, to pursue what Mr Winwood was now convinced would be a lucrative career as a musician. Certainly there was no question of Steve's getting the boot, as he was able to sit his GCE 'O' levels at his old school a few months later.

As Steve had been battling to keep awake during lessons so, on the other side of the city, in Stechford, the dinner register swam before Spencer's budgerigar eyes at Whittington Oval Primary School. With mouths to feed, S.D.N. Davis, BA (Hons), had seen teaching juniors, with its comparatively short hours and long holidays, as an easy option. After each night's performance he'd get

49

home, like Steve, as the graveyard hours chimed, and grab what rest he could. On the bus to work by 8.30 a.m., he'd decide how best to keep the brats quiet today. Frequently he couldn't think straight and would struggle through till playtime on raw power, greeting with a snarl any child approaching his desk. During the lunch hour he'd make use of the telephone in the secretary's office for group business, while glancing over his shoulder for the nosier members of staff. Dozy Mr Davis must surely have been delirious with joy when he had to take football on games afternoons. After five months, Spencer's double life burnt the candle to the middle and he transferred to a less demanding post at a technical college: 'when the kids had to come to my desk some mornings to wake me up, I knew I couldn't do both successfully.'[11]

Driving for his Dad's hardware foundry, Muff took the increasing group workload in his stride, but for Pete York, who had now finished his Chartered Institute of Secretaries course, the strain was showing. Earnings from music weren't quite enough. Under the mistaken impression that this would be the ceiling of the group's fortunes, Pete wondered whether or not to find another, more artistically satisfying, platform for his skills. There wasn't much time for jazz these days, what with tapping out that changeless four-four off-beat with this bloody pop group in the dives they had to play. 'I feel sorry for Pete in these terrible places,' sympathized Spencer, 'because he is a very technique-conscious drummer and the sound just rolls away.'[12] You certainly took your chances in buildings designed for amateur dramatics and table tennis. On nights off Pete would gladly dep for the New Magnolia Jazz Band, pouring out his misgivings during beer breaks. Outside the Edward VII, after the band had wound up for the night, York told Jim Simpson that from now on he'd be more at the New Magnolia's disposal as he'd left Spencer Davis. Rather than tell the boys face to face, he'd posted Spencer a formal letter of resignation.

This news was deemed unworthy of mention by *Midland Beat*, though there was unexpected consternation among the group's now huge groundswell of supporters. Their alarm may have been one of the factors that led to the prodigal drummer's reinstatement a few weeks later. 'He left with a bang but oozed back,' said Jim Simpson. It appeared, after all, that Spencer's lot might be going places, what with the Beatles conquering America. Pete might even achieve his life's ambition to drum at Carnegie Hall where Basie, Rich, Herman and all the rest of them had played.

Whilst in Squaresville, Pete may have sniffed the wind as the Big Beat readied itself for world domination. Glancing up in his armchair from *Melody Maker*'s jazz pages, the drummer might have noticed on TV the Beatles larking about with Morecambe and Wise; the Merseybeats nattering to Val Singleton on *Blue Peter*; the Searchers and Freddie and the Dreamers in *They Sold a Million* and, most piquant of all, the Applejacks on *Top of the Pops* with their first single at number seven. Their walk with destiny had started in a church youth club just a few streets from Solihull's Viking pub, where they used to perform and Spencer Davis' group still did.

That same week, the Rolling Stones showed up on the *Joe Loss Show*. That they did so without compromising their hirsute motley image, as they'd had to the previous year to get on *Thank Your Lucky Stars*, proved that to Hit the Big Time a group didn't have to be like the Applejacks with their red stage uniforms and dinky yuk-for-a-buck record. John Mayall was at large in London while the Animals and Manfred Mann had just charted, as would the 'most blueswailing' Yardbirds, the Kinks, the Pretty Things and Them before the year was out. So too would soulman Cliff Bennett and Georgie Fame, whose 'rockhouse' music embraced both 'Jazz Sage' Jon Hendricks and bluebeat, and 1965 would get under way with – of all people – the Moody Blues at number one. All discernible as rhythm and blues, they'd mined – like Spencer Davis – less confining seams than those defined by Alexis Korner's jazzy horns and Cyril Davies' precious uptown harping, heard no longer owing to his sudden death in January 1964. Surprisingly, it was Alexis who blazoned the strangest symptom of rhythm and blues' new acceptability when he led the house band on *Five O'clock Club*, an ITV children's programme where continuity was provided by guitarist Wally Whyton, who seven years earlier had invited Alexis to join his chart-riding skiffle group, the Vipers. The memory of Whyton's glove puppet compere, Pussy Cat Willum, introducing Korner's gritty rendering of Ma Rainey's 'See See Rider' isn't easy to forget.

Back in the clubs, R and B was no longer the sole property of arty types. Descending on the Crawdaddy, Uncle Bonnie's (under a new name), the Golden Eagle, Glasgow's Picasso, the Maritime – hundreds of 'em now – were diddekoi Rockers and hair-sprayed Mods under a flimsy flag of truce; plus a *nouvelle vague* mixture of 'youths' – responsible for a wave of vandalism in many Birmingham clubs; and, half a class up, 'young people' whose liberal-minded parents might collect them afterwards in Morris Minor 'woody' estate cars. Past 1962's knotted brow appreciation of Cyril Davies perspiring over his harmonica or wholesome sixth Rolling Stone Ian Stewart's boogie piano, young girls would block the view for dismayed longtime R and B enthusiasts. Crowded round the front of the stage, their evening was made if they caught the eye of serpentine Dave Berry, frail Yardbirds singer Keith Relf who looked as if he needed mothering, chirpy Chas Hodges on bass with Cliff Bennett's Rebel Rousers or the youngest Kink Dave Davies with his centre parting and thigh-high cavalier boots. Even in the hallowed Golden Eagle, the first screams had already reverberated for little Stevie Winwood. You could sing like a nightingale or make a guitar talk, but if you suffered from middle age, obesity or baldness you'd never get more than a cult following. Whatever your popularity, booking fees remained at best static because, then as now, most local promoters took no account of inflation.

Not that this bothered the Spencer Davis outfit, who could offer both musical credibility and teen appeal. By spring 1964, the cash flow was such that even family man Spencer could think seriously of packing in his day job. Only one rung above them were the Yardbirds, for whom one engagement per week would net the same as that pocketed by their Paul Samwell-Smith for five days as an electrical engineer. Like the Yardbirds, the Spencer Davis band got chances to back visiting blues legends such as John Lee Hooker and Jimmy Reed. With Steve on piano all evening, one such duty with Arkansas blues balladeer Jimmy Witherspoon was for a total fee of £40 – seven for Witherspoon, eight for each of the group, and a quid for Muff's petrol – which wasn't a bad deal in 1964 when £10 per week was considered a good wage for a young executive. The fondest recollection of that year for thrifty Muff was 'that you could make money while you were still a semi-pro musician. This meant that you could take your time developing. I think myself lucky that I was part of a rock 'n' roll band just at the time when the bubble was really exploding.'[13]

Quite a few straight pop groups in the Midlands traced that R and B scent by ditching stage suits and Beatle winsomeness for a more native denim taciturnity. No more milking their audiences with Merseybeat favourites, the Atlantix of Burton-on-Trent, for instance, played a farewell booking before re-forming the next week as Rhythm and Blues Incorporated. More prosaic still was the Rhythm and Blues Group, all the way from Grantham. Then there were the Boll Weevils from dem ole cottonfields of Erdington, Sam Spade's Gravediggers from Coventry and – inspired by Baton Rouge harmonica man Slim Harpo – the King Bees, whose drummer had been strongly tipped to fill Pete York's stool with Spencer Davis.

From Hereford came the Shakedown Sound who, prior to

mutating into Mott the Hoople, often supported – as did the Davis quartet – major R and B attractions at the newly opened Whisky-a-go-go near Birmingham city centre. With three floors and a four thousand-strong membership, this club was on a par with London's cool Flamingo. Memphis Slim, Jimmy Reed and other American blues giants appeared there while in Europe. Humbler new venues pocked the Midlands, from a regular night at St Andrew's Hall in Norwich – which elicited the *Midland Beat* headline 'R and B ousts Rock in East Anglia'[14] after its inaugural night starring the Pretty Things – to sessions at Digbeth Civic Hall in the very heart of Birmingham where, in October 1964, *Midland Beat* finally got round to reviewing the Spencer Davis group.[15]

Only a number one hit was to put them on its front page – 'the toast is Spence!'[16] – simply because the group had no need to court *Midland Beat* coverage. In a way, being mentioned in the same paragraphs as the ordinary pop outfits that festooned the newspaper may have been detrimental to the band's position as a 'group's group', held in awe by such discerning musicians as young Noddy Holder. Not that they were snooty about mixing socially with other bands – Steve, apparently, taught Denny Laine to play harmonica. It was just that they seemed to operate in a parallel dimension to the Cheetahs, Mike Sheridan and other denizens of the dance halls. *Brum Beat*, a Decca compilation, included no Davis donations – neither did the quartet bother with *Midland Beat*'s Group Register.

For all its laudable aims, *Midland Beat* was not, perhaps, the barometer of taste it imagined itself to be. Its readers' poll in May 1964 to find the Midlands' most popular group showed the Talismen from distant Cheltenham on top. Not canvassing so hard – or bulk-buying April's edition which contained the voting coupon – more likely aspirants the Rockin' Berries made a genuine number eight while, swallowing dust way behind, were Carl Wayne's Vikings and other leading palais draws. The Spencer Davis Rhythm and Blues Quartet didn't rate at all. Neither, for that matter, did the chart-riding Applejacks. Next year's nine-day wonders would be the Moonrakers who, by fair means or foul, presided over a tabulation which slotted the Spencer Davis Group and the Moody Blues – both with records in the national Top Fifty – between ten and twenty. The truest result came in 1966, when *Midland Beat*'s circulation was at its highest. This time, the Spencer Davis Group swept the board – number one group, Davis as top rhythm guitarist, and Steve ruling the lead guitarist, male singer and organist sections. Faintly ludicrous, however, was percussion aesthete Pete York as joint top drummer with ex-Sunday school teacher Gerry Freeman of the Applejacks – whose star by then had long faded.

Not caring one way or the other about *Midland Beat* while enjoying the security of what the journal saw in 1964 as a minority following, the Spencer Davis outfit were none the less grubbing around for the safety net of a recording contract before turning fully professional. After all, the more cautious Dave Clark Five's debut in this capacity was topping the bill of ITV's *Sunday Night at the London Palladium* after a record-breaking US tour. With a mere toe-hold on his own college job, how they managed it without inviting the sack must have baffled Spencer.

Scouring the Midlands for if not *the* New Beatles then *a* New Beatles, a few talent scouts rubbed their chins about the Spencer Davis Quartet before leaving their scotch-and-cokes half drunk on the Golden Eagle bar. 'They liked us as a group,' thought Davis, 'but reckoned our material wasn't right for teenagers.'[17] Despite everything they stuck to their erudite guns, and what tipped the balance was the faith of Brian Allen's partner David Postle that an evening of rhythm and blues at Birmingham Town Hall on Friday, 28 February would more than cover costs. Negotiating with the National Jazz Federation, Postle managed to secure charismatic Mississippi rambler Sonny Boy Williamson, bowler-hatted and vulture-like in posture, to head a bill of British attractions – notably his tour backing group, the Yardbirds, who happened to be managed by the Federation's Giorgio Gomelsky.

From the revolving stage on that night of nights, master of ceremonies Bob Wooler – imported from Liverpool's Cavern – completed his well-modulated build-up. With 'a very big responsibility to launch this sound on your eardrums', the first act on were 'at a sort of turning point in their career because they have decided that following the show tonight, they will turn pro' – like all the other poor sods – 'and we'll have them on the television screens and nationwide tours' – some hope. Led by 'an ex-folk singer', the Spencer Davis Rhythm and Blues Quartet's brief spot enabled Gomelsky and his assistants to adjust the public address system levels, the better to tape on his fancy Ampex reel-to-reel the more important artists who would be coming on later. Monitor speakers were unheard of in 1964 so, with all microphones malfunctioning, Spencer and Steve bawled out 'You're So Fine', a radical rearrangement of John Lee Hooker's 'Dimples', and a number going the rounds with many other R and B bands, Ray Charles' 'Night Time Is the Right Time' – which, because there hadn't been time to amplify the house piano, was the nearest they could get to the showstopping 'Georgia'. Never mind, the group's cracking instrumental thrust – with Muff the unintended hero of the hour – was well received by the admittedly partisan spectators numbering over a thousand.

The group's two lead singers weren't so unnerved that they didn't share a now crystal-clear microphone on the assembled cast's 'I Got My Mojo Working' finale. Even so, they'd been eclipsed, not surprisingly, by participants other than that pedantic, repulsive old delta legend whose performance had climaxed with 'harmonica contortions in which he even played the instrument with his nose.'[18] On Wooler's insistence, second on had been Cavern regulars the Roadrunners, whom George Harrison had considered better than the Rolling Stones – which, prior to their descent into semi-comedy, they might have been. Carrying the torch for Cyril Davies, Long John Baldry's All-Stars had had the advantage of the presence in their ranks of Humphrey Lyttelton's pianist Ian Armit and special guest Ottilie Patterson, singing wife of Chris Barber, who belted out the first 'I Got My Mojo Working' of the evening. Sending Giorgio's recording level off the dial had been 'the powerful rocking singing of young Rod Stuart'[18] (*sic*), briefly one of Jimmy Powell's Five Dimensions in 1963, who was to trouble the world further into the decade. Coming into Steve Winwood's life with deceptive casualness that Friday was another megastar in the making, crewcut Yardbirds guitarist Eric 'Slowhand' Clapton, formerly of the Roosters. Watching from the rabble was one Robert Plant from Bloxwich, who would be among those picking up the pieces when the Yardbirds fragmented in an unimagined future.

When Sonny Boy's bass harmonica was stolen afterwards, blond Viking-featured Plant was a prime suspect. Presumably the best opportunity for larceny arrived when a caretaker, anxious to lock up, pulled the main electricity switch because all that terrible racket was over-running by half an hour and degenerating into 'a late-night Twist session'[18] – 'late' in that innocent era meaning 9.30 p.m. – 'and we were left asking "When is the next R and B festival?" '[18]

There and then, advocate David Postle could answer only that there'd definitely be another one. The following Monday a date was fixed for the autumn, to coincide with Birmingham's Festival of Entertainments. On 11 September, Town Hall ravers could twist the whole night away to Blue Sounds from Leeds, the jazzy Sheffields and, as the main band, the diehard Blues Incorporated. Representing the Second City itself were 'the much-improved

Moody Blues Five'[13] and, promoted to second place, the Spencer Davis Group, who had by then landed that elusive recording deal.

Things had got moving with the logical step of slithering shoulder-to-shoulder round Spaghetti Junction towards Coventry, down the unfinished M1 to London and, at the invitation of promoter John Gunnell and his songwriting brother Richard, a Thursday night residency at Soho's Flamingo – 'the Swinging Club of Swinging London'[19] – where the larger bands of Georgie Fame, Graham Bond and Zoot Money were already established. With the aggressively untidy middle-class bohemians generally heading for darkest Ealing to catch Alexis and his acolytes' blues stumblings spiced with Chuck Berry, the Flamingo worked up a sharper, principally male clientele from a lower caste. Prototype Mods, even back in 1962, would recognize each other by their clean, short-haired pseudo-suavity and whim-consciouis dress sense – clobber that, at the time, only GIs on a pass, homosexuals and West Indians would be seen dead in. Everything had to be just so: double-breasted bumfreezers with back vents precisely seven inches one week, five the next. On the dance floor Saturday, you had to be Frenchified. Go back the following Thursday and it'd be loud American Ivy League. This shirt's got a pointed tab collar which means I can never wear it again.

Musically, of course, you couldn't beat the Yanks but this Spencer Davis lot from Brum were, in a different kind of way, as good as Fame, Bond, Zoot or Chris Farlowe – especially when that nipper Steve took a vocal. As well as singing as though he might mean it, he could handle himself pretty well on guitar and keyboards too. In common with Zoot and Georgie, the Group had kept abreast of the latest developments in R and B which often ventured into what was becoming known as 'soul music' – the Bobby Parkers, Don Covays and Garnet Mimms as well as the more popular Lee Dorseys, Otis Reddings and Fontella Basses.

From this prestigious showcase they gained further West End work – notably at the Marquee on the opposite side of Wardour Street, where other musicians like Eric Clapton, whose Covent Garden flat Steve was often to visit, and Graham Bond sometimes felt the urge to 'sit in' on a few numbers. The Group would still be playing there three years later. However, it was an atmospheric performance at the Flamingo in 1964 that so knocked out Decca recording manager Mike Vernon that the Group were summoned to R. G. Jones Studio in Morden to audition a five-track demo under his supervision. To interest one such as Vernon was a feather in any aspiring rhythm and blues combo's cap. For a start, he knew what he was talking about, having compiled, with his brother, *R and B Monthly*, perhaps the first fanzine of its kind in Britain. Having dropped out of art school, Mike entered Decca on the ground floor; 'I was the general runaround, making tea.'[20] He served his apprenticeship to the strains of such as Mantovani and satirist Paddy Roberts, and his first essay as producer was an LP by Texas-born pianist Curtis Jones, who – like another Vernon job, Champion Jack Dupree – had made Britain his home. As well as the bona fide US article, Mike searched out blues-derived British talent. Among his earlier discoveries were the Graham Bond Organisation, the Artwoods and, shortly before their Birmingham Town Hall appearance, the Yardbirds, who'd recommended the Davis Group to him.

The Beatles had slid from Decca's then unconcerned clutches in 1963, provoking the firm to saturate itself with beat groups in the hope that one of them might catch on like their failed Scouse supplicants had to teeth-gnashing effect when signed by Decca's arch-rival EMI. All the same, it helped if, like the Beatles, groups wrote their own material. This may have explained why Decca A and R department weren't keen on either the Who's demo of Howlin' Wolf's 'Smokestack Lightning' or, arriving on that same afternoon, Vernon's Spencer Davis tape. Oddly enough, it was a version of John Lee Hooker's 'Frisco Blues' – sung, apparently, by Spencer – that stirred most interest. Even with Ray Charles playing to standing room only on his UK tour that very month, it seemed that Decca too reckoned the Group's material wasn't right for teenagers; we know these things, Mike.

It wasn't quite back to square one, however, because the Group's undimmed ring of professional confidence had, by April 1964, chanced on the eye of a self-employed entrepreneur whose will to succeed was stronger than that of any salaried time-server from a major record company. On Saturday, 11 April, West Indian singer Millie Small was booked for two sessions at the Cavern, supported by the Escorts. During the day, it was suggested to her manager Chris Blackwell that, when his client's club itinerary reached the Midlands the following week, he ought to check out two promising Birmingham acts. The one most likely was the polished Carl Wayne and the Vikings but 'it was pop dressed in suits and I don't really feel straight pop'.[21] More rough and ready was the zestful Spencer Davis Group, whose leader was singing when Blackwell walked into the packed Golden Eagle. 'Then Stevie sang ['Georgia'] and I couldn't believe it,' laughed Blackwell, 'it was like Ray Charles on helium[21] . . . it wasn't a matter of having star potential;

57

he was a star right then.'[22] Afterwards, the Group were professional enough to be civil to Mr Blackwell when he bought a round of drinks. Though they were impressed when he spoke of his meeting Miles Davis, Coltrane and Mingus and other jazz luminaries in New York, they had been disappointed enough already to be sceptical when he offered to take them on with the promise of a record out within a month. In fact, it took four. 'Their music was my roots,' insisted Blackwell, 'so I could relate to it immediately.'[21]

Christopher Blackwell was what George Bernard Shaw would have called a 'downstart' in that he came from a family that had once been better off. Related to Crosse and Blackwell – the soup people – his Irish father had married into the Lindos, prominent Jews who had fled to Jamaica from the burnings of the Spanish Inquisition. Over the five centuries that followed, the Lindos progressed from fencing pirate loot to legitimate merchandising – mainly of rum and sugar. By the turn of the twentieth century, theirs was one of the most respectable households in Kingston, but by the time of the birth of sickly, asthmatic Christopher in 1937 the family business was starting to take a turn for the worse.

The boy spent most of his first decade untroubled by trade turmoil in Terra Nova, his parents' enormous mansion in Waterloo Road, Kingston's poshest suburb, worlds removed from Trench Town to the west with its dirt-poor shanties and reeking squatters' camps rife with disease and swarming with undernourished children descended from black slaves. Yet it would be brash, confident Rude Boy music from these ghettos, declaring in no uncertain terms that a change was gonna come, that would be the making of young Blackwell who, by 1947, was enduring the rigours of Harrow, Greater London's most exclusive boys' public school.

A straw-boatered contemporary of the shy Anglo–Jamaican was John Gayden. Taking up the guitar during the hols, he was to form with pianist Michael d'Abo and other ex-Harrovians A Band of Angels, whom some considered a jolly good pop group. The older Blackwell, however, much preferred jazz and boogie-woogie to rock 'n' roll – Lewis, Meade Lux to Lewis, Jerry Lee. Less innocent pleasures than musical appreciation tempted Chris when he joined the accountancy firm of Price Waterhouse. Rather than devoting himself to study so that he might restore the family's prosperity, he mis-spent his youth at dogtracks, racecourses and roulette wheels before his return to the Caribbean. Here he gained more worthwhile employment as, successively, aide-de-camp to the Governor-General, an estate agent and, at the Half-Moon Hotel in Montego Bay, a water sports instructor.

While gallivanting with his pals in a motor boat round the lonely Hellshire coastline near Spanish Town, Blackwell inadvertently found himself at the mercy of dope-smoking Rastafarians, a ghetto religious sect he'd always understood to be 'killers, anti-white'.[23] The adventure began when the launch struck a reef and sank. The party swam to shore and Chris went for help. Hours later, the exhausted playboy approached a hut miles along the desolate beach. When six dreadlocked Rastas emerged, Blackwell almost fainted with shock. However, instead of being tortured to death, he enjoyed frugal hospitality of seafood, Bible readings and back-to-Africa sermons. As well as vaguely reminding him, perhaps, of Harrow, the encounter led Blackwell to sympathy in place of ingrained fear for the island's most shunned sub-culture.

Further against the instincts of his upbringing, Blackwell started hanging around the sound system dives of downtown Jamaica. Owned by various liquor distributors, the sound systems provided recreation for those too hard up to buy record players. From huge speakers poured, at deafening volume, discs from both American rhythm and blues and Jamaica itself. All systems were competitive to the extent of claques and downright thuggery. Much depended on the cunning of the man behind the turntable who, if smart, would search out exclusive sources of new sounds, scratching off record labels to hinder identification of artist and song, thus keeping one step ahead of rivals. Blackwell ingratiated himself with some system operators by purchasing – for a commission – desired records during his periodic trips to New York.

Eventually, one of the foremost sound system record spinners, Clement 'Sir Coxone' Dodd, turned to recording local musicians, thereby ensuring quality control and a ready supply of disco fodder. Others followed suit and so evolved the Jamaican record industry, welding American – and, later, British – pop to West Indian patois and rhythms. As early as 1959, token white Blackwell's career in music had its humble origins in his recording of an LP by the Half-Moon's house band led by Bermudian pianist Lance Haywood. It was pressed on Island Records – named after Alec Waugh's *Island in the Sun* – and sales were hopeful enough for Chris to forsake, on the advice of a fortune teller, a permanent post as film producer Harry (*Dr No*) Saltzman's assistant in order to organize the new record label more earnestly. Events were to prove the wisdom of this decision. In a 1987 television documentary about the company, the presenter justly praised founder Blackwell: 'Twenty-five years later, the role call of stars associated with Island

Records bears witness to his unique talent for fostering some of the great original talents of the music world.'[22]

Like Tamla Motown, Island was launched on a float of a few hundred dollars. However, rather than exploding as Motown did in the States, Island merely ticked over in Jamaica. 1961 brought the first parochial hit – 'Little Sheila' by Laurel Aitken – which enabled Chris to open an office in Kingston. Nevertheless, having learned his craft and finding the cut-throat ambience of the West Indian music business unhealthy, he elected in 1962 to become British licensee for Dodd and other Jamaican record moguls. Setting off from a base in London, he'd ply his wares from the boot of a Mini Cooper to small specialist shops in the suburbs of Brixton and Lewisham, as well as Birmingham and similar areas with a strong Caribbean immigrant population. On this, the truest 'underground' market, the likes of the Maytals, the Wailing Wailers (who had a singing guitarist called Bob Marley), Joe White and Derrick Morgan sold in more or less equal ratio to their standing at home – though Blackwell's own signings tended to do better in England: Island's first UK single, Owen Gray's 'Twist Baby', shifted all of its initial pressing of five hundred.

With no challengers, Chris kept the wolf well away from the door, even venturing later into African high life and Trinidadian music. In 1967, a *Pakistani Soul Session* album appeared via Island, but by then a wealthier Blackwell had long surrendered to white pop, shoving more ethnic material onto subsidiary labels.

Not lost to the Island boss amid the holocaust of the Big Beat was the infiltration of ersatz bluebeat – derived from the ska-mento-calypso melting pot – into the British Top Fifty in spring 1964. An example of the real McCoy – 'King of Kings' by Ezz Reco and his Launchers – had drifted into the lower reaches in March, while soaring into the Top Ten was a revival of Ronnie Ronalde's 'Mockin' Bird Hill' which had been invested with a hiccuping 'bluebeat' lope by the opportunist Migil Five, who'd begun as a cocktail jazz trio in North London publand. More worthy a cash-in that same month was the self-explanatory extended play record 'Rhythm and Bluebeat' by Georgie Fame, who in mitigation had featured the tracks in his Flamingo stage act since 1962.

Overtaking the Migil Five was 'My Boy Lollipop' by Millie (Small), kept from number one only by the Beatles' latest. Over at Island's Jamaican branch had been issued in 1963 'We'll Meet' by Roy and Millie which, imported into Britain, not only shipped a few on the usual circuit but also became a turntable hit at hip London clubs such as the Roaring Twenties and the Crazy

Elephant. Fascinated by the pipsqueak vocal and engaging vinyl personality of Millie, Blackwell flew the sixteen-year-old from the Rude Boy district of Clarendon to London in order to – he hoped – cross over into the national, even international, charts. After a non-starter with her own 'Don't You Know', Chris dug up for Millie 'My Boy Lollipop' on an R and B 78 he'd bought in 1959 on one of his Big Apple expeditions.

Millie's ska arrangement was a worldwide smash and, to Blackwell, earlier enterprises became suddenly and stultifyingly small-time. As Island wasn't powerful enough to go it alone, Millie and, soon, the Spencer Davis Group were signed to Fontana under a lease deal with its parent company, Philips. It would be another three years before Blackwell could afford to declare his independence, without any middlemen taking a cut, with Traffic's debut single on Island.

Arriving at last in the Swinging Sixties by snapping up Spencer Davis, Chris further extended his empire's frontiers by swooping down on folk singer John Martyn when the hunt was up for a British answer to Bob Dylan. Though the job went to Donovan, Martyn turned out to be a steady long-term investment for Island. The previous summer, when in Hamburg with his Spencer Davis Group, Chris had been captivated by another Star Club attraction, the VIPs from Cumbria. 'They were un-be-lievable,' he raved, 'impossible to handle or control.'[21] Yet handle them he did after signing them, as in April he'd signed the Group. On a first-come-first-served basis, the VIPs were left to toughen up on the the Grosse Freiheit while their new manager concentrated on getting the Spencer Davis Group's first single off the ground. 'We really want a hit record,' pronounced bandleader Davis, 'then I could buy a house.'

'And I could buy myself a Hammond organ,'[24] chipped in Stevie, his young sidekick.

4

'Pop Gear'

From the bowels of Broadcasting House in 1986, the Long John Silver burr of Reg Presley transmitted sixties' memories as special guest on a Radio Two wallow in nostalgia. Following a spin of 'Keep On Running', he commented, 'Stevie Winwood, still as good today . . . I met the Spencer Davis Group way back in '65, just before "Wild Thing" in Bristol in a little club down there. They were doing great at the time, and we had a little chat afterwards. They hoped we would do well – well, here we are twenty years on.'[1]

On paper, the Troggs and the Spencer Davis Group were on terms of fluctuating equality. After winning the strongest possible reputation with an R and B repertoire, each had been signed to a Fontana lease contract. Patchy chart placings – either at home or in Europe – were accumulated by both quartets before 1966 yielded two fast British number ones each. On the world stage for two fat years, both left a wound in the United States before going off the boil there almost immediately. After all, however much Davis aficionados refuted the suggestion, both were pop groups.

'Keep On Running' sounded as American as 'Wild Thing'. The main difference lay in the image – contrived or otherwise – that attracted fans to either group. The unconscious humour in the heated studio discussion that constitutes the notorious and illicitly recorded 'Troggs tape' showed that the yokel exuberance that led to their stereotype label as the Unthinking Man's Pop Group was not undeserved. By contrast the Spencer Davis Group came, like the Zombies and Manfred Mann, to get by on the 'intellectual' ticket. None of the Group sported swot spectacles on stage but much was made of Spencer, the first Bachelor of Arts to top the charts. Indeed, before Steve's 'young genius' angle overshadowed this distinction, it was Spencer who handled the bulk of press calls –

from a regular *Midland Beat* column to an *Observer* interview. Often erroneously credited as lead singer, Davis only would be pictured in many hard-core teen comics in his Beatle haircut, slim-jim tie and light blue stage suit – which superseded a Group uniform of thick white woollen roll-necks, impractical under sweaty arc lights.

This threshold of eminence past, a 1966 colour centrefold in *Mirabelle* represented more accurately the Group power structure. Hands on wide-belted hips and sneering gently, Steve and Muff are flanked by narrow-eyed Pete in his neat coiffure, dapper double-breasted grey tweeds and Mafioso black collar and white tie. Of lesser sartorial individuality is Spencer, kitted out like the Wild West Winwoods, whose wan attempt to lean further into lens range is thwarted by Steve's obstructing elbow.

Unlike the other three, it was not to the younger Winwood's advantage to lose a year from his age when annotating his life history for Island's press kit. Common to all on these lists was foreign 'favourite food'[2] in an England where most restaurants which served a late-night square meal were Indian or Chinese. Nothing approached the wit and sarcasm with which, say, the Beatles had invested 'Lifelines' when the Spencer Davis Group's time for publication in the *New Musical Express* came[3] – though Pete and Steve had given 'my left leg' and 'my voice' as their respective 'biggest career breaks'. Uneasily tracing that fading Merseybeat scent, a slang compendium attributed to the Group – Brum's answer to Scouse – appeared in one pop annual.[4] This informed users that 'weird' meant 'strange', and 'face it', 'to examine the facts and accept them'. More unique was 'fluid chariot' for 'a car with a full engine' and 'blow your jets' for 'to get mad, upset'. The probable brain-child of a bored publicist – possibly a Mary Freeman – few of these tortuous expressions ever reached the lips of the Group or anyone else. Yet, gormless as it was, this strategy typified how, in that naïve era, a beat group hoped to impinge on public awareness.

Crasser were circulated photos of Manfred Mann dragging their most hirsute mann into a barber's; the Kinks wielding whips; high-stepping Freddie and the Dreamers; and the Rockin' Berries copying the Beatles' mid-air leap. There was Dave Clark's open apology to Prince Philip over some funny dance step popularized by his Five called 'the Duke'. In an ill-judged publicity stunt the otherwise obscure Primitives had their girlish tresses cut on a television chat show.

Disdain of such exhibitions of toadying to the press did nothing but intensify appreciation of the Spencer Davis Group by other artists. Among the more sincerely loud admirers of the Group's stylistic tenacity and exacting standards were Ringo Starr, Eric Burdon, Keith Richards and the discerning Mick Jagger. Thus blessed, and no longer tied by day jobs to venues within a stone's throw of home, Spencer's boys on their round-Britain itinerary were regarded as a hot act to see by nearly all castes of pop fan. With the release of 'Dimples', their maiden single in August 1964, *Melody Maker* critic Chris Welch wrote, 'if asked to tip one comparatively unknown group for R and B stardom [I] . . . would nominate the Spencer Davis Group from Birmingham.'[5]

'Dimples' went down a storm onstage, but its crude libretto and stylized twelve-bar cycle did not merit inclusion even in a chart that had embraced Howlin' Wolf over the summer. Using Hooker's gutbucket leering as a helpful demo at Pye's Stanhope Place studio off Marble Arch, the Group gingered it up with Spencer's harmonica wailing behind Steve's broader vocal dynamic, which ranged from a semi-screech to close-miked *sotto voce* intimacy. Though the effect was now more dramatic than Hooker's stumblings and the Animals' thuggish cloning of the same arrangement, there was still little indication that the Spencer Davis Group were superior to diverse other outfits plundering those Chicago and Mississippi motherlodes. For instance, Van Morrison's first single with Them – a Slim Harpo cover – was bound for deletion, but cracking the Top Fifty that same month, for better or worse, were both the Zombies and the Pretty Things. It is an instructive exercise to compare each version of the song that, by coincidence, opens both the Pretty Things' debut album and *The Zombies Begin Here* – Bo Diddley's 'Road Runner'. The Zombies' more intricate approach pales beside the mean and hungry smash of the Sidcup quintet. Though it sounds uncomfortable with Colin Blunstone's breathy St Albans' elegance, it is ideal for a lesser vocalist like Phil May. Also, though Rod Argent could crush notes with the best of them, another crucial factor was his keyboard's purer tone and fixed tuning, sounding at odds with the rough guitar heart of the blues.

In the wake of the Rolling Stones, the Yardbirds' 'Good Morning Little Schoolgirl' – aided by publicity shots taken outside Twickenham Girls' Grammar – would shut down Rod Stewart's version for slight chart honours before 1964 was out. Attention to *Muddy Waters at Newport* resulted in worthy readings of 'Hoochie Coochie Man' by Dave Berry, Manfred Mann and Stewart's boss, Long John Baldry. However, giving credence to trad jazz trumpeter Kenny Ball's jaded opinion that it was just 'rock and roll with a mouthorgan' were legion executions of 'I Got My Mojo Working' by also-rans of the Primitives–Gravediggers school of Hohner Bluesvampers and Mick Jagger maraccas.

A better example was taped by Jimmy Powell and his Five Dimensions, who were a regular intermission band at the Crawdaddy. A possible epitaph for this Birmingham sextet is provided in an extract from Reading blues guitarist Mike 'Drivin' Wheel' Cooper's diary, in which he recounts a Dimensions bash at Oxford Street's 100 Club in February 1964: 'Powell is a reasonable harmonica player and vocalist. His rhythm guitarist is quite good too. The rest of the group are mediocre but produce a competent sound which does at least sound like R and B and not rock.'

Before leaving the 100 Club, let's hear what Cooper thought about another act on the bill: 'for me, the evening was definitely made by John Lee's Groundhogs. Lee seems to have succeeded in finding musicians all the same height – short.' Formed in 1963 by guitarists Tony McPhee and Peter Cruickshank, the Groundhogs recorded with and backed John Lee Hooker during one of the Detroit hollerer's frequent visits to Britain during the sixties.

Within a month of the Spencer Davis version, John Lee chose to reissue his original of 'Dimples' and instigate another British tour (with his Groundhogs) to promote it. With the sales territory of the Spencer Davis Group now reduced to loyal Warwickshire, Chris Blackwell remembered with teeth-gritting irony that they'd been among those accompanying Hooker on his previous tour.

Spencer's barrelhouse blues, 'Sittin' and thinkin'', was flip-side of the flop 'Dimples', but any ideas harboured of his playing Lennon to Steve's McCartney were thwarted, as no balancing 'Please Please Me' equivalent was forthcoming; Steve sang lead on all British A-sides by the Group. That Winwood was in another instrumental and vocal league brought about the not untalented Davis citing 'finding out that I can't really sing' as his 'biggest disappointment'. Steve's magnanimous contradiction in print[6] of this mournful 'Lifelines' entry revived Spencer's self-confidence, especially when, after much debate, he took, in October 1965, the main track on 'She Put the Hurt on Me', the Group's only EP that was a product in its own right rather than a mere album chaser or resuscitation of buried singles. Once there was talk of a Davis number, 'Can't It Be You' (arranged with Muff), being an A-side. Yet, even when going down with his ship in 1967, the song's frustrated writer was still insisting 'I want to sing on the next single. We've got a song we'd like to try for the next single that's completely untypical of the group. I *will* be singing. The fact is that

Steve has sung most [*sic*] of our A-sides and I have been getting crowded out. I'm not a first-class singer . . . but I've always enjoyed singing.'[7]

For all his protests, Spencer hadn't a prayer from the start. As their reputation grew, it became customary for the band's billing to be extended with the phrase 'featuring Steve Winwood', as well as the Group itself affirming this prominence in titles like 'Goodbye Stevie', 'Stevie's Blues' and the one-take instrumental 'Stevie's Groove', a time-consuming German B-side. Like piano-pumpin' Jerry Lee Lewis, Winwood on wings of song also began referring to himself by name in the third person: when he knocked on his mama's door in Don Covey's 'Take This Hurt off Me', she said 'Stevie, come on in.' His instrumental activities now extended – with tolerant Pete's approbation – to occasional drum solos, though he later insisted, 'I bash around on drums but that's more a physical exercise than anything else. I can't play any rhythm instruments.'[8]

Absorbing accelerating adulation throughout adolescence, young Stephen was 'considered something of a brat',[9] demonstrated when he ruined hotel guests' sleep by banging on their doors with a tin tray when the Group steamed in after a particularly exhilarating one-nighter. 'I was probably a bit full of myself,' he agreed with early middle-aged candour, 'I didn't really believe it.'[10] Nevertheless, within this teenage trauma continued an artistic quest: 'I want to write songs very badly but I've only ever been pleased with two. The others I've torn up. I get very annoyed when things don't work out; I want to go and kick something.'[11]

A more tangible item he wanted badly was a Hammond organ: 'in fact, last year [1965] when I was practising on piano, I was playing it organ style'.[12] Hit records and increased van space would bring Steve his desire, directly from its Middlesex manufacturers, and allow Spencer a larger piece of lead guitar action. Before its arrival, Steve – having obtained permission from a Hammond owner on the same bill – would roll up hours before the engagement for the privilege of pressing its two-tier keys, trying out its purring effects and struggling for mastery of its bass pedals. Preferring the more *legato* vampings of then fellow Island signing Billy Preston to that of old idol and acknowledged Hammond virtuoso Jimmy Smith, Winwood was also impressed with the sophisticated Alan Haven – who also used a Lowry – and Roy Phillips of the Peddlers, whose respective jazz-pop concoctions were, for much of 1964, heard nightly at Brompton's Annie's Room niterie and the nearby Scotch of St James's. Triggered by a feature on Hammonds in *Midland Beat*,[13] Dave Grounds of

Everett's Blueshounds – an ex-Spencer Davis Golden Eagle accompanist – among others on the Birmingham circuit had also shelled out the necessary £825 for the trendy toy. This was a vast outlay in days when a ten bob note (50p) was considered an adequate consolation prize on the 'Beat the Clock' interlude on *Sunday Night at the London Palladium.*

Steve's new Fender guitar – like those of Spencer and Muff – was now powered by a Marshall amplifier fresh from Ringway Music. Lending further emphasis to his Group's professional status was a public-address system capable of punching out 100 watts – pretty loud for 1965. By 1966, this and other hardware travelled in a 35 cwt Transit driven by a two-man crew answerable to ex-bouncer John Glover who, when dignified with the umbrella rank of production manager, would usually hurtle through the countryside with the band in their fancy Dormobile with fitted record player and radio plus a perpetual crate of Newcastle Brown Ale. Like an army batman without the uniform, Glover would attend to his charges' food, sleep and general health requirements. In a broader sense this meant checking security, prising unwanted company from dressing rooms, buttonholing promoters and signing chits and bills. This was often before the band had played a note. When they did, the fun began. During a fast, heated solo at a Woolwich pub engagement, the stool collapsed and Steve with it (the song was 'Goodbye Stevie'). Scrambling on with a replacement, Glover collided with a stand, wrecking its microphone. Later, the piano's contact mikes went silent, compelling Winwood to switch to guitar. The PA packed up next.

With the M1 still only half-completed, John was also on hand to cope with the tactical problems of moving the operation from A to B: flat batteries, jammed starter motors, snapped towropes, overcharging alternators and long waits for Automobile Association patrolmen were very much part of his day's work. A near-disaster in September 1965 began when Davis, York and Glover set off from London in the early evening for a booking in Droitwich, Worcestershire. Almost immediately, the van's water pump broke. Anticipating the AA mechanic's shaking head, a panting call to trusty Ringway Music, about to lock up for the night, resulted in a replacement part's delivery from a Smallbrook garage. A hundred miles away, Muff had managed to borrow equipment from the supporting Rayvons – an all-girl act from Evesham – who were valiantly over-running as Pete and Spencer reeled into the dressing room after a frightening two-hour dash in a hired London Telecar.

Hot and bothered, the Group shambled on only a few minutes later – to a wild reception. Local engagements weren't so frequent now but – in the teeth of long-term partisans' fears of Beatle-style defection to London with record success – grassroots impact remained strong, having reached its limits by late 1964. In a record booth of a high street department store, Birmingham schoolboy Colin Baylis 'met a girl who was gyrating to the sound of "Dimples". She was clearly an avid fan of the group, and informed me that the lead singer was only fifteen and that she went to see them every week at the Golden Eagle. She was like a living publicity promo for the group.'

Before it died its death, a few scattered airings of 'Dimples' had crackled from Radio Luxembourg's crowded wavelength. A few programme planners' memories were jogged when the next Spencer Davis offering, the driving 'I Can't Stand It', settled among the October releases. As the lead vocalist wasn't specifically named in the four-page A4 handout which accompanied the record, Luxembourg disc jockeys could be forgiven for assuming that this 'Spencer Davis' bore the same all-powerful relationship with his 'Group' as skiffle king Lonnie Donegan had with his faceless backing combo – especially as, in his belated *Midland Beat* review, Dennis Detheridge, who should have known better, implied the same.

Suffocating under bedclothes in the small hours were the conditions under which I first caught 'I Can't Stand It' on my transistor. Idle moments the following Farnborough Grammar schoolday were spent with other C-stream dropouts trying to parrot the strangled agonizing of overnight sensation Spencer Davis. A quick-witted riposte to my go at 'I Can't Stand It' was 'Yes, I don't like it much either.' We'd also been intrigued by his guitarist's trick of sometimes playing in unison with Spencer's presumed singing. Some more radio plugs, spurred by the buzz emanating from Birmingham, throughout the next month yielded sessions on *Saturday Club* and the BBC Overseas Service, eventually pushing this second single to a tantalizing UK high of number 47 over a three-week chart run.

Way above this modest placing was 'One-way Love' by the Rebel Rousers, whose leader, Cliff Bennett of West Drayton, could – like Steve Winwood – sing updated American R and B without departing far from its over-riding passion. Though Spencer's became the definitive treatment, Cliff, along with scores of rivals, had absorbed 'I Can't Stand It' into his own stage set, stretching it out to a five-minute showstopper and, like his Midland counterparts, doubling the tempo of the original, by portly US gospel duo the Soul Sisters[15] from a 1964 album on the Sue label.

To give his Midland boys a clearer run, Chris Blackwell had ensured that the Sisters' rendering of the Smokey McAllister-composed piledriver was not pressed in 45 r.p.m. format until the New Year. Blackwell had negotiated in New York a distribution deal for Sue product in Britain. With rights to material by the likes of James Brown, Ike and Tina Turner (who played Birmingham in 1965), Lee Dorsey and Larry Williams, this specialist sideline – under the delegated management of R and B addict Guy Stevens – spread itself thinly enough to shift thousands of units per release while rarely charting. This was illustrated by Wilbert Harrison's 'Let's Work Together' on Sue, later covered most lucratively by Canned Heat, Bob Dylan and, on Island in 1976, by Bryan Ferry.

Passing a Jamaican record shop in 1963, Chris had first chanced on what became his inaugural Sue single, 'Mockingbird', which enlivened the two otherwise interminable *Ready Steady Go* spots in 1964 of its North Carolina creators, Inez and Charlie Foxx. Pete York, on the other hand, was thrilled when his Spencer Davis Group embarked on its first nationwide tour with Inez and Charlie during this British visit. Another advantage that accrued to the Group through the Sue connection was first grabs at likely items from the label's vaults, such as 'My Babe' from the Righteous Brothers, Ike and Tina's 'It's Gonna Work Out Fine' and, anticipating the late sixties' blues boom, the bottleneck standard 'Dust My Blues' by Elmore James. 'Part of the Spencer Davis Group's success – part of it,' stressed Blackwell, 'was the fact that as soon as I got pressings over from America, I'd send it straight to them and Muff and Steve would do all this material in their way and so they always had really great new material before anyone in the Group was starting to write.'[16]

Via Blackwell too, access was easy to the latest from the West Indies, such as Prince Lala's 'She Put the Hurt on Me', which the Group reworked to showcase not only Spencer's lead vocal but also Steve's unusual solo which combined guitar and scat-singing. Steve was already *au fait* with bluebeat and ska – even African music – through hanging round in Birmingham record shops while waiting for the night's work.

Other repertory sources of the Group's own making evolved from the vast record collections of Pete York and Lawrence Winwood and such as Manchester enthusiast Roger Eagle, who was on the mailing list of untold US independent record companies. From him came 'Strong Love' which, over-ruling Steve's unease, the Group retrod later as a single.

Rival bands had their own erudite goldmines too. From the Animals, for example, who developed an instinct for picking hits, were Alan Price and Eric Burdon, both keen record collectors. Living within the Tyne and Mersey hinterlands, many bands knew friendly Transatlantic seamen – 'Cunard Yanks' – who would import the sacred sounds to be filtered through grinning northern accents. Inland, rare records were borrowed from US air bases and from the collections of ballroom disc jockeys like Jimmy Savile at the Three Coins in Manchester in 1964 – where he appeared between wrestling bouts with Gentleman Jim Skinner – and 'Spinnin' John', who presided over Basildon's Locarno. The Moody Blues' 'Go Now' blueprint by Bessie and Larry Banks came via B. Mitchell Reed, a New Yorker who 'went overboard for the Moody Blues whilst in Brum'.[17]

Along less exclusive avenues, the Spencer Davis Group's re-corded and concert output polarized on the commercial R and B spectrum, ranging – via soul and gospel – from country blues exorcisms to the badlands of rock 'n' roll: 'the Group plays poppy rhythm and blues,' quoth Spencer, 'and they aim for a good dancing beat'.[18] He had illustrated this statement by attempting to work into the act 'On the Road' by fellow 1966 chartbusters the Lovin' Spoonful who, like him, had roots in rural blues and Memphis jug bands. Few were ever seriously rehearsed, but the Group freely admitted preferences in mainstream pop. Though he was contemptuous of the New Vaudeville Band's olde-tyme whimsy, Steve admired the coltish Sinatra-esque emoting of Scott Engel, perhaps feeling an affinity with Engel who dominated similarly his own group, the Walker Brothers. Of the four, the most conspicuous Beatle fan was Davis, whose Christmas present from Pauline one year was the Moptops' then complete discogra-phy. By 1967 he'd also warmed to the disparate delights of the Troggs and Beach Boys, tempering this with self-conscious listening to guitarist John Williams' bids to bring flamenco to the masses. 'I don't really want to become a classical player,' explained Spencer – and no-one doubted him – 'if anything, I feel I might end up in . . . jazz!'[18]

The one who actually did end up in jazz was Pete York. In fact, he never really left it. 'Pete suffered stardom,' said Jim Simpson, 'every chance he got, he'd get out and play jazz.' Despite including items like Horace Silver's 'Sister Sadie', Jim also believed that 'the only jazz things they did were to keep Pete happy'. Belying this was Pete's entering into the spirit of good honest trash when attending to the Group's iconoclastic finales with one of his George Formby party pieces. 'In our group, everyone has their own sense of humour but it all centres on Pete,' chuckled Steve. 'He's always been the funniest member and our fans dig his fantastic George Formby imitations.'[6] A privately pressed album, with ex-skiffle guitarist Diz Disley, of Pete's tributes to the late music hall star has become – in every sense – a priceless Winwood-associated artefact. Stranger still was the dastard who broke into the Group van in March 1964 to pinch Pete's scarf and exercise book compilation of Formby lyrics: will he kiss her under the nose – or under the arch where the sweet william grows?

Of course, the first business of any pop group is to be liked. Lest we forget, a reviewer of the Beatles' second national tour mentioned that a highlight of their act, 'Misery', was 'led into with some good comedy'. Though there weren't many laughs from, say, the Zombies, Them or the Walker Brothers, a lot of sixties' entertainers sugared their sets with varying degrees of conscious comedy. Indeed, for the likes of Freddie Garrity, the Barron-Knights and the Rockin' Berries, audience anticipation became such that to cut the cackle invited professional suicide. More relevant to the Spencer Davis Group, Tom McGuinness was the brains behind Manfred Mann's in-concert R and B send-up of the traditional 'Dashing Away with a Smoothing Iron', which went above the heads of most of their screaming audience.

More attentive to her once favourite group was a Miss J. Cassell of London who, in *Melody Maker*, mourned 'the death of one of the few remaining blues groups in the country – Spencer Davis. They are now just a pop group not caring what performance they give. This was evident at the Manor House recently when not one song was sung seriously. I shall stick to John Mayall's Bluesbreakers and the Cream from now on.'[19] It might have been a bad night. There had been no 'Waving My Little Magic Wand' or 'Stick of Blackpool Rock' from York, but maybe Steve upset the lady by busking a frivolous bossa nova on his Hammond. Anyway, he cared enough to offer to meet Miss Cassell, perhaps to mollify her with a spin of Ray Charles' 1965 *Live in Concert* LP from the Shrine Civic Auditorium, Los Angeles in which the big band jazz-blues of Winwood's own hero is punctuated with a florid burst of Beethoven's 'Für Elise' and, for an encore, an *omnes fortissimo* 'Pop Goes the Weasel'. If he could do it, why not his disciples?

Other old obsessions lingered throughout the original Spencer Davis Group's four-year existence. Near the end, Spencer's adaptation of the Saints' 'Midnight Special' was reactivated, as was ol' Jerry Lee's 'Mean Woman Blues' with 'a Nashville touch of Chet

Atkins'.[20] More often, the Group would revert to the comfort of what used to wow 'em at the Golden Eagle – 'Searchin' ', 'Jump Back', 'Georgia', 'Nobody Loves You When You're Down and Out' – thus endorsing Steve's earliest-known remark to the music press: 'we try to keep up with trends in R and B and yet keep our basic style'.[21]

As a unit, Davis, York and the Winwoods rarely ventured beyond the limits of their rhythm and blues definition. Though this was the frame of reference for similarly motivated artists like the Stones and the Small Faces, the Group's tighter, more polished attack enabled them to cut worthier versions of American numbers simultaneously covered by others. In addition, they dared to record material that less assured British outfits would shun, such as the evergreen 'When a Man Loves a Woman', released within three months of Percy Sledge's first Top Ten probe. And who else had the confidence to cut 'Georgia', Ray Charles' US Hot Hundred number one of 1960, let alone include in their concert set 'Road Runner' from Tamla Motown's singing saxophonist Junior Walker, or closer-to-home 'Down Home Girl' which the Stones had claimed on their million-selling second album? However, the consolidation rather than development of these abilities caused the eventual loss of direction that exacerbated the quartet's disband-ment.

This, though, lay two years in the future as the countdown to 1965 crept closer. Indeed, as the New Year got under way there was cause for optimism. 'I think the public has been vastly educated,' enthused Steve. 'For people between sixteen and twenty-five, music is now a way of life. And who could have imagined Nina Simone doing "You Put a Spell on Me" [*sic*] being played on *Top of the Pops* eighteen months ago.'[22] The *Melody Maker* Pop Fifty for January showed the Stones in retreat from the top with an unrevised 'Little Red Rooster', whose blues pedigree could be traced through Sam Cooke to the Griffin Brothers' US soul hit of 1951 to the first recording by Howlin' Wolf with its composer Willie Dixon on double bass. Colliding with the falling Stones were up-and-coming Them, victims of the same passion with a riveting overhaul of 'Baby, Please Don't Go' by Big Joe Williams, a contemporary of Bessie Smith. At their most rugged, even Blackburn's smooth Four Pennies made a Top Twenty killing with Leadbelly's 'Black Girl'. Not far ahead was the Animals' Top Tenner 'Inside Looking Out' – originally recorded as 'My Rebirth' – as morbid as 'Black Girl' and wilfully uncommercial to boot. With no whistleable melody to carry its harrowing prison narrative, it had first been tried by Eric

Left to right: Muff Winwood,
Spencer Davis and fifteen-year-
old Steve battle with their
equipment at the Golden Eagle,
September, 1963. (*Jim Simpson*)

Steve (left) rocks and Spencer
rolls on their last night as
amateurs, February, 1964.
(*Jim Simpson*)

Finale of Birmingham Town Hall R & B concert on 28 February, 1964, with guitarists (left to right) Chris Dreja, Eric 'Slowhand' Clapton and bass, Paul Samwell-Smith, Keith Relf (tambourine), drummer Jim McCarty, Art Themen (sax) and at the microphones (left to right) Steve, Spencer, Sonny Boy Williamson and Long John Bauldry. (*Jim Simpson*)

Steve gets the blues in a Birmingham nightclub, June, 1965. (*Jim Simpson*)

Assisted by the late Johnny Jones (left to right) Spencer, Pete, Muff and Steve inspect the wares in Jones and Crossland music shop, July, 1965. (*Jim Simpson*)

Steve at the wheel of Jim Simpson's MGTF sports car with (left to right) Muff, Spencer and Pete. (*Jim Simpson*)

Spencer Davis, 1966. (*S. K. R. Photographs*)

Actress Carol White deps for
Pete York with (left to right)
Spencer, Steve and Muff on the
set of *The Ghost Goes Gear*.

Every little bit hurts: Steve calls
for some calomine lotion.
(*Nigel Dickson*)

Soul Man: Chris Wood (left) when saxophinist with Locomotive which included (second left to right) Brian 'Monk' Finch (sax), Mike Kellie (drums), singer Danny King, Richard Storey (sax, organ), Jim Simpson (trumpet), and Pete Allen (bass). (*Jim Simpson*)

Steve knocks back a yard of ale on his eighteenth birthday as (left to right) Pete, Spencer and Muff look on. (*Syndication International*)

Davis and Winwood display quiet good taste, 1966.

Goodbye Stevie: Winwood at
Birmingham Town Hall on 27 March,
1967, during his farewell tour with the
Spencer Davis Group. (*Jim Simpson*)

On the road: Steve, Jim Capaldi, Chris
Wood and Dave Mason hold up the
Traffic. (*Keystone*)

Wood (sax), Capaldi (drums), Winwood (organ) and Mason (guitar) rehearse outside the cottage while the crew keep eyes peeled for irate neighbours. (*Barrie Wentzel*)

Sitar man. (*H. Goodwin*)

Traffic on *Top of the Pops*, November, 1967. *(Pictorial Press Ltd)*

Steve with Francine Heimann – who lisped the 'Hole in my Shoe' monologue.

Burdon during a 1965 jam session with Blues Incorporated under the more genteel title of 'Rosie'. From the hipper Flamingo blackness of soul and bluebeat, Georgie Fame was suddenly at number one with 'Yeah Yeah', co-written by Jon Hendricks.

On the local front, the Rockin' Berries were bowing out with their first smash while the descending piano *ostinato* of 'Go Now' was poised to seize Georgie's fame. As much highbrow connoisseurs as the Moody Blues, the Spencer Davis Group were well placed to capitalize on this, the high summer of both Brum Beat and British blues.

Searching for the right commercial vehicle, the Group weren't to match the Moody Blues' achievement for precisely twelve months. In the meantime, engagement fees continued to increase as each successive release gripped the charts harder before they went for the jugular with 'Keep On Running'.

The antithesis of the raucous 'I Can't Stand It', the third single, 'Every Little Bit Hurts', in February was a solemn *lied* by Brenda Holloway – a Tamla-Motown artiste from whom the Group would be demanding further musical Danegeld. Written by Ed Cobb (also responsible for Soft Cell's 'Tainted Love' in 1981), it was performed by the Spencer Davis outfit in a rendition that echoed that of the Small Faces, who had featured it during their residency at Leicester Square's short-lived Cavern Club six months earlier. Ponderous gospel piano, staccato guitar chords and sessionman Kenneth Salmon's holy organ propelled Winwood's passionate restraint – given wider gesture in an intriguing alternate mix with a supplementary string section. Its downbeat atmosphere and uncommon time signature, amid more extrovert records of the day, were epitomized by the haunted cathedral drama of a *Ready Steady Go* appearance in which Steve's acned countenance was shrouded in shadow.

As its yo-yo chart run peaked at number 41, *Midland Beat* chose to focus on the B-side, 'It Hurts Me So', Steve Winwood's first published effort as a writer. In a Motown mould, it could have oozed more substance than its limited rhymes and chords suggested on sheet music – had not the studio clock dictated such short cuts as Steve singing both the call and response on the chorus. The *accelerando* piano coda provokes further visions of the Group's regular engineer Brian Humphrey's anxiety for his tea break.

On the previous flip-side – an up-tempo blues-derivation called 'Midnight Train', laughably credited to the band's booking agents – Winwood had tackled lead vocal, piano *and* overdubbed guitar solo while Spencer and the rest looked on. Already he was a being apart.

Now accompanying Davis to London to meet the press in this or that office, snack bar or – when he could get away with it – pub, the bored teenager still endeavoured, as he always would, to be helpful. Articulating with guarded deliberation and without cynicism, he became 'pleased to be popular but I'm not pleased about some people I have to meet'.[21] To the more parochial *Midland Beat*'s enquiry about the Group's success, he sighed, 'it's great but people always ask you what it's like'.[23]

What music journalists and Birmingham fans had long understood about the Spencer Davis Group set-up infiltrated a wider pop public during 1965. Davis wasn't The Man after all. Neither was it some grizzled, bearded backwoodsman type like John Mayall, old enough to be your Dad. This lived-in, aged rasp and multi-instrumental command came instead from a spotty, gangling youth, pop-eyed at the microphone. Without belittling them, the other three framed this exquisite's antics – though the drummer's old-fashioned style and, when used, the skittish gospel-esque backing vocals added further character.

Pete's clattering tattoos fired Muff and Spencer's hooting gospel train harmonies to the fore in 'Strong Love' – an attempt at recapturing the 'I Can't Stand It' frantic magic. This was produced by Harry 'Lord Rockingham' Robinson, who'd done likewise for Millie in 1963. Although he delivered the goods as expected, Steve none the less loathed 'Strong Love', issued in May, only singing it onstage when specifically requested. He was obliged to go through with it for the Group's slot in *Pop Gear*, a seventy-minute conveyor belt of musical ephemera B-featured on the ABC cinema circuit. Also among the all-styles-served-here cast were the Rockin' Berries, Nashville Teens and other old acquaintances, as well as crooner Matt Monro; fading Liverpool hitmakers, the Fourmost and Billy J. Kramer; hitless but popular instrumental combo Sounds Incorporated; Herman's Hermits; the Four Pennies, and many other contributors to the rich tapestry of British pop. This exposure guaranteed that 'Strong Love' was as successful as its forbears but, from this holding operation, the next release had to make or break it.

The calculated risk of an album seemed the most sensible stroke to pull, as precedents set by the Yardbirds, John Mayall and Georgie Fame had demonstrated. Appealing to a similar bohemian market, Bob Dylan's first four albums had all been bestsellers before 'The Times They Are A-Changing' charted around the same time as – and far higher than – 'Every Little Bit Hurts'. The Spencer Davis Group's image was likewise bereft of gimmicks, and their mediocre singles figures were a mere surface manifestation of the respect accorded them for their natural vitality and musicianship by sixth formers, undergraduates and the art school mob, while Mods regarded them as fair interpreters of the Americans.

To Chris Blackwell's relief, *Their First LP* sold enough over the six months from July to creep into the album lists and leave its mark at a gratifying number five. Though the Group's prowess was by no means incidental in this, the LP's brown sleeve was under the arms of enough grammar school prefects and parka-ed Vespa riders for *Their First LP* to mushroom into a hip status symbol.

Nevertheless, too soon for the stronger budgetary commitment to albums peculiar to the later sixties, the Group remained geared for *Top of the Pops*. Padded as they were with previously issued A- and B- sides, cancelled singles, blues jams and throwaway instrumentals, the Thinking Man's Pop Group's three Fontana LPs can only be judged as individual tracks rather than as complete entities. Though professional tunesmiths like Reg Presley proffered material,[24] there was almost complete reliance on old crowd-pleasers, newer soul favourites and, to a diminishing extent, their own original efforts.

Half *Their First LP* regurgitated the earlier 45s and their couplings, but no less commercial was 'I'm Blue', which was once earmarked as a follow-up to 'Dimples'. On this Betty Everett revamp, Davis and the Winwoods' spooky three-part lament was augmented by Millie Small's wordless vocal obligato and, much lower in the mix, the ivory tinklings of fellow *Pop Gear* participant four-eyed Peter Asher of Peter and Gordon. Opening side one, 'My Babe' is preserved on an extant TV clip. As his Rosencrantz and Guildenstern, Steve's elder sibling and Spencer mug up to the camera, duetting the kindergarten verses while the lad himself paces in profile like an expectant father – awaiting his capsizing vocal bridge and guitar solo.

5

'Tomorrow Never Comes'

In its first editorial, *Midland Beat* had affirmed 'we are appointing top musical journalists as correspondents in every Midlands county'. Perhaps the most tireless correspondent was a B. P. Finch who, from the onset, scooped the Worcestershire scene. Deemed worthy of a special section – 'Worcester Whisperings' – there was much to occupy Our Man Finch. Not only the last resting place of the much-maligned King John, the cathedral city was also a thriving bastion of beat. By 1965, some county bands had already taken pot shots at the national charts. From Malvern, the Sundowners' 'House of the Rising Sun' – Spencer Davis' Excelsior stand-by – on Pye was totally eclipsed by Mickie Most's melodrama with the Animals. Most produced too the Cherokees, a Whittington quintet whose moment of glory came when their trudging 'Seven Golden Daffodils', five weeks in the Top Forty, almost outpaced a version by the better-known Mojos.

Less than an hour's drive up the A38 from Birmingham, rustic Worcester nevertheless tended to exhibit a certain insular superiority towards its Black Country neighbours with their belching factory chimneys. The county aligned itself more with Wales, an eight-mile hike from Worcester, and the West Country – an affinity provoking the Vampires to become the Severnbeats: was there ever a group called the Ousebeats? Worcester's sixteen bigtime groups in 1963 were more likely to play Swindon's X club or the Rock Garden Pavilion in Llandrindod Wells than Erdington's Pandora or the Moat 'Twistacular' in Wythall. *Midland Beat* reported that the county town's Lansdowne Agency was 'formed with the sole intention of stopping Brum groups playing at Worcester venues'[1] – an embargo extending even to Denny Laine's Diplomatic Sunday show at Kidderminster Playhouse in October.

Home-reared bands also claimed a stronger right over church youth organizations like St John's Young People's Club who, accepting that God would not cast out this Beatle pestilence as He had skiffle, had embraced regular beat sessions. Finger-snapping curates aside, the more secular Pierpont Street Jazz Club – like the Golden Eagle – also capitulated, though much teenage custom defected every Thursday to the plush 'Ot Spot, which boasted a coffee bar, lounge area, liquor licence and record library which stored pressings by Impression, Worcester's own shoestring record label. Of the Fortunes, Hell's Angels, the Renegades and other standardized names jostling for bookings, *la crème de la crème* were the Jaguars who, like their Birmingham namesakes, were one of myriad minor instrumental groups in artistic debt to the trailblazing Shadows. They were the first local band to make a record, and their 'Opus to Spring', coupled with 'The Beat' – taped amidst sound-proofing mattresses at Henwick Road YMCA – was said to have exhausted Impression's unrepeated run of five hundred copies. This may not have been an exaggeration, because rhythm guitarist Michael Mann, drummer Roger Moss and the drummer they shared with the Cossacks were blessed by their volatile lead guitarist's aptitude for selling the band to gruff landlords and wary entertainments secretaries.

Born on 10 May 1944 – the day of Job – David Thomas Mason was impetuous, argumentative and given to bouts of sulking. Yet, like many so-called extroverts, he suffered waves of self-doubt about his musical ability. Indeed, a reason for his Jaguars' concentration on instrumentals was Dave's anxiety about singing in public.

Some nights, the Jaguars would get round this by hauling on a vocalist to be Cliff Richard for a while. None of these were regarded as an integral part of the group – though Mason wondered about a gap-toothed Elvis Presley imitator from Evesham called James Capaldi, but 'I had a bad name – particularly with Dave's parents who thought I was a gypsy, a gangster.'[2]

In his black spiv shirt and white tie, you could see Mr and Mrs Mason's point about saturnine, sideburned Jim. In fact, his own parents, Nicholas and Maria, headed an established Evesham family. They were good Italians and even better Roman Catholics, sending all their seven children to St Mary's RC Primary School in Rynal Road. Music too was in the blood – one of the girls sang in the local opera society and James, the eldest child, had piano lessons, while father Nicholas squeezed accordion in a dance band. Propagated by tidy-minded American journalists was the myth that this combo also once contained Lawrence Winwood. This has no basis in truth – though, unrelated to Muff and Steve, two other

77

Winwoods did touch the lives of Jim Capaldi and Dave Mason.

Leaving Four Pools secondary school in 1960, where he'd excelled at boxing and chess, sixteen-year-old Jim had been bitten by the rock 'n' roll bug, making his debut in this vein as vocalist with the Sapphires at Evesham Public Hall. Perhaps feeling no end of a fool afterwards, he retreated gradually from the front of the stage to become the Sapphires' drummer, purchasing a kit from his earnings as an apprentice factory engineer. He was an admirer of Al Jackson who rattled the traps with Stax house band, Booker T and the MGs, whose reptilian 'Green Onions' was a 1962 million-seller. None the less Capaldi, for all his natural sense of rhythm, did not choose to emulate Jackson's economic disciplined co-ordination, because 'I've always played drums out of feeling – not so much in a technical context . . . I play out of my head.'[3] Furthermore, as his stints with the likes of the Jaguars indicated, he would never outgrow his urge to front a band once again as lead singer.

The Sapphires were semi-professional, and their workload extended as far afield as Gloucester Guildhall, where the town's burghers were scandalized by the tightness of the trousers of the new lead singer, Rodney Dawes. This was in a prudish England that had hounded babysnatching Jerry Lee Lewis from its shores and obliged Billy Fury to moderate his sub-Elvis gyrations. P. J. Proby's splitting strides were yet to come.

A decent interval after this disgraceful episode, Jim left the Sapphires for the Hellions, a trio formed with some Four Pools schoolmates – guitarist Luther Grosvenor and, on bass, Tony Hill. Putting up an impressive show at Malvern's Rock Group Contest in January 1964, the Hellions brushed aside opposition which included Newent's Whirlwinds, led by a Marilyn Winwood – to be beaten by one vote in the last heat by the Seminoles. Within a few weeks they were topping the bill at the second annual Beat Week concert in Worcester, while 'quietly becoming a most important force on the local beat scene, establishing themselves more by personal recommendation than by force of personality'.[4] That they were an unprepossessing bunch is borne out by the Brooding Intensity pose of publicity photos taken when the Hellions expanded to a quartet, having taken on ex-Jaguar Dave Mason who'd fixed up an immediate engagement at Worcester's Flamingo coffee bar. Three months later, Grosvenor – unhappy with the new regime – was replaced by Unit Five's Gordon Jackson, content as subordinate rhythm guitarist. His counter tenor enhanced the deeper vocal harmonies of Mason and Capaldi and also contributed an insane falsetto, put to good use on Donnie Elpert's 'Little Piece of Leather' and one of his own songs, 'Dream Child'.

Now full-time musicians, the four travelled beyond parochial circuits to such alien venues as Victor Sylvester's Dance Club in Chelsea and, more appropriately, Liverpool's Iron Door, which the Searchers ruled as the Beatles had the mildewed Cavern. Among their less celebrated tasks prior to national success, both these Scouse bands had, on various one-nighters, backed Walsall's Tanya Day, who had a Polydor single, 'Your Lips Get in the Way' and an attendant *Thank Your Lucky Stars* slot to her credit. After the Hellions carried out a similar function for her at Lakes Inn on the outskirts of Worcester, Tanya – possibly past her best – agreed to accompany them on a season in Hamburg to satisfy a contract stipulation about a five-piece group.

Since customer complaints that if you'd heard one Merseyside band, you'd heard 'em all, far less of the Grosse Freiheit's imported pop talent was Liverpudlian by the time Tanya Day and the Hellions set up on the Star-Club stage in August 1964. The most popular club in Hamburg 4's red-light district, the Star provided entertainment from early evening till dawn, seven days a week. A far cry from the dungeon accommodation suffered by Rory Storm, the Beatles and other Reeperbahn pioneers three years earlier, the crowded but homely Pacific Hotel housed the Hellions along with, that same month, the Nashville Teens from Surrey and Carlisle's VIPs. More familiar faces greeting the Hellions were Shades Five from Kidder-minster – and, with their new manager, Birmingham's Spencer Davis Group, a cordial encounter and one which had a bearing on Dave and Jim's future lives. Time hung heavily between sets, but the actual time spent playing was greatly reduced from the gruelling eight-hour shifts of 1960. On hot days there were excursions to the North Sea resort of Timmendorf where, sunbathing on the sand, the musicians would recharge their batteries for the labours of the night.

The outside of their van now defaced by the fräuleins' affection-ate messages, the Hellions – though yet to secure a recording deal themselves – were hired to tape demos and accompany others, beginning with the obscure Eddie Curtis, a singer signed to Oriele. Moreover, they were in demand locally as a reliable support act for visiting stars like Adam Faith – on whom they'd pressed a contact address after meeting him outside an M6 service station – and the charismatic Dave Berry, whom they invited to a party after the show. On another occasion they ran into P. J. Proby, who was offered 'Shades of Blue', a group original with Merseybeat overtones, which was also submitted to Fontana recording mana-ger Brian Meecham after a costly day committing it and 'Dream Child' to tape at Hollick and Taylor Studio.

Cumulatively, all this hustling got results. In October, the Hellions' hard-won residency at the Whisky-a-go-go – not the Birmingham club but a night spot within the same building as London's Flamingo – was dignified by the presence of Kentucky songwriter Jackie de Shannon. On the crest of a wave with her 'When You Walk in the Room', a Top Three smash for the Searchers, Jackie was on the lookout for further vehicles for her compositions. Squiring her on this occasion was session guitarist Jimmy Page, who'd heard glowing reports about the Hellions when working with another Worcester quartet, Raynor's Secrets. Astute enough to recognize the Hellions' weathered stagecraft and now cooler professionalism, Jackie promised them a number. With this, the group were able, through the connections of its newly acquired London management, to negotiate a recording contract with Pye subsidiary Piccadilly.

A witty enough paean to lovesick obsession, 'Daydreaming of You' was produced by Hollywood jack-of-all-trades Kim Fowley who, perhaps anticipating the *TV Times* forecast that 'the Brum Beat is all set to take over from the booming Merseyside market',[5] also supervised sessions for Noddy Holder's In-betweens which included a brutal 'Hold Tight', later a hit for Dave Dee, Dozy, Beaky, Mick and Tich. No such luck befell the Hellions with 'Daydreaming of You'. However, they were able to place 'Shades of Blue' with the Rockin' Berries,[6] also on Piccadilly, and with George E. Washington whose version appeared on Decca.

Heartened by this syndication, the Hellions convinced Piccadilly that, rather than seek outside help, a song co-written by Jackson would make a saleable second single. A shattered windscreen while driving to the session may be seen in retrospect as a bad omen, for 'Tomorrow Never Comes', issued in April 1965, also fought shy of the Top Fifty in spite of plugging on the Light Programme. With the soberer skills of moonlighting EMI prducer John Schroeder, a hacienda mandolin lubricated a lyric advising a girl to accentuate her charms to stop her man straying ''cos the girls of today are gonna take him away'.

And good riddance. With Piccadilly's patience snapping, everything hung on the third 45. From Eric Jacobson, a Denmark street tunesmith, came 'A Little Lovin'' – nothing to do with the Fourmost's hit of the same title but, apart from a galloping middle eight, a throwback to the Crickets' 1957 hit, 'Oh Boy'. Showering brighter sparks of Hellion fire, the band's own choice for release, the livelier 'Think It Over', was relegated to B-side – its assignment to the fictitious Fourmost Music demonstrating the group's sarcastic disenchantment. Nevertheless, though it owed its title to

Buddy Holly, Dave Mason's adventurous 'Think It Over' solo, escaping bar line restrictions, was far removed from the late fifties.

Dave was also the first rat to leave the sinking ship. As 'A Little Lovin' ' bit the dust, so did an opportunity to plug it on *Ready Steady Go*. More bitter was the poverty that compelled the Hellions to organize a jumble sale to cover accumulated parking fines. A further drain on group economy was the employment of John 'Poli' Palmer, a new drummer, so that Capaldi could assert himself centre stage for a few truculent weeks. The final blow was the liquidation of the Hellions fan club by secretary Annette Winwood of Dent Close, Worcester.

At grassroots, the Hellions, with their long absences down south, had become very passé anyway. Dominating B. P. Finch's Whisperings now were New Sense, the Daleks, the Buzz, Censored! and the Banned. Also mentioned were the King Snakes who had none other than Robert Plant as lead singer. That New Sense had once been the Phantoms best exemplified the passing of the old order.

Picking up the pieces, the Hellions too toyed with new names suggesting similar abstract leanings. Among these were Emotions – an old idea of Jim's – and the Generation. While their more fortunate Reeperbahn friends, the Spencer Davis Group, topped the charts in January 1966, the Hellions bid an ignominious farewell as their last single, 'Hallelujah', backed with the trusty 'Shades of Blue', was released under an alias – Revolution.

After a radical rethink, Capaldi re-entered the fray with Deep Feeling. Thumping congas as well as singing, among other Hellions survivors with him were Mason's replacement David Meredith, shanghai-ed from Evesham's Wavelengths, and John Palmer – whose talents had been wasted behind the kit – doubling on vibraphone and flute, both of which instruments were yet to achieve prominence in a pop context. With a more pronounced orientation towards both specialized soul music and band originals than the Hellions had known, Deep Feeling's ear-catching line-up netted an impressive tally of London club dates plus sporadic one-shot recording contracts. Marmalade Records put out the self-penned 'If You're Mine' while 'Pretty Colours' turned up in the States on Fontana. Both filled a French EP.

Nowhere as active on vinyl was Dave Mason who, on quitting the Hellions, had intended, so he said, to study formal orchestration and composition. When sufficiently schooled in these arts, he would join the brain drain to North America to pass on the fruits of his knowledge. Dave could hardly have expected to realize this lofty ambition as he drifted with his guitar from pillar to post, from band to unsatisfactory band. One month he played working men's clubs with the Doc Thompson Sound; the next he was on at the Marquee with Herbie Goins and the Nightimers. Late for a rehearsal, he was sacked from Julian Covay and the Machine, a soul band with two drummers.

Intermittently throughout 1966, he served the Spencer Davis Group as malcontented road manager. Humping speakers wasn't exactly the Big Time but it would do while he waited, like Mr Micawber, for something to turn up. Besides, Dave had always enjoyed chatting about music with young Steve Winwood, a lad of hidden depths that he'd come to know very well. Even two years ago in Hamburg, Steve had seemed apart from the rest of the Group. Ray Phillips of the Nashville Teens reckoned Steve was paying court to a German girlfriend or maybe it was the age gap, but he'd rarely joined Pete, Spencer and his brother on Timmendorf beach.

Back in the Midlands, Mason found himself more often in the Birmingham company of Steve and his crowd than in sleepy old Worcester. Conflicting emotions when Capaldi's Deep Feeling went down well at a Salford Park spectacular were appeased when Jim – who couldn't help liking him – invited Dave to join Deep Feeling. This he did on and off, alternating with the more pliant Luther Grosvenor.

Dave was there when Deep Feeling depped for Cream at the Penthouse, a new city centre club in October 1966. Refreshing themselves afterwards, Dave reiterated to Jim – and Steve – his deep feeling that Jim's new group, though it had cracked the bigger nut of Birmingham, could arrive at much the same commercial impasse as the Hellions. Although more optimistic about Deep Feeling, Jim too was tired of waiting for something to happen.

On many an idle evening Jim had fraternized with Ray Everett's Blueshounds, often filling in whenever their regular drummer was indisposed. With the Blueshounds' demise in 1966, after coming second in a *Melody Maker* group competition, some of its members were absorbed into the Kansas City Seven who were led by ex-New Magnolia trumpeter – and *Midland Beat* picture editor – Jim Simpson. The Seven were in transition from mainstream jazz via rhythm and blues to ritualized let-me-hear-you-say-yeah soul routines, and during personnel upheavals over the summer, tenor saxophonist and flautist Mike Burney – who'd played with Spencer Davis – was ousted in favour of Christopher Wood, a twenty-two-year-old neighbour of Simpson's in Cradley.

Like Nicholas and Maria Capaldi, Chris and his sister Stephanie's schoolteacher parents were pleased to encourage musical endeavour in their offspring. Though he had no formal lessons, Chris confirmed his early promise by progressing at his own pace on the piano that always stood in the family flat in Corngreaves Hall which faced the golf course. Acquiring the rudiments of harmony at school, and with a little help from a musical friend who didn't actually squawk woodwinds himself, Chris taught himself to play a second-hand flute, initially approximating the style of Dizzy Gillespie sideman Les Spann. As he had acted in several school plays, this new skill added to his artistic self-image.

By the time he transferred to nearby Stourbridge Art College in 1963, he could also find his way around the saxophone by applying much the same fingering as the flute. According to Jim Simpson, though the boy shaped up OK he 'lacked self-confidence and fell to pieces at times'. Nevertheless, in March 1964 he was working three nights a week mainly in the Kidderminister–Dudley–Wolverhampton triangle with Sounds of Blue, a Stourbridge blues sextet. With Wood in the queue to solo were that old flame of Spencer Davis's, pianist Christine Perfect and guitarist Stan Webb, who'd left a Shades Five yet to share a Hamburg stage with the Hellions.

When Sounds of Blue became Chicken Shack in 1965, Chris landed on his feet in Jim Simpson's band whose stage outfits were made by his generous sister Stephanie, who charged only for materials. Come 1966 it was decided that, as a name, Kansas City Seven was rather too Acker Bilk. More in keeping with the changed repertoire, *Midland Beat* announced the septet would now be known as Locomotive and were 'full steam ahead for the charts'.[7] This statement of intent was amplified by the group's new singer and chief show-off, Danny King: 'we like the crowd to really join in and feel they're actually participating. We try to create a happy party atmosphere.'[7] Since ditching his Mayfair Set in January, King – one of the city's better vocalists – had become a prize acquisition of Simpson's, as were the sensational four-piece horn section and the athletic drumming of Mike Kellie who, unlike the others, kept in trim by laying off the booze.

Birmingham City winger Trevor Hockey – whose living necessitated denials similar to Kellie's – nevertheless bolstered Locomotive's hedonistic image when he bounded onstage at the band's Town Hall concert in November for a boisterous duet with Danny King. With bookings flooding in, even from London, membership of Locomotive appeared a desirable option for a young musician – and so it was for sixteen-year- old Johnny Barry, who took over when Chris Wood resigned in December 1966.

83

6

'Gonna Mess Up a Good Thing'

The fleeting presence of Peter Asher – Beatle girlfriend Jane's brother – on *Their First LP* accurately indicated London In Crowd acceptance of the Spencer Davis Group. At the door of the supercool Ad-Lib, the Bag o' Nails off Carnaby Street, the Speakeasy or the cloistered Scotch of St James's – in Mason's Yard, within spitting distance of Buckingham Palace – the Group were scrutinized through the spy hole and not found wanting. As an alternative to these nightclub-discotheques' deafening dark you could stroll into Soho. Here Steve and, less frequently, Spencer could be prevailed upon to have a blow with Georgie Fame, Graham Bond, Chris Farlowe or whoever else was on that same night at the Crazy Elephant or Flamingo where, earlier that year, the Davis combo had backed sequinned Dionne Warwick. Rufus Thomas and Stevie Wonder were among other Americans who showed up in Wardour Street in 1965 – some standing their round with Steve Winwood and his new-found friend Alan Price in the Ship.

In theory, the most interesting jam sessions still occurred up the road at the less fashionable Marquee. Making a row on its crowded stage one summer evening were chart-riding Denny Laine, who rarely missed such opportunities; two of Manfred's Menn; skeletal London-Irish drummer Peter 'Ginger' Baker from the Graham Bond Organisation; organist Brian Auger, whose EMI single, 'Sixty-five Green Onions', was bound for the bargain bins; the venerable Alexis Korner, with a protégé in Ronnie Jones of the Nightimers; and ex-'Tommy Steele of Scotland' Alex Harvey, on the make with his Soul Band. Beastly drunk at the bar, the zealously unreliable Viv Prince – ex-Pretty Thing and Soho club host of Knuckles – was among those ravers who first welcomed the

Birmingham newcomers to this cabal of pop conquistadors. 'Off to a club', wrote *Melody Maker* of its Second Brightest Hope, 'they were greeted by the Animals, Viv Prince and P. J. Proby. Stevie Winwood was soon up on stage jamming with Brian Auger, Long John Baldry and the VIPs while Eric Burdon bellowed for 'Lucille.'' Adrenalin pumping and talking shop continually, the pack next sauntered into Broadcasting House to gatecrash a late-night show before finishing up at the Scotch.

The Spencer Davis Group weren't above consorting with pro-vincial support bands as they did at Northampton Technical College where, with the inglorious Lynton Grae Sound, an unsteady 'You've Lost That Lovin' Feeling' closed the evening. Steve was as incurable a blower as Denny Laine, and a trip to Nottingham ostensibly to meet Pete's parents, saw him in a Trentside club after supper joining in a hastily rearranged 'Jump Back' with the outrageous Zoot Money Big Roll Band, whom he'd watched from the wings at the Uxbridge Blues and Folk Festival in June.

Never at ease as a West End clubman, Steve gravitated back to Birmingham most weekends. Long a nightbird by vocation, if he wasted time boozing under age in the Rum Runner or the Elbow Room – well, at least he was among friends. Most of these were musicians too and, inevitably, Winwood would find himself on small-hour stages with the likes of Everett's Blueshounds, Ladies' Gentlemen, the Hellions or Jim Simpson's Kansas City Seven: 'we all used to go to this drinking-gambling club where Jim used to play and, like, we used to get up and play with him and jam'.[2] He also fell in with clothes designer Stephanie Wood, a Vivienne Westwood of her day. Steve was quite taken with the circular badges decorating her lapels, collaged from comic dialogue balloons. One he came to wear himself had King Kong making the incredible statement: 'My budgie is 14½ years old. Is this a record?'

Sensible Muff was even more unlikely to be taking part in such as the finals of the National 'Bend' competition – a dance devised by disc jockey Mike Quinn – at the Cromwellian in SW7. The elder Winwood's social circle in London overlapped that of Ray Davies with whom he and Zena spent a quiet evening in a Muswell Hill Chinese restaurant. However, Muff, like Steve, preferred the more familiar hospitality of his Mum and Dad back at Atlantic Road to London.

The more gregarious Spencer Davis, by contrast, continued to cultivate the bright young things down south. One social conquest at a housewarming party was Rolling Stone Bill Wyman, who sold Spencer his stereogram for a knockdown £500. Within minutes of returning to his Kensington mews from the Stones' second US excursion, a jet-lagged Brian Jones was visited by Spencer with Steve and the road crew. Emotionally insecure, Brian over-valued the goodwill of the more revered of his peers – even those still struggling. Banishing sleep, he bid them welcome in his way: 'man, you should see the stuff we've got through,'[3] Jones boasted hours later, indicating the roaches and empty bottles among the album covers, curry leftovers and stoned layabouts littering his front room.

Professionally, the Stones' largesse extended to inviting the Spencer Davis Group – an act much like their former selves – to guest star on their fifth British tour opening at Finsbury Park in September: 'a lucky break'[4] reckoned *Midland Beat*. It was luckier, perhaps, for Unit Four Plus Two who, picking the bones of a worldwide smash in May, had had their fifteen minutes. The same seemed to apply to the waning Moody Blues who were to replace the unit for three dates. Yet the uncritical shrieking pandemonium that greeted even compere Ray Cameron and his attempts to keep order was no barometer of market standing. Though fire hoses quelled the uproar at one venue, the second house at Manchester destroyed the most seats as panicking bouncers fought crazed girls. Among the twenty-one unconscious afterwards was Keith Richards, stunned by a flying lemonade bottle.

The first real experience of fan hysteria proved worthwhile when the Group's own time came. More pleasant was the camaraderie beyond the footlights. In their common confinement to frowsy dressing rooms came anecdotes about what Brian and Bill got up to in Adelaide; Spencer telling Keith how much he liked 'Lady Jane' off *Aftermath*, and Pete agreeing with Charlie Watts – jazzman to lapsed jazzman – that at least it was a living. Before authority complained, Bill, Steve, Brian, Spencer and Pete, back from the local Odeon, had a blow in a Cheltenham hotel lounge. In Stockton-on-Tees, roguish Mick Jagger contrived, during 'Georgia', to spread cold chips on the blind side of the microphone-bound Winwood's piano – not that its auditory effect was noticed amid the tumult. Off-duty japes in Bristol culminated with Spencer in ripped trousers being knocked cold with an aspidistra pot, and Pete's arrest after asking a parking meter for directions to the digs.

More constructively, Steve had investigated the sonic possibilities of the foot-operated fuzz box with which Keith nightly blasted out the 'Satisfaction' riff. It had been intended by its Gibson designers to make a guitar sound like a saxophone but, through Keith, its blackboard-scratching hoarseness assumed a personality of its own. The Beatles had fed a bass through one when preparing their winter album, *Rubber Soul* – another endorsement.

The new device also electroplated 'Keep On Running', the next Spencer Davis chart attack, thus removing it further still from the bouncy ska demo by Jamaican songwriter Wilfred 'Jackie' Edwards. Copying Nat 'King' Cole, Jackie began his lengthy recording career in the late fifties. On Island in 1962 he delved into its Sue subsidiary for his most memorable A-side, Frankie Forde's 'Sea Cruise'. By this time, having been Ben E. King for a while, he had found not only his own voice but had realized a greater dexterity as a composer. 'Keep On Running' was to be his magnum opus.

With no preconceptions, the Group taped three versions – one substituting piano for distorted guitar. Though Steve was integral to the final arrangement, Spencer observed 'often during a run through, Stevie will get an idea and we tell him to keep it in – but he get so involved with his playing that he forgets and we all have to try to remember it for him'.[5] Rejected at first by Fontana's high command, it sliced into the Top Twenty as Britain slept off 1965's Christmas dinner. Back at work, its plain four-to-the-bar rhythm, cemented by Muff's pounding bass, wafted from both factories in Redditch and King's Road boutiques. Pirate Radio Caroline even used the 'Keep On Running' seven-stroke *ostinato* as a station call sign. Finally, a scream-rent plug on *Thank Your Lucky Stars* ended the long reign of the Beatles' 'Daytripper' on 8 January 1966. A spurious vengeance came within seven days when a *Rubber Soul* cover – 'Michelle' by the Overlanders – replaced the Spencer Davis Group at number one. In mitigation, unprecedented demand for 'Keep On Running' had seriously depleted supplies in most northern cities the previous weekend. Nevertheless, sales touched a cool half-million during a fourteen-week chart life.

Front-paged by *Melody Maker*, Steve remarked, 'it's funny, since the hit, they all come running to us, the people that have ignored us in the past'.[6] As 'Keep On Running' raced up the French and German charts too, hasty calls to *Midland Beat* enabled the *Birmingham Mail* to cobble together a story to go with its 'City group top of the pops' headline. Mis-spelling Pete York's name and mentioning Steve's 'jazz-styled singing', the *Mail* also noted that at number two with his Italian translation, 'The River', was Knotty Ash comedian Ken Dodd, currently starring in *Humpty Dumpty* at the Alexandra Theatre. All pop songs are the same, aren't they?

Certainly containing similar qualities to 'Keep On Running', with its trendy fuzz guitar, repetitive lyrics and catchy football chant beat, was 'Hold Tight' by Dave Dee, Dozy, Beaky, Mick and

Tich, unleashed on Fontana in February 1966. Foreseen accusations of 'selling out' sprang from the more committed buyers of *Their First LP*. Denouncing the Spencer Davis Group in a letter to *Midland Beat* was a Lee Stevens, but his feelings may have been mere sour grapes since Lee's group, the Satellites, had been beaten in a beat contest at West Bromwich Adelphi judged by Spencer Davis.

Not all smiles though, was a Birmingham jazz jamboree appearance with the Johnny Patrick Big Band. Backstage the Group were cold-shouldered by bigoted jazzers, while in the hall impatient young ladies fidgeted through endless centuries of toot-tooting for their Stevie to sing two numbers.

Quite used by then to demure requests for autographs and rarer requests to meet girls in, say, the romantic seclusion of a club broom cupboard, Winwood was, none the less, astounded when first mobbed by libidinous fans not much younger than himself at a West Bromwich soundcheck one Saturday in January. Almost despite himself he was becoming a star, although he protested, 'I'd hate to end up in pantomime like the Rockin' Berries.'[7] Not yet a household name, 'Stevie' (as he was in those days) and sometimes the others were nevertheless recognized in motorway service areas, on tube trains and in corner shops. Driving, driving, driving to strange towns, strange venues and strange beds, there were more dates booked than the Group could possibly keep. Though still centred on clubs, ballrooms and colleges, the work spectrum broadened as the van zigzagged across Britain from a palais de danse in Inverness to Margate's Dreamland to the Bird Cage in Plymouth to the Palace Ballroom on the Isle of Man via the Floral Hall in Southport. Often, they'd have to drop everything to fit in *Saturday Club* back in Brum; to Manchester, 'entertainment capital of the north' and home of Granada television; to London, *Ready Steady Go*, new gear from Carnaby Street, photo calls for Fabulous 208 and other promotional necessities. More onerous was the honouring of contracts settled when the band had been only semi-famous. One such requirement was a function organized by Moseley Youth Club on 15 February at Walsall Town Hall, a mere four miles from Atlantic Road. Following three support groups, the Local Boys Made Good plunged in with 'Gonna Mess Up a Good Thing' at 9.40 p.m. before sweeping off thirty-five minutes later to backstage nostalgia and lionizing: I always knew you'd make it, lads. Needless to say, the place was packed, even though the Group had played nearby Smethwick Baths and Nottingham University that same week.

It was a tough old life, but even bookworm Muff forgot himself in the sweep of events. Exhilarated by unexpected applause from the Wembley studio technicians during an afternoon *Ready Steady Go* rehearsal, Muff had leapt from the Group's podium to bawl, 'Hey, we've just heard we're at twenty in your weekend chart!'[6] at an entering newspaperman. There was plenty to get excited about. Steve's 'Lifelines' ambition 'to make an American tour'[8] seemed on the cards as, provoked by substantial US fan mail, a provisional route was mapped out and a Yale University opening on 28 February announced. However, with no *Billboard* bullet for 'Keep On Running', it was decided to look homeward for the time being.

Aborted likewise was a mooted Steve Winwood solo project that would recur with increasing rapidity over the next twelve years. Of a 1966 soul album idea, he commented 'it's been put back a bit as we are rushing material for the next single. It would be an experimental thing – "Stevie Winwood sings the Soul Hits of 1965" – and I wouldn't mind doing it as a demo. It wouldn't be all big band backing. Some of the tracks would feature me on piano and guitar.'[7] A few months later, *Melody Maker*'s Chris Welch again brought up the subject. There would be other occasions when this journalist would prod nerves pertaining to Winwood's career.

During this same hit single hiatus, *Midland Beat* had commissioned a delighted Pete to pen a regular advice feature. Though he was hardly the Marjory Proops of percussion, Pete's way with words was given its head in what became a good read even for non-drumming Midlanders. In between twitting Dave Clark – who also beat a Rogers kit – and lauding Keith Moon as 'the Elvin Jones of the Pop World',[9] Pete dispensed valuable tips from his own strict rota, such as practising with heavy military sticks on a cushion ten minutes a day to improve volume control. Learned critiques of the latest accessories were offset by warmly enthusiastic detail – 'Gene Krupa's chewing, grimacing face' – reflecting his swing roots.

York's inventive absorption of this style was glimpsed in the tempo shift in the showstopping 'Georgia', finally transferred to vinyl with the release in February of the enigmatically titled *Second Album*. Steve's technical immaturity remained apparent in this standard, but his piano runs betrayed a confidence born only from night after night onstage. A laughable Group 'composition', the preceding track 'This Hammer' – B-side of 'Strong Love' – is, none the less, an imaginative grafting of a Beatles-via-Chuck-Berry backbeat to the Leadbelly traditional via the 'new words and music' dodge pioneered by Lonnie Donegan. At least when it was a

Shadows B-side in 1964, Hank Marvin *et al* had had the good grace to put 'arr.' on it.

Much of *The Second Album*, however, evidenced slick, considered covers from the annals of *nouveau* American soul stars of the Don Covay–Impressions persuasion. That it was less hurried and more 'American' than *Their First LP* was exemplified by the calculated arpeggios and quasi-Latin shuffle of 'Let Me Down Easy' and the strident harmony of session singer Madeleine Bell on Gerry Ragavoy's 'Look Away', which was short-listed for the next single.

Also in the running were three more by Jackie Edwards. 'When I Come Home' was a collaboration with Steve, whom Edwards had quickly identified as the main chance. It had been spared a humbler fate as B-side of 'Keep On Running' when its scribbled chords and words were mislaid, thus compelling the Group to knock together the alternative 'High Time Baby' which lived only in its searing riff. The second offering was the more melodic 'Come On Home', but 'we couldn't get enough beef into it and Jack Baverstock, our recording manager, wanted another "bash" number'.[10] Elaborating on the Davis try-out, another Baverstock client, the spirited Wayne Fontana, was restored to the Top Twenty later that spring for the first time since the dismissal of his backing Mindbenders.

The third choice it had to be then. Another 'bash' number as Baverstock had formulated, 'Somebody Help Me' had its predecessor's heavily accented beat with a tambourine adding extra impetus. The hated fuzz box which kept malfunctioning was tamed by vibes pinged in perfect unison with Steve's white Fender. On a separate track was the vocal interaction of the Winwoods, Davis and, so the story goes, Dave Mason, then a transitory road manager getting in on the act. During this two-month stint, Mason had even had the sauce to plug in his flash £160 Rickenbacker guitar and trespass on stage as his employers entertained. It blew Spencer's jets but Steve didn't mind a bit.

Dave's starstruck escapades were minor problems during a difficult period for Davis. As well as procrastination over its commercial viability, an eight-week delay in mastering 'Somebody Help Me' had resulted largely from Spencer's misfortunes whilst driving his second-hand Morris 1000 Estate in the evening of its life. Two planned sessions were scrubbed, first by Spencer's head shattering the windscreen as he swerved to avoid a dog, and next an M1 breakdown involving the police. Pete did his bit when burst tyres on the Hammersmith flyover wrecked his Vauxhall Victor. Two more cancellations were on grounds of ill-health: Steve's poisoned finger and unhappy Spencer's sore throat. All these mishaps were chronicled in Brian Mulligan's press release, which contained the erroneous information that the new record had been set to follow 'Keep On Running' all along.

Breaking the jinx and lingering scepticism, the rush-released 'Somebody Help Me' – straight in at number four – wrenched the Walker Brothers from the top the same March week as Labour's election landslide victory. 'Vote for Spence!' quipped *Melody Maker* in a page one splash which also itemized the treatment meted out to Davis during a painful dentist's appointment that Monday. Davis may have had a good few bites left in his teeth, but on other fronts he was none too hale. Sometimes the urbane mask would slip and the strain would show. 'One thing I don't like is being out of the limelight,' he disclosed. 'I love it all.'[11] Within months, a shattered Spencer on tranquillizers spoke of retirement to a Hebridean island and no one knew whether to believe him. He had, it is true, been deeply shaken at the death of his and Pete's old friend and mainstream jazz guru, Don Campbell, the previous year.

Materially, however, circumstances were much improved. The hits had brought a wage rise to £200 a week, plus a new Mini Cooper to replace the dodgy Morris. He had moved his family from Sutton Coldfield to Potter's Bar, where he'd converted the loft into a music room. He'd also got in with the local gentry. Triggered by the Beatles' MBEs, the upper crust was impressed by British pop as a generator of vast financial power. Former Deb of the Year Judy Huxtable was snapped clamouring for Ringo's autograph as early as 1963, while *Daily Express* gossipmonger William Hickey assured his readers that the Rolling Stones enjoyed social intercourse with high society fledglings. Herman of the Hermits married into European aristocracy, as did Barry Ryan. Moreover, having won the heart of a Stuart, Phil May – ex-Sidcup art student, Pretty Thing and, therefore, social pariah – would be among those privileged to attend the Prince of Wales' wedding in 1981.

Being told by Princess Margaret that 'your music has given me a great deal of pleasure'[12] was all very grand, but Davis and his Group were averaging only one night a week at home to wallow in their royalty cheques. As Pauline was about to present him with a second daughter, Lisa, in April, this was particularly hard for Spencer, a natural nappy-changing Dad. Spencer's parents turned out at the Lido in Port Talbot, when their son's band appeared on All Fool's Day. 'No, he's no different from what he ever was,' decided Mary Davis the morning after. 'When he comes here, it's still "Mum, where's this?", "Mum, where's that?" We treat him just the same.'[13] Embarking on a consoling alcoholic crawl round miners' welfare clubs the following evening, the no-good boyo – with his name in the Glamorgan *Celtic Clarion* – was persuaded to do a turn. He didn't sound much like his records, but he was the bandleader not the singer, see. Middle-aged miners were not subscribers to *Beat Instrumental* in which Spencer had sadly admitted 'unfortunately, I'm not a good guitarist but I'm a functional member of the group'.[14] Under-rating himself or not, he could no longer pretend that he held the Group in the palm of his hand as paranoia split his concentration on the road and in the studio. With Pete sitting on the fence, flare-ups with the other two increased in frequency; in turns more subtle and less courteous.

As his rhythm guitarist became more withdrawn and morose, the Boy Wonder was taking greater celebrity in his stride. 'I got mobbed but mobbing depends a lot on how you carry on,' he advised *Melody Maker*. 'If you run out to a great big waiting Zephyr, then you'll get mobbed. But if you take it casually then the kids won't bother you.'[15] Chronologically he was just a little boy of seventeen himself, as Cliff Richard had been when he donned his pop star mantle. However, when Steve celebrated his next birthday with a yard of ale in a Notting Hill pub near Island's new nerve centre, his childhood was long past.

Though less cerebral, the disciplines and restrictions besetting Winwood were infinitely more demanding than cramming for 'A' levels. Night was day and day was night then. Typical were the twenty-four hours from mid-afternoon on 6 April: a *Top of the Pops* recording, a booking at Farnborough's Carousel, then back to Marble Arch studios till gone dawn. Sleeping through an alarm call at the small Highgate hotel where he usually stayed when in London, he was late for Friday's *Ready Steady Go* rehearsal. As he could not hurry unmolested to Archway tube station, it was fortunate that, having passed his test in December, he could bomb over to Wembley in his new Triumph Vitesse.

In Europe, where the Group were seen less, Steve could still go shopping on days off – though the pace, if anything, was even more hectic. A hiccup even before leaving England was asking permission to go from a Bow Street magistrate, as Steve was still a few days short of his majority. A work permit was granted but Lawrence had to stand £100 surety and the Group's agent, Chris Peers, was told to ensure that Steve reported to the British Consul on arrival in Paris. Steve was also obliged to report back to Bow Street within seven days of his return.

While Pauline Davis recovered from her confinement, her neurotic husband's Group was before the cameras for a Hilversum

TV spectacular, after which they played an Amsterdam all-nighter. A televised concert to six thousand in Bremen next morning was followed, after a few hours' respite, by a round robin set at the Star-Club. As they'd discovered in 1964, the Grosse Freiheit's frenetic gaiety and raving exhibitionism required the Group to likewise '*mak Schau*'. 'They go in for movement,' recalled Spencer in his *Midland Beat* column, 'musical ability doesn't matter so much.'[16] The Group took most numbers too fast; transitions from choruses to middle eights were cluttered; arrangements were shot to pieces. Nevertheless, by the 'Keep On Running' encore, they'd long been home and dry as dancing onlookers congregated round Steve's jerking crotch-level Stratocaster, clapping and stomping in time.

Winwood may have been the darling of the ladies in the Fatherland, but Davis with his fluent German hogged the press. His awareness of West Germany's political extremities had prompted some unfortunate remarks to *Melody Maker* about the election success of the 'new Nazis' in Bavaria.[11] However, having let slip his Hertfordshire address, Spencer precipitated an avalanche of fan mail on its publication by *Bravo* magazine, whose Golden Otto award was won by the Group after a readers' poll put them ahead of the Who and Small Faces but badly behind the Beatles, Stones and Dave Dee. More personal a triumph for Spencer was the sole occasion when he was better qualified than Steve Winwood to sing lead on an A-side – albeit only in Germany. Its bierkeller jollity reined by the revived 'High Time Baby' riff, the Group's medley of Walter Kollo's bawdy 'Det war in Schöneberg' ('He Was in Schöneberg') and the traditional 'Mädel ruck-ruck-ruck' (!) was seen as either an aberration or a breath of fresh air amid an unbroken stylistic diet of blues and blue-eyed soul.

Teutonic organizational efficiency was absent elsewhere *sur le continent*. On *Télé de bois et ages tendres* in Paris, the Group miming 'Keep On Running' was less prominent than a line of choreographed chorus girls. That same June day, they had to squeeze in a spot on a variety show with jugglers and acrobats, as well as two more agreeable engagements, before the breakfast flight back to Heathrow – where, incidentally, they met Acker Bilk's Paramount Jazz Band in the customs queue.

The following month at a humid Norwegian festival plagued by mosquitoes and gremlins, Steve in a rare foul temper stamped offstage as gleeful bouncers laid into an audience fighting drunk on local moonshine. Back home such displays were suppressed though, as John Glover hurled rampaging fans into the pit at Croydon's Fairfield Halls, Steve 'sang viciously against the noise'.[17]

He was also heartily fed up with the tired Golden Eagle chestnuts – even faithful old 'Georgia': 'I tried to put feeling into it every night but it was getting difficult. I was exactly like a machine but it was more a mass-produced feeling.'[18] Where had all the good times gone? Steeling himself to deliver another unheard codswallop special on the scream circuit, he weighed up cash amassed in the hit parade against his self-image as an innovative musician stifled by old-stagers, all over five years his senior and now married. They may have envied him his youth, but professionally he was as battle-hardened as they. Yet with the arguable exception of frustrated Davis, they were a steady back-up team – though, with respect, that's all they were. Even the most casual studio workouts with, say, John Mayall's rhythm section, Aynsley Dunbar and John McVie, affirmed this. 'The rest of us are constantly amazed that one person can have so much talent,' Spencer had enthused in distant 1964, 'and we've got our work cut out to keep up with him.'[19]

What about Spencer? He was very thick with Pete these days. You only had to read the papers: 'I used to say Steve astounded me as a player but now Pete is knocking me out. It's a shame Pete doesn't play more solos' – the patter of tiny Pete, eh? – 'I think people tend to say the Spencer Davis Group is all Steve Winwood and this is not the case. Muff has never expressed any wish to sing his own song but if he did, I don't see why he shouldn't as an important member of the Group. I don't know about Pete singing as he is a bit of an enigma.'[18] My Sunday shirt's got a perforated collar, Mr Woo.

Muff! What charisma! What presence! Whatever next? He could be a great bass player if he practised. More than this, his 'biggest influence' in 'Lifelines' had been 'money'. Not only would he drive his Mini for miles looking for parking metres with time left on them but he also derived a parsimonious kick from balancing the books and chasing receipts. Spencer thought an ideal punishment for tax officers and record critics would be to be thrown from the top of Muff's wallet to certain death.[20] Like his brother, Muff couldn't stop smoking, but he was miserly enough for pious bouts of total abstinence. 'Muff is very narrow-minded and rigid in his opinions,' scoffed Steve, 'and the trouble is, he's usually right.'[21] Fraternal tension was not usually expressed quite so blithely. For every working day since God knows when, Steve had been within earshot of his big brother's drone. Too long had he gazed at old Muff tunnelling into curry and chips across a wayside café's formica table with the jukebox always playing one or other side of the Beatles' 'Paperback Writer' single. Opposite the more appetizing sight of *Disc's* Penny Valentine in the BBC canteen, Steve's disclosure of the pains he took to avoid Mervyn was not surprising: 'we don't get on terribly well so there's no point is there?'[21]

Despite these disturbing erosions in their relationships, Muff, Pete, Spencer and Steve were still bound by common ordeal and jubilation. Outside the context of work, Steve and Spencer loved playing impromptu floor spots together in Birmingham folk clubs as an antidote to the holocaust of fame. Further away from it all, the four comrades-in-arms risked a skiing holiday together in the Austrian Tyrol. While autumn leaves fell on the Spencer Davis Group, Steve expressed 'a combination of happiness, frustration and boredom'.[15]

For want of anything better, an edited 'When I Come Home' reached the shops in September. In spite of scrupulous plugging – including lip-synching for the boys and girls on BBC's *Crackerjack* –it stalled at number twelve. This was a real comedown by previous standards, and reinforced Spencer's perpetual machinations to sing the next one. Rejected during Fontana's customary Tuesday morning board meeting had been the Group's own choice, Brenda Holloway's 'Together 'Til the End of Time', which found its way instead onto the new Davis LP, *Autumn '66*. Marking time with road-tested Americana, *Autumn '66*, matching the single, didn't cut quite the same dash as *The Second Album*. Though signs of danger were imperceptible, 'there was less excitement but that didn't seem to effect our drawing power. It wasn't a concrete thing going, it was the spirit and feeling that went.'[18]

Predictable as it was, staunch fans couldn't complain about any deterioration in overall quality. It was like expecting a racing bike for Christmas and getting one. With much the same evangelical zeal with which the Rhythm and Blues Quartet had furthered the cause of its favoured musical form, younger outfits were avidly taking their cue from the Spencer Davis Group's tasteful image and workmanlike repertoire. Emerging from an Essex scout troop, a quartet called the Avalons contented themselves with a set consisting entirely of deadpan Spencer Davis imitations. They were rewarded by a season in a Parisian club where their adherence to the tenth scout law – about being clean in thought, word and deed – was severely tested.

Also making headway in France were the Habits who, on the 1965 Stones tour, had backed a low-billed vocalist styling himself Charles Dickens after the Victorian writer (whose novels, incidentally, reached a wider audience than his namesake's records). So taken were Spencer and Steve with the Habits that, after freeing them from Dickens (alias photographer David Anthony), the two produced the London-based trio's single, 'Elbow Baby', which, on Decca, crash-landed into oblivion – though Geordie drummer Brian Davidson had better luck with the Nice in 1967. In a semi-official capacity as an Island A and R manager, Steve also supervised and plucked guitar on sessions by Colchester organist Michael Weaver, formerly of the Fairies, who – as Wynder K. Frog – had been commended by reviewers when he opened that troubled Croydon presentation for the Spencer Davis Group. However, a version of Missouri composer Jim Lowe's 'Green Door' was not as fruitful for him as it was for high-stepping Frankie Vaughan in 1956 or for Cardiff rock 'n' roller Shakin' Stevens a quarter of a century later.

Extra-mural activities may have come to nought but, the mild 'When I Come Home' miscalculation apart, the operation was still running smoothly back on board the Davis mother ship even if, at parties with his retinue of lately disbanded Hellions and other Elbow Room cronies, Steve no longer hid his embarrassment when the Group's records shook the stereo. '"Keep On Running"' he said, 'had no artistic content at all.'[15] What had, then? Indian ragas? Jazz avant-gardener John Handy? Maybe it was bursting into a Locomotive session at Hollick and Taylor with a tape of a journey from London made with the cassette recorder tied – at Dave Mason's suggestion – to the Triumph's exhaust pipe. In a candid chat with *Melody Maker*, Steve ventured 'if somebody would come up and tell me I'm crap, I'd start going places'.[15] To amuse his intimates, Winwood – pre-empting Bryan Ferry – sauntered onstage at the *New Musical Express* Pollwinners' Concert garbed in full formal penguin attire for the Spencer Davis two-song segment.

What did Winwood's smart pals think of *The Ghost Goes Gear* – in which the Spencer Davis Group were once again commemorated on the silver screen? Was it Art like Warhol's soup cans? Or did they come up and tell Steve it was crap? At least the Group's role was more than the *Pop Gear* monochrome sideshow. Also starring Carol White (as Polly) and Nicholas Parsons, with Dave Berry and St Louis Union, it was a 'zany' sub-*Hard Day's Night* farce with no highbrow pretensions. It lacked the lyricism of John Boorman's *Catch Us if You Can* with the Dave Clark Five, though there are a few diverting sequences – the Group miming 'When I Come Home' floating on a raft; Pete very Lennonesque in swimming trunks and admiral's greatcoat, holding a bottle to his ear in comic dialogue with a hotel's room service, and Carol White's *salve pudore* cavortings round the Group in a musical routine in the ghost's mansion.

On the cards for 1967 was another movie based on the Hunter Davies novel, *Here We Go Round the Mulberry Bush*. Director Clive Donner had approached Steve independently to assist with the soundtrack. Rather than bother Spencer, Pete and Muff, he chose to pick the younger brains of Jim Capaldi and Dave Mason who, as early as April 1963, had been scouting round London for film music work. He also roped in Chris Wood with whom he, Dave and Jim had now formed a casual group as an escape valve from Spencer Davis. 'Actually, it's not a group,' he assured his public, 'just some friends and a get-together.'[18] However, though this as yet unnamed quartet's aspirations were understood to be no more than having a bloody good laugh for beer money, they voyaged over the edge of the tight-knit world of Birmingham clubs to rent the air in Worcestershire country pubs, once even daring an unannounced bash at the Marquee. For all outsiders knew, it was above board: 'just blowing, having a ball,' to quote a contemporary LP sleeve note, 'what a gas, just blowing, blowing, blowing . . .'.[22]

Spencer's ears strained to catch murmured intrigue as Steve and Dave Mason tinkered on guitars in secret backstage alcoves. 'I wasn't doing anything,' protested Mason, 'except waiting for Steve to leave so we could form Traffic. Almost a year before he left Spencer Davis, we decided to get Traffic together.'[23] Chris Blackwell had also conveniently remembered that 'three years ago when he first signed with the Group, it was agreed Steve would be free to go his own way when he had solidified the musical side of his outstanding talent'.[18]

As the atmosphere thickened, Steve was often missing minutes before showtime. Afterwards, flanked by his retainers, he'd retreat to his hotel room or, if anywhere near where Oxfordshire dissolves into Berkshire, to his secluded two-storey cottage lately acquired for a peppercorn rent from William Pigott-Brown, a wealthy turf gambler young enough to like appalling staider swells by dropping into the conversation the long-haired pop star dwelling on his estate. With the odd poacher and hiker the only intruders, Winwood's new home near the village of Aston Tirrold, unconnected by telephone, stood off a potholed dirt track – necessitating the exchange of the Vitesse for a more practical Land Rover. 'Steve seems to have retired completely,' sighed Spencer indulgently,' and when he does appear, he turns up looking like Farmer Giles, plastered in mud. He roams the Berkshire Downs with his mates in a jeep.'[24]

Perversely, and motivated, perhaps, by the growing tension, the Spencer Davis Group rallied to burn out at a creative peak. Another crucial factor in this short-lived renaissance was an alliance with new Island house producer Jimmy Miller who'd been headhunted by Chris Blackwell, now serving the company better by devoting more of his attention to administration. As a would-be pop singer, New Yorker Jimmy found his early ambition thwarted by a depressing fistful of grounded singles for CBS. Accepting that he wasn't the East Coast's answer to Elvis, 'I soon realised that the aspect of the business that I liked was being in the studio.'[25] When the Beatles broke on his native soil, twenty-three-old Miller – with other entrepreneurial Americans such as Kim Fowley, Bert Berns and Mitchell T. Reed – correctly anticipated unprecedented demand for more Limey talent and flew the Atlantic in 1964 to stake his claim in the musical diggings. Having recorded the backing track of the feverish 'Incense', his own composition, with a session band whom he dubbed the Anglos to signify breadwinning English connections, Miller contacted Blackwell to ask if he could recommend a suitably fiery singer to ice the cake.

Reunited with Steve Winwood in more harrowing circumstances in 1966, Miller's first job was to sort out what was to become the Group's only unassisted original A-side composition, 'Gimme Some Lovin''. 'Muff came up with the riff,' recalled Davis in 1984. 'I had the melody but . . . Steve suggested that we play it in a major key. He went off with a friend and wrote the lyrics.'[26] Winwood's other group added a pot-pourri of polyrhythmic minor percussion, yells of encouragement and – topped by Wood's falsetto – vocal responses to Steve's amorous demands. Along with piano interjections, most of this loose abundance was wiped off the single mix for a starker focus on the growling fuzz organ and Muff's monotonal throb.

Jumping back into the Top Five in November 1966, the Group finally got a fair hearing in the States as 'Gimme Some Lovin'' penetrated the *Billboard* chart. Though the Yanks had started beating us at our own game by 1966, the New World was still fascinated by all things British. At one point in 1964, two-thirds of the discs in the Hot Hundred were British in origin. In the mythical land of Good Queen Bess and Mrs Brown's daughter there were lamp-posts to lean on, fish 'n' chips and long hair. Michael Caine took Twiggy to see *Blow Up* at the 'pictures' in High Street, London before having a 'pint' up the 'pub'. Gor blimey, me plates of meat don't 'alf 'urt. Must be these daisy roots I'm wearing. Better get up Carnaby Street for a new pair. These ones are grotty.

Dropped by Atlantic after 'Keep On Running', the Spencer Davis American breakthrough – like that of the Hollies and the Small Faces – was a long time coming owing to their comparative facelessness, neither being hairy monsters like the Stones nor possessing the impudent jingoism of Herman's Hermits. Before the next single, 'I'm a Man', barged its way up the Hot Hundred, many US radio listeners were uncertain of the Group's skin pigmentation, so exact were Steve's soulful Negroid intonations. Europeans may have been similarly mystified when 'I Can't Stand It' had wavered from the Duchy of Luxembourg nearly three years earlier. In North America, where race was a touchier subject, there were difficulties over airplay until the Group's Caucasian ancestry was confirmed by a promotional film aired on television.

For the Spencer Davis Group, there could have been no worse time for Steve to hand in his notice. Punchier than 'Gimme Some Lovin' ', 'I'm a Man' was also helped by an unusually strong B-side, the lustful 'I Can't Get Enough of It'. 'I'm a Man' was more far-reaching in the States than in Britain where, in February 1967, it teetered on the edge of a Top Ten in which the psychedelics of the Move and Jimi Hendrix nestled uneasily among sweetcorn peddled by Englebert Humperdinck and Tom Jones. Prior to this, the veneration the Group commanded in the States among those in the know was such that Mickey Dolenz of the Monkees, visiting London, regarded an impending presentation to Spencer as akin to an audience at the White House. 'Spencer Davis wants to see me!' he exclaimed to his press agent.

Tom Jones was to cut a piledriving 'Keep On Running' before the year was out. With his beefcake projection, he could have made an equally credible meal of 'I'm a Man' if he'd managed to get his Welsh tongue round its rapid-fire couplets – by Jimmy Miller to Steve Winwood's specifications. Though he wasn't a songwriter himself, even butch Tom – once omnipresent on the Scotch of St James's dance floor – may have sympathized with Miller's visions of off-hand human frailty within the pop star potentate's palace. As to Steve's music, Spencer Davis pleaded that its chiming undercurrent was inspired by Jimi Hendrix.[26] In fact, it was a brutalization of the riff that introduced 'Neighbour, Neighbour', one of Spencer's two lead vocals on *Autumn '66*.

In spring 1967 the Spencer Davis Group completed its last club date. By then a second blow had fallen with Muff's resignation – blood being thicker than service station coffee. On 4 March, *Melody Maker* reported that the 'amicable split' would take place after a British tour that the reluctant Group were undertaking, second-billed to the Hollies. By the final night, on 2 April, amicability was in short supply. As Steve said, 'the vibrations were terrible because I wanted my friends to travel with me. They called us "Steve and his Gypsies." "Gypsies" is a nice name and, anyway, *we* didn't want to put anyone down.'[27]

The last straw for Winwood may have been the next scheduled single. The very fact that 'Back into My Life Again' had come from Jimmy Miller and Jackie Edwards rather than the Group was, in Steve's eyes, a regression. It wasn't as if it was all that special anyway, with its awkward juxtaposition of the salient points from Edwards' two Davis chart-toppers to which had been added a decelerating hook overlaid by a twinkling celeste. The song was then handed to the VIPs, who likewise passed it up.

Fortunately, with 'I'm a Man' remaining its epitaph, the first Spencer Davis Group died easy. In 1970, the song rose again as the global smash that launched jazz-rock big band Chicago (Transit Authority). A decade later, the shifty Blues Brothers ran through 'Gimme Some Lovin'' at a cinema near you. On virtually any Tuesday in 1984, anyone could have seen the Pretty Things close their weekly performance in the functions room in a Little Venice pub with the same number. Fifty miles to the north-west, the Nashville Teens rocked out a wild Spencer Davis medley for the bikers at High Wycombe's Nag's Head.

Beyond these and other tributes, plus the smattering of entries in the *Guinness Book of Hit Singles*, the legacy of the Spencer Davis Group to pop was that, without modifying any stylistic intentions, it extended the commercial yardstick by which the most unassuming local group could judge itself. Furthermore, like Spencer himself, many will always believe that 'Stevie never sounded so good with Traffic, Blind Faith or Airforce as he did with us.'[26]

7

'Berkshire Poppies'

Ending three years of rumour by ratifying Steve Winwood's break from the Spencer Davis Group, *Melody Maker* added the postscript: 'after Steve's "retirement" in which he will re-think his music, he will form a group and musicians expected to join him include Jim Capaldi (drums) of the Deep Feeling, Dave Mason (guitar) and Chris Wood (flute). The group will be called "the Traffic".'[1]

The first major personnel change of the group era was Tony Jackson's ill-advised parting from the Searchers in 1963, likewise to start a new group. Towards the watershed year of 1967, such schisms seemed to occur about once a month. Yet, as with the Searchers, there was no immediate harm done as the Animals, the Small Faces, the Hollies and the Kinks showed by continuing to tramp the well-trodden path up the Top Twenty while their former colleagues mostly fell by the wayside. For every Alan Price Set, there was a Jimmy Winston's Reflections, an Eric Haydock Rockhouse and a Pete Quaife's Maple Oak. 'My leaving was looked upon as a very stupid move,' remembered Winwood, 'because the Spencer Davis Group was just beginning to be successful, and there's me saying "I don't want to do it anymore." So, I mean, everything was against me.'[2]

Because 'apart from fifty thousand hip record buyers in the country, the general public haven't a clue who Stevie is':[1] Chris Blackwell understood the gamble too, having convinced Steve to resist tempting overtures from EMI and remain with Island. A deciding factor was that, after speculation that the level-headed, moustachioed Muff would withdraw altogether from the music business, room was found for him at Island's main office. Further incentives included the best equipment money could buy plus a weekly retainer for all four group members – all courtesy of Chris

Blackwell. As Steve's personal manger, Blackwell even rented the adjacent white bungalow on Pigott-Brown's estate so as to tend more readily to his client's needs.

Putting all Island's entrepreneurial acumen behind Winwood's new venture 'enabled us to attract other talent because Stevie was the hero of all those guys. He was really adored by all the other musicians.'[3] With Traffic as its flagship group and with a depth of up-to-date catalogue that rivals like Immediate, Track and even Decca subsidiary Deram envied, Island became, debatably, Britain's most innovative record company. Over the next decade it drew to its roster Fairport Convention, Free, Sparks, Quintessence and, briefly, Bob Dylan. There were also King Crimson and Roxy Music – both co-managed by John Gayden from Blackwell's old school. As trade figures were to signify, Island would be committing more of its budget to LPs than to singles by these artists – often shop-windowing them via cheap sampler albums. Although by 1972 the company would be averaging four hits every twenty-six singles, a high proportion of these were originally conceived as album tracks.

As well as ruthlessly milking the burgeoning album market, Island and the other firms' rational revision of policy also reflected changes in the music itself. Pop by definition is ephemeral and usually worthless, but by the mid-sixties it had started to move up in highbrow circles, hastily passing through its own classical period – the end of which was probably delineated by the break-up of the Beatles. With their Aeolian cadences and sub-mediant key switches on *With the Beatles*, Lennon and McCartney were described by Richard Buckle of the *Sunday Times* as 'the greatest composers since Schubert'.[4] Less plausible was a gushing lady Juke Box Jurist who cited Alan Price as 'best organist in the world'. Nevertheless, beginning with Adam Faith's intelligent *Face to Face* BBC television grilling in 1960, the notion of pop as a viable means of artistic expression had intensified by the middle of the decade. Adam's successors as 'articulate' pop spokesmen included ex-Oxford undergraduate Paul Jones and the Who's Pete Townshend, the Derek Jameson of British Beat. Pop stars were invited to write books, star in films less vacuous than *The Ghost Goes Gear*, act in the West End, score soundtracks, as Winwood was doing, and even stand for Parliament.

Drama was, indeed, a popular vehicle for cultural expansion. Prior to Mick Jagger's part in *Performance*, his paramour, Marianne Faithfull, had already joined the cast of Chekhov's *Three Sisters* in 1966's Chichester Festival. Ray Davies had taken the title role in one of the BBC's Wednesday Play series while, over on ITV, Dave Dee – a self-confessed 'frustrated actor' – would turn up as Caliban in *The Tempest*.

Since pop rubbed shoulders with the legitimate stage, it was to be expected that some of its protagonists, as well as increasing the membership of Equity, would adopt theatre and multi-media techniques. This was easily and naturally achieved as an integral part of their presentation by such as the unclassifiable Bonzo Dog Doo-Dah Band, Pink Floyd, Crazy World of Arthur Brown and Principal Edward's Magic Theatre.

Ex-art student Pete Townshend acknowledged auto-destructive artist Gustav Metzger as the doubtful inspiration for the Who's practice of closing their act by smashing up their equipment. Two years later, the Move's Carl Wayne would be charging onstage with a chopper to hack up effigies of notable world figures before turning his attention to imploding televisions – and if that's not Art, then I don't know what is. Earlier Who disciples the Creation with Kenny Pickett climaxed their set in more two-dimensional manner by splashing onto a canvas backdrop an action painting that owed less to Jackson Pollock than to Rolf Harris.

As if in reciprocation, many genuine daubers and other acade-mics were intrigued by the pop underworld as a deliciously sordid tangent to more egghead activity. Fine art student Bryan Ferry was to cut his teeth with Tyneside soul combo, the Banshees, before founding Roxy Music. Three of the Pink Floyd met during a degree course in architecture at Regent Street Polytechnic. A more direct indoctrination was flamenco guitarist Chris Britton's acquisition of a Stratocaster, amplifier and subsequent celebrity as a Trogg. Shrewder still was classical pianist Keith Emerson's apprenticeship in Gary Farr's T-Bones and then the VIPs before his graduation to the Nice and, later, an Island recording contract as mainstay of ELP.

Teaming up with John Lennon, Japanese experimentalist Yoko Ono realized a trilogy of controversial non-Beatle albums that showed the couple's awareness of modern composers John Cage and Steve Reich as well as German serialist Karlheinz Stockhausen – who incidentally had been delighted to be included on the *Sergeant Pepper* sleeve photo montage. Infinitely more commercial than *Two Virgins* was electronic boffin Pierre Henri's LP collaboration with Spooky Tooth (a group that evolved from the VIPs). Closer to the mainstream of showbusiness was the Count Basie Orchestra backing a nervous Georgie Fame at the Albert Hall in May 1967.

Less enthusiastic helpmates had to be hired at Musicians' Union rates as pop groups progressed from guitars and drums to mellotrons, tape loops and nascent monophonic synthesizers. Anticipating George Harrison's lessons with sitarist Ravi Shankar, Indian sounds had already been absorbed by the Kinks and the Yardbirds. The latter also investigated Gregorian chant, symphonic tempo changes and dynamics, concrete music and other eruditions, which would be elaborated by later victims of the same passion such as the Pink Floyd, the Misunderstood (with ex-Hellion Tony Hill), King Crimson and Zoot Money's new outfit, Dantalion's Chariot.

Becoming less perfunctorily boy-meets-girl-where-the-action-is, lyrics to later sixties' pop songs reflected the growing musical complexity. Epitomizing the new spirit were Syd Barrett's 'Arnold Layne' of February 1967 – the Pink Floyd's transvestite saga of a washing-line larcenist – and, three months later, Keith Reid's abstract libretto to Procol Harum's 'A Whiter Shade of Pale'. There was also evidence of at least a superficial grasp of political, religious, philosophical and ecological issues, as exemplified in the Kinks' 'Dead End Street', 'Within You, Without You' off *Sergeant Pepper*, Eric Burdon's 'Good Times' and 'Shapes of Things' from the Yardbirds. Though many of its underlying perceptions were ill-conceived in plan, the emerging underground movement crept onto vinyl with the likes of the Social Deviants' puerile 'Let's Loot the Supermarket' and the naïve 'Revolution' by Tomorrow. The Move's horrific 'Night of Fear', the effervescent 'Itchycoo Park' by the Small Faces and veiled references in *Sergeant Pepper* implicated extremes of drug experience beyond mere pills and reefers.

With *Sergeant Pepper*'s expensive and syncretic precedent, record companies found themselves underwriting concept albums, rock operas and other epics requiring months in the studio and long needle time. Island, for example, were to shell out a six-figure sum for ELP's *Tarkus* – although Cat Stevens' first LP for the label cost less than £2,000. Related to this shift of emphasis and an increased technical sophistication was more respect for musical virtuosity and greater scope for instrumental extrapolations that had merely been suggested in the past.

Extended 'rave-ups' on *Five Live Yardbirds* in 1964 and Them's passionate neo-instrumental 'Mystic Eyes' single both streamlined a loose blueswailing structure that could run up to fifteen minutes on the boards. To a lesser extent the Spencer Davis Group had gone in for all that as well but, with Traffic, Steve Winwood entered realms far removed from his old band's rhythm and blues core: 'I'm trying to lose my old identity and gain a new one. I don't want to be

104

the guy who sang "Georgia on my mind" and Muddy Waters. I don't want to deny those things but there is a lot more I haven't done.'[5]

His musical frame of reference had now extended to the new tonalities of twentieth-century composers like the post-serialist Krystof Penderecki, whose best-known work, the dramatic *Devils of Loudun*, is full of free choral babbling, odd tone clusters and the Devil sniggering from within a nun's bowel. Much of Penderecki's Polish school were so stubbornly chromatic as to be almost atonal – and this affected, if not Traffic song structures, then certainly later approaches to soloing.

There was also a preoccupation with Indian culture beyond mere fashion. From messing about on George Harrison's sitar, as Winwood used to on Dave Grounds' Hammond, Dave Mason acquired a sitar of his own from Sweden which – like Harrison and Brian Jones – he treated initially as though it was another guitar. However, although less trendy Oriental devices were introduced, more far-reaching was the application of ideas from the more bookish Winwood's exploration of Eastern musical theories to orthodox beat group instrumentation.

Unlike other pop artists, Steve was aware of – even concerned about – the formal do's and don'ts that traditionally afflict creative flow. He may have been obliged – as were Jack Bruce and John Cale – to unlearn not only the quasi-mathematical rules of institutions like the Birmingham and Midland Institute of Music but also the blues and jazz clichés ingrained from his days with the Muff Woody Jazz Band all through the Spencer Davis Group. Valuable object lessons for Steve were the records and, in September, the first British concert by the Mothers of Invention – which he attended with Chris and Jim. Also an admirer of Penderecki, Mother Superior Frank Zappa, in his pop-Dada musical junk sculpture of rock, jazz, classical modernism and parody, evoked a mixed response from the Traffic party. Wood and Winwood were most enthusiastic while Capaldi thought it chaotic rubbish, genuinely preferring the beery joviality of the Tremeloes – reborn after their split with Brian Poole.

None the less, it was a healthy balance between conflicting tastes that stimulated the group: 'we would talk about records we liked and they would vary so enormously that we made conscious efforts to try and combine all these different styles'.[6] There was common ground in a liking for such disparate pop as the hard-sell chorale of the Association and the Incredible String Band's exotic Gaelic mysticism. In the contradiction of enjoyable depression – the aftertaste of much of Traffic's output – was the less conscious infiltration of the fertile but ill-fated accomplishments of earlier

British bands such as the Zombies, Poets or even Unit Four Plus Two. Sharing the same co-existent vision as Traffic were the 'Waterloo Sunset'-period Kinks and Procol Harum of ponderous majesty. Not for them either were the overdone pastiches of contemporaries like the Beatles or the funny noises of the Soft Machine and Pink Floyd. Nevertheless, like the latter two bands, Traffic – most of them – favoured creating musical moods through improvization.

From these and other sources, Traffic's intention was 'some way to make music that was not American. We didn't live in the States and wanted to reflect that'.[7] The stock angle of Island's press office was the idyll of these four groovy guys, united by a sense of purpose and mutual respect, occupying an isolated cottage in the English countryside and devoting themselves to creating this beauteous music without any outside interference. Sometimes Traffic too believed it. 'It's really beautiful there,' smiled Capaldi from an interview room, 'away from all the concrete and neon of the city.'[8] As much Traffic's spokesman as Spencer Davis had been for his Group, Jim, in the customary 'Lifelines', informed the *New Musical Express* that his best friend was 'the wind'.[9] To *Melody Maker*, old Jim went on about trying to 'get as much colour into our lives as possible. We see movements and roam through the temples of our minds. We get tripped out with the countryside.'[1]

Far out, man! Too much! Swallowing this publicity jive, other bands tried 'getting it together in the country' as well. In a *Disc* colour spread, Humble Pie larked about in a haystack while Yes – yet to warrant press attention – honed their po-faced elaborations down in Devon. Over in the New Forest, future Yes drummer Alan White with Denny Laine, Trevor Burton, Steve Gibbons and other Midlanders – calling themselves Balls – tested their stage act in a nearby village hall. Of similar genital nomenclature, Hard Meat thrashed it out in the wilds of Cornwall, fulfilling part of Ray Davies' personal hypothesis on the matter: 'if I had all my own way and had a country cottage to get together in, I'd write lousy songs and make a lot of money'.[10]

At Pond Cottage in Upper Basildon, seven miles south-east of Aston Tirrold, I too experienced communal living to a musical end as lead singer with a quintet called Turnpike. As a rank-and-file member, I was introduced to the joys of village life as well as the bitter intrigues and jealousies which make pop groups what they are. Unsolicited, I also imposed my own ideas and personality upon the established status quo of Turnpike's folk-rock determination and the rhythm guitarist's songwriting monopoly. It turned out that the two guitarists and bass player were anxious to be rid of me as soon as someone more suitable came to light – such as a girl singer who doubled on flute. When asked what sort of band Turnpike was, the neutral drummer replied, 'We're about three parts Pentangle, one part undecided and one part Shakin' Stevens'. Turnpike's history was punctuated by passionate ménages à trois with consequent punch-ups, rows which continued up the pub, drunkenness, walk-outs, malicious glee, prima donna tantrums, homoerotic camaraderie and a lead guitarist who wouldn't go on stage with a twit like me.

On the domestic front was a ravenous slot electricity meter, arguments about household jobs, body odour, undisguised greed at mealtimes and panic about the state of the place whenever the owner of the property returned to England. Turnpike also developed its own restricted code, superstitions and short-lived folklore. Post-mortems on our few engagements included why we were ordered offstage at Maidenhead Art College, and sabotaged in Slough. There was also The Day We Went To A Recording Studio. On the brighter side, Paul Jones declared us runners-up in a University Battle of the Bands tournament and praised our all-electric arrangement of 'John Barleycorn'.

Imprisoned in tedious drudgery on a flaming June day in Pond Cottage, shuttered against complaints about the noise, the drummer and I discovered that there were only so many fantastic versions of 'John Barleycorn' that could be endured over one afternoon. Finally, we stopped listening. As the other three plotted their hand-tooled guitar potterings, I would improve my mind by studying accounts of Sir Francis Dashwood's Hellfire Club while the drummer scanned *Melody Maker*'s small ads even when needed to tap his kit. By the time of my underhand dismissal in 1974, none of the others gave a damn either and Turnpike packed it in a month later.

In their late teens and early twenties too, Traffic – all admirable young men in many ways – also had their share of young men's follies. 'We were young at the time,' explained Dave Mason, 'just growing up.'[11] They had, however, one vice that they did not share with Turnpike. I know it's distasteful to mention such things but, alas, it's true: members of Traffic took illegal drugs. There! I've said it! With the Stones' bust in the air, rarely were any drugs stashed in the cottage owing to the unwelcome interest the Thames Valley Constabulary had in pop groups living on its beat. Tangles with the law notwithstanding, had Winwood been a responsible father in 1968 would he have risked a statement like 'when you stop exploring with drugs, now that's a bad scene'[12] appearing in print. Yet articles on Traffic by the underground press were riddled with references to contact sheets snapped while on acid, seeing *2001* on speed, and gaga conversation. As with the Beatles, signposts of LSD usage often bled onto Traffic records too. 'I think you have to be on something to understand the lyrics of that one,'[13] said Reg Presley of the trippy 'Hole in My Shoe'. All four were dazzled with acid when recording 'Feelin' Alright', while Steve's falsetto on 'Who Knows What Tomorrow May Bring' from the same sessions delivers a quite explicit hallucinatory epistle.

Such dangerous indulgences were taken for granted by the cottage's visitors, of whom there were many. Producer Jimmy Miller was a semi-permanent resident, as was another inheritance from Spencer Davis, road manager John Glover who was assisted by one Albert Heaton. A pal of Steve's schooldays, John 'Nobby' Clarke served as unofficial major-domo, among whose responsibilities was the welfare of a white Alsatian called Mr Fantasy. In an evil hour, this unfortunate dog suffered a brainstorm and had to be destroyed.

Guests swerved off the A417 down a potholed track which petered out to a rutted path. Vehicles were parked by a barn one mile up, next to Chris Wood's Sunbeam Stiletto. Ambling past lichened fence posts, you'd turn right past Chris Blackwell's shack and the beehives. Then there'd be a spinney hiding the skull-white stucco cottage. I walked past it myself on a muddy New Year's Eve, twenty years after it was all over. There was a fuzzy-diced wally Cortina where the bright pink Traffic van had once stood on the concrete platform built for rehearsals that, under a starry canopy, could be perceived miles away. Bleached in bleak midwinter, sessions beneath more leaden skies were still feasible if participants wore fingerless Old Steptoe mittens. On warmer evenings, with the eight-windowed front of the cottage for back projection, they'd set up the light show they'd loaned from Dantalion's Chariot and, bathed in swirling colour, lose themselves in music till dawn.

Like Tony Hancock in *The Rebel*, for Steve each day radiated a different colour. Saturday, for example, was green.[14] In the roaring logs of the enormous front room grate, he and the others often felt the ghostly presence of a suicide drowned in the well in the very recent past, before water-pipes and electricity reached that far. Inside and out, the cottage's lived-in old-jeans-and-wellingtons frugality suggested to Phil Capaldi, one of Jim's brothers, 'a typical guys' place'. Apart from a farmhouse table and piled electronic paraphernalia, there was hardly any downstairs furniture. With the excuse that 'the soil won't hold together because of uprooted trees',[9] plans to grow vegetables were scotched and the neglected, sprawling garden and its outhouses became receptacles for old newspapers, paint cans, brass bedsteads and further objects which might just come in handy. As a press photographer discovered, at the not unreasonable hour of four in the afternoon the place still slept like the dead. If no one was in the mood to cook or the cupboard was bare, food could be summoned from an Aston Tirrold café which could also be prevailed upon to 'bring out a couple of horses so we can go riding. But I fell off.'[5]

When they weren't playing, evenings might begin in the hospitable Chequers pub where Aston Tirrold meets Aston Upthorpe. Less frequently, when there was something good on like *The Seventh Seal* or the Italian *Passion According to St Matthew*, there were trips to cinemas in either Oxford or Reading. Later, badgers would peer indifferently as overloaded shooting brakes zoomed down small-hour country lanes made by the rolling English drunkard. Rapturously foxed, passengers would bang on the car roofs, shouting out 'yep!' and 'woo-hoo!' It was the life for a roaring boy all right. One observer recalled musicians from Traffic, slit-eyed with stimulants, 'always in a right mess, being helped around the town' of Marlow, a Berkshire Thames-side boating resort.

Though it wasn't quite the Little England arcadia suggested by an investigator from American rock magazine *Rolling Stone*,[15] it was where-it's-at during the peace-and-love summer of 1967. 'If everyone in London were to turn on and turn in,' advised psychedelic guru Timothy Leary, 'grass would grow on the Strand – and the tie-less, shoe-less divinities would dance down the car-less street.'[16] In the north of Berkshire, much of this was laid on already. Protrusions like Harwell nuclear power station and cascading pylons blighted a rural plain surrounding the Great Ridgeway, a prehistoric route cutting into the heart of Wessex. Ancient hill forts and other earthworks scratched the grassy downs where sheep nibbled on Saxon battlegrounds.

When the seasons changed from gold to marble, the flowers wilted and the cold hit north Berkshire like a hammer, with Jim's best friend moaning in the trees. But after the spellbindingly lifeless landscape melted, rust peeped shyly again through the bodywork of Wood's Sunbeam, heralding another endless blue summer almost but not quite as wondrous as the last. Nothing is more erotic than the smell of the earth and advantages could be taken of mellow yellow evenings on Roman Hill, not a leaf stirring, a touch of mist on the sunset horizon and a bird twittering somewhere. You could find peace there, a tranquillity not often found back at the old cottage anymore.

Nowadays, the turning off the A417 is signposted and, as I

stumbled muttering from the cottage, I reflected on the disappointment of a fifteen-year-old Buckinghamshire schoolgirl escorted there by a would-be boyfriend connected to a band called Respect who had supported Traffic at High Wycombe Town Hall in January 1968 – 'As far as I was concerned, I was going to meet Stevie Winwood'. To her chagrin, her idol's abode was as lately deserted as the *Marie Celeste*.

Among many more illustrious callers were garrulous Eric Burdon and his tired wife Angie, Pete Townshend, various Spooky Teeth and, undermining Capaldi's confidence, Ginger Baker. Technically, Winwood – for whom bright city lights had long lost novelty appeal – was the only permanent resident. Jim and Chris had a Cromwell Road flat while Dave favoured the more exotic ambience of Soho, which was also near the group's Oxford Street fan club. 'There's this big social thing in London, and you have to be strong as individuals not to get caught up in it,'[14] elucidated Wood.

During a luckier stay at the cottage, the swain from Respect witnessed, on the cemented stage, Steve working on the skeleton of what was to become 'Sea of Joy'. Helping him in the absence of the others were Eric Clapton, Ginger Baker, Trevor Burton and the bass guitarist from Family. Just for a few moments – subtracting Trevor – the wrong four had found each other.

Though Steve was reserved but pleasant enough to even the most irruptive hangers-on, restless, tetchy Mason had little to do with Traffic's social life. As well as finding the Berkshire Downs creepy at nights, 'Dave was never part of the group like Chris, Steve and I were. He was part of the group's music but that's all he was interested in.'[18] As for the group's music, an early bone of contention was that Dave didn't hold with all this open-ended improvising: 'a lot of Traffic's instrumental things just meander, which has become a kind of trademark of the group. I'd like to hear something a bit more tangible. There's a kind of cast-your-fate-to-the-wind attitude.'[11] Conversely, the other three weren't keen on him presenting most of his songs as a rigid *fait accompli*. It went against the whole Traffic collaborative ethos: 'it wouldn't be important if we were, like, just getting other people's songs together but writing is something almost completely different. A song no matter who writes it, really has to come to all of us, and writing with us is a slow process. And during the time we're writing, it's important for us to be together.'[19] Dave was a solitary mister, and his attempts at using Traffic as a passive vehicle for his own firm ideas generated increasingly more alarm. These ideas were, however, tolerated in the first instance owing to Mason's creative strengths, sealed by his composition of Traffic's most famous song, 'Hole in My Shoe' – inspired by a notepad-by-the-bedside dream. Nevertheless, largely because of Dave, 'Traffic wasn't going wrong except it was always producing internal problems. There were always these silly little things and, in the end, they seemed to be part of the character of the band.'[20]

Undertaking at the outset to keep such rifts private, Traffic presented such a united front that one journalist wrote of their talking 'in a fragmenting conversation that starts at one end and continues round the group'.[21] However, after this particular March interview the group holed up in Berkshire until the June release of 'Paper Sun' backed with 'Giving to You,' while Blackwell turned away newspaper taxis from Didcot railway station. The leaking of a fish-eye lens photograph of a rehearsal in May only deepened their incommunicado enigma. 'We never planned to create this kind of image,' maintained Capaldi, 'but we had always intended to get away by ourselves when the group got together and it just sort of built itself up into a mighty thing quite naturally. We didn't create it but it was pretty good publicity-wise.'[22]

It was fortunate that all concerned had agreed on a brand-name that rolled easily off the tongue. 'The Gypsies' was abandoned because in 1966 Island had issued a flop record by the Belfast Gypsies, a dubious Kim Fowley cash-in on Ulster group Them's percolating American breakthrough. On his way out of either a Birmingham cinema or a London tube station, Jim came up with 'Traffic', which was accepted after a quiet word with the Spectres who had also become 'Traffic' in March 1967. This quintet next tried 'Traffic Jam' but settled instead for 'Status Quo'. As with Cream and Procol Harum, lack of a preceding article was à la mode; if you were the Hedgehogs, it was cool in 1967 to change to just Hedgehog.

To reflect Traffic's delving into the antique, designer Carol Ruskin originated an appropriate identifying symbol. Nodding towards the ambivalence of Celtic art, it was as distinctive in its way as the Nazi swastika.

Unlike Hitler's combo, Traffic endeavoured to be democratic despite Winwood's already established pop stardom. That this was still a potent commodity was demonstrated when, during the Spencer Davis-Traffic interregnum, screams broke the hush as Steve alone, without preamble, sat at a grand piano at the *New Musical Express* Pollwinners' Concert in a single spotlight for an extemporized blues. When Traffic's promotional chores were delegated, Winwood's wider professional training dictated his prompt arrival at *Melody Maker*'s offices for a 9.30 a.m. appointment – as opposed to Capaldi conducting a *Disc* interview from his Earl's Court bed.

With Steve no more conspicuous than the other three, two photo spreads in *Jackie* girls' magazine, six months apart further stressed group equality and at least sartorial concord as well as conformity to prevailing fashion. With Dave's winkle-pickers, Jim's plain green shirt, Steve's Pete Murray cardigan and puckish Chris Wood's grey drape, they retained the Spencer Davis clean-cut Big Beat look in spite of the rosebush backdrop, Winwood's unobtrusive string of beads and the perpetual loud red-and-white cravat of Chris Wood that he untied on the next *Jackie* picture. By then, all had noticeably longer hair, some of it appearing on Mason's upper lip and on Capaldi's long jaw. Winwood hadn't stood very close to his razor that morning either. Neck-belled Traffic now garbed themselves in crushed velvet, chiffon and paisley: Winwood plumped for a bat-winged see-through bolero; Wood a Red Indian fringed waistcoat with mandarin collar and brooch; and Mason a printed women's blouse and a star-spangled jacket with white ornamental clover toggles – the bottom one left artlessly undone.

With depressing regularity over the years, Steve would trot out his 'I want to avoid being the front man of a backing band'[1] litany though, as Dave Mason was the first to admit, 'everyone realised that we were going to get a certain amount of success because Steve was in the band'.[11] Inane reinforcement of this supposition came in music press tittle-tattlers like the *New Musical Express* Alley Cat: 'Chris Blackwell should consider "Traffic Island" as a name for Steve Winwood's label.' Get it? In an Island Records documentary in 1987, it was implied that Traffic was solely Winwood's creation. It was to be expected that Chris Blackwell's alliances would remain with his longest-serving moneymaker – to the loyal extreme of supporting Winwood's doubts in 1967 about the viability of 'Hole in My Shoe' as a hit single.

'The only reason I started writing songs was because I didn't want to ride on Steve's back,'[11] reasoned Dave Mason, but perhaps a green-eyed monster whispered that Dave was easily the most self-contained, prolific and commercial songwriter in Traffic and, if given his head, might outshine not only Steve's Spencer Davis backlog but also his Traffic heritage. 'When Dave started coming on strong, Steve couldn't handle it,' said Capaldi, who collaborated on songs with both, 'and there was a clash of personalities – especially musically.'[23]

With Jimmy Miller as referee, Dave and Steve combined once to compose 'Something's Got a Hold on My Toe'. This was an instrumental with more substance than any Spencer Davis effort in this genre, like Winwood's 'Waltz for Lumumba'[24] which surfaced on the *Here We Go Round the Mulberry Bush* soundtrack among contributions by both the new Spencer Davis Group – and Traffic. Portraying a Scottish sixth former's sexual pilgrimage, this film threw down the gauntlet to the *Ghost Goes Gear* teenpic academy, and helped usher in the tougher pop realism of the quadrophonic seventies.

Traffic's bitty title song – composed by the whole group – had been recorded before the band's official inception and, though proposed for release before 'Paper Sun', tied in instead with the movie's autumn première. Traffic were also considering an offer to perform the Lennon-McCartney title track of the Beatles' laboured *Magical Mystery Tour* – in which was a fleeting glimpse of Spencer Davis – which was screened by the BBC over Christmas. As well as turning down Paul McCartney's invitation, Traffic declined other film work including 1968's *The Touchables*, which went instead to Nirvana, a newer Island act. Also merely discussed were offers to churn out incidental music for television advertisements. Touring commitments blocked these lucrative avenues but, while not denying the group's wherewithal to acquit themselves as well as the Pretty Things and Manfred Mann did in such ventures, extensive involvement was incidental to Traffic's main purpose.

Soon it would be practical for groups that carried any weight to concentrate solely on LPs, no longer merely passing time by providing teenage entertainment. However, at the dawn of this era, in 1967, it was necessary to operate ambiguously with chart-orientated singles to keep investors sweet, and experimental albums to indulge more personal artistic whims. Even the formidable Yardbirds realized this. 'If you didn't have a hit single,' elucidated drummer Jim McCarty, 'you were a fading band.' Because Island had mainly licensed out records prior to 1967, it was now, to all intents and purposes, a new label with one act. After all the hoo-hah since the sundering of the Spencer Davis Group, both Traffic and Island had to make a big splash with that first single.

It wasn't going to be as easy as it looked, as 1967 was also the year of those nurtured on basic marketing techniques established a generation earlier. The antithesis of flower power, though it had started to smell funny by 1966, Tin Pan Alley was still very much alive. However, with internal sources of new material and their own publishing companies, a lot of these bloody guitar groups and their psychedelic heirs had given the business a nasty turn. To the detriment of the usual jobbing tunesmiths of Denmark Street, 'quality' artistes from the more refined realms of jazz and Talk of the Town/Las Vegas cabaret began sifting through the sheet music,

LPs and – if lucky – demo tapes of beat group composers. The most obvious example, 'Yesterday', was a British hit for both rough old Ray Charles and smooth balladeer Matt Monro. In kaftan and beads, jazzman Charles Lloyd extrapolated the Beatles' 'Here, There and Everywhere' amid the strobe lights at New York's Fillmore East auditorium. Peggy Lee, international entertainer since 1938, had been among the first in the queue for Ray Davies' 'I Go to Sleep' fifteen years before the Pretenders.

1967's prize exhibit in the British Top Fifty, however, was ex-palais crooner Engelbert Humperdinck, whose schmaltzy 'Release Me' kept the Beatles' double-sided *Meisterwerk* 'Strawberry Fields Forever'/'Penny Lane' from number one in February. Significantly, Tom Jones, Petula Clark, Frank Sinatra, Louis Armstrong, Des O'Connor and Rolf Harris all scored chart-toppers during this period. After all his blues records had failed, in November Long John Baldry joined this syrupy elite with 'Let the Heartaches Begin', an uncharacteristic hack ballad.

Tacitly applauding this counter-revolution of *decent* music, Alley Cat continued to fawn over the coups and pronouncements of aging publishing and record executives – 'Pye chief Little Louis Benjamin tips No. 1 for Long John Baldry' – while crowing 'this year, Yardbirds absent from Top 30'. On 14 August the Marine Offences Act became law and closed down pirate radio while, on Radio Luxembourg shows were still hosted by Brian Matthew, Sam Costa, future agony aunt Katie Boyle and other leftovers from the fifties Light Programme clique. Reneging on his pirate past, ex-Radio London disc jockey Simon Dee – anxious to keep his plum job on television – hoped, perhaps, to impress his new BBC superiors in prompting headlines like *Weekend* magazine's 'Simon axes hippies on *Dee Time*'.

Aided mainly by the cautious programming of the BBC's two new national pop radio stations, the UK Top Thirty was to become generally shallower and less subversive in content. Had Radio One arrived in 1965, would a record like, for example, Dave Dee's 'Bend It' have enjoyed unrestricted airplay? More bandwagons were jumped by sharp operators like the Ivy League who, as the Flowerpot Men, cashed in on the hot flower power summer with 'Let's Go to San Francisco'. During the succeeding winter, as gangster chic intimidated hippiedom, even a cool cat like Georgie Fame felt obliged to resuscitate a flagging chart career with 'The Ballad of Bonnie and Clyde'. Another old strategy, also employed by Fame amongst others, was covering American chartbusters purely for buyers at home. Mercilessly, Love Affair heisted two consecutive 1968 releases by soul singer Robert Knight, serving him in much the same way as Tommy Steele had Guy Mitchell eleven years earlier. Almost as lucrative were similar time-honoured thefts in 1969 by Amen Corner and the Dave Clark Five. Ironically, the Five copped a sneaky US-only smash with a version of Amen Corner's only British number one, 'Half as Nice' – as did the ailing Yardbirds with Manfred Mann's 'Ha! ha! Said the Clown'.

Pitting their stoned hippy image against Britain's citadels of squaredom, Traffic – as close as they were willing to be to a conventional pop group – left deep chart wounds with their only three hard-line singles before a calculated retreat from the pop mainstream. With a weather eye on the hit parade, yet with enough sophistication to be considered 'progressive', 'Paper Sun' – 'a sunshine supersound', declared *Melody Maker* – rose without effort to number five in Britain. This achievement was repeated to varying degrees throughout Europe – topping the chart of Dutch pirate Radio Dolfijn was typical. In the Netherlands, incidentally, it was issued on bible-black Fontana rather than pretty pink Island.

Between the thudding conga-tumbledown sitar preamble and the coda's faint reminder of the Hellions' 'Shades of Blue', the Kinky lyric – about a desultory summer romance and a simultaneous search for work at a seaside resort – mingled a sympathetic humour with gloom as mournful as a seagull's cry. Musically, 'Paper Sun' conveyed most effectively impressions of noisy beaches full of cardiganed holidaymakers determined to enjoy themselves despite the whims of British Augusts; self-catering slum attics with crumbling plaster and a one-ring cooking area; turnstiled Victorian piers; fish and chips eaten from last month's *Daily Sketch*; and the lonely hours between boarding house teatimes and eight o'clock. The first time is sometimes the only time. No other Traffic single – especially the post-1967 album chasers – ever recaptured this early glory.

New Musical Express reader John Wynne boasted infinitely briefer fame when Alley Cat – recognizing a kindred spirit – printed his crack that a revival of the Mastersingers' psalmodic 'Highway Code' ought to be Traffic's second 45. Back at the ranch, the matter was considered with more gravity. As usual it was Dave versus the others. Only on his most fervent ally Jimmy Miller's insistence was 'Hole in My Shoe' even completed, so that an Island round table decision could ride roughshod over the other possibility, the stately 'Coloured Rain' constructed by Chris, Jim and Steve one wet afternoon.

Dominated by Mason's sibilant voice, sitar and mellotron, this single in stereo – unusual in 1967 – was recorded in a post-haste spirit of evaporating bad grace to scud up the charts. The contradiction between Steve's protest at the time that 'Hole in My Shoe' was 'the best we have made'[25] and his later contention that it 'wasn't the kind of direction Traffic ought to be taking'[23] tempts theories that it was one in the eye for the nineteen-year-old prodigy when, not counting 'Det war in Schöneberg', he found himself for once in a supporting role vocally on an A-side – a smash hit too. Whether he really wanted to or not, Winwood had indeed avoided being the front man of a backing group.

However, Mason had kept his trap shut long enough for the Utopian inter-verse bridge which, as it hadn't lent itself to adult reverie, was lisped by six-year-old Francine Heimann during her Whitsun holiday at stepfather Chris Blackwell's Berkshire bungalow. The disc's picture sleeve of Traffic festooned in buttercups buttressed this child-like aura. 'Dave influenced a lot of people with what I call the "Toyland" scene in lyrics,' acknowledged Capaldi, 'but it got overdone . . . and became sickening.'[26] Sickening or not, pop's gingerbread-castle hour was cornered by Dave more than by Keith West's 'Grocer Jack', 'Lucy in the Sky with Diamonds', the Stones' 'Dandelion' and lesser pretenders like Syd Barrett's 'Gnome' and Billy J. Kramer's 'Town of Tuxley Toymaker'. In November, aspects of the 'Hole in My Shoe' arrangement were borrowed by Simon Dupree and the Big Sound for 'Kites', a windswept dose of Top Ten yellow peril. A particularly obvious plagiarization was Chinese actress Jacqui Chan's sensual mumblings in the vernacular for sixteen bars before the last chorus. Prototypical of this style, 'Hole in My Shoe' repeated its chart performance in 1984 – this time as a spin-off single from the BBC series *The Young Ones* by neil, a hippy-drippy anachronism played by Nigel Planer. Two years earlier there had also been a more imaginative but less funny arrangement by the News, omitting Francine's monologue.

Present at the original 'Hole in My Shoe' session had been Steve Marriott and Ronnie Lane who, with the other Small Faces, mucked in on 'Berkshire Poppies', the most light-hearted number on *Dear Mr Fantasy*, Traffic's first LP. Cut on the joint birthday of Winwood and Small Face Ian McLagan, 'Berkshire Poppies', a gymnasium waltz, borrowed more from the late conjuror Tommy Cooper's 1961 chart entry 'Don't Jump Off the Roof, Dad' than from the Devils of Louden. Subtler humour permeated 'Giving to You,' – loosely derived from the Spencer Davis instrumental 'On the Green Light' – which, in its uncut album form, has Miller pretending to be a jazz critic.

The genesis of the LP's title track was four lines pencilled one evening beneath Jim's drawing of a long-robed bardic figure, the neck of whose stringed instrument vanished into his fingers rather than machine heads. As a *Beat Instrumental* portrayal of him bent over a typewriter implied, Capaldi's creative input was primarily as a lyricist; however, on this occasion his muse deserted him and he hit the sack, leaving the tireless Chris and Steve to polish off the words, to be repeated three times over the simple five-chord melody.

Dear Mr Fantasy serves as a reliable guide to Traffic's recording methods at London's Olympic Studio, where the album was made. Frustrated by the inescapably bland precision and slick sterility that made them sound uncannily like all the other groups, the ambience of cottage rehearsals was approximated by dispensing with acoustic separation and headphones, and piling into *Dear Mr Fantasy* 'on impulse with practically nothing worked out because it was almost jammed. The initial spirit of the whole thing was captured on record which is very rare.'[19]

This homespun approach to arrangement was also epitomized in the ragged spontaneity of 'Heaven is in Your Mind' with its busked vignette from the Association's 'I Got Rhythm' on the fade. This, however, belied the acute attention to detail characterizing other tracks such as the one-sided telephone conversation on Mason's 'Utterly Simple' and the ensemble riffing of 'Coloured Rain'. With overdubbed clockwork motor, 'House for Everyone' span out Dave's fairytale fixation, but of no such pixified scenario was Capaldi's cantering 'Dealer'. Because of its tragic associations, the haunting melancholia of 'No Face, No Name, No Number' will always be, for me, Traffic's greatest moment. To another Island band, the Smoke, was accorded the first Traffic cover – 'Utterly Simple,' produced by the composer with the Yardbirds' Jeff Beck, while a Newcastle trio under the aegis of promising Geordie songwriter Alan Hull named themselves Coloured Rain.

'Once you get it down on tape,' said Steve, 'it can sometimes change into something else that you don't expect.'[27] The ultimate ideal was to record masters in the cottage environment as the mood took them – perhaps thus tempering Dave's increasingly more frequent vanishing tricks. Demos could already be managed beneath its low ceiling on a two-track stereo tape machine. 'The room in the cottage where we do rough takes of the songs has its own special quality,' argued Winwood, 'because it is an old house and you can tell what kind of room the sound was recorded in when you listen to the tape.'[20] Placing action over debate, an attempt was made – too late for *Dear Mr Fantasy* – to lay down a fresh Winwood-Capaldi opus, 'Withering Tree' by removing the necessary equipment to the hollow where the said tree withered.

'Withering Tree's' heavy-hearted compound of time signature switches, dynamic shifts and references to Deuteronomy, chapter 33, verse 27 encapsulated many of the group's musical aspirations and glimpses of the eternal. It was one of many Traffic moments that made hippiedom seem in retrospect not so corny after all – you forgot that record company backing was Traffic's refuge and underneath were the everlasting public. Fleetingly, you were convinced – as arch-flower child Donovan was – that God had seen 'all the ugliness that was being created and had chosen pop to be the great force of love and beauty'.[16]

Yeah, well . . . with income dependent on the day-to-day mundaneness of selling records came the litmus test of transferring the product onto the boards in September as 'Hole in My Shoe' was inexplicably blocked at number two by the smarmy Engelbert, and *Dear Mr Fantasy* stopped at number eight in the LP lists. With Dave in very green elephant cord trousers and with six stitches over his eye after an accident at his Dean Street apartment, Traffic pressed ahead with their planned Swedish tour, opening at Gothenburg where the set began with a confident if shadowy 'Hole in My Shoe'. High on the proscenium arch, a spotlight homed in on a flat wooden horse hanging before Carol Ruskin's symbol.

After plugging the same number – with Dave cross-legged at his sitar – on French television, the quartet flew back for the all-important British debut at Shaftesbury Avenue's Saville Theatre. *Sundays at the Saville* was the brainchild of disquieted Beatles manager Brian Epstein, who'd bought the art deco auditorium in 1965. One week his NEMS organization would put on, say, the Bee Gees, the next – John Mayall's Bluesbreakers. Buried among the sea, stars and naked flower girl on the theatre's hapshash poster was the information that 24 September would see Traffic's turn.

Introduced by Wonderful Radio One's David Symonds were a variety of acts chosen for their affinity to the main event. First up at 8.30 p.m. and dying an unnatural death by nine were the fragile Nirvana, signed by Muff on Mickie Most's recommendation. Steve's A and R discovery Wynder K. Frog – with his Nigerian conga player, Rebop Kwaku-Baah – was next for the chop, but building on this inauspicious beginning was the polished Jackie Edwards who reminded the customers where Spencer's number ones and Wayne's 'Come on Home' were from.

After the beaming Jackie's exit, Traffic forewent laid-back unpunctuality to maintain this belated goodwill with a *moderato* 'Smiling Phases', a B-side plea to keep cheerful under difficulties – flower power's answer to 'Cheerful' Charlie Chester. Their Laney amplification set amongst the cardboard ramparts left from the weekday presentation of Shakespeare's *Midsummer Night's Dream* seemed entirely appropriate as Traffic worked through the rest of their recorded repertoire. Even 'House for Everyone', with Steve winding the clockwork, proved that 'we're not using any recording tricks. There are no effects on the record that we can't reproduce on stage.'[21] Though Capaldi stuck to his kit, instrumental switch-overs were so rife that the remaining three all played organ at differing points. The high point of the show was a devastating 'Dear Mr Fantasy', dedicated by Wood to Frank Zappa plus footballer and 'beautiful person' Nobby Stiles. 'It was like a rehearsal,' declared Capaldi ambiguously, 'only this time with an audience.'[22] All the same, a four-minute ovation brought Traffic back for an encore – 'Feelin' Good' – during which a rapturous Winwood finally broke sweat, hammering his eighty-eights like Jerry Lee Lewis.

From the mixed gathering of hippies, young fans, bemused parents and provincial riff-raff, the cream of the In Crowd filtered backstage. Among these were old friends from the Davis days – Brian Jones, Scotch regular Jonathan King, the Hollies, Zoot Money, John Mayall – as well as all the young dudes (and some not so young) come to pay homage. With the Herd and Keith West was bubbling Jimi Hendrix bass guitarist Noel Redding, who mitigated his barracking of the support bands by handing round a bottle of Sauternes.

Traffic came down with a bump soon afterwards at a Finsbury Park Astoria extravaganza in October that was marred by an unbroken series of foul-ups. As omnipresent as the groups themselves, road technicians blundered onstage to replace dead microphones and adjust other faults within the ear-shattering decibels. After the opportunist Flowerpot Men in all their regalia had tossed dead chrysanthemums into the front rows, the first London appearance of the melodramatic Vanilla Fudge was truncated by a mistimed falling curtain, resulting in savage oaths feebly censored by keening feedback bleeps. Containing their weary fury better, Traffic – coldly professional – went the distance in a blizzard of distortion and loud unbalanced sound.

No night this bad – or as satisfying as the one at the Saville – occurred on the round-Britain package show which wound up at the Slough Adelphi on 10 November. Innocent of London's *sangfroid*, girls still screamed at pop stars as they had on the 1965 Spencer Davis trek with the Stones. By coincidence the compere from that tour, Dave Clark lookalike Ray Cameron, had been hired to officiate likewise for Traffic, special guests of the bill-topping Who.

119

On that same bill, Capaldi's fave raves the Tremeloes pulled rank over chart newcomers the Herd – who'd suffered the Astoria debacle too – and then-hitless Hibernians the Marmalade, glad to be away from the grim Highgate flat they'd shared since migrating from Glasgow. Judging from the *en masse* photograph of the participants, the tour looked a laugh a minute for Traffic too – Jim was sticking his tongue out at the camera while Chris, gesticulating with a cigarette, might have been cracking the joke that was clearly amusing Keith Moon and pie-eyed Marmalade guitarist Junior Campbell. More impassive, however, were old pro Winwood, inconspicuously squatting in a white cassock, and Mason, standing self-consciously in the front row.

Though Traffic broke many a heart on this jaunt, a Birmingham University engagement immediately afterwards was a more personal triumph, proving Capaldi's point that 'really playing to university audiences is more our scene. People sit and listen and know what you're doing – they can appreciate it.'[18] Jim also had an idea for a console whereby audiences would be completely surrounded by speakers arranged in a circle.

All seemed well. Like the Spencer Davis Group, Traffic had been voted Second Brightest Hope in *Melody Maker*'s poll. With Steve back on lead vocals, 'Here We Go Round the Mulberry Bush', with its tempo change borrowed from the Hellions' 'A Little Lovin''', returned Traffic to the Top Ten, even meriting them a *Dee Time* spot on which Steve sat mockingly bolt upright at the organ. There was high-spirited conjecture about working American colleges and the Fillmore in March. None the less, everybody close to the group knew the game was up, and an uneasy press couldn't keep silent for much longer.

Dave finished with Traffic on 22 December at *Christmas on Earth Continued* – an Earl's Court spectacular featuring the top drawer of British psychedelic pop. One after the other they appeared on the stages erected at each end – Pink Floyd, Tomorrow, Soft Machine, the Move, you name 'em. It begged the doubtful concept of a last hurrah to flower power, so passé by then that it was gag fodder for end-of-the-pier comedians. In an Al Capone slouch hat and shoulder-padded zoot suit (with a belt at the back), I was staking out the stage where the Jimi Hendrix Experience were due on when 'Coloured Rain' boomed from the opposite end. Even from half a mile away Mason seemed the most animated, playing up to the audience more than the circumspect Winwood, limited to the fixed microphone at his keyboards. Nevertheless, the fervent efficiency with which Traffic attacked song after familiar song awed me –

though nearly all wandered, as did my attention, into exuberant jamming. Though often swamping the music's fundamental elegance, the set still confirmed Capaldi's remarks in *Disc* the previous week: 'it's a funny feeling onstage with Dave knowing that by Christmas he'll be gone. It gives you a feeling of Auld Lang Syne. We're like old comrades and it's a bit of a sad thing but it's making everybody play like crazy and the dates we've been doing lately have been the best yet because of it.'[18]

As in the Abdication crisis of 1936, each faction had right on its side. Nevertheless, as Dave's Traffic songs became increasingly distant from the other three's team efforts – often doodled in hotel rooms, soundchecks or those interminable jam sessions – his departure seemed the least inconvenient alternative. Furthermore, Mason was dissatisfied with Island's financial settlement which led eventually, so he claimed, to Chris Blackwell submitting to him a worrying demand for £6000.[11]

Traffic subscribed to the leading fortnightly underground journal *International Times*, which often preoccupied itself with propagating ancient creeds. Linking this with Traffic's back-to-the-land aura, some saw the schism with Dave Mason to be of deeper portent than that of Tony Jackson with the Searchers. Maybe it was like some fertility rite by which Traffic would be saved by the sacrifice of one of its figureheads in his prime. Capaldi said as much in *Disc*[18] and, sure enough, Mason never had a bigger commercial smash than 'Hole in My Shoe'. If you want to believe that, go ahead. But upsetting this theory of peculiar goings-on in Aston Tirrold was an open invitation for Mason to continue contributing material and even rejoin one day. According to Winwood, it was always 'oh no, man, no rows; I get on well with Dave'.[20] All the same, someone saw fit to obliterate the errant Mason from the cover and credits of Traffic's first LP in the States – issued with Capaldi, Winwood and Wood's 'Heaven Is in Your Mind' as title track. However, it was 'Dear Mr Fantasy' that picked up most airplay there.

So then there were three. Trios were popular in 1968 though, like Cream, the Experience and Rory Gallagher's Taste, most harked back to the Big Three's guitar-bass-drums Merseybeat test case. Traffic did not bother to compete against the prevalent leaning towards heavy blues, and more intense than gut-wrenching was their flute and keyboards empathy, with only drums providing the steadiest pulse – although the sound frequently reduced to only one instrument before surging to climaxes all the more rewarding for their low-volume restraint. Others took hints from Traffic's refreshing example – perhaps the most staggering conversion being that of John Mayall who, not stopping at lead guitar, also dispensed with drums for an unrepeated undertaking, closer to the jazz end of Traffic than to his beloved blues.

Of course, some Traffic numbers were unworkable without Dave, though nobody objected to dropping 'Hole in My Shoe'. While some still found his loss noticeable on stage, he'd figured little in certain pieces anyway – such as the new stop-gap single, 'No Face, No Name, No Number,' which, for all its TV plugs and saturation plays on Radio Caroline, expired at number forty. Nevertheless, Traffic's solemn hit parade farewell lasted well. Most immediate was a plaintive refashioning by Marsha Hunt, star of *Hair*, in which producer Tony Visconti substituted for Winwood's organ a string octet drifting into *legato* counterpoint.

A mainstay of Traffic's concert set for the next six years, 'No Face, No Name, No Number' had its place in the band's bill-topping forty-five minutes on a thrifty UK tour in January, using local heroes as supports. It was less hectic than autumn's outing with the Who, and the capacity crowds' residue of autograph hunters and stargazers were well-behaved and often lucky. Admitted to one particular inner sanctum, an Aylesbury pop correspondent[28] had the rare treat of watching Winwood seizing the first opportunity to shave in days.

Steve had more time to attend to his toilet during the swiftly ensuing and long-awaited visit to North America. They travelled by car and culminated with a week in San Francisco, where they were required to play only three dates. Steve even drove over to an Indian reservation where – like Billy J. Kramer before him – he shook hands with Chief Shooting Star of the Dakota Sioux. Thanks largely to Anglophile musician Al Kooper's eulogy in *Rolling Stone* – 'I regard Stevie as the finest white blues singer I have ever heard regardless of age or environment'[12] – and the hip approbation of such as psychedelic chemist Owsley Stanley, who welcomed them to San Francisco, Steve was deemed worth a look himself. Reflecting a healthy turnover for the *Heaven Is in Your Mind* album, reaction to Traffic's US tour was such that, in Jim's words, 'besides it, England becomes rather like Sweden or Germany – it doesn't seem to matter so much. The audiences are so great there . . . they live for music. It makes you feel that what you're doing is really worthwhile – and we're playing much harder now.'[8]

They were too. 'There's no more fantasy stuff,' continued Capaldi. 'I feel we're going towards not so much a freaky scene but a simple natural sound. Total reality is such a beautiful thing and you can reach it just as easily with unamplified guitar, bass and drums.'[8] No doubt Jim had fallen under the spell of the *John Wesley Harding* LP, Bob Dylan's austere, understated new morning which was steering pop away from the backwards running tapes, sitars and clutter that disguised many essentially banal artistic perceptions. Unhappy with diluted sound levels from home pressings, Traffic spoke too of recording or, at least, mastering a second album in high-tech New York where, it appeared, there were more British rock 'n' rollers than in Britain itself.

In their midst was Dave Mason, in a vocational slow movement. He was, perhaps, deflated by the fact that his presence in North America had fired no great enthusiasm. Clogging the ether then was Elvis Presley's latest hit; nobody wanted to hire a guitar man. However, an evening at the Scene Club led Mason to the Record Plant a few blocks away and round-the-clock sessions for the Jimi Hendrix musical self-portrait, *Electric Ladyland* – including the one that yielded the hit single version of Bob Dylan's 'All Along the Watchtower'. With Hendrix hot property in the States, a piece of *Electric Ladyland* action was not to be sniffed at, as Al Kooper, Larry Coryell and other top-notch US practitioners already knew. As incorrigibly partial to a jam as the pliant Jimi himself, Winwood and Wood – loitering in the Big Apple after the tour – also found themselves with what engineer Eddie Kramer described as the 'tremendous influx of musicians that made the studio a breeding ground for creativity'.[29] On 'Voodoo Chile' – a sort of 'Hoochie Coochie Man' in orbit that occupied nearly one side of what became a double album – with the Experience's regular drummer and Jefferson Airplane's Jack Cassidy on bass, Hendrix and organist Winwood earn overdubbed stoned applause for intermingling obligatos; but, from a lunchtime Dansette twenty years on, more impressive is the segue from the cacophony following the requisite drum solo back to the slow blues pattern.

Just as spaced out back in Britain was Capaldi's production of 'Lovers in the Sky' by Contact, 'which fits in,' said Capaldi being Capaldi, 'with the interest in UFOs. In fact, they're members of a much bigger organisation which is out to get in touch with visitors from space.'[17]

Closer to Earth, Mason – in thick with Jimmy Miller – had co-produced *Music in a Doll's House*, an LP by Family whom he coaxed into recording his 'Never Like This', which ended up sounding like a *Dear Mr Fantasy* out-take. On 23 February, just after Traffic had hightailed it to America, Dave descended on the cottage to tape an all-acoustic new single, 'Little Woman' with assistance from, among others, some of Family. As much a variation on 'Greensleeves' as those of Ralph Vaughan-Williams, 'Little Woman' was the most successful field recording tried at Aston Tirrold. Its archaic instrumentation of shawm, recorder and consort of viols was entirely sympathetic to Mason's reproachful tale of a local poacher who, even in 1968, was an archer rather than a rifleman. Had 'Little Woman' been able to command the same media attention as 'Hole in My Shoe', a thrilled Dave might have faced the logistical problem of presenting it on *Top of the Pops*.

Better than a mere hit record, perhaps, was how much Jim, Steve and Chris liked 'Little Woman'. Dave, blast him, had achieved on his own that 'simple, natural sound' that they were still chasing. With old affections flooding their hearts, Dave Wasn't Such A Bad Bloke After All – and, God knows, they were fresh out of material for the new Traffic LP. They could have done with him in America too. Sprawled across side two of a posthumous Traffic album, *Last Exit*, are two straggling prolongations, recorded on cassette from the first row of the trio's set at the Fillmore West in February 1968. Documentary rather than recreational for the listener, these curate's eggs lack the discipline of the quartet. 'Feelin' Good' was a Capaldi choice from the catalogue of Leslie Bricusse and Anthony Newley – the all-round entertainer on whom David Bowie once modelled himself. Not so much the roar of the greasepaint as a Graham Bond Organisation number gone to seed, 'Feelin' Good' preceded the bluesy 'Blind Man' from Bobby Bland's trumpeter Joe Scott (alias Malone Deadric), which likewise took a long time to get going. Steve had never found pumping those Hammond bass pedals easy – so much so that he was agitating for a bass player, possibly Rick Grech from Family.

For all that drove Dave from Traffic, by April it abruptly made sense all round for him to remount the old rehearsal platform beside the other three and give it another whirl. 'He came back mellow,' exclaimed Capaldi, 'suddenly he was super-cool. He'd gone to the other extreme.'[23] Adaptability, it seemed, was a guitarist named Mason.

No fewer than five of his songs – one co-written with Capaldi – wound up on the eponymous album that had to be completed before the restored Traffic took to the road again. Though the other half of *Traffic* came from Steve and Jim and the front cover portrait gave Winwood pride of place, it was shifty-eyed Mason who'd won on points. Of the only two tracks considered as a promotional single A-side, both were Dave's. Written about nothing in particular, the maddeningly catchy hoe-down 'You Can All Join In' was vetoed by Chris and Jim, only to give its name to the first of Island's budget samplers and anticipate Malcolm McLaren's 'Buffalo Gals' by fourteen years. All fingers pointed finally at 'Feelin' Alright', which Dave had composed during a Greek holiday in March. Its bareboned paranoia was heightened by Mason's croaking vocal as well as the rawer sound quality of its mastering from cassette. On 45, 'Feelin' Alright' shared the unhappy commercial fate of 'Little Woman' and – to Mason's rage – an inferior take was included on *Scrapbook*, a seventies' compilation. None the less, it was the Traffic composition most assiduously covered by outsiders, among whom were Three Dog Night, Grand Funk Railroad and Gladys Knight.

Dave's other two numbers aren't quite so hot, but at least he'd jettisoned the airy-faerie nonsense. Mind you, though far removed from twee 'House for Everyone', Steve and Jim's minor-key 'Forty Thousand Headman'[30] had a touch of Treasure Island about it; as late as 1973, I heard a band crucifying it in a Brentford pub. In almost as narrative a style, 'Pearly Queen' – born of American skylarking – had its stronger melody paced by clipped unison guitar and provoked another group, Tramline, to record a most commendable version on their Island LP *Moves of Vegetable Centuries*.

Whittled down from its original conception as a double album, *Traffic* was still a more ambitious, polished affair than *Dear Mr Fantasy*. Bolder and less fussy arrangements were illustrated in the Chinese block as the only percussion on the quasi-acoustic 'Vagabond Virgin', the timpani on Jim's favourite track, 'No Time to Live', and the direct Beatle harmonies in 'Don't Be Sad'. The four's North American labours came to the fore technically in the employment of Eddie Kramer, and were evidenced musically in the predominance of abrasive saxophone as opposed to the lilting flute – which didn't put in an appearance until the non-stop second side. There was also the Chet Atkins tinge to 'Means to an End'.

One of two tracks left in the can for, hopefully, the next album was the 'Is this all there is?' sweatshop window-gazing of 'Shanghai Noodle Factory' – laying ghosts of Jim's Evesham apprenticeship, perhaps – coupled with a deceptively perky arrangement with jarring staccatos, a trebly snare drum setting and a snatch of ye olde backwards-running tape. Such detail pertained also to Mason's 'Just for You,' which, though it featured Jim on tabla, Steve and double-tracked flautist Chris, had – with strings overdubbed later – already B-sided 'Little Woman'.

Typified by Winwood's singing of a passage on Mason's 'Don't Be Sad', a spirit of appeasement exuded from the grooves. Yet before *Traffic* ascended the British and US charts, signs of danger

125

were already identifiable. Within the gatefold sleeve, the group photographs taken at the Uffington White Horse chalk monument showed only Steve, Jim and Chris. More ominous was Steve's known unhappiness with the musical end product. Having bitten back as hard as Dave, probably he'd compromised too much for the leaderless group's own good.

Whatever Steve's feelings about *Traffic,* the bookings between the sessions had gradually taken on a depressing familiarity as super-cool façades cracked. Across Europe, from the group's odd pairing with Bill Haley and the Comets in Paris to a pop festival in Budapest, slowly but surely last winter's unresolved impasse loomed again. Vague and unlikely schemes for a trip further east to Moscow were thwarted by the immovable second American tour, timed for the LP's October release there. Traffic were still in erratic shape onstage – walking a tightrope between near magical inspiration and rubbish. As well as the nebulous 'musical differences', the emotionally uncertain Wood's mixing of stimulant intake with work was causing concern. Giggling drunk or on another planet, on more than one night he'd looked as if he'd never totter on stage. Although he always made it, sometimes it might have been better if he hadn't.

When Chris was on form, however, he was great. Furthermore, as his behaviour could then be contained and he didn't want to sing lead, he was no threat to Steve. This wasn't the case with Mason who, unlike Spencer Davis, wouldn't moan ineffectually before resigning himself to just fretting guitar. Steve could wipe the floor with Dave as an instrumentalist – on any instrument – but, as a songwriter, Dave had always checkmated him. Even so, Winwood was still trying with all his might to compose songs entirely on his own. It had been a long time since 'It Hurts Me So'. Dave couldn't be palmed off with merely side two, track four every album. He wouldn't let you help him either. It was simply that he didn't function in groups – not this one anyway.

With the differences between Mason and himself causing a far deeper ruction than the mere irritation of, say, a horn player who can't hold his drink or a road manager who hums all the bloody time, Winwood decided by the second US date that he couldn't stand it any more. Even if it meant organ-pedalling again, Mason had to go – and now there would be no welcome back.

Dark nights of the ego past, Traffic or, if you prefer, the Steve Winwood trio embarked on a series of British one-nighters to break in the trio format once again. 'It wasn't very honest onstage because we made a different sound on our records,' thought Winwood, 'we did things like double-tracking. This goes on practically every record made but I still think the group should play live as it sounds on the record.'[20] At the Starlight Room in Boston on 25 November, Steve reeled offstage feeling pretty rough. Overnight his glands became swollen, thus curtailing the group's forthcoming college tour with Family. As a barometer of Traffic's popularity, it was thought prudent to contract both Ten Years After and Jethro Tull to deputize.

No one realized then how long it would be before Traffic performed again. Though the tour itinerary kept many university students from their studies, the indisposed Traffic weren't so far above the adoration of schoolgirls that Winwood couldn't be quoted in a *Jackie* survey of How The Stars Spent Christmas: 'I won't be working – we won't play over that period.'[31] Capaldi especially hadn't been convinced about Dave's second expulsion. One alternative had been that, as Mason wasn't keen on losing sleep on the road, he could stay at home instead and write hits for Traffic as Brian Wilson did for the Beach Boys. This was thrown out on the grounds that – though one was in the pipeline – Traffic were no longer a singles band, thank God.

This was, after all, the silver age of the Marmalade, the jolly old Tremeloes and the winsome Love Affair – spiritual elder brothers of the Bay City Rollers. As well as this grinning triumvirate, *Top of the Pops* was also constipated with harmless purveyors of popular song who clocked in with a couple of chart entries before faltering. Let's have a big hand for Vanity Fayre, the Casuals, Cupid's Inspiration, Picketywitch, the Ides of March, Butterscotch, Arrival and all the rest of them.

Between the limits of these disposable cash-ins and the most way-out 'progressive' groups, pop artists in the latter half of the sixties tended to become polarized in particular styles, as jazz had been for years. There was a traditional school wide enough to contain both mucho macho Tom Jones and the drippy New World. Mainstream could be represented by orthodox pop organs like the Honeybus ('I Can't Let Maggie Go') and Amen Corner, while the likes of Fleetwood Mac and the Jeff Beck Group had enough class and style to muscle in among modernists like the Move and Traffic. No more providers of teenage entertainment in their way than Engelbert Humperdinck, in the distant reaches of the avant-garde roamed Soft Machine and the Third Ear Band.

Some acts belonged in more than one of these categories – often in awkward combination, as the Beatles were when recording both vaudeville ('Honey Pie') and freak-out tape collage ('Revolution

Nine') on the same album. There were also numerous overlapping sub-sections, some more easy to place than others. For instance, folk music in a pop context varied from the squeaky-clean wholesomeness of the Seekers to the early vigour of Steeleye Span. However, where did that leave, say, a band like East of Eden who, though in a predominantly jazz-rock mould, are best remembered for an alien one-off smash with 'Jig-a-jig', a barn dance reel like 'You Can All Join In'.

Traffic – able to feed off albums – were best off out of the Top Fifty rat race. Another 'Hole in My Shoe' could even be damaging in the long term. By the end of 1968 the traumas of the year had taken their toll, and Traffic weren't much of a group any more. 'There were three instrumentalists and it became frustrating for *either* one of them over a long period of time' was Winwood's side of it – to which he tacked on 'I suppose the public think you are obliged to stay together out of loyalty.'[20]

Winwood had upped and quit, you see, sending up in smoke tours of the Netherlands and, again, the States. Recuperating alone in the cottage one late November weekend, he packed his gear and, stopping to ask Blackwell to inform the others, left for Amsterdam for an indeterminate stay. 'I don't think Jim expected the group to break up although Chris did,' he surmised, 'it was all too complicated and when you are trying to write, you should be doing nothing else.'[20]

Having had leadership thrust on him at last, Steve had never been out on a longer limb. In his previous group, big brother Muff had shouldered many of the trials and tribulations of the road, and there had been far less pressure to come up with original material. With Wood no longer casting his net into the songwriting pool and lyricist Capaldi malcontented, Steve sweated blood to create while ministering to day-to-day matters that hadn't troubled him when busy Chris Blackwell had only Traffic on his books. Ultimately the twenty-year-old, cocooned by stardom since he had left school, may have heeded the first verse of 'Feelin' Alright' by his ill-treated former colleague – about wanting a change of scene before he starts to scream.

Flogging a dead horse, Island flung together from B-sides, out-takes and concert recordings the patchwork *Last Exit* to wring what was presumed to be the last monetary drops from Traffic. On a sleeve consciously loaded with cryptic imagery, how many trees died for the inner gatefold soft focus of Steve and Chris standing twenty feet apart in a field of grey clay? Maybe it was from a contact sheet snapped on acid. Its back cover profile featured only mainman

Winwood munching an apple; only more engrossing was the front, largely assembled from shots of the withering tree hollow session.

In the interim before the May 1969 release of *Last Exit*, Capaldi, with Wood's approval, telephoned Dave Mason on the rebound. Dave, through Jimmy Miller's sponsorship, was attempting to make a go of it as a freelance producer in Los Angeles. But with Winwood gone there was no impediment to Dave reuniting with Jim and Chris for a new group. Sold on the idea, despite misgivings about the Island link-up, Dave checked in at the inevitable pastoral retreat they'd rented in the Wye valley. To fatten out the sound, the three called in Mick 'Wynder K. Frog' Weaver, who now had a brace of Island LPs to his credit. Mason, Capaldi and Frog went back quite a way. With Deep Feeling – and the VIPs – Frog had supported the Pink Floyd at the Marquee as long ago as 1966.

Under the prosaic nom de guerre 'Mason–Capaldi–Wood–Frog' – pet-named Wooden Frog – the group daringly secured major engagements, such as one at the Albert Hall with Jimi Hendrix, having barely rehearsed. Naturally, the majority of originals belonged to Mason – including 'Look at You, Look at Me', composed with Capaldi. Sharing lead vocals, the ex-Hellions duetted on the murder ballad 'Long Black Veil' that Bob Dylan's backing Band had lately resurrected. As an instrumental, Albert King's 'Born Under a Bad Sign' was tackled when Wooden Frog made their radio debut – as Traffic had in October 1967 – on Radio One's *Top Gear*. Though they accumulated enough material for an album, studio time under an intrigued Chris Blackwell's supervision was botched when a girlfriend's hash cakes got the better of them. This was unfortunate as, in Wood's words, 'our future is bound up with Island Records and what is profitable and what won't work out'.[32]

With this door closed, the quartet shrugged their shoulders and saw out the remaining bookings. By March, Wooden Frog was no more. Poignantly, the last hop had been in the Hellions' old stamping ground and, like the others in its short existence, Wooden Frog's show at Kidderminster Town Hall had gone down a storm. Nevertheless, there had been no second chance from Blackwell because – Dave believed – 'Steve wasn't involved any more.'[11]

8
'Well . . . All Right'

Too late for Christmas 1968 came a posthumous postscript from Traffic. An oblique tribute to Booker T and the MGs was the two-chord single 'Medicated Goo' from the final session. Attributed to Winwood and Jimmy Miller, its desperate libretto read as if scribbled during a tea break – some drivel about freaky Freddie Frolic gathering green flowers in a field of snow. Since this pig's ear lacked the instinctive commitment of, for instance, 'Wooly Bully' or Wild Man Fischer's 'The Taster', no silk purse was forthcoming, despite Steve's spirited squealing against an ersatz Stax soul stew of crescendoed bridge, lowdown Bar-Kay saxophone and agitated fretboard lacerations. Traffic signed off sounding like any merely competent dance band who fancied themselves as composers.

As 'Medicated Goo' saturated deletion racks, Winwood – back from Holland – wintered alone in Aston Tirrold, holding at arm's length any decisions about the future. 'We feel that today's scene is moving very much away from permanent groups and more towards recognition for individual musicians,' he explained in royal plural to Chris Welch, 'the trend is going more in the direction of the jazz scene when musicians just jam together as they please.'[1] In tacit endorsement in December 1968 came A. N. Other, an *ad hoc* quintet with John Lennon, Yoko Ono (enveloped in a sack), Eric Clapton, Keith Richards (on bass) and Jimi Hendrix drummer John Mitchell, all performing Lennon's 'Yer Blues, on *The Rolling Stones Rock 'n' Roll Circus*. A month prior to BBC Television's shooting of this hitherto unscreened spectacular, Clapton had been invited also to a less glamorous all-day function in a Staines warehouse where many of the ablest musical technicians of two continents dissolved outlines between rock and jazz. Among those captured on rarely seen film were guitarist Steve Stills, veteran multi-instrumentalist Roland Kirk, Nebraskan drummer Buddy Miles and Jack Bruce, who – with two other participants, saxophonist Dick Heckstall-Smith and drummer Jon Hiseman – would cut a one-shot jazz album the following year. Buddy Miles' former Electric Flag colleague, guitarist Mike Bloomfield, had already been the prime mover in a series of less erudite get-togethers in the likelier setting of a US recording studio. With the likes of Stills and organist Al Kooper, the edited result, modestly titled *Super Session*, was the best-selling CBS album of 1968.

The clouds parted again on the gods at play when the producer of both the Moody Blues and the Move, Denny Cordell, assembled a star-studded cast to assist windmill-armed Joe Cocker, blues constrictor and ex-East Midlands Gas Board fitter, who in November had wrenched from Welsh songstress Mary Hopkin the UK number one position with a funereal-paced overhaul of 'With a Little Help from My Friends' from *Sergeant Pepper*. Containing Wynder K. Frog, ex-members of Dave Berry's Cruisers (and one former Argonaut sessionman) from his native Sheffield, Cocker's Grease Band were among more famous friends on the subsequent LP. Intrigued guests included Jim Capaldi, Tony Visconti, ex-Tornados drummer Clem Cattini, Chris Farlowe's guitarist Albert Lee and members of Procol Harum, Joe's Regal Zonophone label mates. Constituting one big-name rhythm section was, from the ashes of the Yardbirds, Jimmy Page plus two old acquaintances from Birmingham – Spooky Tooth's Mike Kellie and, on bass, Steve Winwood.

Hinging on Cocker's sweaty bellyaching, items veered from the Great War sentiment of "Bye, 'bye, Blackbird' to, more poignantly for Winwood, Dave Mason's 'Feelin' Alright'. Contributing keyboards too, so compatible was Steve with Cocker's crew that he volunteered his eager services for future sessions. This offer, however, became impossible to fulfil.

As his extempore musical wanderings already indicated, Eric Clapton – with his curling-tonged Hendrix frizz growing out – was at a loose end. He had made no contingency plans since – opposite a Traffic article – *Beat Instrumental*'s interview with his drummer Ginger Baker, had reiterated Cream's calculated disbandment on 26 November 1968. Two years earlier on British boards and, later, in the retractable spheres of the recording studio, Cream's output contained piquancies of blues, experiment and humour. Most of the group's originals came from the pen of Glaswegian six-string bass guitarist Jack Bruce who, in adventurous use of cello and other acoustic subtleties, demonstrated that his adolescent studies at the Royal Scottish Academy of Music had not been in vain.

From the cramped Angel at Godalming or Camberley's seedy Agincourt ballroom, Cream removed themselves to grander but more impersonal showcases where American collegiate youth seemed fair game to buy anything British labelled 'heavy', 'progressive' or – surely taking coals to Newcastle – 'blues'. Their name justly implied their virtuosity and twenty-three-year-old Clapton was deified as a guitar hero, but in the US climate their sensitivity and clever ironies were warped by high-decibel diddle-diddle-diddling: 'endless, meaningless solos,' reflected a bemused Clapton, 'we were not indulging ourselves so much as our audience . . . because that's what they wanted'.[2] As long as such customers headbanged, mimed to fresh air guitars and went ape as much over strings of bum notes as the group's most startling moments, Cream in stagnation broke box office records in Uncle Sam's baseball parks and concrete colosseums. Their original intention expressed at their Willesden scout hut rehearsals in 1966 had been to work Home Counties clubland as a blues trio; they were not quite so humble two years later with a double album going gold across the Atlantic. Forever in America, Cream had slotted few UK dates into their taxing schedule. Therefore, for old times' sake, their final recital was staged at London's Royal Albert Hall. The set included their usual triple-forte workout of Willie Dixon's basic 'Spoonful' – about the transience of fiscal cares – which on the *Live at the Fillmore* half of *Wheels of Fire* they cut, dried and dissected for nigh on twenty long minutes to snowblinded applause.

When the Cream idea was first mooted, Bruce agreed to undertake the bulk of the singing only after other possibilities had been investigated. Baker, for example, gave first refusal to Weybridge rocker Ray Phillips, leader of the Nashville Teens who were still Top Fifty contenders. After two consecutive chart-toppers with Spencer Davis, a similar invitation to Steve Winwood by Clapton fell on even stonier ground. Unlike Ray, whose Teens – hitless after 1966 – would travel a mighty rough road, Steve had no qualms about misplaced loyalty. Praising Cream in print, he would acknowledge the particular influence of Clapton, with whom he had mixed socially since March 1965, the month that the Yardbirds swept to joint top of the *New Musical Express* chart with 'For Your Love', after replacing disgruntled blues purist Eric with Wimbledon art student Jeff Beck.

Clapton taught himself guitar, to the detriment of his own coursework at Kingston Art School with Keith Relf, but his only ventures into the extraordinary had been in his taste in clothes. From made-to-measure threads of 1963, he metamorphosed over fifteen months to the workmanlike *Beano* reader on the LP sleeve of *Bluesbreakers*, his *pièce de résistance* with the formidable John Mayall, whose blues came down from Macclesfield. 'He'd discovered these Sta-Fast paints for painting his shirt,' recollected Vivian Stanshall of one dressing room encounter – to which he added, 'no-one was under the impression that Eric was about to become a world-class musician'.

'Clapton Is God' evolved from Marquee toilet graffiti during his time with Mayall – for whom he twanged the wires with better grace than with the chart-riding Yardbirds. This was despite the parsimony of his new paymaster. Though his over-amplified fretboard eloquence helped ease Mayall into the LP lists, Clapton only received a standard Musicians' Union fee before knocking off for the night. Yet former Royal Engineer Mayall commanded respect for his unconcern about the hit parade, his painstaking vocational dedication and his disciplined enforcement of his own order. As the suspensions of bass player John McVie during six Bluesbreaking years affirmed, Mayall wouldn't tolerate intemperance – and if he caught you with drugs, God help you. This regime didn't suit everybody. Barely twenty, Clapton enjoyed a two-month absence without leave on a hedonistic odyssey to Greece, with pianist Ben Palmer and four other pals, before his prodigal reinstatement. Back with Mayall, Clapton earned the exalted status not of 'God' so much as 'best guitarist in the country – and so unaffected',[3] according to one fan, Steve Winwood.

Mixing autocracy and chance operation, Mayall's purposely unstable band allowed a rapid turnover within the ranks. The roots of Fleetwood Mac and Colosseum, for example, were embedded in the Bluesbreakers, who also schooled future Rolling Stones, Mothers of Invention and Free among many others. More pertinently, both Jack Bruce and Ginger Baker had been Mayall men too.

Spencer Davis and Steve Winwood had been among the multifarious passers-by roped in by Mayall for extra-mural one-nighters – Winwood was attracted initially by the prospect of having a go on Mayall's Hammond organ. Some musicians were asked by Mayall to sit in literally minutes before showtime merely because they happened to be holding a musical instrument or because Mayall liked some facet of their personality. Mayall and Clapton would often reciprocate, as they did at Birmingham Town Hall in December 1965 when they joined in with the Spencer Davis Group who, owing to an engagement at the Flamingo, did not arrive until 3 a.m.

Clapton and Winwood with Bruce and Pete York had also recorded together as part of the Powerhouse, a sudden sextet convened by Ben Palmer and mouth-organist Paul Jones of Manfred Mann. Following a cursory rehearsal, producer Joe Boyd's tapes rolled for thirty ragged minutes in an otherwise deserted Marquee. Among extant tracks by this after-hours ensemble is – sung by Winwood – a nascent 'Crossroads', then the subject of a Sue reissue by elderly bottleneck guitarist 'Homesick' James Williamson, who was flavour of the month with London's In Crowd. Composed by 'king of the Delta blues singers' Robert Johnson – an icon of Clapton's – 'Crossroads' developed into a mainstay of Cream's interminable American treks.

While the final note of Cream's Albert Hall encore – a further Powerhouse blueprint, the instrumental 'Steppin' Out' – yet vibrated in the Kensington air, imaginative journalists shorthanded rumours. So ecstatic were the home crowd that Cream considered not splitting up after all. Deadly enemies Clapton and Bruce, with a backing combo apiece, would tour simultaneously as rival attractions. As he couldn't sing, Ginger favoured a group concept with a more pronounced percussion emphasis, which had been stifled in Cream. Eric was going to produce a Hollywood movie.

As the press debated Cream's fragmented future, Steve Winwood, in his chat with Chris Welch, mentioned a possible private visit to the States. In the same edition as this interview, *Melody Maker* reported Clapton's intended search for US accompanists 'because most of the good English musicians I know are already in groups and settled'.[1] Hunched over his typewriter the next day, it occurred to Chris Welch that as Winwood and Clapton might be on the same landmass at possibly the same time, next week's *Melody Maker* could drop hints about their collaborating on an album there. And why not? It would lend tidy credence to premature comments a month earlier: 'now both Eric and Stevie are free with the break-up of their groups, there is a strong possibility they may get a group together or at least record'.[1]

Anxious about his intolerable guitar divinity, Clapton the man listened to Welch, his old flatmate's advice and in January 1969 telephoned Winwood. Sure in retrospect that 'at some point we would play together',[4] Steve duly slammed his jeep door in the forecourt of Hurtwood Edge, Eric's newly acquired twenty-four-room Surrey mansion, on 5 February 1969. 'When we started rehearsing,' recalled Clapton, 'it was just me and Steve and other people that we had around, and it was so completely different – almost a jazz thing.'[5] From these casual improvisations within temporary refuge from fame, there was only the perverse joy of making uncommercial music. Yet since their living relied on selling records, the medicine had to be dispensed more neatly. So they sharpened the musical focus, and what smouldered into form, with the expected hybrid, was evidence of Clapton's particular liking for an album of insidious impact, *Music from Big Pink*. By the Band, from their communal home in rural upstate New York, it demonstrated a True West blend of electric folklore that had been nurtured over years of rough nights in hick dance halls before the musicians landed a job backing Bob Dylan. As Wooden Frog were also discovering, *Music from Big Pink* was a difficult yardstick for any group – let alone one yet to be formed.

The most urgent requirement for Clapton and Winwood was a permanent drummer. Arriving for rehearsal one day, Steve noticed Ginger Baker's Jaguar outside Eric's: 'if Ginger, who was exhausted after Cream, hadn't wanted to do it, Jim Capaldi would've probably been drummer'.[6] As for Eric, 'I wanted no part of Cream again but didn't have the heart to say no [to Ginger].'[7] Exploratory recording included a Dylan number from his legendary *Basement Tapes* with the Band, but Clapton, via matchmaker Welch, parried the outside world with 'as far as Steve Winwood, Ginger Baker and myself are concerned, we are just jamming and have no definite plans for the future'.[8]

With his own fretboard skills a wasted resource, and obliged doggedly to stamp bass pedals as well as press keys and sing, Winwood sought relief by procuring Richard Roman Grech, a twenty-two-year-old bass guitarist he'd heard at various cottage get-togethers. Grech and Winwood had also been present the previous year when Traffic had been among the team on Dave Mason's production of Gordon Jackson's album *Thinking Back*, which, as John Palmer and Luther Grosvenor also played, effectively reunited – bar Tony Hill – the Hellions. Additional input was provided by former Yardbirds' fan club secretary Julie Driscoll, then on the crest of her 'Wheels of Fire' hit, plus hand drummer Remi Kabaka and members of Grech and Palmer's group, Family.

Born in Bordeaux, Rick moved with his family in 1953 to Leicester, where he scraped violin in the city's Youth Symphony Orchestra. The onset of puberty found him looking for an opening in pop. He was hired by the Farinas as bass guitarist, and a *Midland Beat* feature[9] in July 1966 indicated that he also fronted the quintet as singer during their repertory transition from rhythm and blues to soul, which necessitated the incorporation of saxophonists James King and, from Danny Storm and the Strollers, ex-croupier Roger

Chapman. As the Roaring Sixties they cut 'We Love the Pirates', a topical 45 on the Marmalade label (who had also recorded Julie Driscoll as well as Jim Capaldi's Deep Feeling) before becoming Family. With Chapman now centre stage as lead vocalist, Family migrated to an uncertain future in the Smoke.

From their unsmiling 1967 publicity shots, they looked, frankly, a nasty shower, but in a year when another son of Leicester, Engelbert Humperdinck, ruled British pop, Family emerged as darlings of London's underground movement – with regular engagements at the Roundhouse and clubs like Middle Earth and UFO. This was supplemented with sessions on *Top Gear* and their off-duty frolics being chronicled under an alias in Jenny Fabian's racy *roman à clef, Groupie*. Supervised by the prolific Kim Fowley, Family's demo of the traditional 'Silver Dagger' caught the ear of Liberty Records, who signed them in early 1968. They were self-consciously 'weird', and by then not the least of their distinctions was Chapman's developing tortured goat vibrato and Grech's intriguingly quirky fiddle overdubs on their debut LP, produced by Jimmy Miller and Dave Mason, who'd met the band through their manager, John Gilbert. None the less, epitomized by an in-concert punch-up in the wings of the Fillmore between Chapman and promoter Bill Graham, who reckoned they were the worst group he'd ever heard, Family's troubled American tour in 1969 was capped midway when Rick – after refusing an invitation to join Atomic Rooster – slipped his cable when summoned by Winwood to Surrey.

Their line-up now complete, the four cats grooved while their respective handlers slugged it out. With Baker and Clapton on its books, the Stigwood Organisation called the shots, placing the act on Cream's label Polydor 'by arrangement with Robert Stigwood and Chris Blackwell' – Winwood appearing 'through the courtesy of Island Records'. Who was Rick Grech anyway? After naming the commodity Blind Faith – Clapton's suggestion – the wheels were set in motion. 'I knew it was a hype as soon as it was called "Blind Faith",' muttered Winwood later. 'We were handled wrongly – sold as a product, and people were hip to see that. We just wanted to play music – not even supermusic – but I hardly knew what was happening.'[6]

Those who did were still dividing up the swag generated by Cream's US barnstormers. Dollars danced before the gleaming eyes of the new group's investors as Stigwood's office rang with merchandising deals, advances against takings, franchises and estimates, spewed out at a second's notice to American entrepreneurs yelling 'Klondike!' Within days, a six-week multi-megatour of the States was set for summer; 'the first to feature a true supergroup'[10] wrote *Melody Maker*'s New York correspondent. The asking prices per show were reported to be comparable to the million greenbacks palmed by David Bowie for one notable US concert fifteen inflationary years on. For Blind Faith, there was now no turning back.

As these blizzards of notes subsided into wads, the rehearsing supergroup, though still in a protective bubble amid the howling publicity, stole nervous glances at the increasing depth into which they would plunge should they not live up to their selfish public's expectations. 'Blind Faith fail?' gasped a letter in *Melody Maker*'s Mailbag. 'Someone has to be joking. I feel sure they are a success even before they produce a single recording. Almost Beatle status.'[11] It seemed Clapton's tacit resignation as God hadn't been accepted. Therefore if, as Clapton remarked, 'Steve is really the focal point',[12] what did that make Steve?

In April it was announced that the four-man Master Race would shape up, as Traffic had done, with some Scandinavian dates before a concert in London – which would be free of charge! Actually, no Nordic invasion transpired but – defying belief – the buckshee bash was pencilled in by organizers Blackhill Enterprises for 7 June in the Cockpit, Hyde Park's natural amphitheatre.

As an ex-Family man, Grech was an old hand at these altruistic happenings. So common were they in post-flower power England that reaction, when scanning billings in *Time Out* or *International Times,* had shifted from a cynical 'Yes, but how much is it to get in?' to a jaded 'Hmm, is that all that's on this time?' Typical was a rain-drenched affair in May near the tumulus in Parliament Hill Fields. This was headlined by Procol Harum, promoting their latest epic, 'A Salty Dog', supported by stars-in-embryo Yes – still stark enough to be accessible to the Average Joe. Preceding Yes were pixieland acoustic twiddlers Forest. Present but not bothering were, of less trivial renown, jet-lagged American guitarist John Fahey and, fixture of earlier free concerts, manic Mancunian Roy Harper. Not digging either the vibes or the PA system – as quality-checked by Forest – both mingled among the multitude sprawled across muddy Hampstead Heath.

Favourites of master of ceremonies Sam Cutler of the sad gaucho moustache, protracted whiffs of the Orient and elsewhere from the Third Ear Band put some in a trance while others wondered how much longer. There they were again at 2.30 on Blind Faith's sunnier afternoon a month later, their oboe, cello, viola and bongo meanderings boring 'em stiff on the low wooden stage a few yards and two thousand light years from us common herd beyond the crash barriers. This ubiquitous quartet were also to kick off the Rolling Stones' memorial for the drowned Brian Jones at the same venue on 5 July. With their Hell's Angel stewardry, Beggar's Banquet backdrop, potted palms, six television crews, sky-clawing scaffolding and Cecil B. de Mille crowd of 650,000, the Stones made Blind Faith's debut seem rather rustic. Though equipment from Watkins Electronic Music served both events, the Stones' chaotic sorcery, transmitted from speakers twenty feet above them, was loud enough to impinge upon ears in Putney. Blind Faith's far fewer columns stacked on the boards were quite sufficient for Park Lane listeners, thank you. A calculated risk about the weather meant a stage open to the sky. Neither was there any obvious security.

Shouldering a movie camera, an operator would flit fitfully across the front press enclosure, collating images that would be eventually edited to a one-song snippet in *Cucumber Castle,* a sixty-minute television vehicle for longer established Stigwood clients the Bee Gees. Indeed, two of the Gibb brothers, with John Lennon, various Rolling Stones and other backstage wellwishers were glimpsed Chad-like behind performers' heels by those in the front rows, who could also decipher what was daubed inexpertly on a bedsheet banner stage right: 'Blackhill with the help of Robert Stigwood + Chris Blackwell + WEM'.

Some seven thousand fans had unzipped their sleeping bags round Charlie Watkins' electronic fastness at dawn that Saturday. A number had come over from continental Europe. Some had even crossed the Atlantic. Of these, a few had spent Friday evening across the road at a concert by fellow American Richie Havens at the Albert Hall. Depending on what Sunday journal landed on your doormat, audience estimates ranged from 36,000 to 150,000. However exaggerated, it was certainly and briefly the largest assembly for any cultural event ever accommodated by the capital.

With the deranging pallor of dawn, I slumped in counterpaned readiness in Hampshire for my own forty-mile pilgrimage via Waterloo to Hyde Park. Past sleep by five, I tempered a cold water hairwash with an illicit slug of my father's Johnny Walker. Though I was feeling one hell of a fellow by then, ten minutes of backcombed titivation had been already flattened fractionally by sweat when my twelve-year-old sister Kate and I joined our fellow travellers – two Waitrose checkout girls plus Malcolm, a doubtful friend who none the less owned an electric guitar and Rangemaster amplifier. Even at Fleet railway station for the 6.20, the day was promising to be a scorcher, and I regretted burdening myself with a blue linen jacket which hid an alarming floral shirt a year old.

Among the hordes in Hyde Park's heat, luck led us to settle mere feet from the stage area near the portly possessor of the first cassette player I'd ever seen. Clad only in Levi's, at least he ensured no overcrowding of our spot with his running perspiration and plummy commentary on the Strawbs, who brayed incessantly from his new toy. As suntan oil and joss-sticks mingled with denser odours of people and food, our morning vigil was measured in expeditions for tepid soft drinks and melting ice cream. Unless you had an iron bladder, concealing bushes *en route* were not ignored.

The gathering tension infiltrated from the buzzing tribes around us. 'Almost biblical'[12] we were, according to one newshound, in our massing like the Israelites at the foot of Mount Sinai. For many, it was more than just free entertainment by a pop group. Veiled in flesh, the gracious idols had deigned to allow us to worship them in person. More than the Word made vinyl in the comfort of your own home, they'd impart their epoch-making Art via electronic vibrations hanging in the clear air. Wouldn't they? Riding rough-shod over drug-bust martyrdom, acid visions, secret doctrines from India, sympathy for the Devil and other distant worlds known only by Beatles, Stones and by proxy, the anticipated fusion of Cream's resounding violence with a generous shot of Traffic's mystical glimpses would uplift us infinitely and, like a sort of musical Billy Graham, turn us into more aware, more creative human beings. No one really expected the waters of the Serpentine to part, but we'd surely descend the tube escalators afterwards, having participated, however passively, in making history – the proverbial 'something to tell your grandchildren about'.

Near noon, a squeak of feedback drew us to the stage where Sam Cutler's continuity this time would include – amongst news of lost youngsters and inadvertent reading of messages in restricted code – cautions about climbing surrounding horse chestnut trees for a better view. One determined soul clung to the top of a lamppost for the duration. Similarly enterprising was a whiskered scruff squatting on the roof of a Bedford van parked stage left, causing its outraged satin-suited owner to marinate the air with rage at this 'motherf***er' – a trendy new swear word from the States.

This loss of cool apart it was, indeed, as *Rolling Stone* reported, 'a nice day in the Park'. There were few arrests and, other than litter, little environmental damage. Furthermore, the programme ran with hardly a hitch, each performer, however humble, commanding attentive silences and considered ovations. As the crew furnished the stage during one intermission, a mildly amusing mime involved what even we Hampshire yokels recognized as an invisible giant spliff. Projecting the good vibes further, having interrupted his European tour itinerary, singing guitarist Richie Havens prudently punctuated his Brooklyn busker bark with exclamations of 'Peace! Peace!' as he retuned and pedantically replaced a broken string. Real, real gone by his big finish, he bowled offstage still hammering that E chord.

In feyer vein, the unscheduled Donovan, fresh from an unlikely studio liaison with Jeff Beck, ambled on in a linen jacket just like mine. Unlike his interminable gatecrashing at the Bath Festival the following July, he stuck to the point – which was a handful of his British smashes. Asking for requests, he by-passed yells for his US chart-climber 'Lalene', unheard by most and available only on import. Instead, he gave us the predetermined 'Colours' from 1965. His merry minstrelsy rewarded, he warned us not to go away because 'these young boys are going to blow up a storm'.

Though Donovan meant Winwood, Clapton *et al*, the only act that *did* cut up rough was the Edgar Broughton Band from the Midlands, whose superficial grasp of issues political and social secured their high standing in the country's agitpropism. Specializing in free concerts, long ago they'd thwarted Warwickshire County Council by playing from the back of a lorry after being refused space in a local recreation ground. Though they weren't quite my bag, Edgar and his brothers utilized time interestingly enough from the inappropriate 'Love in the Rain' to their genuinely reluctant encore plug of their latest single, 'Evil'. Actually, they set the place alight like gin-sops at a temperance meeting. Edgar's Yogi Bear bellow palled in due course but whirling idiot dancers, familiar from Parliament Hill Fields, warranted distracted sneers and some shirt-sleeved bouncer-types became suddenly evident manning the low barricades as spectators rose during the audience participation number, the rabble-rousing exorcism 'Out, Demons, Out'. Primed for the main attraction though we were, the Broughtons came within an ace of stealing the show.

'When we went onstage, it was already over somehow,' lamented Clapton, 'the heart, the core of what Blind Faith could have done was all wrapped up in the time before we were actually exposed.'[5] A disaffected onlooker's angle might have been this: these four blokes piled onstage at quarter past six. The guitarist in a striped pirate's vest and denims was swigging from a can of Coke which he perched on his amp. The drummer with a fag in his mouth cracked a joke about it being the first rehearsal. Then they had a go at an old Crickets song – which wasn't bad. Neither was a subdued version of the Stones' 'Under My Thumb'. They *had* been practising after all. The rest of the set – which went on for about an hour – had some good bits too, but all of it was new and, thinking about it later, it was like one long number. Still, it was easy on the ear and the singer at the organ seemed to enjoy himself. Yeah, they were all right, I suppose.

Unfortunately this wasn't a beer-sodden evening in the jovial atmosphere of someone's local. Only a miracle could have rescued Blind Faith, even if the media build-up forestalled instant damnation. Facing facts in the public eye, Clapton would admit 'we weren't ready . . . but we had no choice'.[13] God and axe victim Eric had been unable to deflect that merciless eye onto Winwood. Like Tommy Cooper's comic nervous procrastination prior to a complicated trick, there persisted a 'Will he? Won't he?' suspense whenever a looming instrumental interlude presented a chance for Eric to ignite some Fillmore fireworks as the sun sank that Saturday. Instead, grinning beneath his wavy fringe, Clapton remained supinely integrated into the combo's restrained elegance.

Not as enigmatic was Ginger, who forced a disruptive memory of his immediate past when he put his back into a truculent frenzy of cross-patterns and ringing silverware. His fans loved it, but whispers would soon come of Jim Capaldi – without a drum solo to his name – replacing the flamboyant Baker, whose testy Jaguar almost flattened two hippy pedestrians as he skidded past Lancaster Gate too soon afterwards.

With less to prove and a beard that hadn't really taken, Rick Grech toiled at his guttural Fender, very much the junior partner. None of his compositions made it into the set but, over Baker's splashing ride cymbal shuffle, he'd been allowed to regurgitate his lot while Steve and Eric took five. For another arranged passage – in 'Sea of Joy' – he switched from bass to tea dance violin – the only tangent to the drums-guitar-bass-keyboard prototype.

From the piano stool, Winwood seemed the most enthusiastic and relaxed about the failsafe situation, which was a closer approximation to his old band than most outsiders had imagined. Despite his characteristic hunch over the eighty-eights and a boyishness emphasized by a recent haircut, it was much as a morning-after letter to *Melody Maker* opined, 'Steve Winwood and a backing band'.[14] As with Spencer Davis and Traffic, it had been that precise, soaring ashtray tenor that had craned distant necks, reducing even those of greater global fame to grey mediocrity.

Winwood also dominated Blind Faith's eponymous only album, which topped lists both home and abroad by late summer, for much the same reasons as teenybopper dreamboat David Cassidy would be voted Top International Guitarist by *Record Mirror* readers in 1972. It was for who Blind Faith were, rather than what they did. As well as goodwill and advance sales, it was buoyed by King's New Clothes reviews. Determined to like it, the rock magazine *Zigzag*'s scribe, while conceding that 'at first it's slightly disappointing like the debut concert', thought the selections were still 'landmarks in contemporary British music'.[15] Expecting magic, all he got was forty minutes of mere music, recorded over an April fortnight.

Vaguer about the LP's directional motivation than the lads themselves, Jimmy Miller had been commissioned to apply his detached console objectivity to the goods after an abandoned attempt at self-production. Drawn largely from outside sources, in the can was enough to fill a double album, but under Miller's quality control this was whittled down to the group originals plus the Buddy Holly and the Crickets revamp 'Well . . . All Right'. An instrumental showcasing Clapton was circulated to five hundred showbusiness recipients as one side of a pressing giving notice that, from 2 June 1969, Island were at a new address. Titled 'Exchange and Mart', it surfaced on a 1987 Blind Faith compact disc with the previously unissued 'Spending All My Days', a one-take sketch.

Likewise cut *au naturel* was the album's most aimless exercise – Baker's 'Do What You Like'. Here, the few verses of doggerel sandwich an irritating samba chant which underpins the group members' immortalizing of their own arrogance for a few expensive plastic minutes each – the most arresting aspects being Steve's flatulent organ tone and the diverting stereo separation of Ginger's tom-toms. Blighting the other offerings are lesser symptoms of self-indulgence. With its cowbell clatter, catchy snake-charmer riff, lyrical update and double-tracked jangling of Steve's ivories, 'Well . . . All Right' was on the cards for single release. Yet a superfluous blow over a fade, prolonged for this very purpose, couldn't be resisted.

This was followed by Clapton's contrasting 'Presence of the Lord' which had least ostentation. Flawed by Ginger's walloping fills, this stately hymn's pious litany is jarred by a tempo change worthy of the Yardbirds, wherein a wah-wah Eric bares his teeth for a thrifty twenty-four bars.

Both nearest to Traffic and holding half-hidden clues of the Winwood yet to come was one of Clapton's eternal favourites,

'Can't Find My Way Back Home'. Steve's concise acoustic entreaty
to a drug-addicted friend is emoted in a near-falsetto, sliding into
wordless cooing where Chris Wood's flute might have entered.
Less 'pure' were his other Blind Faith efforts: the nine-minute 'Had
to Cry Today' – saturated by its recurrent run-down which is
dismembered in the coda by intertwining guitars – and, more
dependent on arpeggio than ostinato, 'Sea of Joy' – originally meant
for Traffic, which swims with modal switches and dire symbolism
though, lest we forget, half its melody reared up four years later in
Slade's 'Merry Christmas Everybody'.

Born of unconsolidated panic, *Blind Faith* stands as a curate's egg
of an album. Like the recital in the Park, it was all right, I suppose.
Zigzag, however, concluded that it was 'classic'.[15] 'Prototypical'
was more the word. *Melody Maker*'s Brightest Hope of 1969 pooled
every ingredient of a standard late sixties' progressive outfit:
trundling heavy riffing, anguished vocal attack, smart alec instrumental intricacies and, crucially, enough soloing misery to
soundtrack drying paint. For good measure, there was the softcore
rock 'n' roll retread, some acoustic calm and a dash of religion.
More subtly than Cream, Blind Faith endorsed dangerous imitative
patterns: the ten-minute drum thrash, for instance, continued to
drive paying customers out for a swift half of lager way into the
seventies. Moreover, Blind Faith's crass supergroup precedent was
detected most blatantly in Humble Pie, which amalgamated Small
Face Steve Marriott, Peter Frampton from the Herd, Spooky
Tooth's Gregory Ridley and ex-Little Women (!) drummer Jerry
Shirley. Into the bargain, Humble Pie even dragged up another
forgotten Buddy Holly item.

Blind Faith fell back on a second-hand strategy themselves with
their album's UK front cover. Neither sexy nor winsome, for that
vital US sales territory the nude study of Ginger Baker's eleven-
year-old daughter gripping a toy space rocket was dropped for an
innocuous band photograph on a non-gatefold sleeve. After all, it
was for North America that Blind Faith were intended.

Tell-tale signs that the troupe were, if not yet perishable, then
fallible, lent piquancy to Blackwell and Stigwood's discussions
about the impending assault on the States. In a quest to take the
continent for every cent they could get, additional matinees had
been crammed into already alloted coast-to-coast evenings in
leisure complexes, large-capacity auditoriums and stadiums designed for championship sports. 'It was just a rush,' pleaded
Winwood, 'and as soon as Robert Stigwood got hold of us, we sort
of played where he put us.'[2] Though impetus had slackened at

home, Beatle-sized headlines, a *Time* colour spread and screaming foyer posters trumpeted the Ultimate Supergroup's messianic July arrival in New York.

Cushioned within luxury suites, limousines and private jets from all but their most necessary underlings, the four stars were, according to Eric, 'still enthusiastic about the future of the group at the time',[5] despite a shaky American debut before 23,000 on the revolving stage at Madison Square Garden. Mitigating the increased labour intensity of each date were enough consecutive days off for all but Eric to risk flights back to English peace and quiet. Time hung heavier for Clapton, who preferred killing it in the purchase of vintage cars to be shipped back to Surrey. After dark, he began loafing around with some of the package's small fry such as Free, a young band new on Island's roster. Soon Eric sought the particular company of another supporting group led by Deep South guitarist Delaney Bramlett, which also included his wife Bonnie and – of all people – Dave Mason. When Blind Faith next performed, Eric was, as he put it, 'one step ahead from them'.[5]

To clarify this oblique remark, Clapton's feelings about this phase are worth quoting: 'After the first couple of gigs in America . . . it was just a question of getting up on stage . . . and trying to find some sort of pattern that you could fit into that would make it secure . . . and do the same numbers in the same order and try and get them polished so that people couldn't say that we were just a hype, like they were saying we were.'[5] Eric's rapid disenchantment with the Blind Faith routine, against his pleasure at bashing tambourine whilst hidden in the larger ranks of the preceding Bramletts, may have been kindled by press criticism aimed directly at him. The cruellest caption was *Rolling Stone*'s childish burlesque of Eric's thoughtful 'Presence of the Lord' chorus: 'Everybody knows the secret/Everybody knows the score/Stevie Winwood is a winner/Eric Clapton is a bore.'

So apathetic was Clapton that his upstaging provoked no friction. There was none, for example, when Winwood – as had been intended anyway – began alternating between singing behind his keyboards virtually in the wings, and occupying a central microphone while plucking joint lead guitar with an expertise that at least equalled that of his colleague. 'There was no focal point in terms of the band having a leader,' observed Dave Mason, 'yet neither Steve or Eric wanted to step out and take the limelight.'[16] Compared to the situation in both Cream and Traffic there was a marked lack of bickering and prima donna jealousies in Blind Faith, but that created its own problems. 'It wasn't alive,' groaned Ben Palmer, then the group's road manager, 'it never lived at all.'[17]

Inherited from previous bands were more private and sinister worries. 'We'd been doing drugs,' confessed Cream's old producer Felix Pappalardi, 'yeah, there were big piles of heroin . . . and cocaine in the studio.'[2] Baker's 'works' were still an established if discreet part of dressing room paraphernalia. Before the year was out, Clapton too would live only for junk. Not inexperienced with drugs himself, Winwood was not immune from temptation, though it must be noted that he'd once cut down on booze to avoid a pot belly. 'Steve had a lot of his own problems,' confided Clapton to a journalist's tape recorder, 'and, you know, at the time we were doing Blind Faith on the road, I had more than him and I needed help but he couldn't actually come out and help me . . . because he was actually struggling to keep it together himself.'[5]

Yes, they were a fine bunch to pay six dollars to see and no mistake. A good view wasn't guaranteed either. The antithesis to Hyde Park's tolerance of Blind Faith's gentle surprise was 'Acclamation by Riot!' – a typical critical summary of US audience conduct. With the universal surge towards the protective cordon of hired police, onstage silences and pianissimos were undercut by a ceaseless barrage of stamping, whistling, discomforted snarls and, worst of all, bawled requests for the good old good ones like 'Spoonful', 'Dear Mr Fantasy' and even 'Gimme Some Lovin'.' Maddened by body pressure and dripping stink, one hot-headed riot squad was so goaded by Ginger Baker's reprimands for their arbitrary manhandling of fans that the drummer himself became a recipient of their punches and kicks. Was Baker berating the uniforms that guarded him as Blind Faith's initial low volume led dismayed bottles, cans and even seats to be hurled stagewards? In a travesty of legitimate admiration, the receding, homely 'high priest of percussion'[16] was once scragged behind his kit by maverick souvenir hunters who fled with his sticks as the tardy cops waded in.

In much the same boat, Clapton elucidated 'the minute you get onto the stage at Madison Square Garden, first thing you think is how to get out. You just battle through and get it over with as soon as possible.'[5] Already drearily familiar to Eric and Ginger was Steve's exasperated discovery that 'we could play really terrible and get the same reaction as if we played f***ing good'.[18]

Amid the cash and chaos, Rick Grech – in pop terms the cliché Hollywood chorus girl thrust into a sudden starring role – remained cheerful. Coming up for air mid-tour in London, he regaled *Beat*

Instrumental with his group's grand design to cut the next LP in Memphis plus the carrot of a few British dates. 'The band has got better and better,' he explained, 'and as long as we swing happily together, then we'll stay together.'[19]

He was hopeful. The 'supergroup of all times'[20] threw in the towel – its virtue all gone – at the Los Angeles Forum on 15 August, with amplifiers now flat out and Ginger's rataplans 'impossible to hide from, spelling out messages and moods on the instrument he has received as a medium'.[21] With Cream and Traffic numbers in the set, 'Blind Faith's rumbling, churning sound conjured up the colorings of a full rock symphony in the throes of a disaster scene'.[21]

Within a day of winding down, the retinue scattered like rats disturbed in a granary. As Blind Faith's Surrey mansion ideals were perverted to blaring ham-fisted resignation and with half its number – Ginger too – slumming it in Delaney and Bonnie's tour bus, Steve had started thinking aloud to anyone who would listen about either looking up Jim and Chris to reform the old firm, or going it alone.

Chris Wood's travels since 'Medicated Goo' had led to marriage when he won the heart of Jeanette Jacobs, a feathered, beaded chanteuse in Doctor John's voodoo circus. Himself trilling flute within the echoing wails, throbbing murk and choreographed aetheria, Wood's gris-gris path had often crossed that of Blind Faith's less stylized zombie trail across the States. When the Night Tripper vanished back to the Louisiana swamps – and his alter-ego Mac Rebennack to Los Angeles – the now redundant Mr and Mrs Wood drifted back to London, where Chris landed on his feet in Airforce – Ginger Baker's post-Blind Faith big band.

'There was a great atmosphere [in Airforce],' Wood enthused, 'and the two concerts we did were the first I had made in Britain since the Mason-Capaldi-Wood-Frog group.'[22] Retaining Rick Grech, Ginger had belatedly confirmed the old gossip by forming a percussion-heavy outfit. Beating the skins with him and his fellow sticksman, the jazzy Phil Seaman (whom Winwood had seen backing Roland Kirk at Ronnie Scott's), were conga players Speedy Acquaye (whose Jamaican patois inspired the Beatles' 'Ob-la-di Ob-la-da'), Rebop Kwaku-Baah and fellow Nigerian Remi Kebaka. Also among Airforce's distinguished flux of players were the late Nassau trumpeter Harold McNair and, quite at ease playing alto sax and organ simultaneously, Baker's old boss Graham Bond – awaiting a mysterious death on the rails of Finsbury Park Underground in 1974.

146

As Ginger had also roped in some under-employed Brummies, Birmingham Town Hall was a fitting venue for their Air Force debut early in the New Year. As well as Wood, there were Trevor Burton and Denny Laine – whose Balls were in neutral – and Laine's old harmonica tutor, Steve Winwood.

While Winwood recognized that 'Ginger knows how to get people under control',[6] Baker's idiosyncratic adherence to the leadership principle caused a few over-sensitive souls to stride out from the few formal Airforce rehearsals to dissect their chief's character with bitter intensity. Though taken more seriously than actual performances, rehearsals degenerated into social occasions owing largely to interruptions as late arrivals set up their gear, as well as premature departures motivated either by thirst or by Baker's ruthlessness at sticking to the job in hand. 'May I make a suggestion?' asked Graham Bond. 'Yeah – shut up!' snarled Ginger. With one eye on the clock and another on waning patience, Airforce would run through numbers speedily and incompletely. Yeah! Cut! OK! That'll do. It goes on like that for another chorus then there's a standard middle eight. After that, someone takes a solo. Get the picture? Right, let's have a go at . . . 'He's totally off his nut,' said Clapton affectionately of Baker in 1970, 'if I joined a band of his now, I'd probably go round the twist. I mean, his escapades . . .'[5]

Marking time, 'Squadron Leader' Winwood and 'Flight Officer' Wood – as their flame-headed 'Wing Commander' dignified them – stuck it for one more engagement. At the Albert Hall was captured on tape for all eternity Airforce's rambling and unrepentantly loud concert set, from which was salvaged an exquisite single – 'Man of Constant Sorrow', delivered in Denny Laine's hurt voice. At least it wasn't weak or, as George Harrison aptly summed up Blind Faith, 'put together because they were all famous'.[23] Structurally, Airforce – falling to bits within a year – depended too much on too many variables, even if November 1970 saw them headlining at a presentation in Brighton over Pink Floyd, Tyrannosaurus Rex and, in small type, Status Quo. By then, of course, Chris Wood and Steve Winwood were long gone.

9

'On the Road'

It was another Battle of the Bands tournament during the University of Reading Rag Week. Suddenly all the other competitors' Deep Purple grimness was forgotten when Big D and the Deltas took the stage.

Clothed only in sheets and monochrome Hammer Horror facials, Big D and his riparian quartet had, apparently, rolled up in the late afternoon from a Portsmouth art school. It quickly became clear to the organizers that they weren't like the other bands in the contest. Their appearance apart, none of them could play a musical instrument and the singer couldn't hold a tune. I suppose they anticipated punk rock by about four years. Nevertheless, the belligerence that this movement would embrace was belied by the hirsute bonhomie that Big D's combo assumed in order to scrounge a drum kit, guitars and attendant amplification from rivals backstage or in the bar who were more apprehensively awaiting their turns.

Shambling onto the boards for their ordained fifteen minutes, Big D and the Deltas approximated versions of 'Pinball Wizard', 'Tulips from Amsterdam' and, as their climax, 'Purple Haze'. With impressive self-confidence, they also premiered a number they'd composed during their journey that day. Their unfamiliarity with the common chord, rhythmic consistency and harmonic scale was worsened by a lager-induced vagueness and the sheets more obstructing than possibly Solihull's Batman and his Wonder Boys had found their capes in 1966. Random notes chased up and down fretboards amid feedback lament while unco-ordinated, relentless drumming clattered behind a lead vocal ignorant of tone and key.

Most of the audience welcomed this comic relief as the curtains descended to an amused cheer. On the spot, one of the judges – a

BBC executive – offered them a booking at some funny party he was attending in St John's Wood the following night. Rejecting the fleshpots of London, the group stumbled back to their beer to be on call for *Melody Maker* critic (and future *Times* editor) Richard Williams' patronizing remarks about them before he announced the shock winners – the Thames Valley Stompers, a semi-traditional jazz outfit who'd played last.

The Deltas and Big D departed as elusively as they came and nothing was ever heard of them again. Though there were ponderous discussions about whether they'd been making an Art Statement or not, most agreed that they'd been merely a clique of students playing silly buggers. I was entranced by their trash; into the spring night I wandered lost in dreams and half-formed ambition. Well, I was only twenty. A sleeve note on a Scott Walker LP sprang to mind on which Albert Camus was quoted: 'A man's work is nothing but this slow trek to rediscover through the detours of art, those two or three simple images in whose presence his heart first opened.'

Next morning I decided that this conclusion was rather extreme. All the same, I felt that Big D had been the product of a mind similar to my own. It told me much of what I had already realized by 1972: pop was and is always years behind the major movements in art, but now it had touched the twentieth century. Recognizing that Queen Victoria would never recover from being dead, pop would soon be self-consciously embracing bruitism (the art of noise), Dada, the theatre of the absurd and the notion that, put crudely, all art is muck. Developments by the end of the decade would prove this judgement to be correct.

Though Big D, the incomparable Portsmouth Sinfonia, AMM, Billy and the Conquerors and other cells of pop music's lunatic fringe were nurtured by collegiate youth free from real-life responsibilities, the year of the Thames Valley Stompers' victory was pretty dull in the wider world of pop. In starkest contrast to the exhilarating, lurid Big Beat of the mid-sixties was the bland uniformity of the Woodstock Generation – a Bridge Over Troubled Waters indeed. The three years from 1968 had seen a petrification of pop's turbulent adolescence. Certainly, the impetus of British pop had relaxed on a world scale as our Transatlantic cousins beat us at our own game on many fronts. As a reprisal for the 'British Invasion' of 1964, Anglophile 'garage bands' such as the Standells and the Barbarians had crawled out of the sub-cultural woodwork. Across the same continent, power trios like Mountain and Grand Funk Railroad had modelled themselves profitably in the Cream image. At one end of the spectrum had been the Monkees' calculated bowdlerization of Herman's Hermits, mid-period Beatles and similarly clean-cut English groups. Conversely, the Fugs, Mothers of Invention and MC5 exaggerated the outrageousness of hairy monsters of the Stones–Pretty Things–Them persuasion even more than the garage bands.

In Britain itself, 1971 had been bracketed by the undiggable sounds of 'Grandad' Clive Dunn and Benny Hill's 'Ernie', with plenty of chirpy-chirpy cheapness in between. True, T. Rex and Slade made their chart debuts at this time, but both these harbingers of glam-rock were conspicuous by their absence on most technical college and university jukeboxes, full of depressing album-enhancing 45s of heavy business by Status Quo, Humble Pie, Black Sabbath and their ilk. The excesses of these 'brilliant' craftsmen appealed to male consumers recently grown to man's estate.

From a female perspective, the outlook was even worse. Emanating from the bedsits of many young women in higher education were the 'beautiful' cheesecloth-and-denim banalities of singing songwriters such as Neil Young, Elton John and – most precious of all – Melanie. The Royal Couple of the genre were probably Joni Mitchell and James Taylor. Among their many subjects were solemn abominations like Dave Crosby, Cat Stevens, America, Smokey and – for specialists – the Natural Acoustic Band, blank perfect harmonies and lyrics that made you embarrassed to be alive. Even a purring Mr Wonderful like Andy Williams enjoyed a period of being thought Truly Hip.

What chance had I in the early seventies, when it seemed that every other female in Reading had lost her marbles over a broad-shouldered hunk of PE student called Steeeve with a cowboy shirt, sensible jeans and a small shy smile. His dark facial hair came and went as he kept pace with the cosmetic caprices of His Folksy Winsomeness, James Taylor. To his own acoustic guitar tiddling, Steeeve would warble precise copies of his idol's *lieder* in local folk clubs and at college socials, where shameless hussies vied to join the half-finished pint of Breakspear's beer near the wretched fellow's feet.

All the old heroes had gone down. There'd been the fragmentation of the Small Faces, the Animals, Traffic, the Dave Clark Five, the Zombies, and, with Paul McCartney's High Court action in 1970, the Beatles – leaving a residue of splinter groups and solo performers to add to a growing pile. Three of the groups named were to re-form, but such a possibility was denied to the Jimi Hendrix Experience after the death of its figurehead in autumn

1970. Exacerbating a shortage of new original talent, more old acts had simply gone to seed. After the disaster of Altamont, the Stones luxuriated in St Tropez and tabloid gossip columns. The Kinks' sojourn in the Top Twenty was, apparently, nearly spent while the Hollies – now minus songwriting pivot Graham Nash – were driven to seek outside help in order to continue delivering the goods. The Nashville Teens, Unit Four Plus Two and Spencer Davis had long been brought to their knees, while Alexis Korner, Georgie Fame and Manfred Mann had been drawn into television commercials. Steve Marriott and Van Morrison – both now with receding hairlines – had Gone West with Eric Burdon, tempted by either Hollywood indolence or lucrative US tours with their tedious new backing bands. Marking time were the Searchers, Dave Berry, the Swinging Blue Jeans and the Merseybeats who, in an outer darkness of cabaret and the back-of-beyond dance hall orbit of northern Europe, were displayed as lovable curios from the recent past. Less wantonly unfashionable but struggling to keep the faith as the sixties faded had been the exhausted epic vulgarity of Dave Dee, Dozy, Beaky, Mick and Tich and the lost peasant aggression of their blood brothers, the Troggs. Finally, both John Lennon and Cliff Richard turned thirty.

Falling apart the same year as the Beatles' more sweeping exit was Love Affair, latecomers whose eldest member was barely twenty-one. Of the same age was Steve Winwood, whom striplings like Love Affair, paradoxically, regarded as an old-timer of a different pop generation. He was a lucky man, possessing both his magical youth and an artistic pedigree that, unlike that of Love Affair with their five run-of-the-mill UK chart entries, could be taken seriously by the so-called intelligentsia. Furthermore, he had – despite fighting shy of adulation – remained so much in the public eye since collecting his cards from Spencer Davis that he was still pestered for autographs as he was once over a salad in a Carnaby Street restaurant in 1969. The manageress, no less, obliged him to scribble a long message for her daughter who was in hospital.

More to the point, he still rated as a musician amid the deluge of virtuosi ushered in since 1966 during pop's short classical progression. In a 1969 readers' poll in *Beat Instrumental* – too expensive to rig results effectively – though Traffic made a humble posthumous twenty-three in the Best Group On Stage section compared to the equally lifeless Cream's number one, it was neck-and-neck between Winwood, Brian Auger and victor Keith Emerson in the keyboard stakes. Old Wynder K. swallowed dust at fourteen, with Manfred Mann and Georgie Fame barely getting a look in. As Best

Vocalist, Steve had shut down current fave Rod Stewart and crazy Arthur Brown as well as fellow old-stagers Mick Jagger, all the Beatles and golden-throated Scott Engel, to breathe down the necks of only Joe Cocker, Tom Jones – whose vocal magnificence smothered his squareness – and Cream's Jack Bruce.

Of course, his rhythm and blues rather than straight pop roots were instrumental in the escape from his previous incarnation as Stevie the 'Keep On Running' teenage heart-throb. Nobody, for instance, was ready to disconnect, even as DBMT, the much maligned Dozy, Beaky, Mick and Tich from their earlier scenarios with Dave Dee – not even when they cut a perfectly reasonable 'progressive' album in 1970. Not switching as naturally or as expediently as Winwood had from Davis to Traffic, DBMT's volte-face was, nevertheless, more plausible than attempts by the despairing Love Affair (as 'LA', for gawd's sake) and the foolish Tremeloes to crack the 'serious' market.

Conditioned by then to think only in terms of LPs – 'singles are so shallow'[1] – in 1974, Winwood was making music that was not as undercut by the general drift of seventies 'rock' as it might have been. Possibly he'd had enough of adhering to the state of the art during Blind Faith's last dinning weeks. Disregarding how easily the Who, Humble Pie and Deep Purple were subjugating their audiences with decibels, Steve's next band would have no more than one hundred watts per man: 'freaking out with volume is over. Everybody seemed to think volume was the revolution in the music. That's OK theatrically but not musically.'[1] However, Steve could be as self-indulgent as the worst of them, and his succeeding albums with his reformed Traffic contained fewer but longer tracks. Onstage, seventy-five-minute sets would contain but eight numbers. Though he admired the complex and innovatory extrapolations of the Mahavishnu Orchestra and the Mothers of Invention, he was often guilty of merely soloing aimlessly over static riffs as in his 1973 wah-wah exercise in 'Roll Right Stones' [*sic*] – which proved only that he was no Frank Zappa.

In common with bands like DBMT, Blue, the latter-day Searchers and Marmalade, and the Shadows – as 'Marvin, Welch and Farrar' – Winwood displayed a predilection for paeons to pastoral yearning. Instead of looking to the States and wooden Crosby, Stills and Nash (and Young), however, Winwood's revised Traffic vision was shared with British folk artists such as Steeleye Span, the Young Tradition, Pentangle and others who acknowledged the influence of, well, traditional folk music: 'It means a lot to me because it isn't documented. I don't think rock 'n'

152

roll is a tradition. Things that are steeped in history I like because I think that lends more meaning, more resonance. The points of reference go further and further back.'[2]

Unhappily, when these mists of Avalon cleared, Traffic made homespun attempts to address contemporary issues. Like every other aspect of culture, pop cannot avoid being part of the social conditions that produce it. Winwood looked at it like this: 'our music hasn't anything exactly to do with street fighting but, then again, I don't think that the music leaves it out. I feel we're part of it without trying to force it on anyone.'[3] While they refrained from protest marches or writing to the *Daily Mail*, Steve and Traffic's hearts were still in the right places. Jim Capaldi spoke of 'using musicians that wanted to play for free so that we could give all the money to the whales and seals and eagles. I've just discovered this woman who's into all that, saving whales, and I'm gonna send her some bread.'[4] Yet, when pinpointing iniquities and espousing worthy causes such as that of the Friends of the Earth, as well as taking part in a benefit concert to raise the court costs of the celebrated *Oz* obscenity trial in 1971, Traffic wrote and endorsed lyrics that were often pretentiously on the nose.

Because it exposes a point of view, even the soppiest lovey-dovey or self-pitying couplets – even Traffic's 'Empty Pages', 'Evening Blue' and 'Love' – may be construed as political, but as the seventies got under way there were myriad less clichéd topics. Was it only 1968 when *International Times* had exclaimed: 'Charlie Manson is just a harmless freak?' 'I've just been given a flower – the second in two weeks,'[5] wrote one of its columnists, John Peel, whom some considered the most beautiful person who ever lived. As the decade turned, mothers still moaned about their sons' long hair, but it wasn't the obsession it used to be for most families. With 'Mud Slide Slim' by James Taylor or Deep Purple's 'Machine Head' in the background on stereo altars, college hostel room hosts might offer guests a joint as they'd once shared a communal cigarette behind grammar school bike sheds two years earlier.

Manson was no longer the harmless freak he'd never been and, if you gave out flowers to all and sundry, sooner or later you'd get a kicking. There wasn't much to get worked up about any more. There'd been a ritual tub-thumping from clean-up television campaigner Mrs Whitehouse when ghoulish Alice Cooper with his macabre props hogged *Top of the Pops* over summer 1971, but who cared when, on the *Nine O'clock News*, the Sharon Tate bloodbath, American boy-soldiers missing in Indo-China, slaughter at anti-war demonstrations, terrorized Palestinian children and Ireland, bloody Ireland now horrified viewers about as much as a shoot-out in a spaghetti western.

And how did pop react to this ghastly awakening from the Swinging Sixties? I mean, like, war is wrong. People get killed, you know. Well, like the Dadaists in the aftermath of the Great War, there was nihilism all the way down from Alice Cooper to Big D. More self-conscious was Wings' naïve 'Give Ireland Back to the Irish'. And what about John and Yoko's slogan-ridden *Sometime in New York,* an entire double album which changed the world about as much as Barry McGuire's 'Eve of Destruction' had in 1965? Then there was the mawkish but bankable 'Ruby, Don't Take Your Love To Town' from Kenny Rogers – about a crippled war veteran's shocked return to domestic life. More credible was the Kinks' moving dirge 'Every Mother's Son', which protesters sang *en masse* outside the White House during the Vietnam moratorium.

Neither Winwood nor Capaldi could match Ray Davies but, running out of steam *circa* 1973, they gave James Taylor – to whom Steve was to grant a small part in *Back in the High Life* in 1987 – a run for his money. As its pigeon-holing intimated, the 'self-rock' ethos of Taylor and others was of being so bound up in yourself that every trivial occurrence or emotion seemed worth informing the whole world about in song. Melanie wrote one about tuning her guitar; Dave Crosby about *almost* cutting his thinning hair. Traffic – with the possible help of a rhyming dictionary – told us about being uninspired through feeling tired, hired and the room's been wired. Luckily, they pulled back from this abyss in time to go out, if not with a bang, then with the full honours of war.

This 'Uninspired' doggerel filled the best part of one side of two Traffic in concert albums – one a double – released over the group's final and most public journey. The proliferation of this type of output reflected the fact that, though there were still periods of hibernation, Winwood spent a greater amount of time on the road than he'd ever done with the Spencer Davis Group: 'I was supposed to be so successful but I was still sitting in a van and travelling somewhere. I'd always been doing that anyway so there's not much difference in it.'[6] In the end, just before the Brazilian leg of another world tour, he decided that enough was enough and that Traffic should be locked in the garage for all time.

It hadn't always been as bad as that. In the two years after their comeback in dim blue light at the Roundhouse in April 1970, Traffic had averaged only one engagement a month. The first post-draft US tour under the new regime began gently at the Fillmore East, followed by four stops over a fortnight in Texas,

154

Chicago, Detroit and Atlanta. There'd been time for the band and
manager to take in the three hundred miles of scenery between San
Antonio and Houston by car instead of flying as usual, as was
necessary for the home stretch of New York again, Toronto and,
lastly, the West Coast of fond memories.

With record sales – and quality – falling off, Traffic's investors'
anxiety about the group's commercial evolution urged a more
intense concentration on touring. There was even talk of procuring
another hit single to stay possible relegation to the middle league of
the adult-orientated rock hierarchy that had newly sprung up its
head – to three-thousand – rather than twenty-thousand-seaters.
When their first British 45 for six years, 'Walking in the Wind',
issued in October 1974, worked no such miracle, all that was left
was to go right on playing. The alternative was to quit while they
were ahead.

This may appear a silly metaphor but, if Blind Faith was a
technicolour trailer for a movie that never made it to the cinema,
then the next Traffic was, perhaps, a full-length monochrome
B-feature remake. Blind Faith's dramatis personae may have been
bigger box office, but this edition of Traffic – at first anyway – was
more in sympathy with Winwood's original musical concepts
when he left Spencer Davis.

Back from California and shot of Blind Faith, Winwood had had
his fill of being in a group, thank you. Recovering from America,
he wandered briefly into a wilderness of the ramshackle Airforce as
well as sporadic sessions for the Ian McDonald–Mike Giles duo –
lately parted from King Crimson – and, also in London, multi-
instrumentalist Leon Russell, whose perpetual onstage top hat and
star-studded album credits were indicative of his elevation to hip
omnipresence after years of anonymous studio work. Not on such a
vocational high then was Jimi Hendrix; his last authorized LP, *Cry
of Love,* also featured Winwood who, in spring 1970, had got down
at last to a project of his own – an album – since he owed two to his
US record company, United Artists.

Made under the working title *Mad Shadows*, and produced by the
late Guy Stevens, Steve 'had a lot of ideas about what I wanted to do
and I wanted to get them down but it was difficult. It seemed a bit
inhuman to make records by overdubbing which was what I was
trying to do. It seemed to remind me of a telephone directory – sort
of dialling the instrument I wanted next.'[7] Later in the decade he
would revise this view, but in 1970 he was not yet ready to function
beyond the context of a group. After one backing track, 'Stranger
to Himself', with misgivings and possibly a guilty conscience about

excluding his old friend from Blind Faith, Steve contacted Jim Capaldi.

After Wooden Frog Jim could have lived, like Leon Russell had, as a backroom hack. With Winwood, he'd had a hand in Joe Cocker sessions of 1968 – notably on an early take of 'With a Little Help from My Friends'. On the spur of the moment, he'd deputized in the Bonzo Dog Doo-Dah Band for 'Legs' Larry Smith who, at the first Isle of Wight Festival, had been 'off in a helicopter, getting out of his mind with Keith Moon'.[8] Appealing from the stage for someone to 'thrash the drums,' Bonzo Dog interlocutor Vivian Stanshall had been flattered when, from the backstage enclosure, Capaldi volunteered. As intrinsically English an artist as Frank Zappa was American, Stanshall regarded Traffic as 'the only English rock 'n' roll band'. He was also fascinated by the antics of world heavyweight champion Muhammed Ali, and during a backstage conversation with Jim, a more general boxing fan, there was an amicable exchange of telephone numbers.

The most bizarre of Capaldi's 1969 furloughs from Traffic was when *Time Out* reviewed the fictitious Heavy Jelly – the most underground of underground groups – in reply to the cloak-and-dagger 'We Are the Moles', a mysterious record that its manufacturers, Parlophone, neither confirmed nor denied was the Beatles in disguise. In fact it was a shifty manoeuvre by Simon Dupree and the Big Sound, trying to recapture their lost 'Kites' glory. With even less substance, Heavy Jelly was given vinyl life when – after a counter-satire in *Private Eye* as poet E. Jarvis-Thribb's fave raves, Heavy Sausage ('Time Out the long wait') – a Heavy Jelly single was released by a studio band which included two of Eric Burdon's New Animals and ex-Undertaker and Apple recording artist Jackie Lomax. An existing band signed to Island, Skip Bifferty, took advantage of the interest in assuming the name and even gaining a Swedish chart entry with it. When the publicity died, they reverted to their previous identity but, with members of Aynsley Dunbar's Retaliation, Jim Capaldi was commissioned to rehearse a new Heavy Jelly to hit the road. This idea, however, was aborted when Capaldi reunited with his old songwriting partner.

As well as taking Steve's writer's block by the horns, Jim was drawn more and more into the sessions themselves, from his one-line cowboy harmony on 'Stranger to Himself' to anchoring Winwood's instrumental pile-up on 'Every Mother's Son' – not the Kinks song – with his comfortably familiar drumming. With over two-thirds of *Mad Shadows* still to go, Winwood and Capaldi tired of the alarming, overworked Guy Stevens, who was also endeavouring to finish off a prior professional commitment to a Mott the Hoople LP.

Much debate concluded with Steve's jettison of both Stevens and the *Mad Shadows* title – that went to Mott the Hoople. Recoiling also from striking out alone, why not put it out as a Traffic album? Though Jim had flown the Atlantic last year to help out on some Dave Mason recordings, Steve wouldn't wear that particular Traffic. The old trio format – now that was something else. Chris seemed to be in much better shape these days, and his confidence had been much boosted when he had been voted third best in *Beat Instrumental*'s Brass and Woodwind section. Albeit one place above Ringo, Jim had only been twelfth best drummer. Chris was sounded out at the next Airforce show. Of course, he jumped at the chance.

The dithering over, the record was in the bag – most of it being aired at the Roundhouse concert to uplifting response. As *John Barleycorn Must Die* it swiftly rose by late summer to number eleven in Britain's album chart, also becoming a student bedsit essential. Considering the lay-off of over a year, this was good going.

The four-minute-plus track length precedent set by the last Traffic incarnation continued, but gone were the gimmicks: no more clockwork, backwards tapes or Shanghai noodles. Less pronounced lyrical and instrumental detail came forth only after repeated listening – canine welfare in 'Every Mother's Son'; a triangle in 'John Barleycorn'; Chris Wood's 'Freedom Rider' bongos. There is little discernible difference between the two Guy Stevens' efforts and the rest, other than the use of *legato* electric for Wood's absent horns. With Traffic down to three lanes, substantial overdubbing – mostly by Winwood – was still necessary to realize an orchestration of up to eight instruments.

The sparsest arrangement was reserved for the title track, which was Worth-the-Whole-Price-of-the-Album. Pulling a bold stroke, it pervaded too the buff graphics and commendable sense of historical perspective on the record jacket. What folksong archivist Cecil Sharp regarded as 'one of the most common, the most characteristic . . . the most beautiful of English folk airs'[9] was, fittingly, one of the last Traffic numbers to emerge from the cottage environment where the centrefold portrait was taken.

Twenty miles from Aston Tirrold as the crow flies is Bampton, where Sharp collected a version of 'John Barleycorn' from a Shepherd Haden.[9] Ostensibly concerning a harvesting ritual, 'John Barleycorn' was traced back further by A. L. Lloyd, another archivist, to the Egyptian Passion of the Corn. There are also analogies – as Chris Wood noted[10] – between 'John Barleycorn' and the Resurrection, although the concept of a Divine Victim was neither new nor confined to Christianity. The fertility rite in which a kingdom is saved by the sacrifice of its leader in his prime could be applied to certain Greek, Roman and Norse gods, King Arthur, Harold II, William Rufus and even Charles I – beheaded in his climacteric seven-times-seventh year. The more credulous might also apply this theory to John F. Kennedy and John Lennon, who were both assassinated in their early forties. The Victim's awareness of his role is irrelevant. The point is that the common people may have believed he died for them and their land. This was illustrated very well in *The Wicker Man*, a 1973 film starring Edward Woodward and Christopher Lee that Winwood may well have seen, in which a remote Scottish island reverts to pagan ways in the hope of fertile autumns. Primitive man did not think of himself as being separate from nature: I'm a part of it's a part of me. The fertility god, whether Nerthus (Mother Earth) or the Green Man, was the kernel of his belief – if Anglo-Saxon, his 'weird' – in which growth, death and rebirth were the eternal verities around which the Earth's seasons revolved and in which he was inescapably involved.

It is certain that there are mystical implications which go much deeper than the Home Service *Singing Together* adaptation that schoolboy Stephen heard in the fifties. A turntable fixture for a while at the cottage had been an acapella rendition by the Watersons, a family trio from Hull. Traffic exchanged their modal harmonies for plain acoustic instrumentation – guitar, unobtrusive percussion, flute interludes and one-finger piano for bass – and Winwood's understated vocal, supported by Capaldi, was further from Ray Charles than any 1965 Spencer Davis Group fan could have imagined. So far removed was it that Traffic's 'John Barleycorn' was thought 'purer' than that of more recognized folk performers Steeleye Span, who, ironically, had broadened their scope by adding a rock rhythm section. At a greater distance from the Watersons' blueprint was Turnpike's unsettling electric version.

Plunder of our national musical heritage at bedrock level has always been a common if intermittent ploy of British pop. One potent advantage was that items from time immemorial were public domain – which meant that the artist's publishers could cream off composing royalties. Such mercenary rewards, however, were often deserved. In 1963 there was an imaginative rocking-up of the Cornish Floral Dance by the Eagles from Bristol (nothing to do with Joe Walsh). The Liverpool children's play rhyme 'Johnny Todd' was most effectively transformed into the theme tune for BBC Television's police series *Z-cars*, while 'Danny Boy' – from the Gaelic ballad 'Acushla mine' – had long been a sentimental favourite of cabaret stars like Tom Jones and Matt Monro. However, even if they were not the originators, Traffic with their daring 'John Barleycorn' definitely instigated what could be considered as a trend. Recorded the previous year had been the Beatles' 'Maggie May', the Liverpool shanty, but in the wake of 'John Barleycorn Must Die' came such as the Nashville Teens' spooky 'Widecombe Fair' and versions of the traditional hymn 'Amazing Grace' by both Judy Collins and – a 1972 number one – the bagpipes of the Royal Scots Guards. There was also Alan Price's 'Trimdon Grange Explosion', written in 1882 as a 'whip round' song after a County Durham mining disaster.

Probably the most memorable post-Blind Faith Traffic recording, 'John Barleycorn' rather overshadowed its companion tracks, which veered mainly towards medium tempo interspersed with clever dynamic changes. There was much else to praise too. Not significantly 'poetic', the lyrics, if less direct than those of the 'Paper Sun' period, at least sidestepped much of the cornier pretension of later releases as well as the negative symbolism of 'Medicated Goo'. Even so, there persisted a tendency for Traffic metaphysics to approach the bombastic rhetorical flights of a bad actor – souls crying out from hell and all that. Sometimes it was a bit obscure – particularly in 'Freedom Rider' – but the freewheeling 'Every Mother's Son' as verse is far more pleasurable than 1971's twee international hit 'Me and You and a Dog Named Boo' by Lobo, which it seemed to have inspired.

As would always be the case with Winwood, the music was stronger than the words. The first half of the opening thirteen-minute suite, 'Glad'/'Freedom Rider', managed without any. An attractive *introit*, it made earlier Winwood instrumentals seem throwaway with its recurrent bouncy piano descent and sax flutters breaking into disciplined solos. This led to a protacted *diminuendo* dominated by sombre keyboards as the prelude to 'Freedom Rider' which, after a suspended riff bereft of drums, resolved also to A minor. Over the long flute solo, keyboards and drums got progressively more agitated towards the climax.

Issued as a US single, 'Empty Pages', with its plink–plonk ivories, crept to number 74 in the Hot Hundred, possibly because Steve's voice was here closest to the 'Gimme Some Lovin'' intonations of yore. It was also only fractionally longer than the shorter (4 minutes 2 seconds) but less commercial selection, 'Stranger to Himself', which none the less neatly intermingles acoustic and electric guitar in the mix. On the other Guy Stevens offering, 'Every Mother's Son', Winwood's organ, entering like a ringing telephone, was the only throwback to 1967 with its Rick Wright 'See Emily Play' tone colour and overall mood, but puzzling is the song's abrupt fade – reminiscent of a music hall hopeful getting pulled offstage.

No thoughts of Traffic getting the bird in this way occurred to anyone attending the trio's April dress rehearsal in an Island studio. Later, Steve was to admit,

> I most enjoyed the Traffic trio which was very creative. It was a fantastic thing to do. There were lots of heights reached – probably more in the way of 'live' performances than records . . . the group was mainly intended to improvise but also to sound rehearsed. We were able to go places within the music that we had never gone before. Improvised wanderings can sometimes get a bit too much but, within such a small group, we could improvise and go somewhere and also play with other people easily.'[11]

Eric Clapton, who drove up to see Traffic in Oxford, was one who was invited to sit in:

> I didn't think they were any better with me . . . but I felt they needed another instrument. . . . I was hoping that after the gig I would be asked. If I had been, I would have joined – just like that. I don't think Steve needs a guitarist. I'd been thinking that a guitarist would've made the group more versatile. In actual fact, it would have given it a more rigid structure. It would have meant that, being as I can only play guitar, he could have played organ and piano. Maybe we could have had two guitars but, you see, I'm a very unversatile musician because I can play one instrument and maybe dabble on bass so it wouldn't have actually been an improvement for me to have joined, whereas having a bass will because it gives Steve more opportunity to jump about.[12]

Eric hit the nail on the head. Though the three-piece was much more surefooted than in the final shirty, reproachful months of 1968, technical difficulties were unchanged. Steve was never to be over-enthusiastic about 'jumping about' but, though no Jagger before the footlights, he resented again being bound to keyboards, co-ordinating every limb – hands on keys, feet on the hated pedals –

like some one-man band, whilst struggling to put some emotion into his hard-bought songs. Not only did he miss strutting his stuff on guitar, but he also remembered from last time that numbers like 'Heaven Is in Your Mind' just couldn't be done without an extra pair of hands. Why had he thought things would be any different? Nevertheless there were still magic moments, and makeshift arrangements of the *John Barleycorn* music just about walked the line. For 'Freedom Rider', for instance, Wood's sax held the bass part with the aid of an octave divider until his solo, when Winwood took it up on organ. As usual, the Americans were the least inhibited in showing their appreciation when the three toured there later in the year. Every stop of the way there were standing ovations and even scattered screams until Traffic lurched back on for the fixed 'Dear Mr Fantasy' encore.

It often felt OK at the time for both band and audience, but you should hear it back on tape afterwards! An in-concert album, *Traffic Live '70*, was scheduled for November release. Though it was taped at San Francisco's Winterland on more sophisticated equipment than that used on the 'Last Exit' side, Steve's unease nipped it in the bud even as white-label promo copies were posted and advertisements placed. Its catalogue number went to Quintessence's *Dive Deep*.

The last straw was a Dutch mini-tour with a new organ in a dodgy condition after being dropped during unloading. Someone had suggested Steve Stills, who was still at large in London then. No, it had to be a bass player as with Blind Faith. Rick Grech! Why not? It'd be easier to get him out of Airforce than even Chris Wood. Ginger's band was washed up anyway.

With Grech's bass once more unburdening Winwood, Traffic decamped via Morocco for the sands of the Sahara, where director Antoine Coyas was tearing his hair out shooting what would never be a film called *Nevertheless*. They were there to score the soundtrack, but the movie's delays and ultimate scrapping found Traffic 'getting stoned and lying in the sun all day',[13] though Capaldi and actor Michael J. Pollard made desultory attempts to form a songwriting team. Steve's penchant for Moroccan decor from Christopher Gibbs' King's Road emporium dragged him away from the other layabouts to browse round the bazaars and haggle for finely woven rugs and curios straight from source.

Failing through no fault of their own to get it together in the desert, Traffic left the chaotic set to resume an interrupted European tour. In Sweden they ran into Wynder K. Frog's former hand-drummer, Rebop Kwaku-Baah who, after his brief stay with

Airforce, was – with Bob Marley – among those involved in the incidental music for a film starring soul-reggae crossover singer Johnny Nash. Rebop had been a frequent overnight guest at Chris and Jim's Cromwell Road flat in 1966. 'Rebop was one of those people who could fill a room with music,' reflected Vivian Stanshall, a later Traffic associate, 'bashing away on congas which he made sound like bongos as he'd hit the things so damned hard – yet he was the gentlest of men.' Already contemplating further augmentation in Traffic, 'we just adopted him'.[14] Next it was a toss-up between frustrated front man Capaldi's proposition of hiring another drummer, and Steve's more enterprising idea of a French horn player – possibly the gifted Al Kooper who'd blown one on Jimmy Miller's eye-stretching production of the Stones' 'You Can't Always Get What You Want' with the London Bach choir on *Beggar's Banquet*.

Pragmatism ruled and Jim had his way. He was dabbling now on occasional piano, extra percussion and vocals, and his emergence from behind the kit would lead to his becoming almost as cosmic a buffoon on the boards as Beach Boy show-off Mike Love. It began innocently enough – 'I add atmosphere,' he explained, 'I'm essentially a back-up man. If I was lead [singer], I'd just blow it but' – ominously – 'I'm working on it.'[15] Perhaps I'm being unfair because, although his up-front encroachment didn't appeal to me especially, it was Jim's springboard to modest acclaim in a solo capacity later on.

In Jim's stead came American sticksman Jim Gordon, who'd been in Delaney and Bonnie's outfit on the Blind Faith tour as well as on the Leon Russell sessions with Winwood – while a member of Eric Clapton's Derek and the Dominos. In common with Capaldi, he'd also worked on Dave Mason's *Alone Together* album. And, beyond belief, onstage with Traffic for a handful of dates was none other than old Dave himself. The combined eulogizing of the two Jims about what a great guy he was nowadays might have done the trick, though this may not have been what Steve had heard from Eric Clapton, in whose new group Mason had lasted precisely one engagement. 'He might play on a sort of casual basis but he wouldn't do it too seriously,' shrugged Winwood, 'we're all much more tolerant than we used to be.'[16]

After watching Blind Faith plummet, Dave had given notice to the Bramletts while borrowing their band to help out on 'Alone Together'. Laden with numbers that he'd tried originally with Wooden Frog, this LP was a US best-seller when released on Blue Thumb, to whom Chris Blackwell had sold Mason's contract.

Joining forces with portly Mama Cass Elliot, Dave was less successful with his second album despite – or because of – the pair's spot on Andy Williams' nationwide TV show. Behind the scenes Mason, as well as Jimi Hendrix, had assisted George Harrison on the *All Things Must Pass* triple album as had Eric Clapton. For his old champion Jimmy Miller, Dave had done his bit during the Stones' preliminaries for *Beggar's Banquet* which, learning from his experiences with Traffic, Miller had advised they conduct in the ambience of a Surrey village.

With Clapton and Gordon, Dave had also been present on albums by Carl Radle, Bobby Keyes or any one of those inter-changeable funky cats from Delaney and Bonnie. One such front centrefold cover had the opportunist whose name it bore sitting on a stool, head back, eyes screwed shut, holding a Jumbo acoustic six-string in mid-strum. You didn't need to hear the LP to know what it was like – maybe four flabby tracks a side, all 'laid-back' and incredibly boring. The self-written songs, delivered in a 'raunchy' dixie drawl and hip restricted code, might be about snorting cocaine, loving the one you're with and other overworked myths of the rock band lifestyle. All these guys were, needless to say, hung like horses.

More insecure than conceited because of their profession's peculiar exhilarations, miseries and unsocial hours, rock 'n' roll outlaws tended to stick together offstage as well as on – which is why pop, like theatre, achieved a reputation for being a cliquey, inward-looking closed shop. Every pop generation, even punk, has, by its very nature, thrown up a self-contained privileged caste, an In Crowd, but none was so insufferably smug as that of the early seventies, which traded licks round the good-time Bramletts, Nashville's Allman Brothers Band, the Los Angeles studio crowd and *All Things Must Pass*. Exchanging smirks across the console with ol' Leon, it was as if rock 'n' roll couldn't be done in any other way or with any other people than that self-absorbed, worthless elite whose only contact with real life out in Dullsville was through narcotics dealers, gofers, chauffeurs, managers and bodyguards. The rest of us, it seemed, didn't count.

Sometimes an inkling of some fad that the early seventies' Anglo-American 'superstars' had latched onto would leak to Joe Public through *Rolling Stone* or some other magazine. Overlooking exceptions like Keith Moon's nonsensical frenzies, there was nothing too outrageous or original. They'd lay down a groove with the Memphis Horns at Muscle Shoals or tour the States backed by Tom Scott and his LA Express. They'd be 'into' Jesus, heroin or

Buddy Holly B-sides. They'd dress down in a flurry of long print dresses, pre-faded Levis embroidered with butterfly or mushroom motifs, clogs, bell-bottomed loon pants, cloche hats, cowboy suits, coke-spoon earrings, grandad vests, air force greatcoats, buck-skins, T-shirts printed with a favoured band's logo, and stars-and-stripes singlets revealing underarm hair – predictably, so would all those who bought their records. Then they'd truck on down to the Whiskey on Sunset Strip to get into Stoneground, or hang out backstage at the Strand Lyceum on 14 June with George, Steve Stills, Ringo and other heavy friends, 'toking', swigging Southern Comfort, deciding who you were going to 'ball' later on, digging the vibes while Eric picked your brains for a name for his new band – who were due on an hour ago, but that was cool. Let 'em wait.

That was the 1970 day Dave Mason played his one and only booking with Derek and the Dominos – as the group was finally and facetiously called. The other Dominos were Gordon – who co-wrote the love-lorn 'Layla' – and two more from the Bramlett rank-and-file. 'My playing isn't as good as I want, nothing like Eric's of course,' admitted Dave, 'but being in the band will enable me to get it together again.' He saw possibilities 'for each of us to do our own things together. If we could do that, it would be beautiful but I want to retain my own identity, because that's very important to me.'[17] So important was it that when the outfit reappeared in public, Eric/Derek was looking for a replacement second guitarist though, bless him, he continued to include in the set and, indeed, recorded Mason's North American hit single 'Only You Know and I Know' from *Alone Together*.

In microcosm, Dave's brief sojourn in Derek and the Dominos had familiar flashes of his life with Traffic. Though by no means overawed by Eric, Dave had been excited at becoming his lieutenant, but 'I guess I got too pushy again. I wanted everybody to say "O.K., let's get it on and rehearse every day and do it." But Eric would be up in London doing George's album and nothing was really happening.'[18] It has to be said that Clapton wasn't the easiest person to rub along with since contracting his heroin dependency during rehearsals in May.

Back with the old firm not quite a year later, Dave was disappointed too by Traffic's 'real sloppy'[19] preparations to tour, even with the liberated Capaldi very much in charge, darting hither and thither on whipcord legs. Perhaps they pulled their socks up when Mason breezed in from California. Certainly this 1971 line-up's six shows were punchier than those of the trio. When the septet opened up at Croydon on 6 July, curbing much improvisory excursion, some numbers were actually rattled off in less time than the studio originals. It wasn't first night nerves either, because the same snappy precision pervaded the other bookings from the Great Hall at the University of Kent to a couple of hours for nothing at the Glastonbury Fayre knees-up – *the* hippie happening of 1971.

Containing no new material, the set was a cross-section of the main protagonists' recorded highlights, together and apart. Almost tearing the show from Winwood's grasp, Mason provided the latest sounds with extracts from *Alone Together*. 'Sad and Deep as You' was performed solo bar Wood's querulous flute obligato replacing the original's piano, and 'Shouldn't Have Took More Than You Gave' – Dave's most unwieldy title yet – left its mark via the composer's scorching cry-baby fretwork. Mason was also featured singer on 'Look at Me, Look at You', dating from Wooden Frog. By a hair's breadth, Steve – with his more voluminous backlog – prevented Dave from upstaging him, especially on the surprise encore. Lending itself comfortably to the band's strong percussive emphasis, a jittery, neo-military introductory backbeat was not recognizable until a swooping organ *glissando* brought it all back home with a rearrangement of 'Gimme Some Lovin''. To close each evening with this Spencer Davis smash transfixed the greatcoated audience in much the same way as Irish tenor John McCormack did in the thirties when, after a hushed recital of classical arias, he'd wind up with 'The Rose of Tralee', 'Mollie Malone' or like sentimental chestnut from the Auld Sod.

Its composing royalty giving Spencer's bank balance a welcome shot in the arm, this 'Gimme Some Lovin'' reprise as a US single scrambled to the middle of the Hot Hundred. The in-concert album from which it was taken, *Welcome to the Canteen*, taped at Croydon and the *Oz* Benefit Concert, did even better in its field, as well as settling Winwood's vinyl debt to United Artists. It was more a hi-fi souvenir than the sub-standard second side of *Last Exit*, and, to many *Canteen* customers, the most thrilling moments were on the playout of 'Dear Mr Fantasy', with the wild duelling guitars of Steve and Dave. But though some parties – notably Capaldi and Island – were optimistic about Dave's permanent reinstatement, 'there were too many conflicts between me and Steve for that ever to happen'.[19]

That Steve remained Chris Blackwell's blue-eyed boy was emphasized – possibly unconsciously – on the album's monochrome front cover, on which a smoking Winwood is, apparently, holding forth to the other six seated round a green room dining table. Mason, silent in sunglasses, is obscured by Jim

Gordon's Hendrix-haloed bulk. Moreover, the word 'Traffic' appears neither on the sleeve nor on the disc label, which both merely list the musicians' names – starting with Winwood's. Setting aside the cutting edge born of warring egos that character- ized this unrepeatable band's music, it was charitable to conclude that Dave Mason had only been in it for the laugh.

A few months later, he wailed harmonica for Capaldi as the sessions got under way for Jim's first solo LP. From their Hellion days came the title track, Al Jolson's 'Oh! How We Danced'. Most of the other tracks, too, had been accumulated over a long period, though some, like 'Trickie Dickie Rides Again' were blatantly topical. The stand-out, no question, was the fetching 'Evie' which, though not a hit, gathered enough airplay for the occasional new-born daughter to be launched into life with that name.

In London, Jim had been able to call upon the likes of Trevor Burton and ace guitarist Paul Kossoff from Free, as well as most of his Traffic cohorts. However, the album was completed in rural Alabama at trendy eight-track Muscle Shoals studios – 'very laid-back and relaxed,' said Leon Russell – where Chris Blackwell as casting-vote co-producer stumped up for the crack house rhythm section of drummer Roger Hawkins and David Hood on bass plus, when required, the keyboards of Barry Beckett. These had all been hired also by Arif Marden when producing Aretha Franklin. So efficient was this service that Blackwell and Capaldi wondered whether the three sessionmen could somehow be tempted into Traffic should vacancies arise.

Behind shop counters by March 1972, *Oh! How We Danced* scored in the States – far less so at home. In this respect, it basked in the afterglow of Traffic's *Low Spark of High-heeled Boys* – a title suggested by Michael J. Pollard – out in a hexagonal *trompe l'oeil* sleeve with jumbled track listing to grab buyers the previous Christmas. The biggest-selling of all Traffic's LPs, it almost touched a million units in North America while not charting at all in Britain. Like the Dave Clark Five before and Fleetwood Mac after them, they'd have been foolish not to have followed up this US success – especially when Jim Capaldi calculated that 'for one night in the States, I earned more than my old man did in all his working life'.[20]

It was unfortunate that this attitude chagrinned all but the most devoted of their British following who, no longer caring about Traffic as personalities, regarded their UK television and concert appearances as those of ghosts from the recent past who'd returned to haunt them after being spirited away to the New World by

Mammon. It was true that albums didn't dominate the market as much in Britain, but there'd been a swing back to the flashy glamour and cheap thrills of classic rock and the Big Beat after an age of parched wasteland. Inter-related with tacit weariness of heavy metallurgy, pomp-rock and cloying Melanie-esque songsters, this was most explicitly instanced by a kind of Melanie Depreciation Society in 1972 whose activities, according to *Melody Maker*, included loud disruptions of Miss Safka's London recitals. More gratifying to me was the discovery that a few girls at college genuinely preferred Shakin' Stevens to both the real and pretend James Taylor. They hadn't read *The Once and Future King*. Tolkien left them stone cold. Like me, they'd never read *Watership Down*, though they'd passed some of its stars sightlessly staring and bloody in butchers' windows. They'd never drawn flowers in felt-tipped pens on scuffed white plimsolls either.

Another factor was that while Mud Slide Steeeve's jeans, checked shirt and intense socks stage presence had the charisma of a sack of potatoes, the Top Thirty looked more hopeful as Marc Bolan, Slade, Alice Cooper and the Sweet – none of whom meant half as much in America – had paved the way by sheer tenacity for the greater sartorial excesses of Gary Glitter, the revived David Bowie and Roxy Music. With hip-hugging biker leathers and fair hair dyed black, also in the ascendant in the UK hit parade was former *Saturday Club* regular Shane Fenton – now exhumed as 'Alvin Stardust'. Down-home patched pastels were smart no more; making triumphant entrances were sequins, form-fitting lurex, shiny shiny leather, chains, gaudy leopardskin, kohl, stiletto heels, gold lamé and mascara-ed men dressed up as ladies.

In the broadest sense, undramatic Traffic embraced elements of all that was anathema to glam-rock, though Jim Capaldi felt 'we've kept going for so long because we've never really had an image – which has kept a lot of interest going for us. Maybe in England there is not so much whereas in America, there has always been a lot of mystique.'[18] With a certain mental athleticism, you could lump Traffic with the outmoded Deep Purples, ELPs and Melanies as some blinkered scribes did when sharpening their quills for *Low Spark of High-heeled Boys*. If they'd only been reviewing Richard Polak's back cover photograph, you could see their point. On first sight, Traffic were disadvantaged by Rebop's army fatigues and, especially, Wood's vacant, unshaven slovenliness – whatever did his mother think? Though garbed in a quasi-Teddy Boy drape, Winwood seemed the most slumberous of all six.

Theoretically he was executive producer, but 'I don't dictate. If I haven't written a song, I'm not going to dictate how it should be played.'[21] Perhaps he should have put his foot down, because it was the numbers that involved him least that were the major flaws of *Low Spark*. Both sung stridently if unastonishingly by the otherwise under-employed Capaldi, Grech and Gordon's 'Rock 'n' Roll Stew' and Jim's own 'Light Up or Leave Me Alone' were played slickly enough but contained not an interesting idea between them – though I must add the raw information that, issued on 45, 'Rock 'n' Roll Stew' with its sub-Deep Purple riff paid a fleeting visit to the US charts. Cast from the Bramlett solo mould, it covered the old ground of being on the road with the band, lovin' every doggone second of it, while the little woman minds the house. Presumably Jim's brutish grunts over the 'blistering bluesy axework' exorcised his thwarted eroticism in 'Light Up or Leave Me Alone' which, within its descending four-chord cycle, perverts an *ostinato* from Offenbach.

Capaldi had done his worst but it was no death touch. Despite those loutish aberrations, *Low Spark* – with *John Barleycorn Must Die* – could claim to be the most distinguished product of Traffic's second coming: one million fans couldn't be wrong. Instrumentally, the album belongs to Chris Wood, whose flute gambols through lush Arcadian woodlands, down lonely valleys and up to a white-boy-in-Birdland tour de force, free of trying to copy Roland Kirk and Les Spann. At the fade-in, he whipped out his sax, but his obbligatos and crescendos over the title track's twelve minutes convinced the layman that he was on a par with Frank Zappa's sensational woodwind protégé, Ian Underwood. In other respects too, this piece justified nearly all its occupation of half a side, because so smoothly executed is the convoluted arrangement that switches from ponderous bass *ostinato* peppered with finger-snapping to Steve's fast piano babble à la 'Riders on the Storm' – the Doors' hit, heard often on the radio the month *Low Spark* was recorded – flow quite naturally. Winwood's desolate contemplations invest the words, always a weak link now, with a vengeful if naïve reproach for their clichéd targets – men in suits ripping off artists but getting what was coming to them. Did record company heads still bother with suits in 1971? Chris Blackwell didn't. And were they all male? Anyway, the Pink Floyd were as bad with all their 'Have a Cigar' business – young record tycoons of the seventies were likely to smoke more exotic substances than Havana tobacco.

If composers Winwood and Capaldi were merely suspected of sacrificing nitpicking detail for scansion on the LP's title song, they

Wood, Winwood and Capaldi.
(*Stuart Booth*)

Love that necklace . . . Steve
contemplates a shave. (*Barrie Wentzel*)

Steve, Jim and Chris, November, 1968. (*S. K. R. Photographs*)

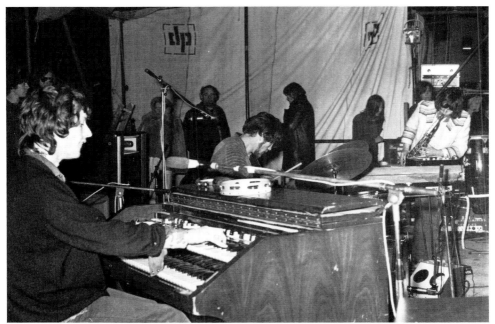

Right and below: Winwood, Rick Erech, Ginger Baker and Eric Clapton yuk it up at a Blind Faith photo call.

Below: Steve and Eric at Blind Faith's Hyde Park concert. *(Roger Barnes)*

Dave Mason (right) plays his one and only engagement with Derek and the Dominos led by blueswailing Eric Clapton (left), 14 June, 1970. *(Barrie Wentzel)*

Steve (left) and His Friends The Stars – (second left to right) Ron Wood, Rick Grech, Eric Clapton and Pete Townshend – at Clapton's Rainbow concert, 1973. *(Barrie Wentzel)*

One of the last of the few.
From rock's agit prop period.
(*Robert Ellis*)

Steve models his *Arc of a Diver*
haircut. (*The Picture Library*)

Winwood and mandolin, attuned. (*Janet Macoska/Retna*)

Onstage in New York in 1983, Sean and Julian Lennon let Winwood show them how it's done. *(London Features International)*

Spencer Davis (left) with Alan Clayson, April, 1988. *(Paul Tucker)*

Back in the high life: Steve with Gina Crafton at the British premiere of the film *Hearts of Fire*. *(Syndication International)*

Winwood with one of the two grammys he won for 'Higher Love', February, 1987.
(London Features International)

could be accused outright on 'Many a Mile to Freedom', where verses concerning bluebirds singing from the heart of a wishing well made pretty listening but verged not so much on the abstract as the meaningless. So did 'Wooly Bully', but Sam the Sham never believed it was much else. None the less, Winwood's singing and sweet melody to a jangling electric guitar give the libretto an undeserved 'beautiful sadness'.

On the next album, Steve would rely on scat-singing and repetition to hide textual shortcomings, but on the *Low Spark* opener, 'Hidden Treasure', these devices are integral to the song, which has a soothing intimacy akin more to Japanese koto music than to Indian raga. All acoustic bar Rick's bass, the accompaniment is dominated by guitar and flute embroidering a meditation on the wonders of nature beneath inland waterways that suggested, not obviously, that someone had read the relevant pages in George Orwell's *Coming Up for Air*.

An inversion of this hydrological study is 'Rainmaker', drawn possibly from Steve's tourist perspective of primitive culture and definitely the Steeleye Span end of the folk-rock spectrum. In its stark essence, it is a Winwood-Capaldi original in the 'John Barleycorn' genre, but here arcane practices are implied more in musical than in lyrical textures, its lengthy and discomfiting coda closing the album.

Who played what had not been specified on the cover because, throughout the sessions in London, there had been frequent absences with or without leave. Cutting corners, those present often found themselves with headphones on, playing an unfamiliar instrument. Jim Gordon, reputedly, took a guitar solo, though 'Light Up or Leave Me Alone', used, on different takes, drummers Gerry Conway from Fotheringay and Mike Kellie, who had assisted on Capaldi's solo LP. However, on his return Gordon insisted that it be redone to accommodate him. All this to-ing and fro-ing was symptomatic of grave, drug-related internal problems which, during *Low Spark*'s promotional American trek in December, led to the cashiering of Grech and Gordon, in whose places stepped the fellows from Muscle Shoals. No matter what Hood and Hawkins got up to elsewhere, they were at least punctual and tidy on the boards.

Whilst with the Spencer Davis Group, a spotty teenager had spoken of leading 'an eight- to ten-piece band in a few years time – get myself a vocalist like Herbie Goins or Ronnie Jones'.[22] Not much like either of these gentlemen, Capaldi had imposed himself as Steve's second-string singer and was yet unwilling to take a back seat again behind the drum kit. Never mind, the new Alabama boys had been worth the money and, hopefully, they'd be retained for the impending world tour – even if it was postponed.

Steve, you see, had felt rather off-colour in the States. Had it been, say, Rebop going under, somehow the show would have gone on. But without linchpin Winwood, Traffic devotees might get upset at being short-changed. No fewer than four doctors attended the unhappy young pop star, who was now complaining of abdominal pains. The English one reckoned it was bronchitis. One of the Americans thought it was something he'd eaten. The final diagnosis was peritonitis, which required an operation. Putting the group on ice, Steve was under the scalpel by February. Taking four depressing months to recuperate, he'd decided that, unless Blackwell signed up the Muscle Shoals team on a fixed contract, Traffic was finished as far as he was concerned.

While Winwood thus wrestled with vocational variables, ambitious Capaldi became involved, so he said, in a feature film with personable West Indian actress Esther Anderson and Lee Jaffe, a New York artist he'd met during that calamitous winter tour. However, on location in the Caribbean the movie was forgotten when Jim, Lee and Esther, with Esther's boyfriend, Bob Marley, plus Chris Blackwell and his Jamaican friend and sometime employee, Richard Jobson, indulged themselves in a leisurely island-hop to a carnival in Trinidad in a DC3 – the aeroplane usually chartered for Traffic's crew and equipment transportation. As all the seats had been removed for this purpose, the party sprawled on cushions spread over the deck. Growing tired of play, Capaldi returned to Jamaica to record at Blackwell's Strawberry Hill studio – the result appearing on a reggae sampler under the pseudonym 'Zap Pow'.

As the sales areas of Island's new signings in the very late sixties had testified, it was as cool for hip white sixth-formers and freshmen to own *In the Court of the Crimson King* or Fairport Convention's *Liege and Lief* as for their elder siblings to have had *Autumn '66* or *Dear Mr Fantasy*. However, a rather snooty attitude had persisted towards more ethnic Island product – especially ska, bluebeat and further shades of West Indian sounds which would amalgamate into the primeval atom of reggae. Though Desmond Dekker, Prince Buster and similar upmarket practitioners had enjoyed isolated hits, and a few Caucasian pastiches were attempted – like 'Ob-la-di Ob-la-da' by the Beatles and Marmalade, and 'To Ransaan' by Island's own Blodwyn Pig – reggae had been despised by most of the so-called intelligentsia as 'skinhead music'.

Perhaps to inspire confidence in its new 'progressive' customers, hard-nosed Island had issued few Jamaican records over the four years from 1966. Wishing to withdraw still further from its black origins, Island merged with Trinidad-based Trojan, which facilitated the channelling of remunerative reggae – such as the *Club Ska '67* compilation – from credibility-damaging association with the new rock money-spinners on the main label. Via the auspices of Bob Marley, Sly and the Revolutionaries *et al*, reggae in the seventies would outflank even blues as the new 'twisted voice of the underdog' and student disco accessory. Mentioned as long ago as 1966 by Spencer Davis in his *Midland Beat* column, Montego Bay ska exponent Jimmy Cliff – after a significant transfer from Trojan to Island – had been a catalyst in this with his 1970 UK smash 'Wild World', written by 'progressive' singing songwriter Cat Stevens, whose jerky 'Can't Keep It In' hit in 1972 was, in possible reciprocation, his idea of reggae.

Starring Jimmy Cliff as a West Indian gunman, the film *The Harder They Come*, underwritten by Blackwell, was on general release that same year. That this violent film and its soundtrack album were patronized by white college students demonstrated the distance Blackwell had travelled since *Lance Haywood at the Half-Moon*. No longer was Jamaican culture an alien commodity to the general pop market. Furthermore, Blackwell could now take the gamble of moving to the Bahamas to set up a lavish new studio at Compass Point near Nassau.

Capaldi preferred the more downbeat ambience of Strawberry Hill and, on arrival back in England, sought to persuade Winwood to cut the next Traffic LP there. Winwood had more or less recovered but, never robust at the best of times, he now appeared even frailer. However, he'd cheered up considerably and favoured Capaldi's scheme, because 'Jamaican music is itself particularly English and African for obvious historical reasons and that's what attracted me to it.'[23] Besides, it would be pleasant to escape the wet English winter for tropical sun. Furthermore, Hood, Hawkins and Beckett had been retained, which removed barriers to the reconstitution of Traffic.

As it was more expedient for Steve to overdub all the keyboard parts himself, Beckett – though present at Strawberry Hill – was neither heard on the album nor pictured on its sleeve. In the shops by spring 1973, *Shoot Out at the Fantasy Factory* – a title attributed to actor Ben Carruthers, another Capaldi social conquest – was packaged in a six-sided illusory sleeve to stress affinity to its more illustrious predecessor. Thanks partly to the Alabama contingent was the record's no-frills precision but, for that very reason, *Shoot Out* lacked guts. The second half of its 'Tragic Magic' instrumental with its tracked horns, for example, is like a hip musak ensemble sight-reading for its coffee break. It was as if the hand-picked craftsmen in the Kingston studio could not accomplish what the Traffic of Aston Tirrold – for all their casually strewn mistakes – committed to tape instinctively and without complacency. The cottage's three veterans on *Shoot Out* weren't in good form, either. Steve, poor lad, had been ill and it showed in his strained, almost listless singing. On 'Tragic Magic', Wood's only opportunity to shine this time round, he merely honked an inane saxophone. 'Tragic Magic' was his only published solo composition, too. It was a pity he never got the chance to write any more.

After *Low Spark* there were to be no more new Capaldi lead vocals in Traffic, though he continued to churn out his lyrics for them. Most, so it seemed, were completed with the nonchalant ease of an Ernie Wise play or Yoko Ono concept. The very inclusion of Wood's instrumental must attest to the dryness of that particular well. Perhaps to cover up the lyrics was the voice distortion and rapid-fire delivery on 'Shoot Out' itself, and the wordless sung prelude and thrice-repeated verses on the long melody of 'Roll Right Stones'. The latter refers to the neolithic circle about one mile off the A34, not far north-west of the farm that Steve had just bought. The idea is that, in this space age world, we'll never know what it was like long ago. Whatever tomorrow may bring, we'll still have those seventy-six Rollright stones.

There was surely more to write about the place than Winwood and Capaldi's passive evocation of these banal platitudes. One persistent legend that springs to mind is that, but for the timely manifestation of a witch, the Rollright Stones would have become animate and conquered England. Maybe that was what chilled Winwood to the bone – or else it was the knowledge that, long ago, if you had peritonitis you were a goner.

On *Shoot Out*, the words could not be rescued by the music. Even with a chord structure recalling Frank Zappa's 'Mr Green Genes', 'Evening Blue' still sounds like Mills and Boon – and then there's 'Sometimes I Feel So Uninspired', in which unchanged to the pressing plant went one odd line about not worrying because there's no reason for *not* failing. Unlike that of the quicksilver *Low Spark*, the scoring of *Shoot Out* leaned more on long-winded soloing over sorcerer's apprentice jazz-rock riffing, often with clattering percussion for good measure.

Once more, there was nothing else for it but to take the new album on the road – and this one would take seven months to circumnavigate the globe. With Barry Beckett at the organ, Steve could concentrate on guitar, piano and, of course, singing: 'it allows me a lot more freedom and I can move about the stage a bit.'[21] Technically speaking too, he had no complaints: 'in some ways, that was the best band because there was never really a bad night. If it was bad, it was still f***ing good. The Muscle Shoals lot wanted to work with us and I definitely wanted to work with them. I think at first they tried to emulate the sounds we had made before but we had to say "no, no, we don't want those at all." '[21]

Prior to setting off on the tour, there was something special that three of Traffic's British residents had to do. In the throes of preparing *Quadrophenia*, his next rock opera, Pete Townshend had been approached by Robert Stigwood and Lord Harlech – respectively, Eric Clapton's manager and his girlfriend's anxious father – 'to see whether I would help Eric put a band together for a concert which was for one of Harlech's charities, and I agreed to do that. To be quite honest, the only problem I saw was that Eric had been out of the scene for a long time.'[24] Rarely seen outside his country retreat, let alone by the villagers of nearby Ewhurst, for nigh on two years, Clapton had been out of more than just the pop scene. Heroin had now condemned him – and Harlech's daughter – to a self-imposed house arrest during which the lethargic hours between fixes were passed asleep or in front of the television, nourished by fast food. When able to tear himself from the News in Welsh or the Epilogue, Eric might strum his guitar a bit before slipping back to monosodium glutamate and optical chewing gum. Since he'd ditched the Dominos – with Duane Allman – halfway into the second album, he'd made no long-term plans. How could he?

Succumbing to Pete's persuasion, however, he resolved to haul himself from his pit, albeit temporarily, for a so-called 'comeback' concert at the Rainbow Theatre – formerly the Finsbury Park Astoria – for two shows on Saturday, 13 January, supported by the Average White Band. An 'instant supergroup' would accompany him, howled the press as all tickets sold out within a morning. Townshend's first telephone call had been to one whose presence would probably be most positive in the reinforcement of Eric's fractured confidence. Winwood and Townshend had appeared at the Rainbow together only the previous month, in Lou Reizner's stage production of Pete's done-to-death *Tommy*, along with other stars such as Peter Sellers and Rod Stewart plus the London Symphony Orchestra. During the opera's rehearsals, Townshend had concluded that 'Steve does have to be bullied'[24] before committing himself fully to a new enterprise.

Over the wire, Steve said he'd be pleased to play keyboards. Like the Who guitarist, he'd maintained contact with poor old Eric during his seclusion, respecting his artistic integrity and recalling his many kindnesses such as the gift of a vintage black 1956 Stratocaster purchased in Nashville in 1970. The following year, with Bill Wyman and Charlie Watts, Winwood and Clapton had even recorded together again on *London Sessions*, an album produced by Glyn Johns for blues sexagenarian Howlin' Wolf. Since the 'blues boom' of 1968, many major black bluesmen in the evening of their lives had aimed more directly at the rock market by reprising their music on vinyl with eminent white musicians whom they had influenced rather than merely employing them for stage work as John Lee Hooker had the Spencer Davis Group in 1963. Though Wolf had been disappointed with the American band used on his first venture in this vein, the respectful humour and sympathetic playing of Johns' London boys had been more than satisfactory as Howlin' Wolf growled 'Little Red Rooster', 'Sitting on Top of the World' and other classics that his white admirers had popularized.

Quite a few blues standards had been shortlisted by Pete and Eric for the Rainbow concert. Well acquainted with these and the more contemporary items proposed, Winwood was initially rather lackadaisical: 'yeah, that was really nice to do. There was a lot of unnecessary rehearsal going on beforehand – well, not unnecessary, but I knew most of the tunes. . . . I said I'd go to the rehearsal on the first day.'[21] However, for his non-appearance at the next one, a cursing Townshend bawled out the Traffic leader. At the other end of the line was a stunned silence after which Steve ate humble pie and promised not to let the side down again.

With Clapton, Townshend and the contrite Winwood were Los Angeles session drummer Jim Keltner and, on bass, Ron Wood of Rod Stewart's Faces. In Wood's eight-track studio extension at The Wick, his Richmond Hill home, rehearsals often continued all night, while the drugs flowed freely. Recalled to California, Keltner was supplanted by Jimmy Karstien, borrowed from the band of J. J. Cale, an ex-Bramlett guitarist whose 'After Midnight' had been a US hit for Clapton.

Less than a week before the reckoning, the hospitable Wood reverted to his natural role as a guitarist when Rick Grech volunteered his services. For all the rights and wrongs of Traffic's last US tour, relations between Steve and Rick had been cordial enough for both to have played together on a Muddy Waters album that had won a Grammy award as the Best Ethnic/Traditional Recording of 1972. Furthermore, Grech had so mended his ways that, at five o'clock on the dot, only he had been punctual at the Rainbow group's Wednesday dress rehearsal at Guildford Civic Hall. When things shifted into gear three hours late, it was noticed that Jim Capaldi's drums were standing next to Karstien's but – perhaps worried that the less heavy-handed American might show him up – instead of settling behind them, their owner traipsed about like a lost sheep, striking a desultory cowbell or tambourine and singing along with Clapton if passing an unused microphone. However, when Karstien proved unable to get to grips with 'Pearly Queen', Jim found the composure to stick to his kit.

At Friday's soundcheck, like chartbursting Gary Glitter's Glitter Band, the band now had two drummers, though when 'the Palpitations', as they'd been dubbed by Rick Grech, trooped on, this percussion artillery had been supplemented further by the ubiquitous Rebop with his timbales and congas. Despite cohorts then and now having the majority, only the inevitable encore, 'Pearly Queen', came from the Traffic catalogue – even if Steve also sang 'Nobody Loves You if You're Down and Out' from *Autumn '66*. He was to the fore elsewhere too, duetting with Eric on 'Roll It Over' from Derek and the Dominos and, with his piano, bridging Cream's 'Badge' and 'Blues Power'. Yet, if his energetic keyboards on the latter cut Leon Russell's performance on Clapton's first solo LP to bits, Winwood throughout 'instilled his own personality without upstaging the star', according to one observer, John Pidgeon. In the front row was the usual showbusiness faction which included 'Badge' co-writer George Harrison, who 'thought it was a bit raggedy . . . and what was going on behind the amplifiers between each number was a bit strange'.[24] More forthright was Glyn Johns, who'd been responsible for taping the show for rush-release on Atlantic. So disconcerted was he at the Palpitations' wall of sound that he surrendered the mixing of it to a road manager.

The fans loved it. Eric, who'd been so tardy that the others almost went on without him, had been touched by the Rainbow ovations but was not yet ready to fight his addiction. Within days he was slumped once more before afternoon television. The overblown event and its star's rapid relapse was the climax of all the condescending supergroup arrogance streamlined by Blind Faith and, largely through Clapton's infiltration into Delaney and Bonnie's Friends, carried like an Olympic torch into the next decade.

Seeing the transparency of it made many scour junk shops, deletion racks, charity stalls and jumble sales for overlooked artefacts from earlier musical eras – anything to hold the ghastly *Eric Clapton's Rainbow Concert* present at arm's length. One of the few vintage record shops in existence before the advent of 1979's *Record Collector* magazine, pop memorabilia auctions at Sotheby's and matrix number bores was Let It Rock in Chelsea's World's End. Its proprietor was a chap called Malcolm McLaren. With the Sex Pistols less than a twinkle in his eye, more overt precedents for the future were being forged not only in the glam-rock hard-sell on *Top of the Pops* and in the rock 'n' roll revival, but in many London pubs with music licences. In time, certain individuals would be swept from the nicotine clouds of the Nashville or Hope and Anchor into the Top Forty – though, by definition, 'pub rock' precluded stardom. Even in its slowest moment, British Beat was preparing once again to bare its teeth to the world.

With a few bites still to go, Traffic embarked on the eagerly awaited world tour. If the writing was on the wall in Great Britain, the biggest sales territories – the Americas and Germany – still appreciated good 'progressive music' and, as Traffic would be visiting many areas for the first – and only – time, much of the aura of a fresh sensation could be engineered. With over half their number on salary as company employees, Traffic had mutated into more a commercial merger than a bunch of Midlands hippies playing together for the hell of it.

Though in theory he had the most far-reaching power of veto in the organization, there was still much of the flower child left in Steve. While necessarily drawn into the complexities of Traffic finance, he maintained a liberal front on the illegal practice of bootlegging. Defying every known copyright law, these recordings had been common in jazz circles for years but came into prominence in 1969 when an illicit Bob Dylan double album, *Great White Wonder*, sold in sufficient quantities to qualify for a gold disc. The floodgates then opened for hundreds more releases of this type, culled from studio out-takes, concerts and other recordings not meant for public ears, by the cream of the pop world. Under-the-counter Traffic LPs tended to be of questionable clarity through being taped on domestic equipment from the audience – though some compared favourably to legitimate Island releases. As Winwood told a Dutchman who confessed his part in such an enterprise, it was OK by him as long as Traffic had done a show worth hearing again.

Bootlegs of the 1973 world tour contained mainly lengthier

extemporizations of the five *Shoot Out* tracks – though some old favourites from as far back as 1967 were thrown in too. It was understandable why so few of these older artefacts were included. Who wants to look forward to the past? The problem was that the latest material – 'Uninspired' *et al* – was not strong enough to merit such domination of the set. Even so, four weeks after the world tour terminated at the Rainbow in September, Island – battling the bootleggers – issued *On the Road*, a double LP recorded on the Rolling Stones Mobile and edited from the homeward leg in Germany. 'Roll Right Stones' had gone on too long – just blowing, blowing, blowing – to fit in comfortably, but you could still fork out for Traffic's onstage stabs at three of its four companion tracks. It was mixed by Muscle Shoals guitarist James Johnson, and the presence of the footlights certainly lent drive and ferocity, especially in Winwood's dexterous guitar soloing in 'Uninspired', while even 'Tragic Magic' sounds less like an amphetamined Northern Dance Orchestra.

For the most part, *On the Road* was an instrumental album – and it was the sound of Traffic at any given moment that mattered more than individual numbers. Not everyone was ready to accept this. Once, when listening to it in company, I was interrupted at intervals by somebody whose knowledge of Winwood began and ended with the Spencer Davis Group. 'When's he going to start singing?' she kept whining, succinctly summing up *On the Road*. When he did get going, he was in good voice – edgy and without the irritating embellishments that some vocalists, like Capaldi, are prone to before an audience. Less idiosyncratic was Steve's self-defeating fretboard offerings which, however skilfully fingered, invariably wah-wahed a no man's land between Frank Zappa and that stifled 'Shaft' chukka-wukka, omnipresent in the early seventies. Underpinned by Barry Beckett's endearingly dinky organ, Steve's unflagging invention on piano – which frequently escaped into atonality – compensated for this, though more unpredictable was Chris Wood's somersaulting sax, particularly towards the ascending *glissando* that linked 'Glad' to the group's swift disposal of 'Freedom Rider' which was Wood's only flute excursion.

'Light Up or Leave Me Alone' was Capaldi's excuse to introduce the boys in the band, from Winwood down to the expendable Rebop, who'd been the most obvious butt for heckling. He'd been impelled to drown his sorrows one night when a cry of 'Can the gentleman from Africa stop playing please?' sparked off a snigger from the crowd. To beef up Hawkins' tasteful tapping, Capaldi would cease his more flamboyant ministrations to more effectively double up on conventional drum kit. Early in the tour he'd been a bit rusty, but the defiantly economic bass of David Hood had steered him out of danger.

Whether crouched behind the piano or centre stage with guitar, Steve Winwood held the Traffic whip, conducting with nods and eye contact. There was no more of that 'avoiding being front man of a backing group' nonsense any more, as evidenced by his *On the Road* centrefold portrait looming behind a smattering of smaller photos snapped mainly in the luxury coach chartered for the band.

Concentrating on the possible, the group filled comparatively small auditoriums such as Hamburg's Musikhalle and the kitsch Capitol Theatre in Philadelphia's Port Chester. Local acts usually supported, but in Europe throughout March and April, Traffic was joined by one of Winwood and Capaldi's favourite bands, Spooky Tooth, who were a fusion of the VIPs and singing organist Gary Wright, an ex-child actor from New Jersey, whom Chris Blackwell had spotted in an outfit low on the bill at the very first Traffic engagement in Sweden. Wright was persuaded to form Art with former VIPs Mike Kellie and ex-Hellion Luther Grosvenor; pianist Mike Harrison being joint lead vocalist, and they became Spooky Tooth after appearing on Traffic's catastrophic Astoria show in October 1967. Though to his mind they 'were never as good as the VIPs,'[25] Blackwell saw them through lean times when their mediocre record sales were always out of proportion to their talent. After all, there but for Winwood went Traffic. In 1970, Spooky Tooth disbanded, to regroup in 1973 after Wright and Harrison's disillusionment with other ventures such as Harrison's solo LP at groovy Muscle Shoals. In West Germany with Traffic they played John D. Loudermilk's 'Tobacco Road', which had been in the repertoire of the VIPs and the Nashville Teens when both had played the Star-Club in 1964 with the Spencer Davis Group and the Hellions.

Old times were sometimes forgotten when Spooky Tooth and Traffic tried to socialize after engagements. Tired and hungry, they'd find that, instead of reserving tables in a quiet restaurant, the promoters had laid on a loud disco with flashing lights and junk champagne so that exorbitant admission charges could be levied on autograph hunters and groupies keen to meet the stars. Mixing metaphors, a road manager remarked of such impositions and the general running of the tour: 'It's been like a mediaeval carnival: Hannibal and his bloody elephants.'[26]

Up the other end of the hierarchical scale, Winwood had hoped to detach himself from the hedonism and the squalor of the road to compose items usable for, at long last, a solo album, 'but it was so hard that in the end I gave up'.[26] With less at stake, Capaldi was all set to cut his *second* LP at – you guessed it – Muscle Shoals. It was titled *Whale Meat Again*, and it promotional single, 'It's All Up to You', actually climbed to the middle of the British Top Fifty in 1974.

By that time, Traffic were working as an all-British four-piece. With Hood, Beckett and Hawkins in demand back in Alabama, there'd been the inconvenience of geography and expense. As supplicants for their services, Traffic had been at a disadvantage, as Winwood understood, by the inherent transience of pop: 'if you have a band, you can't just say "well, O.K., we've done that, that and that – now we're going to do something else" – because if that "something else" isn't as financially productive, then the band suffers and the pressure starts'.[26] Deeper than this, perhaps, was the suspicion that, despite healthy chart placings abroad, the Traffic big band with its extended jamming had become as remote (yet predictable) as what the now more radical *New Musical Express* lampooned as 'dinosaur bands' – over-the-hill acid freaks like the Grateful Dead, or wholesome and Americanized like Fleetwood Mac who were now far removed from the tougher blues quartet they once were.

Occasionally, Steve would accompany his Island talent scout brother on his London rounds, during which up to ten bands would be checked out in one evening. During these excursions he was able to see for himself how the 'street level' acclaim given to pub rockers such as Kilburn and the High Roads, Duke Duke and the Dukes and the formidable Dr Feelgood, as well as Teddy Boy revivalists like Crazy Cavan and Shakin' Stevens, was a reaction against the distancing of the humble pop group from its essentially teenage audience. Festering beneath this, the Sex Pistols' exploratory rehearsals in 1974 hinged on forgotten sixties' classics from Dave Berry, the Small Faces and Love Affair, as well as more contemporary material of the Stooges-New York Dolls trash-rock persuasion. Accompanied by growing coverage of these trends in *Zigzag* and lesser journals, plus the snowballing of specialist 'fanzines', these haphazard cells of archivist-performers continued to grow in impetus and, to a certain extent, become more cohesive.

Winwood had more sense than to brutalize Traffic, as Ian Anderson was to do to Jethro Tull in 1976's 'Too Old to Rock and Roll, Too Young to Die'. Nevertheless, there was a conscious attempt to regain lost ground at home where encouragement and

179

praise for Traffic had long faded. Axed were not only fifteen-minute instrumental interludes between verses but also most of last year's model's thirty-five-person entourage and such auxiliary bric-à-brac as Rebop's tom-tomming. No more stalking the stage rattling a tambourine, Capaldi – possibly to secret relief all round – had been induced back to his kit permanently. Melodic undercurrent to Jim's rhythms now came courtesy of bass guitarist Rosco Gee, formerly of Gonzales, a band built from top sessionmen like pedal steel guitarist Gordon Huntley and saxophonist Chris Mercer, who'd previously worked with John Mayall and Wynder K. Frog. Gonzales vocalist Carl Douglas had zipped in sharpish during a craze for martial arts with his smash hit of summer 1974, 'Kung Fu Fighting'.

Electing to break in the new band on the road before getting down to another album, Traffic conformed to many Muff Winwood's comments in a press release: 'there is a resurgence of the old Traffic spirit and they are more professional now. Jim going back to drums has made all the difference and Steve has that happy attitude he used to have in the early days of the Spencer Davis Group and Traffic – and he's working non-stop.' This last incarnation of Traffic's renewed omnipresence in Britain was marked by an energetic Rainbow show and, over the bank holiday, a plum job following Georgie Fame at the Reading Festival on an evening stage in imposing floodlights.

Two numbers taped during the British tour – one of them 'Vulcan', another Wood instrumental – were originally meant for inclusion on the next LP, *When the Eagle Flies*, but, when shipped in September, this contained only studio recordings. There were six by Winwood and Capaldi plus 'Dream Gerrard', an epic with lyrics by the remarkable Vivian Stanshall who, since Jim's gracious intervention in the Bonzo Dog Isle of Wight crisis in 1969, had become a popular and – when in the mood – hilarious confidant within the Traffic fraternity: 'the people who surrounded Traffic had an emotional commonality and it was easy to be with them whether fustian intellectual or Rebop coming from Nigeria. We just got on. Trust had a lot to do with it.'

The making of Stanshall's first post-Bonzo Dog LP, *Men Opening Umbrellas Ahead,* was the subject of a 1974 BBC Television documentary. The album drew much of its supporting cast from the Traffic circle – Rebop, Rick Grech on violin, Zoot Money and Doris Troy – who also sang on a Spencer Davis album called 'Catch You on the Rebop' around this time. Stuck for a bass guitarist one day, Vivian – urged by Capaldi – asked Steve Winwood. Of the

obliging Steve's contributions to the record, Stanshall commented:
'he was great every time. If you use someone of that calibre, you
don't presume to say to them "I think you should've suspended the
ninth" as with the old band. I'd talk about the emotion – "this is
someone crying;" "this is someone who discovered his father
wasn't such a bad bloke after thirty years." '[12]

Falling in with this approach and charmed by Viv's witty
personality, Steve was to collaborate with Stanshall on various
other projects over the next few years. Their mutual admiration
and friendship appeared superficially to be a collision of opposites.
Vivian was an East Ender, the son of a chartered accountant who
'equated artists with gypsies and ne'er-do-wells', and his adolescent
aspirations to enter art school were not encouraged. Through his
own persistence, none the less, he gained a scholarship at the Royal
College of Art in Kensington. There, as well as learning painting
and illustrating techniques, he grasped that 'clever people could also
have Geordie and Mancunian accents' – Brum ones too. From here
and other central London seats of learning was pieced together the
Bonzo Dog Doo-Dah Band, for whom Stanshall began writing
songs – many with Neil Innes, another founder member. The
group's eventual modicum of chart success, however, was secondary to its devastating stage act, which earned a weekly turn on
ITV's *Do Not Adjust Your Set.*

Though the Bonzo Dog Band's *raison d'être* was usually centred
on musical comedy, they weren't like Freddie and the Dreamers.
Also, on first glance at most Bonzo publicity photographs, the first
face you're drawn to is Vivian's. Though his main instrument was
the euphonium, he composed on ukelele, guitar and accordion –
albeit master of none. In *Magical Mystery Tour*, quite negating his
yellow Custer tresses, moustache and octagonal specs, he proved a
marvellous Elvis Presley impersonator – purposely less so six years
later with his portrayal of a rock 'n' roll has-been in the feature film
That'll Be the Day. However, from his earliest youth, Vivian's 78
r.p.m. record collection reflected a love for the verbal gymnastics
and humour – rather than 'humor' – of the English language.
Random examples included 'The Lion and Albert,' 'The Laughing
Policeman', Stanley Unwin and, by Billy Hill and his Boys, 'The
Farmyard Symphony' coupled with 'The Village Jazz Band'. More
unconsciously amusing were later items on 45 such as pundit
Godfrey Winn's sanctimonious monologue 'I Pass', which was
among record rarities aired by Viv when guesting on a Radio Four
chat show.

Partly from this melting pot of influences came 'Big Shot',

'Canyons of Your Mind', 'My Pink Half of the Drainpipe' and further Stanshall donations to the Bonzo Dog vinyl output. By no means snorting at their musical fabric, the lyrics to these numbers could have led as separate a life from chords and melody as Vivian's evocative Bonzo Dog sleeve notes: 'I'm very careful with every word – mosaic work almost. For me, it has to be as correct as I can make it and I can justify everything. I weep blood when I write lyrics. Those are quite a lot of people I wouldn't write them for' – adding with a chuckle – 'I should say that there are also quite a lot of people who wouldn't ask me.'

One who never did again was the late Matt Monro, who commissioned a B-side. 'I sang it through to his manager,' guffawed Stanshall of the resultant 'Blind Date', 'who collapsed under the desk. I just couldn't write a straight song.' Other pursuits since the Bonzo Dog Band's 1969 demise found him in the Pasadena Roof Orchestra and, over Mike Oldfield's 'Tubular Bells' grandilo-quence, intoning a valediction with such perfect enunciation as to make his working-class-posh parents proud. Whatever did Mr and Mrs Stanshall's neighbours think when they read Master Stanshall's gluttonous *Melody Maker* interview in 1970? Pictured with shaven head dotted with plastic flies, Vivian was simply publicizing his new fly-by-night outfit the Sean Head Showband's new single 'Labio-dental fricative', on which was heard the 'woman tone' guitar of Blind Faith's Eric Clapton, an old acquaintance from the art school crowd: 'I sent him some lyrics that he liked so he came over. We recorded the number at three in the morning.'

Four years on, Vivian and Eric's mutual chum liked one lyric by the surprised Stanshall so much that he immediately set it to music. Suffering a bout of depression so severe that he had been prescribed a course of Valium, Vivian

> was staying at Steve's house and he said 'We're going off for dinner. Are you coming?' I said 'No, I'm reading about this French poet and I don't feel very well.' So he went off and I wrote not more than a quatrain about Gérard de Nerval. When he came back, he said 'Right! That's a chorus. We need a verse for that.' And he went into the front room and started plonking away on the piano.

Precipitated by the unruffled dispatch of 'Dream Gerrard' [*sic*] and the title track on BBC Two's *Old Grey Whistle Test, When the Eagle Flies* scraped into the Top Thirty of Britain's LP chart. A market killing compared to the two previous Traffic offerings, it was also better value for money, cramming more songs and less time-serving blowing into an increased needle time. A further incentive was – a first for Traffic – an inner sleeve lyric sheet. Inspection of this revealed more substance than the *Shoot Out* non-starters. On the shortest track, 'Something New' – a lean three minutes and a quarter – Capaldi, endorsed by Winwood, described spiritual consolation after erosion of human love with matter-of-fact flair. Of less insight, the semi-autobiographical 'Memories of a Rock 'N' Rolla' just about passed muster, though it may have rather idealized Jim's Hellion past – and the bit about a sixty-acre country estate being a heavy load might have touched a raw nerve or two in the queue at the labour exchange.

With the concerned detachment of one who had been long and, perhaps, guiltily isolated from the everyday, Capaldi railed against privilege – heads of state who don't 'pay their dues' like prostitutes have to – as well as the go-slow wage slaves of trade unions and shop stewards. After all, Capaldi might have been languishing in Straightsville himself if he hadn't joined Traffic. Many of his ideals were highly laudable – you should give more than take; pollution is wrong because flowers get killed. Outlining his lyrical articulation of these soapbox opinions and truisms, Jim pontificated to *Melody Maker*: 'very often it comes from the flash of someone saying something. I've always dug life, you see, and the reality of life' – and then, ambiguously – 'That's why I dig the Stones.'[15] That's cool, man, but Martin Hughes' back cover drawing of an eagle hovering vengefully over the dark Satanic mills of somewhere like Birmingham was far more expressive a statement than any of Capaldi and Winwood's indictments which rhymed – often using the same word – and scanned almost as tortuously at times as those of the Great McGonagall.

The non-rhyming 'Dream Gerrard' – standing as a poem in its own right – brushed aside the other selections like matchsticks. 'One criticism of Viv,' said Winwood, 'is that often his lyrics are a bit obscure.'[23] Admittedly, it helped if you too had read a biography of de Nerval, a precursor of the French surrealist poets. Recognizing the dream as a bridge between reality and the supernatural, de Nerval's writings, which investigated the symbolism of his own dreams, could be inter-related with his periodic committal to mental institutions until 1855, when he was found hanged from a Parisian lamppost. Anyone aware of de Nerval's work and behavioural vulnerability – as Winwood was – could only be moved by Stanshall's lines.

Lyrics aside, the music of *When the Eagle Flies* is among the strongest – and strangest – in the Winwood canon. Fractionally contorting his diction, Steve stretched the word 'of' over four bars before gabbling 'Mother Nature's Gown' in a *sotto voce* snort at the close of the title track. Far from rendering his singing unlistenable, the quirkiness unprecedented in that versatile larynx was as enchanting in its way as that of Captain Beefheart, P. J. Proby and other gifted vocal extremists. Further instances of eccentric phrasing crop up throughout the record. Perhaps he was trying to distract attention from some of the passages he'd been handed to interpret – such as one about snowballs hurtling through the membranes of yer mind in 'Walking in the Wind'.

A better choice for a promotional single might have been the more rounded and accessible 'Something New', with its fat unison combine of saxophone and twanging Stratocaster unadulterated by artifice. With his foot now forever off that wah-wah pedal, only necessary sounds were shaped mainly on the oscillators of Winwood's newly acquired Moog synthesizer. It was likely that this device also lent sparkle to the 'Walking in the Rain' organ section. With Elton John as his model for a 'good' pianist, Winwood considered himself 'lucky enough to have never had a piano technique as good as I'd like. I'd never call myself a pure piano player because I don't think my technique is good. So fortunately, it enables me to adapt more easily to synths which have totally different techniques than pianos.'[23]

The use of both electric and grand piano on 'Dream Gerrard' are among the LP's other keyboard subtleties, though an agitated piano riff and morse code Moog dominate 'Graveyard People', which in its overall drift rather than the actual notes played gives away the group's recent captivation by the music of Billy Cobham, Chick Corea and like jazz-funk pioneers – though such flavouring had been introduced more blatantly in 'Pretzel Logic', the third album by 1974's toast-of-the-campus Steely Dan, a New York band. An earlier jazz age brought traces of Thelonius Monk and even Cecil Taylor to Winwood's piano dissonances in 'Dream Gerrard', against Wood's immovable eight-note insertions on sax which insidiously breaks into a solo, subjugating the piano to the riff.

Traffic's improvising throughout the LP was suddenly more controlled and directed. At last they were reacting to the aesthetic spirit of the songs rather than intellectually to basic chords and rhythm. Removed from pop standards of discernible verses and choruses, 'Love' worked almost as a tone poem, while 'Dream Gerrard' again, layered in cinematic mellotron, had all the other-worldly deliberation of a dream's slow motion – so much so that, unlike, say, on 'Roll Right Stones', its eleven-minute permeation of side one does not induce restlessness in the listener.

Though not as joyous as past product, *When the Eagle Flies* still represented a Traffic renaissance. Even after savaging Capaldi's lyrics, many critics agreed that the band finally might have 'got it together'. 'Finally' was too real a word for, blighted masterwork as it was, *When the Eagle Flies* also proved to be Traffic's epitaph. 'By making it smaller, we were trying to get back to an earlier spirit or mood,' Winwood lamented, 'but it's always difficult to go back to things like that. Also, there were personal problems. People in the group wanted to work at various paces and it just sort of drifted apart.'[27]

On the same stage was light-fingered Rosco Gee, the most adept bass player Traffic had ever employed, scowling with disgust at Chris Wood who, from 1966's slight therapeutic tipsiness, was now lurching on with his woodwinds and catherine-wheel eyes to collapse semi-comatose with pills, powders, resins and old John Barleycorn. Said one onlooker at Traffic's show at Bracknell Sports Stadium in 1974, 'I vividly remember Chris Wood spending most of the time on the floor on his back playing very screechy sax whenever he felt like it. It was almost as if he wasn't with the band.' Winwood didn't even bother to introduce him when the time came.

Far from his dream home in the Cotswolds to be shared with the girl he hoped to marry, there Steve was, trying to cover up as Wood in a shell-shocked frenzy enters a full tone flat in 'Dream Gerrard'. With an eye-crossing headache on the coach a week later, and a whiter shade of pale after the last lot of overpriced lard and chips from a nameless roadhouse hours of torpid warmth ago, Steve with Traffic nears a soundcheck in High Street, America. Loved ones back home wonder night after ancient night until headlights in bedroom windows signal one more deliverance from the treadmill of the road. 'During that time,' said Winwood, 'I never felt I could do anything beside just tour, do the record and tour again. I found myself in this never-ending rut.'[27]

He wasn't kidding. It often transpires that singing or playing an instrument is your only saleable trade, and that you're in pretty much the same endless highway dilemma as an olde-tyme rocker or black bluesman of a pre-Beatle era. At least Winwood hadn't died in hell like Hendrix or Brian Jones, and a blending of his established pop star grandeur and hip sensibility had kept Traffic's head above water financially – but there was always the worrying psychological undertow, compounded in a dictum of another travelling man, Dave Berry: 'The thing about this business is that you never know

what's waiting for you round the next corner.' Johnny Kidd, killed
in a road accident near Preston in 1966, didn't – nor did high-flying
Buddy Holly and Otis Redding. Lynyrd Skynyrd's date with death
lurked only a couple of years ahead.

Not as absolute were smaller deaths along the way. You'd take a
good book for idle hours, but after endless centuries of self-loathing
in Holiday Inns, Ramadas, Crests and Trust Houses, it would occur
to you that you'd scarcely glanced at it the entire trip. Travelling
with Traffic in 1972 had been Richard Jobson. At the New York
stop of that year's American tour, he invited Bob Marley – then
about to defect from CBS to Island – to a party at Traffic's Windsor
Hotel suite. Sitting quietly in a corner, Marley drank in a scene not
so much *Satyricon* as a BBC play mock-up of an imagined pop
group drugs-and-sex orgy. In a dark spliffy haze, pushers, groupies
and loud-mouthed showbusiness periphery all competed for the
musicians' attention while, over on a makeshift stage, Jim Capaldi
was life-and-soul of an interminable blues jam.

At Liverpool Stadium there are blood stains on the toilet ceiling
above where someone has been shooting up heroin. Outside, the
police cannot control random attacks with bottles on the rowdy
queue. After the show, a gang rape is reported by the *Liverpool
Echo*.

Back in New York a year later, all Steve Winwood's guitars are
stolen. Often beyond sleep and alert with hunger, you could
soundcheck forever. Instead, you're steered into the artistes' bar
until it's time to steal onto the boards again. Afterwards, as you're
feted by fans, only fellow sufferers are aware of your glazed eyes. In
tomorrow's armpit-and-marijuana dressing room, you wait as
shiftless equipment changeovers keep the second house in Detroit
hanging about until two o'clock in the morning. The support
band's obnoxious drummer piddles down the washbasin.

10

'Boy in Shadow'

After a short childhood and the merest artistic prelude, Steve had grown to manhood in the hothouse of British Beat and its endless North American aftermath. Like a food pigeonhole in a self-service cafeteria, it seemed taken for granted that he and his kind existed only to vend entertainment with a side serving of cheap insight. To those for whom a thousand miles was a few inches on a map, the attitude seemed to be: 'Well, the group's latest has just gone into the US Hot Hundred – with a bullet. This, therefore, is the optimum period to maximize on capital expenditure. What are we going to do about it, then? Better get 'em over there on tour pronto. Make a fortune, eh? [pause.] America's a pretty big place, isn't it?'

In Think-In, a *Melody Maker* word-association column, Winwood's weighty reaction to 'solitude' in 1966 had been:

> It's important because people don't have enough time to think these days. I use it, not consciously but I sometimes end up that way and other people don't understand. When I get my cottage, I can just think about music and I can link up solitude with practice. I don't feel solitude when I'm playing. I just like to be alone sometimes. It's a hang-up with people pressing round you.[1]

Even up on the isolated Downs, there'd almost constantly been someone else imposing on his privacy. With Traffic's passing, an opportunity presented itself, after a decade on the run, for Steve 'to let my breakfast digest. It wasn't low key for me but people say that.'[2]

One who did say that was Muff, who felt that his brother's retreat verged on indolence. Town dwellers like Pete Townshend didn't understand either: 'this guy is an absolute genius and there he is, walking the dogs and combing his country estate for sheep ticks. I mean, what's the guy about?'[3] Chris Blackwell, however, was more diplomatic:

> He hasn't actually been doing very much at all. . . . I've seldom met anyone who loves the country so much. He's really into everything about it . . . how it works and fits together. He's got a house with a few acres in a lovely part of Gloucestershire where he just spends a lot of time walking – and he's used his time well in my opinion. In this business, so many people are casualties of drugs but he's really healthy.[4]

Better than dressing room fug was the smell of honest dung. In wool trousers, pullover and gumboots soon muddy, 'Squire' Winwood would stride forth on a clear dew-sodden morning with his gun dogs through the orchards and flower gardens to the woodlands and sheep pastures of his forty-three acres. In the rural postal district of Northleach, these were situated not far from Swinbrook, home of the aristocratic Mitfords. With but one employee, 'there's always jobs to be done around the farm and I'm a great believer in mindless physical things for relaxation'.[5] Whereas they might have pressed ivory or fret, the twenty-eight-year-old musician's fingers were now hardened from fencing, logging and moving bales. Against the winter, he was to purchase a Mercedes Gelandvagon with fitted snow plough.

Life revolved round the ivy-clung manor house dating back – as its exposed oak rafters and stone-flagged floors attested – to the Plantagenets. He first saw the farm in the pages of *Country Life*, and thought the £400,000 asking price in 1970 was money well spent. With no telephone until absence of one became a false economy, he could only be reached through the post or – with no glad welcome assured – by surprise visit. Otherwise, all that he needed to remind him of the holocaust he had left behind were mementoes like the Blind Faith gold disc hanging in the downstairs bathroom.

After the facile superficiality of showbusiness, it was pleasant to mingle with the eighty souls who populated the nearby hamlet of Turkdean – whose grocer provisioned the Winwood larder. Though Steve was present at many local events – fêtes, clay pigeon shoots, beagling – there was one pastime for which he was better qualified. More often than not, the hymns, canticles and psalms at Matins in All Saints', Turkdean, would be accompanied on the church's pipe organ by the former Perry Barr chorister. Like other worshippers, Winwood dressed for the occasion in sober suit and tie. 'Some people might think it odd that we have such a famous person as an organist,' commented the vicar, the Reverend James Webb Hugues, 'but to us he is just another villager – and he plays very well.'[6]

The diversion of divine service notwithstanding, 'I wanted to get involved with different aspects of music – probably the more oddball or unusual projects which I did get involved with. I was looking for a more varied diet, I think. Music was something I was much more interested in than being a star.'[7] Now that the *bête noire* of Traffic's tour-album-tour sandwiches no longer loomed, Steve could pick and choose 'obviously people I liked or was interested in in some way. So at the time, I was doing as many sessions as possible with people like Sandy Denny, George Harrison, Marianne Faithfull – although Marianne's *Broken English* was different. I didn't produce it but I did have more of a creative role.'[8]

Steve earned legion credits on LP record covers during the fifteen years he lived at Turkdean. Marianne he'd met when she and the Spencer Davis Group had both been on the bill at Uxbridge Blues and Folk Festival in June 1965. After a heroin odyssey of greater wretchedness even than that of Eric Clapton, *Broken English* confirmed a comeback with a voice grippingly shot of any former soprano purity. From this album 'The Ballad of Lucy Jordan', her first chart placing for twelve years, was sung by a woman profoundly changed from the convent girl whose party dress Mick Jagger had splattered with wine in 1964.

Recording his 1973 *Berlin* LP in London, another drug casualty, Lou Reed, tempted Winwood from his Cotswold fastness for a date at Morgan Studio with Jack Bruce and drummer Aynsley Dunbar. On another *Berlin* session, organist Blue Weaver observed that 'if you didn't get a performance out of Lou early on in the evening when the drugs really got going with the alcohol, then you didn't get one at all'.[9] Surer that same year, but less interesting, was *Road to Freedom*, the first solo album by Ten Years After's high-speed guitarist Alvin Lee; as 'Alvin Dean' in Nottingham's Jaybirds in 1964 he'd been 'considered by many the best guitarist in the Midlands'.[10] As well as Winwood, assisting Dean-Lee were others who'd also warranted mentions in *Midland Beat* – Jim Capaldi, Chris Wood and, from Norwich's Breakaways, Mike Patto (then briefly of Spooky Tooth) – plus old stagers from outside the region such as George Harrison, Ron Wood, Mick Fleetwood and Rebop Kwaku-Baah. Supporting on a 1974 Traffic tour had been Sour

Grapes, led by Richard Thompson who, with his wife Linda, recorded with Steve the following year, as did drummer Tim Donald who'd earlier worked with Spencer Davis. With other of her former Fairport Convention henchmen, Linda Thompson was present on Sandy Denny's *Rendezvous* LP with such odd bedfellows as Winwood, Acker Bilk and guitarist Julian Marvin. Killed in a domestic accident the following April, this was the last record on which Sandy would ever sing.

By no means confined to the established, Steve Winwood turned out too for the likes of Amazing Blondel, Jade Warrior and, in 1979, Gong – whose avant-garde line-up of bass, vibraphone, drums and glockenspiel had accrued a cult popularity – mainly in France. Further afield, Steve tried his hand at South African salsa with Puerto Rica's Fania All-Stars: 'I'm intrigued by traditional music that has a twist of the city about it.'[11] Through overproduction, Fania's *Delicate and Jumpy* LP fell rather flat compared to its ebullient concert performances, in which Latin American blended with jazz and Caribbean music with shades of Santana's big band tijuana-rock. Steve felt genuinely honoured when invited to join in on guitar at an All-Stars Lyceum show in spring 1976. In summer, he brushed up his reggae with Toots and the Maytals, returning to it in 1978 on Ijahman's *Haile I Hymn* with a 'Hi-ho Silver' on hand percussion plus drummer Sly Dunbar and, on bass, Robbie Shakespeare – a Jamaican rhythm section rated highly by many, though James Brown, a bandleader of some discernment, reckoned that they had no idea.

The opportunity was also seized by Winwood to make music with Remi Kabaka, a Nigerian percussionist less flashy than Kwaku-Baah but of more inventive resource. Steve and Remi's paths had crossed often enough in the past – from Gordon Jackson's LP back in 1968 to John Martyn's *Inside Out* album six years later, which introduced the echoplex pedal to folk music. They had also worked together on *Aiye keta* by Rastafarian band Third World, whose timbale and conga rhythmic emphasis was to reappear on *Higher Love*. Recruiting other Afro-Londoners, Kabaka began well under Winwood's aegis but, after a few tracks, Steve 'was getting very stuck for time as I had agreed to start rehearsing with Stomu [Yamash'ta] so it was a bit impossible to do anything else. Therefore, it was just kind of left. It wasn't African music. Let's just say "Afro-cosmic-punk-disco." There was good stuff on it.'[12]

That this of all Winwood's explorations had foundered was a particular disappointment, as his faith in Kabaka had been such that the African's had been among the first projects to be associated with

Fantasy Songs, Steve's new publishing and production company. Combatting self-doubt, Winwood had also splashed out a massive chunk of his fortune on a sixteen-track studio in the barn adjacent to his house; later he sank a further £60,000 for urgent structural alterations. It was comfortable enough for five musicians to 'not keep banging each other's elbows',[8] and both Third World and Kabaka recorded there. Its building was motivated 'because of the pressures in a [commercial] studio – like how much it's costing you – you're not allowed to mess about and make mistakes'.[8] Furthermore, its owner – taking a leaf from 'non-musician' Brian Eno's book – believed 'that it's possible to go into the studio without any prepared material and come out with something good. It seems that my best work generally occurs in that way but I was never allowed the liberty to mess around and try things out when I was in studios costing £200 a day.'[13] Christened 'Netherturkdonic', this electronic den was used by Steve – testing and experimenting with the aid of a manual – to tape, by multiple overdub, several long instrumental pieces which he then preserved for a non-specific purpose that was impossible to bring to full fruition just then because, for much of 1976, he was preoccupied with *Go*, a multi-media creation of Japanese classical percussionist and composer Stomu Yamash'ta – 'the Samurai of Sound'.

Revered as a virtuoso by both doddery late Romantics like Khatchaturian – whose 'Sabre Dance' was a 1968 Top Ten smash for Love Sculpture – and younger post-Schoenberg composers such as Cage, Stockhausen, Maxwell Davies and, especially, Hans Werner Henze, Yamash'ta was a 'wild child of a cultured family'.[14] Though he was at least as precocious as Winwood, Stomu's musical education was structured more formally by his father, a conservatory director. Studying percussion from the age of eight, the boy also mastered piano, cello and harp when attending Kyoto Music Academy. Winning an academy place in the United States in 1964, the seventeen-year-old Stomu was under the same Boston tutorship as modern jazz drummers Elvin Jones, Tony Williams and, in Yamash'ta's year, Chick Corea. Relaxing, like Corea, in downtown jazz combos must have been a liberating experience for the former Kyoto Philharmonic Orchestra timpanist.

By 1966, when he was undertaking solo performances, arrayed on stage would be up to fifty percussion instruments, including inverted prayer bowls and water-filled hub caps. So heavily was Yamash'ta brought to public notice that in 1971 he was collaborating with Peter Maxwell Davies on the dramatic film soundtrack for Ken Russell's *The Devils*. That year saw the formation in Japan of the Red Buddha Theatre, with Stomu as its producer, director and composer. This tableau of Japan's history as seen through the eyes of a beggar came to Europe in 1972, where it was the toast of the Avignon Festival, before Stomu accepted a residency in Paris which extended into 1973 until the company did a month at London's Roundhouse. Among the thirty-odd dancers and musicians were several from the field of rock such as guitarist Gary Boyle and, on bass, Hugh Hopper from the Soft Machine, whose free-form style Stomu admired.

Yamash'ta was awarded a classical Grammy for his first solo album, *Floating Music,* which contained items by Henze and Maxwell Davies, and until 1977 his destiny was bound up with Island, who saw rock star potential in this long-haired, exotically garbed, mannered young Oriental. Banging out as much Yamash'ta product as the traffic would allow – three LPs in the first fiscal year – Island pulled out all the stops for *Go* the minute Winwood got involved. The promotion drive embraced a *Melody Maker* competition – a quiz plus a sort of 'I like Stomu's music because . . .' in under thirty words – and a photo session at the Albert Hall where, on 29 May, *Go* – the first part of a trilogy – would be premiered. As the cameras clicked, Steve was obliging but fed up while most of the talking was done by Stomu and a third *Go* senior partner, drummer 'Maitreya' Michael Shrieve who, like his former employer 'Devadip' Carlos Santana and 'Mahavishnu' John McLaughlin, was a disciple of Bengal mystic Sri Chinmoy. However, chatting about *Go* to the press, with his 'Boy, don't take acid when listening to this one' drivel, he seemed more a soul-mate of Owsley Stanley. 'Like, Stevie Winwood had always been one of my heroes,' he gushed, 'I always hoped I'd get a chance to work with him some day.'[15] Not as aware of Winwood's pop stature as Maitreya Mike, Yamash'ta – armed with the relevant records – had undergone a surreptitious crash course on the music of the Spencer Davis Group, Traffic and Blind Faith.

'Tubular Bells' having paved the magniloquent way, 'works' were very much the order of the day in the mid-seventies. Jethro Tull, Yes and Hawkwind were three prominent outfits who cut albums as a continuous unity teeming with interlocking themes, links and leitmotivs. Even Dave Dee, several worlds from *Zabadak*, sang on one – 'Few and Far Between', composed by Jean Musy – which, overlooked in 1975, was perhaps the least overblown and lyrically obscure of the genre.

Go, however, had the most extravagant visuals. Yamash'ta's props included gymnasts, acrobats, jugglers, dancers, a tiger, a swan, kung fu displays, banks of television screens and multi-beam back projection. The music matched this presentation as it mashed up jazz, sci-fi psychedelia, classical modernism, atonal expressionism and the most abstract tonalities of Satie and Mahler – plus obscurer ingredients like the 'ur-concept' imagery of George Crumb. All this was held together or not by a rock 'n' roll backbeat. And, as Hans Werner Henze reminded us, Yamash'ta 'remembers the ceremonial gestures of his ancestors' music as signals for anxieties or threats. He is not bothered by conservative conceptions whatsoever',[16] an attitude ensuring an injection of traditional Japanese music, kabuki and Nippon jabber into the proceedings. What might have seemed mindless chaos was held in check by Stomu who, when all was said and done, had recorded music scored by Henze for the wreckage of a motor car, harmonica and electronic tape in collusion with the Fires of London and the Gunter Hampel Free Jazz Ensemble for highbrow Deutsche Grammophon. What further credentials were needed?

As Winwood noted, the show was better than the studio album. As well as composing the ballad 'Winner/Loser' and exhibiting his instrumental prowess, Steve also had the onerous task of singing the metaphysical libretto – by Mike Quartermain, a mutual friend of parties concerned – without affectation:

> Mike had the lyrics all prepared in poetry form and that's not always the easiest way of writing a song so some things I took straight, while other things I mutilated to suit the shape of my voice. But really it's all Mike's writing; the basic idea behind the meaning of the lyrics is his. Stomu talked the play concept over with Mike and then he came through with the lyrics.[17]

As always, when required to pick the bones of meaning from oblique verses like Quartermain's 'Ghost Machine' – about catching the thread of time when the said spook surrenders its mind – Winwood emerged with credit.

In Paris, it was thought prudent to record the second Go concert. As well as being Steve's farewell performance, the troupe was now loaded with semi-famous names from the realms of pop. Stomu's first choice, Mike Gibbs, had been too busy, so conducting the pit orchestra was Paul Buckmaster; since leaving the Third Ear Band he'd been hired by the Rolling Stones (to Mick Jagger's apparent dissatisfaction) and Elton John. From Roxy Music was Phil

Manzanera, guitar hero of the moment, while supplementary keyboards were played by a Brian Gascoigne whose bespectacled brother, Bamber, had achieved television celebrity in the sixties on *University Challenge* with his 'It's your starter for ten' catchphrase. Winwood had supplied percussionist 'Brother' Robert James from Toots and the Maytals; and, from redundant Traffic, Rosco Gee and – It's That Man Again – Rebop Kwaku-Baah.

Having done his duty by Stomu, 'after the kind of things I had been through with it, to make a solo album seemed easy. Needless to say, it wasn't but I just felt it was necessary to do an album on my own.'[11] Steve listened again to some backing tracks compiled both alone and with Remi Kabaka, but 'that idea was scrapped just because I wanted to start afresh. I wanted it to be spontaneous – not just a collection of old things.[11] He had, none the less, some glimmering of intention as he'd taken to carrying a micro-cassette on his countryside rambles to note down musical brainwaves. Furthermore, he'd 'relearned to write things down, write the music out. I may not be so much a slave to the tape machine which I always have been.' Enigmatically, he went on, 'I can remember distinctly things I've remembered and forgotten and never remembered again.'[5] This was, I think, a refinement of an earlier statement: 'it's like the story of someone asking some guy who was just sitting around if he was working and he said "well, I'm just thinking of a sax riff". I don't think you have necessarily to be in any particular place to write.'[18]

Sufficiently schooled in Netherturkdonic's aural possibilities, from September he disciplined himself – like any self-employed worker – to a strict timetable. In his case, it was, after breakfast and exercising the beagles, eight hours a day, six days a week – 'Then,' said Viv Stanshall, 'we went out for a few pints at night.' 'From my point of view,' explained Winwood, 'the situation is simple. When you want to get something done, then you really must cut yourself off from everyone else . . . it's difficult getting something together when everybody is trying to get at you.'[19] As Steve laboured, the gloom encircling the studio sweetened the pill: 'on those dark winter days, you've got to have something to do otherwise it gets really depressing'.[20]

Recording began in earnest in December. Since he was still an uncertain engineer, Winwood's masters were taped in London and, on one occasion, at Mike Vernon's Chipping Norton studio three miles south of the Rollright Stones. However, most of the mixing was completed at leisure back at Turkdean. Chris Blackwell's function as producer was, in his own words, walking in the studio and just being something he can bounce off . . . I would be involved in what songs would go on the album in terms of, would there be X amount of songs? If Winwood was performing, he'd perform then come in the studio booth, and we'd discuss it. I was a sounding board. When the other guys were doing their parts, Winwood would be in the booth with me.[21]

Anchoring four of the six numbers selected for release were bass guitarist Willie Weeks and, on drums, Andy Newmark. Both had recently served David Bowie on his 'plastic soul' LP, *Young Americans*, recorded at Philadelphia's Sigma Studios – the 'Muscle Shoals' of 1976. Moreover, Winwood and Newmark had already scraped acquaintance at sessions earlier that autumn for, respectively, John Martyn and, with guitarist Russ Titelman, on actress-singer Julie Covington's hit version of Alice Cooper's 'Only Women Bleed'. Though they demanded higher wages than their British counterparts, Steve was not immediately impressed with Weeks and Newmark's detached precision: 'I very much wanted them to invest their own things and, whilst they did, they weren't very happy about doing that. They wanted to be given the parts more than make it themselves which, at a certain stage, I didn't particularly want. Obviously, I wanted someone to play something I hadn't thought of before.'[11]

The Chipping Norton track, 'Vacant Chair', featured British-based soul band Kokomo's rhythm section, who were used to cudgelling a red-eyed, unshaven objectivity as engineers twiddled for a small-hour floor-tom sound. Against this possibility, they unpacked sleeping bags. Present too were 'Brother' Robert James and another Jamaican-born musician, Julian 'Junior' Marvin, who took the biting guitar solo. Having first noticed his playing on Sandy Denny's 'Rendezvous', Steve further discovered that, after emigrating to the States, the young Marvin had backed the likes of Billy Preston, T-Bone Walker and Ike and Tina Turner as well as making a brace of albums with his own band. Midway through 'Vacant Chair', Chris Blackwell dropped by. On impulse, he offered Julian a post that had arisen in Bob Marley's Wailers – starting right away. As Winwood seemed inclined not to want to tour in the foreseeable future, there was no harm done, was there?

However, to Blackwell's relief, Steve felt, with reclusive Beach Boy Brian Wilson, that interviews were a necessary evil for publicity, even if 'for a musician, doing an interview is like being a fish out of water'. Titled plain *Steve Winwood*, the album was filed

under 'Popular' in the shops on its maker's birthday in May – a date
he shared with one of Viv Stanshall's old art tutors, Ian Dury. From
Kilburn and the High Roads, Ian Dury was crippled, pugnacious
and described with vague accuracy in a tabloid as 'a sort of dirty old
man of punk'. The antithesis of slight, countrified Winwood, Dury
spat out in Oi! Oi! Cockney his perspectives on London seedy-flash
low life. Unlike Winwood too, he had entered pop late, his casually
amusing discoveries taking form as literary-musical wit. In 1977,
Ian Dury possessed some genius if little talent.

On *Steve Winwood*, it was vice versa. With keyboards as his main
instrument this time, Steve's understated skills still shone through,
but the material demonstrated that he hadn't quite extricated
himself from many Traffic excesses. Though Capaldi and Rebop
had only fleeting and minor hands in the recording *per se*, there was
more than a suggestion that *Steve Winwood* was a surrogate Traffic
album. Unlike certain ex-Beatles, Winwood had not reneged on his
past. Compliant as always, he'd put in time – as did Kwaku-Baah
and Rosco Gee – on Jim's third solo LP, *Short Cut, Draw Blood,*
which in late 1975 had spawned 'Love Hurts'. This, more like the
Majestics' 1987 cover than Roy Orbison's original, clambered to a
painless number four in Britain's singles chart. A true star now,
Capaldi gathered about him as many of his *Short Cut* minions as he
could to reflect his new glory for a two-song spot on the *Old Grey
Whistle Test*. In the throes of his on-camera cavortings, Jim
introduced Steve, who smiled without looking up from his
keyboards.

Capaldi was on hand as he'd been six years earlier for *Mad
Shadows*, when, predictably, Steve hit a blind spot over lyrics. Only
too pleased to help, maybe there was half a chance of putting the old
firm back in business. This wasn't to be, but Jim managed to leave
his mark in the words of four *Steve Winwood* tracks. 'Let Me Make
Something in Your Life' was almost moving in its clumsiness, but
when he stepped outside the role of a swain, Jim's capacity for
crassly expressed socio-political tenets was undimmed. Telling it
like it was about overpopulation, advertising and street crime, he
was no Ian Dury. Relating the wider world to personal problems,
Winwood endorsed a hint of Capaldi sexism on 'Time Is Running
Out', the track lined up for single release.

Again, as with *When the Eagle Flies*, Vivian Stanshall dismissed
Jim's harangues with one blow. 'Because of our agreement
spiritually,' Vivian had been 'sort of' commissioned by Winwood
to write more lyrics. Like Lennon and McCartney, Stanshall and
Winwood were unalike temperamentally – yet mild-mannered

Steve and Vivian of extreme behavioural strategy had found enough common ground, such as an interest in Arthurian legend, for Stanshall to have been a frequent guest at Turkdean during the apocryphal period since 'Dream Gerrard': 'We go out for walks and agree philosophically. We have a good sort out with each other before we approach whatever the damn thing means. Sometimes I will write the lyrics and say "What do you think of that?" but usually Winnie does the melody and I say "I think this feels like this" and he'll agree or not. I go ahead and write a poem and we'll see if it sings.' More was written than performed by this method. Both having read Mervyn Peake's grotesque yet tangible Gothic trilogy of the life of Titus, 77th Earl of Groan, the two were motivated to investigate financial backing for a film of *Gormenghast* – the middle book of the fantasy, written in 1951. Sketching its soundtrack in anticipation, the pair's hopes were scotched when Gordon 'Sting' Sumner, pop star turned thespian, stole a march on them in his acquisition of the necessary readies to buy a *Gormenghast* property in 1982. Some Stanshall-Winwood incidental music is extant, however, including 'Boy in Shadow' – for Titus when in the Hall of Bright Carvings – which features Vivian on euphonium, clay drums and basso profundo. Lead vocalist Winwood, at his most technically adept, leaps a full octave in the space of a bar before the melody is lost to an elongated percussion interlude pertinent to imagined visual drama.

Other plans of Steve's and Vivian's – theatre work, children's stories – likewise came to nought, but one film idea (which, ironically, contained elements of *Gormenghast*) became reality for Stanshall. His second album, *Sir Henry at Rawlinson End*, a development of a Bonzo Dog running joke, was adapted for the silver screen in 1978 with the late Trevor Howard in the blustering title role. Naturally, Winwood was heard on the Rawlinson soundtrack as he was on the next item on the Stanshall agenda – a third long-player, *Teddy Boys Don't Knit*.

On *Steve Winwood*, Vivian's was the text to 'Vacant Chair', based very much on the death at twenty-eight of his best friend, bass guitarist Dennis Cowan:

I was appallingly upset for a week and I phoned Gaspar Lawar [who played on *Men Opening Umbrellas Ahead*] and I was lachrymose and self-pitying and he said (in Nigerian), 'Only the dead weep for the dead,' so I said to Gaspar, 'That's very cool of you.' He said, 'No, just get on with life', so the sentiment of the lyric is: although,

197

sadly, people must die, most of grief and mourning is pity for yourself. But it's called 'Vacant Chair' because there are funeral parlours that actually sell floral chairs called 'vacant chairs'.

The most disturbing and personal outpouring on *Steve Winwood*, however, is by the man himself. Once more, he'd overcome his verbal inferiority complex and proved a capable, idiosyncratic lyricist. Possibly Winwood's equivalent of Van Morrison's harrowing 'TB Sheets', 'Midland Maniac' is a veiled and morbid articulation of a tragic person or incident. While the words convey a sense of bleak resignation similar to pieces by the more literarily accomplished Bryan Ferry, disconcerting breaks in tempo heighten the suddenness of the subject's elations and depressions prior to suicide.

Working almost as well is the arrangement to 'Time is Running Out' which, more than its lyrics, stokes up a rushing feverishness particularized by fragmentary electric piano and a jarring slow-motion cymbal effect near the end. A more melodic creation on Winwood's monophonic Moog is the unconvincing 'saxophone' break on 'Vacant Chair' during the repeated chant of Lawar's homily 'Oku nsukun oku' – the song's original title. Winwood's synthetic emulation of known instrumental timbres on this album was, as future more pukka-sounding recordings would reveal, only the tip of the iceberg.

This was offset by the cosy hum of his faithful Hammond trotted out to sweep some of the languor from 'Let Me Make Something in Your Life', the tune of which crosses the Beatles' 'Something' with Pete Dello's 'Do I Still Figure in Your Life'. More heavily disguised is the syncopated opening of 'Luck's In', which is close to the central riff of Pentangle's 'Night Flight'. After slumping into a heavy-handed blues-derived stalk reminiscent of Free, the six-eight time signature riff, as an extended coda, underlines Winwood's neo-Latin phased guitar solo. Less open to accusations of plagiarism is 'Hold On', attractive through Steve's dubbed vocal harmony as its perfunctory lyrics converge on a virtually acapella hook line.

Favourable reviewers implied that Winwood was British opposite number to Tamla Motown's cosseted former child-star (Little) Stevie Wonder. In the broadest sense, singing multi-instrumentalist Wonder indeed paralleled Winwood, his self-expression reflecting current trends from a 1962 debut album called *Tribute to Uncle Ray [Charles]*, recorded at the age of eleven, to 1977's *Songs in the Key of Life*.' If you wanted to nit-pick, Junior

Marvin had once been a Wonder sideman. However, Winwood – if flattered by the comparison – denied that any influences from Wonder or anyone else had been conscious: 'I decided that I was not going to listen to any other music while I was making this album. Obviously, I couldn't help overhearing some things but I tried not to. I sometimes find that there's too much music around and I haven't the capacity to listen to it all.'[11] Besides, *Steve Winwood* certainly failed to reflect current trends in Britain where, rather than being compared to *Songs in the Key of Life*, it might have sold more in the teenage market place had it been likened to, maybe, *Damned Damned Damned* or *Never Mind the B********, *Here's the Sex Pistols*. 'It was the punk era,' he admitted, 'and I couldn't have timed it worse.'[22]

Though *Steve Winwood* had thrown up a few weird shudders, it was easy on the ear and, let's face it, dated. This meant that it was ideal for North America where Neil Young, James Taylor and other Woodstock Nation comedians still held sway. Also with *Steve Winwood* in the US album Top Twenty was a 'work' by the Alan Parsons Project glutted with English producer Parsons' superstar pals; soporific West Coast country rock by the Eagles with Joe Walsh; Britons Supertramp – whose third album's cover art was inspired by that of Traffic's *Shoot Out* – and Peter Frampton, outmoded at home but never off American 'progressive' FM radio, which would remain amenable to him until the New Wave storm broke.

Steve Winwood's new album – his 'comeback' if you like – found enough buyers in Britain to enable it to enter the album lists there also. Nevertheless, many loyal fans would now be listening to successive Winwood records *before* purchase, a widespread viewpoint being that *Steve Winwood* had been something of a false dawn.

11

'Without the Little Barleycorn'

In 1979, Nora Mason died. On the flight from England after the funeral, her musician son David – long resident in lower California – decided to make the public gesture of dedicating to her memory his forthcoming album, *Old Crest of a New Wave*. Staring him in the face was the end of the CBS contract he'd inked in 1972, a year after *Welcome to the Canteen*. Shot of Island and the Blue Thumb limbo, he'd considered his debut album for CBS, *It's Like You Never Left*, his first real solo album, unfettered as it was by emotional obligations to critical familiars like Jim Capaldi who, while ostensibly assisting him, had, through that very familiarity, tended to cramp his style and undermine his creativity. Steve Winwood, of course, had never been involved: too many old wounds might have reopened. Though time didn't heal, and many of Dave's misfortunes since *Welcome to the Canteen* were traceable to Traffic, there lingered memories of 1966 when Steve and Dave had been intimate in the preparation of the new music. That was when they'd really been friends and, no matter how much they feigned indifference or neglected to send Christmas cards, each stayed in the picture by circuitous enquiry about the other's activities. In 1977, with a single, 'We Just Disagree', doing well in the US Hot Hundred against the lukewarm reception for Winwood's first solo album, Dave's mask slipped: 'I'd love to play with Steve – he's a great talent but he should learn to give more. I can't forgive him for not using my talents more fully.'[1]

When pressed for comment in the years before 'We Just Disagree', Mason had been more cryptic. Inveigled into law suits against various dumped managers and publishers of excessive thift, he'd assimilated caution. Unlike Winwood, there'd been no figure of Chris Blackwell's allegiance to shield him. Guarded in press interviews, he was much changed from the voluble Hellion of old who, in Jim Simpson's view, 'invented the art of posing'.

Unavoidably, living on the West Coast had affected his accent and vocabulary – 'sidewalk' for 'pavement', 'trashcan' for 'dustbin' – though other Englishmen in the Hollywood Raj weren't so phonetically pliant. Retaining his nasal twang was Mancunian Graham Nash, who'd left the Hollies in the lurch in 1968 when he'd emigrated to Los Angeles to become a darling of the Woodstock generation as the 'Nash' in Crosby, Stills and Nash. Invited to play guitar for these warbling old hippies, patriotic Mason afterwards paired off with Nash alone on the latter's anaemic solo LP *Wild Tales*. Affirming the respect still felt for him in the superstar firmament, a Dave Mason song was whinged by Bob Dylan during a concert at Blackbushe aerodrome in 1978. To sing harmony on 'Old Crest', Dave had anticipated Paul McCartney by reeling in Michael Jackson, whose *Thriller* of 1983 was to be the biggest-selling LP in history.

For all the august company he kept, Mason had lost touch with British consumers virtually from the moment he touched down in Los Angeles after the *Canteen* tour. Half-seriously, he contemplated burying himself in a band – planning to call it Destiny – as he'd done in Traffic. However, commercial pragmatism ruled and a 1975 European tour to promote *Split Coconut*, his third CBS album, saw Dave backed by a faceless quartet of American session musicians. Almost entirely on musical merit, 'We Just Disagree' was a shock turntable smash in London, reaching number eight in *Time Out's* Top Ten which, admittedly, was compiled from the personal selection of disc jockeys and journalists rather than from sales. This chart position was shared with 'Wild Youth' by Generation X, pretty boys of punk, whose singer, Billy Idol, like Dave Mason before him, was to try his luck across the Atlantic when his band broke up.

Unlike Billy however, Dave's face had never been his fortune – nor was his singing and guitar-picking exceptional. None the less, he realized some extraordinary visions as a pop songwriter, and his thwarted ambition provokes a measure of sympathy. Family commitments caused a long vinyl silence following the expiry date of the CBS option, but in 1987 a new Dave Mason LP, 'Some Assembly Required' was released on a small Los Angeles label. With the right song, Dave's return to a qualified prominence might not be as improbable as some may think.

You only have to look at Jim Capaldi who, five years earlier, had made a standing jump into *Billboard's* Top Thirty with 'That's

Love'. Jim too had no hard core of fans uncritical enough to keep the wolf from the door, so whether his records sold or not depended entirely on their commercial suitability. Despite unflagging attempts to colour him as a pop star in his own right, as with Ringo Starr, few were prepared to disconnect him from his previous incarnation – a situation that was aggravated further by his appointment as lyricist on *Steve Winwood*.

Vindicating accusations of over-dependency on such a bond was Capaldi's removal from Island to Polydor through the offices of his new manager – John Glover, that same ex-bouncer on the Spencer Davis Group payroll in 1965 who'd stayed on for Traffic too. While unissued Capaldi masters mouldered in Island's vaults, the next opus of the artist concerned came to maturation – an album entitled *The Contender*, consisting almost totally of self-compositions. As usual, he'd put in time at Muscle Shoals as well as London. Conspicuous by his absence from sessions in either hemisphere was Steve Winwood. However, Jim made up for this by weight of numbers. No fewer than eight drummers could claim a *Contender* session, including trusty Roger Hawkins and, from the Peddlers, Trevor Morais who – like Ringo and Keith Hartley – had also served Rory Storm and the Hurricanes. The biggest name summoned was that of Paul Kossoff, founder-guitarist of the extinct Free, who, despite conquering heavy drug addiction, was to die a few weeks later of a related heart-attack.

To break in the new album, Jim Capaldi and the Contenders embarked in 1977 on a sixteen-date British tour, mainly at the universities, where Traffic had always been treated well. There were also some more roughhouse bookings like Folkestone's Leas Cliff where, on the Saturday before Jim's visit, the hall's security guards had to eject some hooligans who were pelting the Argonauts and myself with plastic beer tankards. The week before, Generation X had been victims of a similar rubbishing – though the contrasting Steve Gibbons Band knew comparative peace on this circuit, as did Capaldi's band from whom, more often than not, encores were demanded. Pleased to oblige, Jim – shirtless and pouring with sweat by then – would bound back on, his hands clapping above his head like Ozzy Osbourne, late of Black Sabbath. As peace signs flashed and the mob clapped along as well, Jim knew he had them eating out of his palm in the way he'd always imagined when daydreaming during physics at Four Pools Secondary. Observing his eldest brother's dazed ecstasy was auxiliary percussionist and backing vocalist Phil Capaldi, who'd left his Evesham semi-pro band in neutral to assist with the recording and promotion of *The Contender*.

Also notable amidst Jim's backing group were in-demand session musicians like Gerry Conway on drums and, in Winwood's shoes, ex-Bo Street Runner Tim Hinkley on keyboards.

As his onstage mobility indicated, Jim was in rude health. Always stimulated by the celebrity of others, he had cultivated the friendship of star athletes such as Olympic swimming champions Sharon Davies and Duncan Goodhew. From an open truck, he was serenading cricketer Ian Botham on the 'Hannibal' charity walk across France in April 1988. These friends' disciplined regimen for fitness rubbed off on Jim, who'd excelled at school sport and had since been tough enough to survive the drug-crazed debauch that often characterized rock 'n' roll.

Angie Best, estranged wife of corrupted footballer George, was to rent Capaldi's rambling rectory in Marlow, which Jim left until 1978 for nearly the last place you'd expect to find him. He had been disappointed that Steve hadn't stuck Traffic for a few more weeks to tour Brazil, homeland of the woman whom Capaldi had married in 1976. Laughably, Capaldi and Winwood tried to compose songs over long-distance telephone. None the less, while Steve engaged co-writers to whom Turkdean was more accessible, Jim in his equatorial remoteness continued to foist his music onto a falling quantity of consumers until the 'That's Love' windfall turned his thoughts homeward to the distant roar of the crowd and, as the title of his LP two years earlier had it, *The Sweet Smell of . . . Success*.

Capaldi had put action over debate, whereas Chris Wood had merely pencilled 'travelling and disappearing' as his hobbies in 'Lifelines'[2] back in 1968, without actually daring to move somewhere as outlandish and unreachable to a Cradley lad as Rio de Janeiro. Indeed, he seemed quite content, prosperous even, at a chance meeting with another former Locomotive horn player at King's Cross Station in 1983. He was, he said, off to visit his parents who still lived in Corngreaves Hall. Like Steve Winwood, he'd been talking for years of recording a solo LP and, once again, he'd got round to starting one. 'Exotic African influences'[3] were reported on an earlier attempt, so perhaps the weeks lazing around in the Sahara on the *Nevertheless* jaunt hadn't been wasted. Bouts of ill-health had slowed things up, of course. Sometimes, he couldn't think straight enough to practise, compose or even perform domestic chores. When the Chelsea drug squad swooped in 1978, they'd damaged his front door and, trying to repair it later, he'd locked himself out. The coppers had found nothing, fortunately, but their intense and unwelcome interest had hardened Wood's resolve to steer clear of drugs.

Not as robust as Capaldi or even Winwood, Chris had long overdrawn on a misspent youth. Drowsily mooching to the newsagents for cigarettes, it was as if he'd never made those records, played those solos or won that acclaim. There was still a lot of session work when he could manage it, but dejecting in their curtness were old associates 'too busy' to call him back. These brush–offs hadn't all been self-induced by unreliability, either. He'd figured prominently on an album by Crawler who, after leader Paul Kossoff's passing, had regrouped in hopes of re-creating Free. However, in 1977 this notion fell hirsute victim of the inspired amateurism of rising New Wave groups as diverse as the Damned and Television. With Crawler castigated by many as another outmoded 'heavy' band, Wood was guilty by association. However, disembarking at Birmingham New Street in 1983, he seemed confident as he bid farewell to his train companion.

Unhappily, the studio time Chris had booked for autumn 1983 to finish his solo project had to be reallocated. In the early hours of Tuesday, 20 July, Chris had been rushed unconscious to Birmingham's Queen Elizabeth Hospital. At thirty-nine, his abused liver had finally collapsed and, before the city woke, Chris Wood had been pronounced dead.

An earlier Traffic fatality was that of Rebop Kwaku-Baah, who died in 1981 of a brain haemorrhage during a Scandinavian tour with a jazz-funk outfit. He too had been heard on the Crawler record, but more fulfilling was, with Rosco Gee, a British tour in spring 1977 with Can, a Cologne band whose lengthy but hypnotic improvisations depended on repeated rhythmic patterns. Issued in North America only a few years previously had been an eponymous solo LP on which Rebop had been assisted by many of his famous friends including Steve Winwood – and Jim Gordon, whose tragic life since Traffic led to incarceration in an asylum for the criminally insane for matricide. His story was the basis of a ballad by up-and-coming British country star Terry Clarke.

Gordon's songwriting confrère Rick Grech's post-Traffic history had a smaller portion of drama, generally casting him as an onlooker. Between *Low Spark* and Clapton's Rainbow Concert, he'd co-produced in Los Angeles the first album by former Byrd and Flying Burrito Brother Gram Parsons who, with Keith Richards, had discussed possible fusions of country and classic rock for an audience then biased against one or the other. With Grech at the helm, Parsons was on the way to achieving this when he died mysteriously in the San Bernardino desert shortly afterwards in September 1973. A week later, his corpse was stolen and consigned to the flames at the Joshua Tree National Monument by a road manager. This, he explained, was the way Gram would've wanted it – and it sold records.

To a less traumatic end, Grech and other Parsons' sidemen – including pedal steel guitarist 'Sneaky' Pete Kleinow – were also hired by the Bee Gees for *Life in a Tin Can*, an album prelude to the first of the trio's many successful comebacks. Prior to *Jive talkin'* in 1975, however, was a missing link – an entirely scrapped LP which contained 'A Lonely Violin', a Grech showcase.

Next, Rick served the Crickets – formerly Buddy Holly's backing band – before a reluctant sojourn in KGB, another 'supergroup' founded on quicksand more treacherous than that of Blind Faith. After both he and Mike Bloomfield bowed out of KGB at the same time, Grech assembled a new combo to develop – like the Eagles did – the style pioneered by Gram Parsons. When this fizzled out, he continued with treadmill session work.

In the stylistic mayhem that was 1977, November saw a trio called 'Grechmas' – Rick, guitarist Keith Christmas, and, from Boxer, drummer Keith Ellis – take the stage at Covent Garden's Rock Garden the same week that Capaldi's Contenders knocked 'em cold down in Folkestone. Quickly, Grechmas petered out and, by the new decade, its bass guitarist was living in Leicester where it had all started. Reportedly, he was nursing debilities not unrelated to the drugs that had been common currency when he'd been a 'superstar'.

Rick's Airforce commander Ginger Baker had tracked percussion to source through his financial and professional commitments in Africa. When he set up his kit within a chorus of claves, congas, talking drums, bongos and sekeres, Ginger's was the only white face in the troupe of energetic Lagos high life entertainer Fela Ransome-Kuti, who had entered into polygamous marriage with all his dancing girls. By 1972, Baker had graduated to leadership of Salt, another mainly Nigerian band that he later brought to Europe.

Back in London two years later, Ginger joined forces with Adrian and Paul Gurvitz, two-thirds of the Gun – 1968 one-hit wonders with 'Race with the Devil' – shortly after guitarist Adrian had completed an album with Graeme Edge of the Moody Blues. In 1973, Edge's old colleague Denny Laine had, with Paul and Linda McCartney, recorded Wings' first platinum album, *Band on the Run*, at Ginger Baker's studio in Akeja, Nigeria – his pride, joy and major source of income.

After three albums, the Baker-Gurvitz Army, as it was known, demobilized. Since then, from his château in Provence, Ginger has tended towards selected sessions, including several in 1985 for Public Image, a conglomeration headed by former Sex Pistol Johnny Rotten who, with Baker, was of London-Irish descent.

Ginger's ponderous Lewisham whine had been heard in commentary ten years before on a BBC documentary about his field trip into the Nigerian outback. However, by far the most chronicled ex-Blind Faith member is Eric Clapton, whose reassuringly more ordinary albums have continued to be bought en masse in the eighties out of habit. Regardless, Eric forged a second career with his psychiatrist-couch discourses to television interviewers and glossy adult-orientated journalists about his life, his soul, his torment. With retrospective honesty, he told 'em like it was about his vices, his women and his music – thus playing into the hands of his respectful biographers and drivelling eulogists. Always he bitched about the Yardbirds, who'd been far better off with Jeff Beck – as Blind Faith might have been. That's by the by. Clapton got the job. Perhaps the myth of him as the Greatest Guitarist Who Ever Lived would have run less risk of exploding had he been killed in a plane crash after 'Bluesbreakers' or before 'For Your Love'.

While I recognize a certain self-satisfied drollness about him, to me there were hosts of other sixties' guitarists – Dave Davies, Peter Green, Tony Hicks, Steve Winwood, George Harrison – who, if not on equal terms technically, plucked the heartstrings harder by directing their talent to their groups' general good with subtlety untried by flashier Eric – even when he was with Blind Faith. I know you'll think I'm terrible but my opinion since hearing him in person at Hyde Park in 1969 is unaltered. I thought it then and I'll say it now: not only as a guitarist but as a singer and composer, he was all right, I suppose.

None the less Clapton – and Ginger Baker – may be praised for, unlike other Traffic and Blind Faith associates, they conquered hard drugs: *pars sanitatis velle sanari fruit.*[4] 'Poor old Stephano,' commiserated Vivian Stanshall, 'his band has just died around him. The people I know that are still alive had to fight to be alive and they're just not there.' Vivian himself wasn't well, not having slept or eaten for several days, when he conducted me into his Muswell Hill flat one rainy September evening in 1987. Neither drunk nor sober, he sprawled like a sultan on his double bed while a girlfriend of timorous beauty filled our glasses at regular intervals as we talked of many things – of Gérard de Nerval, Crazy Horse, the Afghan War, the Abdication Crisis, animal rights and, every now and then, of Steve Winwood. More Shakespeare's Falstaff than Webster's Flamineo in appearance these days, Stanshall was still one of the few

I've ever encountered who could be described as a mystic – even if, in an ITV advertisement a few weeks later, he was extolling Cadbury's Creme Eggs via a voice-over rewrite of his 'Intro and Outro' monologue from the Bonzo Dog Doo-Dah Band. More abiding projects in the pipeline include a libretto to a tape collage of animal sounds which, from the snatches I caught, hint at an aesthetic if uncommercial brilliance. It seems also that the world has yet to hear the last of Sir Henry Rawlinson. Should Vivian ever be fit enough to return to the stage, among those likely to accompany him are Rosco Gee and Mike Kellie, both regular visitors to Stanshall soirées, though not beyond the bounds of possibility are the sporadic services of a friend more seldom seen – Steve Winwood.

I gathered that Muff Winwood too hadn't got much to do with his brother either when, after protracted one-sided negotiations and pestering by me, he finally declined to be interviewed. 'Muff doesn't want to get involved,' confirmed his secretary. 'The only connection he's got with him these days is that he's his brother.' After six years behind the scenes at Island, Muff declared his independence by becoming a freelance producer though still controller of the company's Basing Street studio – with a tacit agreement that he would bring all his discoveries to record there.

While still at Island, there arrived on Muff's desk Love Affair's demo of Robert Knight's 'Everlasting Love'. Hearing a potential smash and anxious to steal a march on the Knight original, Muff hastily booked a session with the young group to record a master for release on Island. One of his first production jobs, Muff also supervised a Love Affair version of the cancelled Spencer Davis Group single, 'Back into My Life Again'. For all Muff's efforts, Love Affair slipped through his fingers to earn a fortnight at number one with an orchestrated 'Everlasting Love' on CBS – given an extra push with a £200 back-hander from the group's manager for forty plays a week on Radio Caroline.

Nevertheless, having proved that he had an ear for a hit, Muff was the power behind the initial success of Sparks who, from the indignity of being booed offstage at Guildford Civic Hall in 1973, enjoyed – after Muff's intervention – half a dozen UK chartbusters for Island, beginning with 'This Town Ain't Big Enough for Both of Us', noted for its manic arrangement and wide stereo separation between the bass guitar part and singer Russell Mael's twittering falsetto. Muff also worked his magic on such as the Bay City Rollers, Mott the Hoople and Dire Straits. During his work on 1972's 'Lifeboat' by the Sunderland Brothers and Quiver, Muff was able to enlist his brother to play keyboards on three tracks – including one with an extended piano solo – using the rhythm section of Fairport Convention's drummer Dave Mattacks and Pat Donaldson on bass.

When CBS made him an offer he couldn't refuse in 1978, Our Man Winwood shot up the executive ladder through his signings of hitmakers like Shakin' Stevens and Adam Ant, who both dominated the UK charts in the late seventies. Other Winwood A and R hunches included Bonnie Tyler and Altered Images. In his own field Muff became, if not as rich as Steve, then commanding of at least as much respect for his shrewd judgement and steadiness of character as his younger sibling did for making gramophone records. I'm sure he'll be anxious to follow up a request in December 1982 from the Musicians' Union for M. Winwood (bass) to contact his branch secretary to verify his current address as the Union may be holding monies on his behalf.[5]

The Union was also uncertain then as to the whereabouts of Pete York and Spencer Davis. After the flight of the Winwood brothers in 1967, British Top Forty strikes by the Spencer Davis Group could be counted on the fingers of one offensive gesture because 'even when the Spencer Davis Group was in its heyday, it was Stevie's period not mine, and when the split finally happened, it affected me badly as I really had no direction in which to go and things began to collapse'.[6]

The paradox of Spencer Davis in April 1967 fogged even his own acute intellect. As *de jure* leader of a world-famous group with its heart ripped out, Spencer vacillated between a guarded optimism – 'Brian Wilson left the Beach Boys and they kept going'[7] – and despondent chagrin – 'At one time, I felt like jumping off Tower Bridge.' Countering loud predictions of a golden future for him by an initially supportive Chris Blackwell and, at grassroots, the struggling *Midland Beat*, came depressingly sympathetic fan mail and later instances of oafish barracking such as that at the Cannes Festival: '*Steve! Steve! Où est Steve?*' A recital by Denny Laine's Electric String Band at the Speakeasy that April marked the first public encounter between Davis and Winwood since the schism. Conducting himself with observed good humour, Spencer gave credence to his press remarks about 'no bad feelings between myself and Stevie. If there is any at all, it is with other people. To be honest, I didn't expect the split to be so soon. Although it couldn't be helped, I still think it was premature.'[8]

Spencer's less moon-faced similarity to Paul McCartney and his comparative youth were belied by an ill-concealed collegiate demeanour, and together these attributes expressed vague discomfort at his brittle pop star status. Yet with transient success in his blood and the lure of the dollar, he shelved recurrent thoughts of the securer anonymity of teaching German or studying comparative philology in either Birmingham or Berlin. With few consoling moments then for re-reading Goethe and Rilke, Spencer held his misgivings at bay and, with Pete York, sorted out a band to cut a new record and play bookings long scheduled.

Having spawned one wunderkind, it seemed prudent to adopt another. A cult celebrity and former guitarist with Great Yarmouth's Peter Jay and the Jaywalkers, Terry Reid had had (on the recommendation of Screaming Lord Sutch), first refusal but, following an arranged meeting outside Battersea Magistrates Court where Davis was appearing in connection with a traffic offence, the job went to Dulwich school leaver Edward William Hardin. With only a layman's knowledge of his new employer's distinguished past, young Eddie's worth lay in his familiar Ray Charles-with-a-hernia voice and a keyboard dexterity born of five years of piano lessons – with parental encouragement stretching to the purchase of *two* Hammond organs. Noticed by Davis and York in the Bag o' Nails club in Regent Street, bass guitarist Philip Sawyer from Les Fleurs de Lys completed the line-up for the second Spencer Davis Group.

As Blind Faith did, the New Spencer Davis Group rehearsed a brace of Bob Dylan numbers but Spencer's Indian summer began with his new Group's maiden A-side, 'Time Seller', out within a fortnight of 'Paper Sun'. As far removed as Traffic were from the old Group, 'Time Seller' rode roughshod over previous criticism of Davis not attempting to reach wider markets: 'a wonderful record,' declared *International Times*. As evidenced by their 'King Midas in Reverse' three months later, the Hollies had listened hard to 'Time Seller''s heady double basses and violas sawing a driving *ostinato* behind Spencer's quasi-toytown libretto. Though not as negotiable a money-spinner as even 'King Midas' became, 'Time Seller' was popular in regions as diverse as Western Australia and France – where the new band made its television debut on the ignoble *Music Hall* show, a sort of Gallic *Billy Cotton Band Show*.

Hot on its heels, a *Top of the Pops* plug shoved 'Mr Second Class' to number thirty-five – and that, as far as Britain was concerned, was that for the Spencer Davis Group, unless you counted two close shaves in 1968's 'After Tea' (accompanied by a photo call at the Tetley tea stand at the Ideal Home Exhibition) and 'Catch You on the Rebop' five years later.

'Time Seller', its lyricist told *Midland Beat*,[9] concerned the fact

209

that there are not enough hours in the day. In the immediate afterglow of its surprisingly modest chart run, the Group certainly led a full life. Taking the plunge at the *New Musical Express* Pollwinners' concert, Spencer and his boys limbered up with a few English club dates before embarking on exhausting back-to-back tours, spending the summer of 1967 in Scandinavia, Hungary and, at last, North America, where 'Somebody Help Me' was enjoying much belated airplay. Though audience enthusiasm had stretched to igniting concert programmes in Hungary, it became painfully transparent that all that Spencer's fans, old and new, wanted were the sounds of recent yesteryear, as proved by indifference towards items from the Group's latter-day albums against countless requests for 'I'm a Man' and even 'When I Come Home'.

Spencer's creative parameters as a composer were always proficient but limited, which is why an LP like *With Their New Face On* could never match the recycling of the big hits with Steve Winwood. Beyond Island repackagings, 'Keep On Running' helped extol the virtues of Andrex toilet tissue in an ITV advertisement as late as 1982.

Commercial pragmatism fourteen years earlier had obliged Davis to moderate his 'progressive' aspirations to 'much more entertainment . . . like the old Spencer Davis Group', as a press release via the offices of Peter Walsh, manager also of the Tremeloes and Marmalade, intimated. Despite the loss of Eddie and the faithful Pete, Spencer rallied again with 'a rock 'n' roll band – well, almost'.[10] Trying hard to live up to this with him were guitarist Ray Fenwick, who'd been added in January 1968 after work permit irregularities had ended a stint with popular Dutch outfit After Tea, plus – awaiting a platinum future with Elton John – bass guitarist Dee Murray from Mirage and, fresh from a one-shot collaboration with singer Brian Keith as 'Plastic Penny,' drummer Nigel Olssen.

Still the Spencer Davis Group couldn't get another hit to save its life. Supporting Pauline and the girls on the consequently reduced engagement fees, the homesick Spencer, tormented by persistent buzzing from a damaged eardrum, rotted in transit along the autobahns of Europe. Fuelled as well by second-in-command Fenwick's frustrated rancour, failure and disappointment did not yield dignity in Spencer Davis but a rapid emotional disintegration, which came to a head in some cockroach dressing room in Italy.

Shortly afterwards, a cryptic announcement reached *Melody Maker*: 'Spencer Davis has left the Spencer Davis Group.' With managerial disagreements thwarting a liaison with Plastic Penny guitarist Mick Grabham and session pianist Kirk Duncan (with whom Davis and Fenwick had written the last Group 45, 'Short Change'), Spencer enjoyed a period of convalescent sloth in the Fatherland, subsidized perhaps by a shameless solo single in German of 'Aquarius' from *Hair*.

Light years from Berlin, with his very name a millstone round his neck in Europe, Davis moved his family to California where, for a time, employment as a singing guitarist remained the ceiling of his ambition. From local venues like the Troubadour in Los Angeles, Spencer's work spectrum widened. By the early seventies, as Traffic jetted overhead, Spencer would be boarding a train, clutching guitar and luggage. His partner for many of these ventures was bottleneck guitarist Pete Jamieson, whom he'd met at a blues club in London's East End. In 1970, this led to an all-acoustic LP collaboration titled *It's Been So Long*.

A wild dream from the Golden Eagle came true when Spencer cut another album with blues legend Mississippi Fred McDowell. From similar Delta obscurity was the late Robert Johnson, to whom Davis paid more quantitative homage than Eric Clapton had done during a Chicago studio session in 1969 which had embraced contributions from Jon Mark, who had previously shared stages with, among others, Marianne Faithfull, and John Mayall and Alun Davies. Both these guitarists had worked the year before with Together, a vehicle for the compositions of ex-Yardbirds Jim McCarty and Keith Relf. A project by Mark and Spencer came to nought, but more fruitful was the Davis and Davies duo's offensive on the folk scene before Together's producer, Paul Samwell-Smith, persuaded Alun to team up with a new client on Island, Cat Stevens.

A bigger amalgamation by Davis was with an Australasian rhythm section and 'Sneaky' Pete Kleinow who, after his spell with the Bee Gees, had been behind the console on 1972's *Mousetrap*, Spencer's United States-only solo album. Epitomized by a Lincoln Festival spot that one discerning observer found 'boring beyond belief', this colonial combine quietly died when another New Spencer Davis Group – which included York, Hardin and Fenwick – reached back over the years with two Vertigo LPs and attendant 45s before likewise falling apart, as did similar attempts at seventies' rebirth by the Byrds, the Animals and the Small Faces.

After briefly working as a technical translator in 1974, Spencer gladly accepted a post in Island's Californian office. With lost business innocence, he later speculated in management and production, eventually landing a lucrative video contract with his old girlfriend Christine Perfect's Fleetwood Mac in 1983. The following

211

year, a new Spencer Davis LP was cast adrift on the vinyl oceans. Among its highlights were arrangements of the murderous 'Careless Love' from his Birmingham University repertoire and 'A Pretty Girl is Like a Melody', the Swansea Gang Show favourite. Less ancient a revival, Judy Clay and William Bell's 'Private Number' from 1968 was the album's promotional single, performed with an old friend from the sixties, Dusty Springfield. With Booker T. Jones on organ, a retread of 'Don't Want You No More' – which had been covered by the Allman Brothers Band – was its B-side, as the original version of this Davis composition had been on 'Time Seller' – which, despite Spencer's tenacity in the twenty years since, still stands as his best-remembered post-Winwood moment.

Giving Spencer their notice a year after 'Time Seller' fell from its British high of number thirty, Pete York and Eddie Hardin had teamed up as 'Hardin and York – the smallest big band in the world'. However, despite being blessed with greater mobility and fewer overheads than a group, this promising and original duo threw in the towel after a couple of well-received albums. At their 1969 apogee York and Hardin could fill moderate-sized auditoriums, but most people regarded them as a reliable support act to such as Black Sabbath, recipients of a glowing and amusing review by Pete in *Big Bear* which, under the editorship of Jim Simpson, was a gazette that linked *Midland Beat* to '*Brum Beat* – the Music Mag of the Midlands', launched in March 1980.

With Black Sabbath's Bill Ward and Locomotive's Bob Lamb, Pete had played in an experimental percussion band. With Led Zeppelin's John Bonham, these were the hottest drummers in Birmingham but, in the wider world, the names of Dave Clark, Ringo Starr and Ginger Baker were more likely to trip off the tongue when discussing pop drummers. Nevertheless, if less ornate than Baker, Pete York was an abler technician who could wipe the floor with mere thumpers like Clark and Starr.

Never short of work throughout the seventies, Pete sprang up in the most unlikely settings – with Birmingham power trio Bakerloo (with guitarist Clem Clempson, later of Humble Pie) or endorsing Zildjian cymbals in a *Beat Instrumental* advertisement.[11] At continental jazz and blues festivals and on television, the sharp-eyed would spot Pete sweating it out with some band or other. More often than not, he'd be backing artists booked by the enterprising Jim Simpson for annual Blues Legend tours. If the likes of Lightnin' Slim and Snooky Pryor weren't as immortal or even as old as Muddy Waters and Howlin' Wolf, at least they were more available to trudge round Europe.

Having replaced the long-serving Graham Burbridge in Chris Barber's Jazz and Blues Band in 1977, one strenuous but well-paid obligation for Pete after a Barber engagement in Scandinavia involved diving on a plane for Heathrow for an Albert Hall appearance the following January night to perform in David Bedford's *Odyssey*. This 'work' also featured Mike Oldfield and the keyboards of Jon Lord, Mike Ratledge and Dave Stewart as well as a full orchestra, the Queen's College girls' choir and, possibly, the kitchen sink.

With this kitsch and that endless twelve-bar was another string to Pete's bow. Having discovered that a healthy diet contributed to the stamina necessary to his musical calling, Pete and his wife decided to open a restaurant in Lambourne – not far, coincidentally, from Aston Tirrold – which one patron, Muff Winwood, described as 'an upper class place where they get all the horsey fraternity'.[12]

Leaving the Downs gentry to feed themselves, in 1980 the Yorks moved to Munich, more convenient for Pete's commuting to an ever-increasing European workload. One of his more inspired ventures was taking Jim Simpson's idea one step further. The brains behind the yearly 'Blues Reunion' tours of the eighties, Pete would lead bands composed of white British musicians whom the blues had made more famous than it had many of the black originators who'd captured their adolescent imaginations. Among those old pals persuaded to assist at these events were Brian Auger, latter-day Kink Andy Pyle, Chris Farlowe, Zoot Money and, direct from California, Spencer Davis.

Blues Reunion '88 – a quintet this time around – played at the Wyvern Theatre in Swindon one Saturday in March. Though not musically ambitious, there was a friendly, downhome ambience about the proceedings as Pete and Zoot Money swapped bantering continuity about the old days between songs old and older. There was 'Key to the Highway' from the forties and, with guitarist Miller Anderson on vocals, J. J. Cale's 'After Midnight'. The first half finished with a Chuck Berry medley, but more special was an earlier number sung by Spencer and rearranged to accommodate an extraordinary drum solo – extraordinary because, unlike similar ploys by other bands, this one wasn't an excuse for the other personnel to take five. Pete York's skill had matured like a good wine. With sticks, hands and beaters, Pete – still looking as though he was loving every minute – chose some quite unpredictable rhythmic sequences as he rode 'em on down for several exhilarating minutes. At his signal, Spencer and the others strode back on to re-enter what happened to be 'Somebody Help Me'.

213

12

'Still in the Game'

Since the Spencer Davis days, Winwood's celebrity had assured that he need never go without female company for long – even allowing for his narrow shoulders and the teenage spots that no hit record could stop exploding onto an otherwise fairly presentable face. Perhaps identification with this vulnerability and Steve's absence of common pop star airs and graces was part of his allure. Readers of *Jackie* and its American equivalent, *Sixteen*, had wanted to take him to the pictures; their older sisters – among them photographer Linda Eastman – had wanted to cook him a decent meal and look after him. What more could he have wanted? Now, passing thirty, his skin was clearer and he'd become, in pop terms, more Grand Old Man than Boy Wonder.

One of the landed gentry, Steve Winwood inhabited a world more exclusive than even that of the Eric Clapton Rainbow Concert superstars. The boy from Atlantic Road was now huntin', fishin' and shootin' with the upper crust. One of Winwood's particular friends was George Fleming, nephew of the millionaire James Bond novelist who knew Chris Blackwell. At George's Scottish lodge Steve had an open invitation to partake in a new and disgusting passion for stag hunting.

A different sort of hunt, however, had been brought to a conclusion. On 31 August 1978, at Cheltenham register office, Stephen Lawrence Winwood married Nicole Weir. It had been a quiet ceremony attended only by immediate family. Steve's parents signed as witnesses, Lawrence giving his profession as 'foundry manager (retired)'. Driving home to Northleach, they passed the parish church, where lay buried Brian Jones, Steve's jet-lagged friend who'd died, as a Sunday filthy would have it, 'strangely old at twenty-five'. More than ever, thirty seemed a good age to settle down.

A twenty-seven-year-old American-born divorcee, blonde Nicole was the daughter of French writer Charles Tacet. She appeared to be ideal for Steve: attractive, amusing, supportive – and musical. Furthermore, from the bluster of the United States, she was more than willing to adapt to the sedate domesticity of Turkdean:

> When I first came to England with Steve, I never thought I'd want to bury myself in the English countryside – beautiful as it is – but very soon I felt unable to face life in the fast lane. A trip to London became an ordeal rather than a pleasure. I grew to hate parties, the buzz, the fake excitement of the rock business. Village life and the peace and quiet of the countryside mean everything to me now.[1]

Other than for the wedding, Nicole's most exciting excursion from the manor that summer was to Cirencester, stone-built 'capital' of the Cotswolds, for the Rough Hill Festival. A low-key event, an untroubling ten miles from Turkdean, this was to mark her man's first official stage performance since Go. Focusing mainly on songs from its leader's solo album, the warmly-received 'Steve Winwood Band' had included Bryan Ferry's bass guitarist John Porter and drummer Terry Stannard from Uncle Dog plus a 'Demelza' as trademark Nigerian percussionist. As Linda Eastman had long assisted her spouse Paul McCartney in Wings, so Nicole was up there next to Steve at Rough Hill, harmonizing on lines and choruses she had and hadn't sung on Steve Winwood. During the time that was left at Turkdean, Nicole would also be heard on subsequent records of Steve's.

There weren't going to be many of these. Three LPs in the ten years since Steve Winwood was not prolific enough for Record Collector to consider publishing a solo Winwood article.[2] There was a discomfiting suspicion that – the unmistakable voice apart – had Steve Winwood been offered anonymously to major record companies, it might have courted rejection, as an actual marketing experiment of this kind by Jack Bruce humiliatingly proved.

Flipping through a summer issue of Melody Maker,[3] there is no doubt that 1977 was a bad year in Britain for Grand Old Men. The re-formation of the Moody Blues was dutifully reported, and one valiant reviewer scratched out nigh on half a page about a new Grateful Dead double album. The jazz and folk sections were still intact, as was one concerned with reggae and soul. Nevertheless, though resisting the fawning saturation coverage granted by rival music journals, there was a pretty strong dose of punk rock. Staged it might have been, but 'Teds versus Punks' bawled the front page about a confrontation in Sloane Square. A Sex Pistols recital in Copenhagen ('Rotten spews up charisma'); Tommy Ramone says, 'Why should young kids have to listen to the music their older brudders listen to?'; Generation X's contract with Chrysalis; the Stranglers awarded a Silver Disc – with the Pistols racing towards number one with their banned 'God Save the Queen'. . . that's what sold music papers in 1977.

It was a fierce time and no mistake. Like skiffle, anyone could do it. As punk fanzine *Sniffin' Glue* pointed out, all you needed were three chords. Not a week went by without another hot New Wave group ringing some changes. Somehow most of them sounded just like the Sex Pistols: provincial punks half a step behind London with their ripped clothes, safety pin earrings, slim-jim ties and expectoration. Woolworth's guitars open-tuned to a vague major chord thrashed at speed to machine-gun drumming behind some ranting johnny one-note who'd given himself a self-denigrating name like 'Kenny Awful': onetwothreefour dah dah dah dah dah-dah DAH! We mean it, maaaaaan! Individual pieces from this aural debris were irrelevant – what counted was the attitude. I hate your guts, you long-haired, complacent hippy git. For all its two-minute bursts of self-conscious racket, at least it wasn't weak. God knows what disaffected youth might have got up to if it hadn't wasted all that energy shouting and banging. Superficially riveting but lacking the musical strength of both the sixties' beat boom and psychedelia, punk was always doomed to be ineffectual.

Where could long-haired Steve Winwood fit in all this? *Melody Maker* slotted an interview with him well towards the back, just before the box adverts for disco equipment and Allan Jones' 100 Club review of Clayson and the Argonauts ('a premier position on rock's Lunatic Fringe, challenged only by Wreckless Eric'). What did Steve reckon about punk? Well, he didn't mind the Stranglers – punk with musical ability – but 'it's very showbiz. I don't think it's particularly good to explode a thing like what's happening at the moment . . . whilst punk rock is an opening for a lot of people who want to express in a certain way, it's in danger of overdoing itself'.[3]

Overdo itself it did. The Sex Pistols disbanded after an American tour, their separate parts never equalling the whole. With their departure came a mopping-up operation as the grubbing music industry stole its most viable ideas and got the more palatable punk entertainers to ease up, grow their hair, talk correct and get ready to rake in the dollars. The aptly-named Billy Idol couldn't sing but he was to outstrip Andy Gibb in the US dream date stakes, having been groomed by Chrysalis as an updated Ricky Nelson: by Jove, I think he's got it! By 1986 the Damned, if unlucky in the States, were smooth enough to score their biggest UK hit with 'Eloise', lovingly copied from Barry Ryan's string-soaked 1968 original.

During the initial stages of this taming, Winwood bided his time as usual. Punk may have passed him by, but not disco fever, which got into its groove in 1977 with Donna Summer's 'I Feel Love' and its sexy sequencer putting 'God Save the Queen' – reflections on Elizabeth II's Silver Jubilee – in its place at number two. The following year, the Bee Gees' soundtrack to *Saturday Night Fever'* – disco at its apogee – filled dance floors all around the world, selling millions in the process. While he may have cut the occasional rug with Nicole at All Saints' parish shindigs, Steve didn't indulge in disco either immediately or obviously, but its influence had taken hold – to lie almost dormant until *Back in the High Life*.

In 1978, with but one mediocre solo opus under his belt, such a glittering Album-of-the-Decade prize was a far-fetched after-thought for Steve Winwood, grappling with his muse in the heart of rural Gloucestershire. Starting work in January 1979 on what would become *Arc of a Diver*, 'I began ideas and scrubbed them and then I would try to resurrect them and end up throwing them away. But basically, it wasn't until March '80 that all the material was finished.'[4]

A Vivian Stanshall number, 'If This Gun's for Real' – though a demo prepared at Netherturkdonic still exists with organist-singer Winwood and Stanshall on guitar playing along to a drum machine – was among items thus remaindered. Even in – or because of – this rough-hewn state, this chilling ballad of imminent mortality bites hard, too hard perhaps for much US airplay. Other than the title track of *Arc of a Diver*, it was to be several years before Steve was to record another Stanshall lyric – the comparatively straightforward 'My Love's Leavin''.

Another ingredient in *Arc of a Diver's* lyrical cauldron was to have been Robert Hunter, who wrote for the Grateful Dead. Resident in England from 1979, Hunter had known Winwood since an embarrassing incident in the late sixties when Traffic's leader

> jammed with the Grateful Dead somewhere in America. They were playing 'Not Fade Away' and did this very, very long instrumental intro and were looking round and smiling at me and I thought they were waiting for me to sing. I waded in but, of course, didn't know the words so

217

they went back to another very, very long instrumental jam and I felt a right idiot. The audience were so out of it they didn't realise anything was wrong . . . mind you, so was the band.[5]

Winwood's creative liaison with Hunter seemed to follow a similar path and, though a few ideas were tossed around, none of these got as far past the drawing board stage as even 'If This Gun's for Real'.

If a thing's worth doing, it's worth doing pedantically. Nevertheless, the making of *Arc of a Diver* was a costly business – 'when I finished, I was virtually out of cash'.[5] Though hardly left destitute enough to consider re-forming the Original Traffic for nostalgia cabaret, 'if the record hadn't been a success, I would have completely lost confidence'.[5] The delay from *Steve Winwood* was, he said, 'due to writing relationships'.[6] Viv Stanshall was still on call, but Jim Capaldi's emigration to South America rendered his lyrical participation inconvenient. On this excuse, Winwood had carte blanche to find new collaborators whose literary eloquence was more nearly comparable to Stanshall's. Contacted through Van Morrison, a mutual friend, was American wordsmith Will Jennings, whose bond with Winwood was to prove more productive – and lucrative – than any that either of them had experienced before. For Steve, the most telling recommendation on Jennings' curriculum vitae was his work with Joe Sample, keyboard player with the Crusaders, a revered free-form jazz-rock quintet from Texas. In 1976, they had recorded with Van Morrison who, since withdrawing from Them, had been in a position similar to Winwood's. After a shaky start as a free agent, his second solo album, the impressionistic *Astral Weeks*, began his climb to an introspective international stardom.

Astral Weeks had been finished in two days flat and was still selling as the recording of *Arc of a Diver* entered its nth month. The difference was that Morrison's LP had been more or less extrapolated on the spot, whereas Winwood's *modus operandi* – to Van's amazement when Steve let him hear it – was personally to hand-tool every note in the privacy of Netherturkdonic. Without the emotional and financial overheads of a hired studio, Steve had gained enough confidence to start a day's taping with nothing prepared. Assisted by John Clarke and learning all the time, 'I engineered this album and it gave me a whole insight into how engineers hear things and how they look at things in a different way.'[6] Instrumentally, he'd broadened his scope too. Since sitting in on Pete York's lessons with Lionel Rubin, Steve had taken tentative steps towards teaching himself drumming during the Blind Faith–John Barleycorn interim. Like Sly Stone and, I suspect, Dave Clark before him, Steve's recording methods involved building up instrumental layers using a metronome or retractable 'click track'. Drums would then be added last, when the rhythm had already been invested into the number.

An exercise that became an achievement,

> while I was doing this record, because there was really so much involved with doing the different parts, I found that if I got bogged down with a particular aspect – maybe the vocal on one track – there was always so much to be done that I would leave that and spend a week working on something else. I found that I could get back to this other piece and say 'of course, that's exactly what to do.'[7]

In mid-September, Steve's magnum opus was finished to the last detail. Too late to catch the Christmas sell-in period, it was as much as Island could do to get *Arc of a Diver* out by the final week of 1980 in the hope that John Citizen wouldn't waste Santa's record token on something else.

The long wait worked to Winwood's advantage, creating much of the aura of a fresh sensation. His new short haircut distanced him further from his Traffic past and obscured some memories of *Steve Winwood*. He looked at least as young as current chart incumbents like Bryan Ferry, Sting or David Bowie. Many were intrigued about how he'd reacted artistically to the hurricanes that had swept through pop since 1977. Possibly in the light of John Lennon's pavement assassination just before that creepy 1980 Christmas, others felt vaguely reassured that Steve Winwood's wrung larynx was still going strong. Besides, after punk there had been a move towards more melodic fare, of which there was no shortage on *Arc of a Diver*. This time, Steve couldn't have timed it better.

In Europe, its green cover was almost as much of a fixture in student halls of residence as Che Guevara's mug had been years earlier. However, across the continent that mattered, the ramifications had spread out of the campuses and instantly into *Billboard's* Top Five – much to Winwood and Chris Blackwell's relief. In similar ratio, the attendant single, 'When You See a Chance', while sneaking up to number forty-five in dear old England, sliced to number seven in the United States as a wire through cheese.

This Winwood–Jennings composition was a sound choice. As if welcoming an All Saints' congregation to Evensong, a funereal fade-in is startled into a rural romp as the chorus theme is stated by a contrasting nasal synthesizer. Ideally conveying lyrical intent, the catchy tune of 'When You See a Chance' takes you to a stile by a dewy pasture under an ominous sky. Leaving an aftertaste of pleasurable regret and no time to sit and stare, it hardly matters that the singer's voice has floated effortlessly over layers of treated state-of-the-art sound. The faintly hymnal 'I Will Return', a forgotten UK instrumental hit by Springwater, had a similar effect – and that too resulted from the multi-tracking of one musician.

'People have done albums like that before but to me they sound like an overdubbed album,' said Winwood, reminding us of contrivances like Jon Anderson's *Olias of Sunhillow*. 'I worked at trying to make it sound like a band.'[6] Try he certainly did, but the technology wasn't yet up to it in many areas. It was true that 'making records, like making movies or anything else is trickery. So is arranging music because you do it so some things have an impact. You lead the listener on to believe it's a sax. The actual programming isn't difficult.'[4] With a very basic Mini Moog, he had sought to 'lead the listener on to believe it's a [alto] sax', but it didn't fool many. Perhaps he should have persisted with Muff's clarinet a bit longer. Any instrument would have been an improvement on the ghastly swimming pool synthesizer noise on 'Second Hand Woman.'

Nevertheless, his stark use of percussion was endearing – and accurate. In 'Dust', it co-ordinates precisely with the bass part carried by the left hand on the piano. Avoiding gratuitous frills, there was subtlety in its simplicity – a good example being the deployment of bass drum on 'Spanish Dancer', which also drops appropriate hints of disco in the seductive fluttering sequencer rhythm.

As its title suggests, the mood shifts to a shuffle for 'Night Train' – the only 'blowing' number – with a guitar section that swells from flecks of sound, as the carriages hurtle through landscapes blackened but for distant pinpoints of light, to a furnace flame coda in which Steve drives the express to oblivion with Eric Clapton way back in the guard's van. Though four of the seven tracks likewise fade, there was to be a greater – and healthier – tendency for Winwood's arrangements to feature more definite endings, indicating his more disciplined attack.

Of the three lyricists employed, Will Jennings was the one most aware of his client's new requirements. Winwood often had 'difficulties with a writing relationship – it takes a long time to get relaxed. As far as music is concerned, I prefer to write on my own.'[8]

Nevertheless, Jennings was a professional. Rather than burden the listener with clumsy tracts about the wrongs of the world, Will approached the songs with the reasonable argument that the words should blend with the music. With detached efficiency, he provided four sets of lyrics – not poems – in which meaning did not take precedence over phonetics. If they were repetitive, they none the less rolled off Winwood's tongue without pomp; neither did they conflict with his artistic motive. In 'Slowdown Sundown', for instance, the cartoon sadness of Traffic's 'Evening Blue' shifts in locale – via the lilt of a mandolin – from the confines of a cottage to a ranch veranda, where the subject's tipsy musings take on a breadth of gesture that is simultaneously universal and personal. Feverish 'Spanish Dancer' turns you into a pleasure-seeker with money to burn in an evening street of wanton perfume, languid music and temptation. With dawn a year away, the clanking 'Night Train' powers across a Europe on which the sky is falling.

Selling well when issued as a single in Australasia, more mysterious is Vivian Stanshall's sole contribution. He explained,

> Arc of a Diver was effortless. I used to think that there were lamas in Tibet that could write perfect verse – that, perhaps before the end of his life, Dali could paint and know that he was going to make marvellous and astounding works. I don't think that's going to happen to me. I don't think it happened to them but I think it's a marvellous idea to be able to flow perfectly. I don't know much about Indian mystics but I figured that once you'd got past a certain age, if you could forget nuts and bolts, you could just play, sing or speak. You wouldn't have to consider your words or the next thing that occurs. You could actually do it. Arc of a Diver is about that.

Though Vivian's lyrics again had the most substance of any on the album, they weren't as 'made to measure' as Jennings' were to Steve's designer music, which from the attention-grabbing synthesizer sweep of 'Arc of a Diver' to its 'quartz clock' cadence kept American FM radio in tasteful focus.

During one Hibernian deer stalk, George Fleming might have mentioned that it might be rather jolly if he too dashed off a few verses for a couple of Winwood's tunes. Inspired no doubt by his famous uncle, he'd already half finished a novel but 'he'd never written a song before, and he wrote these two songs. I liked them and used them.'[4] With these completing the LP, there was no middle way with George. The words of 'Second Hand Woman' were so corny in their heterosexual chauvinism and strained Americanisms that the most verbally impoverished heavy metal group would have thought twice about trying them. Yet the tender 'Dust' might have come from a totally different author. Chosen by Winwood as what had become his customary album slow ballad valediction, 'Dust' is a compassionate meditation of two old friends who used to be lovers.

Without the questionable aid of the lyric sheet, I first heard 'Dust' on a car cassette deck. To me, the opening line came out as 'Time, Nicole, (i)s a universal healer.' Life at the manor was no more the epitome of marital bliss for the childless couple. While her technocrat husband was engrossed in computer manuals or tapping on his latest keyboard toy from the States, Mrs Winwood had veered by contrast towards the morning of the Earth. No more feeling like the stock Connecticut Yankee in the Court of King Arthur, the apple-cheeked farmer's wife was attending rectory coffee mornings and chatting about field drainage, jumble sales and muck-spreading with the best of them. Steve too had 'loved it for the first few years but, strangely, as he became restless, I found myself completely at home. Gradually, we grew apart. He began spending more and more time away while I immersed myself in life here.'[1]

She was no Yoko to Steve's John, so most of the outside world weren't even aware of Nicole, except as an album sleeve credit. Was she his sister? He never spoke of her to the press but, knowing as they did his characteristic reserve, that signified little. He'd never been the sort to wash dirty linen in public. It was noted, none the less, by Turkdean folk that Mr Winwood was spending increasingly longer spells away. 'In danger of becoming arty in isolation',[9] he flew frequently to meet Will Jennings in New York to compile material for a third solo LP, intended to snap at the heels of *Arc of a Diver*.

Furthermore, pop star as he was, he was considered an Artist in enthusiastic America. At grassroots extremes, he was on what seemed an irreversible slide in Britain. With readers' votes counting, both individually and as part of Traffic, he would be rated low down in *Record Collector*'s poll of 1985 – the Spencer Davis Group being unlisted. In a rock musician's magazine the following year, he'd figure nowhere in every category. He was, it seemed, merely as-good-as-his-last-record for all but those fine minds who always guaranteed him a moderately high but short-lived spell in the British album charts. 'It doesn't upset me really,' he said, 'obviously it shouldn't because Britain is not, in terms of the amount of people, a big market so in theory it doesn't bother me but I suppose it does in a way but not to the point of being an obsession because I think that is not the way to go about getting hit records.'[7]

What did such a minor territory like the United Kingdom matter when even in hitherto unvisited and bigger sales areas like Australasia and Japan, he was still very much on a winning streak? Back at the farm, he'd be getting the next US blockbuster ready. One February morning in 1987, Steve took the gun dogs and their puppies for their run as usual. Later that day, he left – back to the High Life.

The inevitability of this strange day became perceptible around 1981 when, though it had 'been a relief not doing it for a time',[10] after six years' grace Winwood began talking about touring again: 'I've learned a lot and achieved a certain amount but really music is about playing with other people. Now I need to play with a band again, partly because playing to a "live" audience gives you instant criticism which you don't get when you're alone in the studio. The audience lets you know straight away whether you've got it right or not.'[11] Some British dates were pencilled in for autumn 1981 and, though no such undertaking was in fact to take place for two more years, the wheels were cranking into motion.

'When I eventually tour with a band of my own,' he said, 'I'll play mostly keyboards and have someone else playing guitar.'[10] Compensating, perhaps, for general underestimation of his guitar playing, the esteem of American musicians for Winwood's keyboard forte was exemplified by his nomination in three categories – Rock Organ, Rock Piano and Multiple Keyboards – in a readers' poll in *Keyboard*, a specialist US glossy. In his enthusiasm for one particular digital sampling synthesizer, Steve's reserve so evaporated that in a trade advertisement his photograph appeared above his quoted endorsement: 'I need to get to my sounds quickly and also create new patches when I'm on tour. The Dss-1 gives me that flexibility. It's a very responsive instrument.'[12] With such innovations as electronic drums, programmable desks and graphic equalizers to do battle against adverse auditorium acoustics, the notion of taking to the road with a backing group was almost attractive enough to erase flashbacks of how dreadful it had been in 1975. With a rescued reputation and his own man at last, Winwood could now pick and choose musicians and even venues. As to 'when', he was too long in the tooth to take pot shots. There was little point in publicizing the million-selling *Arc of a Diver* any more, so he decided to see how the new album fared before venturing on stage again.

Pieced together at Netherturkdonic between November 1981

and the following summer, *Talking Back to the Night* was – with one aberration – a consistently strong collection of songs. Steve's melodious adventures were rife with unexpected but attractive modulations and chordal juxtaposition, leanly arranged with discernible beginnings, middles and endings. At its most minimal ever was Winwood's instrumental soloing.

There wasn't a guitar in sight. Bar the vocals, everything – percussion included – was the product of keyboards. More machines and US sound laboratories receive 'special thanks' on the LP's inner sleeve than do people. Anachronistic among the multi-Moogs and polysynthesizers was a Hammond organ, lugged from the attic to emit one of the record's more pleasant sounds on 'And I Go' – which, with its simple love lyric, sketches hazily how the first Spencer Davis Group in sombre mood might have sounded in the eighties. It remains a mystery why this organ wasn't employed on 'There's a River', the blissful spiritual that closes the album. Instead, there's the festering impassive synthesizer that pervades most of the earlier selections too. Surfacing as frequently as rocks in the stream is the snotty grate previewed on *Arc of a Diver* as substitute for sax or single-note guitar lines. No matter how cleverly played, it still seemed gutless against the real instrument's grit and potentially more thrilling margin of error. The title track in particular screamed for a flesh-and-blood musician to cameo the out-of-work saxophonist of the first verse.

Nevertheless, Steve was in good voice – as was Nicole on backing vocals – and some of the processed sounds were highly authentic, especially 'bass guitar' which nowhere yielded to the 'twanging plank' disco trendiness that plagued eighties' pop. Yet all this expensive equipment lent no drive, no transcendental edge.

The Japanese had invented a drum machine that would make a deliberate mistake within bar lines – perhaps fluffing a floor tom fill – every now and then in order to preserve some vestige of humanity. Winwood's Linn electronic programming made no such allowances. None the less, despite its perfect time-keeping, nothing appeared too impossible an accomplishment for any competent studio drummer. The Linn sound was accurate too – apart from the hi-hat which was especially irritating on the start of 'It Was Happiness'.

Once I asked a certain faded sixties' pop star why he'd never composed anything. 'Dunno,' he replied. 'Could've written some great ones, though.' *Talking Back to the Night* had the material already, but this kicked vainly against the one-man-band ethos of Netherturkdonic. Subsequent events showed that Winwood himself became aware of this but, had he twigged sooner, *Talking Back to the Night* produced in New York rather than Turkdean might have surpassed *Back in the High Life*. It could've been a great one.

Me? Well, if I'd been producing, I'd have axed 'Help Me Angel' altogether. Although, like 'Wooly bully', it didn't seem to be about anything much, rhyming 'find' with 'sunshine of yer mind' condemns it without trial. Furthermore, elements in its chordal and rhythmic structure are maddeningly familiar – 'Sympathy for the Devil', I think. Also, Steve's 'whoa-oh' near the end clones the way Ray Collins sings it on the fade of Ruben and the Jets' 'Jelly Roll Gum Drop'. If Steve had insisted on doing it, I would have plagiarized the piano figure and 'wam bam boom wam bam de-boom' background chant of Anthony Newley's 'Idol Rock-a-boogie' of 1959 and hoped that no know-all would notice.

I'm nothing if not vulgar. The difficulty was that, long before *Talking Back to the Night*, Steve Winwood had lost me. You see, if you were a child of the sixties, you could either regress as I did – heart pounding in anticipation while hurrying towards a pile of scratched 45s on a bric-à-brac stall – or else start saving up for one of these new-fangled compact disc players in order to hear the dandruff falling from the hair of Dire Straits, Fleetwood Mac, Steve Winwood, Paul Simon and other purveyors of cultured 'contemporary' pop for the over-thirties. The only concert I bothered with in 1981 was Gary Glitter's Rock 'n' Roll Circus in a field near my house. Poorly attended but devastating, sequinned Gary was, at one point, suspended wired and boggle-eyed on a gleaming Harley-Davidson some sixty feet over our frenzied heads while, down on the sawdust, the band cranked out one of his ancient smashes – 'I'm the leader of the gang (I am)' it might have been.

Others my age would have preferred the more dignified atmosphere of a Steve Winwood show. Though four years younger than gross Glitter, Winwood had matured with his audience, as the situations outlined in *Talking Back to the Night* showed – all in collaboration with Will Jennings only this time. Incidents in a life of rich refinement included Paris in the rain, nude sunbathing in California – from 'It Was Happiness' – and the admonishing of the kind of wasp-waisted gold-digger that an upper-class fledgling might pick up in Stringfellow's ('Big Girls Walk Away'). What was escapism for most of his consumers was the world in which Winwood lived.

Nor were the lyrics solely the vision of Jennings. Unlike other teams such as Rodgers and Hart or Procol Harum's Gary Brooker and Keith Reid, there was no strict delineation between the functions of Jennings and Winwood because 'I don't like a strict music-words relationship really. The only thing that matters is what comes at the end. There's really no formula at all because, as soon as you try it one way, you find that other things work better . . . it's a funny thing to actually plan to write.'⁴ With workmanlike application and a shared sense of humour, the words on *Talking Back to the Night* are the most sophisticated from any of Winwood's records, even if nothing especially original is expressed. A possibly unfair generalization is that in both 'Still in the Game' and the title song is the 'keep on keeping on' adage of seventies' soulman Curtis Mayfield. They tell of the artist's lonely craft and the hard knocks of which Winwood had had nil experience – even if he was pictured on the cover in the citrus smog caricature of New York's Chinatown, scene of some of the action.

Traces of 'The Rose of Tralee' and 'The Lark Ascending' touch 'There's a River'. References to *Jazz on a Summer's Day* and 'Ticket to Ride' mingle with yearnings for an old flame in 'While There's a Candle Burning' and the single off-cut 'Valerie', which leapt into the US Top Forty. Winwood would have been amused rather than exhilarated had 'Valerie' repeated this feat in the marketing sideshow that was Britain. 'I think it will be a hit – my first since 1967,'⁵ he chortled the same month that Valerie stopped one place short of his homeland's Top Fifty. 'Valerie''s time was yet to come.

For Nicole Winwood, time was running out. Unconscious though they might have been, lines on *Talking Back to the Night* about the best times being over, lovers wanting it all until it's gone, and the singer becoming a mere memory to his soul-mate one day – most of them on 'It Was Happiness' – were the writing on the wall. With decreasing inclination to play Darby to his wife's Joan, and vaguely despising contentment, Steve was reverting to type. Sixties' soul music – never off the record player once upon a time – at full blast would transport him, however temporarily, from the suffocating country quiet. As his calling-card youth ebbed, he said, 'I'm trying to get more rock 'n' roll. I'm casting off the brogues, tweed jackets and wellies – which are really sensible when it's cold and muddy. I'm starting to wear T-shirts and maybe I'll get an earring.'¹³ Now that his North American resurgence had rekindled his drive, was he still 'just another villager'?

'He doesn't tear his hair out to be a star,' brother Mervyn had surmised blithely in 1977, 'and he doesn't want to be a star.'¹⁴ Maybe that was still the case ten years later, but being a star by then was the lesser of two undesirables – the other being an eternity in Turkdean with Nicole.

Especially as *Talking Back to the Night* was yet to match the fiscal heights of *Arc of a Diver*, there was no rest for Steve as – on top of reassessing his lifestyle, wardrobe and art – his return to the stage became ever more crucial. Other than the Rough Hill scratch band bash and a brief appearance with Georgie Fame's band, there hadn't been much more than promises unfulfilled. However, by late spring of 1983 Steve Winwood, with a hand-picked multi-national six-piece group, was ready to hit the road again.

Fresh from the British segment of what was becoming a standing-room-only world tour, Steve was among those persuaded by multiple sclerosis sufferer and ex-Small Face Ronnie Lane to do their bit in a gala concert in aid of Action for Muscular Sclerosis at the Albert Hall in September. He took his place on the semi-circular stage with a cast of fellow stars – among them Ringo, two Rolling Stones, Andy Fairweather-Low and three successive Yardbird guitarists – Clapton, Beck and Jimmy Page. Appreciated for who they were rather than what they did, these musical philanthropists were rewarded with much clapping and cheering, though those doing so weren't so impolite as to leave their seats.

Also appreciated for who they were rather than what they did, the Spencer Davis Group had played the final date of the Stones tour there in 1966. After repeated warnings about rushing the stage, the show had been stopped by Authority as tidal waves of screams flung clutching, hysterical girls towards and onto that same stage as PA columns toppled and pop stars were mauled.

More interesting than behavioural analogies between audiences, what Fleet Street tittle-tattlers in 1983 noted was the presence of both Ringo's wives and Bill Wyman's ex-lover and present girlfriend at the party afterwards at the Hard Rock Café off Hyde Park. These social tangles distracted attention from Steve and Nicole, whose partnership was nearing breaking point. A man suddenly preoccupied with his job is apt to be an inattentive husband. While Nicole wondered whether divorce would mean her losing the house, Steve began spending weeks on end in re-energizing and romantic New York, a city that he found 'extraordinary, not only for the vitality and excellence of its musicians but because there is more playing going on'[15] – more than in Turkdean anyway.

Apart from the inclusion of occasional audience-milking guests such as Julian and Sean Lennon in New York, the format for Steve's tour had been fixed for every stop. He was not well-travelled by rock star standards, and the itinerary did not initially broaden his mind further as it stuck mainly to the States. Nevertheless, the two-and-a-half-hour show gave the people what they wanted – though there were some mild surprises. Coming to terms with his past and present situation, to balance material from Winwood's two latest albums were ambles far down Memory Lane. As well as a 'Low Spark of High-heeled Boys'/'Dear Mr Fantasy' medley, he delved back to the Spencer Davis Group for refashionings of all the big British hits and one unrecorded Davis showstopper – Junior Walker's 'Road Runner' – presumably referring to himself. He resisted giving 'em 'Georgia' as there were enough more recent slow ones already.

Damn him, he actually seemed to be having a high old time up there. Less cold-blooded in a concert setting were the many synthesizers at his and auxiliary keyboard player James Hooker's command. Though Steve looked uncomfortable as a guitar hero cynosure of four spotlights, greater attention was paid to theatre than ever before – mainly because Steve-as-extrovert had rarely been seen since his days in Hamburg clubland. Sometimes at the central microphone, unburdened by any instrument, he'd slip off his jacket to reveal patterned braces, unclip the hand-mike and accommodate within the songs suitable dramatic gestures and facial expressions. Bob Dylan's world tour around this time had also featured such unexpected tangents, as well as the integration of his twenty-year-old lyrical enigmas into the eighties – 1963's acoustic guitar reworked for radar-amplified rock band and female chorus.

From the Rockin' Berries on the chicken-in-a-basket trail to Steve Winwood packing out Madison Square Garden, it seemed that all acts still intact from the sixties had somehow become archetypical units of their own spanning, with differing emphases, every familiar avenue of their professional careers – all the big hits, every change of image, each bandwagon jumped. With repackaging factories in full production by then, it made as much sense to plug recordings thirty years old as well as the most recent output. However, even Steve's youngest ticket holder, for whom 'Keep On Running' antedated conception, could not pretend that this is what it must have been like in the Golden Eagle in 1963.

Epilogue
Autumn '88

Perhaps the worst trauma an artist can suffer is a dream coming true. 'When you first start,' said Steve Winwood, 'there's no pressure except the desire in your heart . . . that you've got something to say and you're damn well going to say it as well as you can.'[1] When you've totally Made It and are as close as anyone to a pain-free existence, maybe there's not much left to say. Your dream became reality and the feeling you had when you were young and struggling somehow becomes the new dream – more far-fetched than Getting Rich And Famous had ever been. From the colour supplement Art of *Sergeant Pepper*, the Beatles' endeavours to get back to their Merseybeat womb, for instance, only hastened their bitter freedom from each other.

One day we change from children into people who can't do the Madison – who walk the dog when *Top of the Pops* is on. Yet once in the forest primaeval, we used to dance with the diddekois. Some of us even aspired to a Hell's Angel wedding with a motorcycle manual for a Bible. In those roaring years, she didn't give a tinker's cuss but today a former night café rocker girl is hitched to some sports car Tony – because all the bikes ran out of petrol. Those wedding bells are breaking up that old gang of mine.

Happily married himself – with a second baby expected in November 1988 – could anyone begrudge Steve Winwood his joy? With no blues getting bluer, his latest album, *Roll With It*, was the product of a satisfied mind, reconciled that 'if you sing songs to people, you're an entertainer whether you like it or not.'[2] He hasn't been called a genius for a long time. What's a genius anyway? Among the many blessed with this dubious title are Einstein, Dali, Ray Charles, Horst Jankowski, Brian Wilson, Jocky Wilson, Ian Dury and Screaming Lord Sutch. 'Genius?'

mused Winwood, 'No, I felt I was pretty good but I wouldn't go that far.'[3]

True to precedent, *Roll With It* – album and title track single – shot to triple platinum Number One in the States. Back in Britain, the 45 nudged the Top Fifty – a significant 30 per cent of sales on compact disc – while the LP was straight in at Number Four before a foreseeable slide downhill. I wondered if his home faithful and the Yanks only bought Steve's records to complete the set like Buffalo Bill annuals.

The problem with *Roll With It* was this: I didn't want to like it. Firstly, Virgin wouldn't send me a pre-release copy. Therefore, with a kind of despairing triumph, it eventually dawned on me that I'd have to buy it new – the same as everyone else. Secondly, to promote this latest venture – and consequent forty-date tour – Winwood allowed interviews by the *Guardian, Daily Express, Radio One, Q, Channel Four* – anyone, it seemed, but me. Months before this re-emergence, I'd weighed each word as I wrote several letters to him requesting his co-operation. Via his lawyer, his U.S. management, Viv Stanshall, his Dad, Muff and, finally, to one of his private addresses, I assured him that I wasn't some scum reporter but an artiste like himself. Yet, as I near the end of the saga, there is still no word from its hero.

Gleefully, I alighted on factual errors by those to whom he had spoken: one writer thought that Winwood had first met Clapton in 1965 – another implied that Dave Mason had played on *Low Spark*. Otherwise nothing appeared to contradict my own more thorough research. As far as I was able, I tried to stop both this nitpicking vigilance and childishly making a rather impolite sign at *Roll With It* advertising hoardings picturing a plainly-dressed Winwood mocking me with that slightly criminal look associated with passport photos.

One afternoon, I saw him on television at the Montreux festival, miming with bemused confidence to his single and lording it over the ghastly cross section of Euro-pop that had preceded him before the Club 18–30 audience. As the boys in Bros – Winwood fans, apparently – jerked about to their latest hit, Steve nattered in the control room to the BBC presenter. Because his old-young looks hadn't been marred by noticeable hair loss or podginess, only his known maturity set him apart from the likes of Bros, Danny Wilson, the Sisters of Mercy, a hard-faced tart whose nose wrinkled as she attacked consonants, and an Italian Donny Osmond with a slop-ballad and dry ice. Nonetheless, the other acts' synchronized frenzy, coy androgeny and weedy ersatz soul – puppets copying other puppets – made *Roll With It* sound like Albert Ayler jamming with the Sex Pistols.

I decided then to suspend my annoyance with Winwood and Virgin, and listen to my *Roll With It* with fresh ears. One track – 'The Morning Side' – he'd said, was about 'going through hard times and coming through the other side:'[4] the darkest hour is just before dawn. 'Hearts of Fire,' composed with Jim Capaldi, after Steve and Gina had attended the premiere of the film of the same name starring Bob Dylan, sounded like the Spencer Davis Group, he reckoned. With a sly reference to 'While You See A Chance,' it seemed to be about chatting up some bird in a bar until the narrator philosophizes that you're nobody until someone loves you. Though not as shy-making as the self-centred soul-baring of John and Yoko or Mrs Simpson of Edward, there is still much declamation of the thrill of courtship, two hearts beating as one. In Winwood's most personal statement to date, he dedicates one song to Gina-as-mother. Another is for Marie-Clair. He sings of his change of life, the light at the end of the tunnel and his new freedom (from Nicole, maybe, snapped at a decidedly non-rural Hollywood shindig in May 1988). He tells of his dreams coming true. He dispenses advice like a curt agony aunt: *quidquid praecipies, esto brevis.*[5] If things get bad, roll with it, baby – about as meaningful as saying 'when life's too much, do the Zoot Bop, boy!'

Without necessarily hearing it, you got the idea, from the lyric sheet, that Steve's new LP was tinged with a playful but middle-aged nostalgia – mellower, cosier than *Back in the High Life*. Maybe *Roll With It* had been the goal back in 1977 when his solo career swayed unsteadily into its stride: 'it's not to draw attention to any problem. That's not what I want to really say on a record . . . music has a soothing and healing effect. The way I put my records together is how I mix my medicine. It's a pick-me-up. I think that if a record has that effect, then I've said what I want to say.'[6] Little Richard said as much in the fifties but his was, many would argue, the wildest rock'n'roll ever recorded.

For all its lyrical ponderancy, most of *Back in the High Life* had still been dance music as much as 'Tutti Frutti' or 'Lucille': its passion born, perhaps, from Steve's domestic limbo. Three years on, he mixed his musical medicine in a professional and personal condition never more relaxed, striking a balance between an enjoyment of beer and eating, and at least cursory nods towards physical exercise – ownership of a stationary bicycle, stairs rather than lifts – and repudiation of marijuana ('there's no way I can get near it now'[7]).

Regarding his stage shows 'like going into the office,'[4] the snail's pace ambience of the recording studio – no spectator sport – had long become a more satisfactory setting for creativity. With a nucleus of Tennessean musicians – few big names this time – Steve lit out from Nashville ('like Warwickshire but 100 degrees in the shade'[4]) for the colder climes of Toronto and Dublin. All the same, 'it came out like another Steve Winwood album because a studio's a studio.'[2]

More 'Otis Blue' than 'Dance to the Music,' *Roll With It* also came out like a sixties soul record with eighties polish and without an executive brief to produce an album's worth of two-minute singles. The wildest Hammond organ in town, unobtrusive guitar obligatos, rhythm section solidarity with mainly human drums – the instrumental backbone was more southern Stax/Volt rather than Michigan Motown. Stressing this further was the presence of the renowned Memphis Horns, a trio whose beefy riffing serviced *Roll With It* as it had on passionate Stax set works like 'Knock on Wood,' 'Sweet Soul Music' and 'Hold On I'm Coming.' More subliminal were structural undercurrents – here, Marvin Gaye grapevine stealth; there, into the seventies with a George McCrae 'Rock Your Baby' fade. 'Put On Your Dancing Shoes' even has a touch of *Saturday Night Fever*. More minute attention to detail is exemplified in the evocation of a world waiting for the sunrise in 'The Morning Side' as the voice drifts in and out of echo amid a Fairlight synthesiser cross between a guiro and a chirping cricket.

Effortlessly, the singing has a more convincing crackle than that of, say, Phil Collins or David Essex. Without the over-emotional histrionics that would tempt others, Steve imposes his vocal magic on the expected grey areas in the libretto – mostly by Will Jennings again. At times, it's none too clear in diction but that's no criticism as – despite lyrical directness – there's little substantial 'message' per se – but whoever thought there would be? The music works sensually rather than intellectually – like the Rolling Stones' claustrophobic *Exile on Main Street*. Like that seeming faux pas, it's possible that the slicker but less immediately attractive *Roll With It* may be fully appreciated only in retrospect.

Nevertheless, Steve Winwood in late 1988 just about shapes up without resting on many laurels. *Roll With It* isn't up to its predecessor's Times Square excitement but, as a holding operation for the new Virgin deal, it'll do for now.

Finally, it struck me that, rather than specific items, the most astonishing trait of Steve's latest effort lay in passages within them – such as the synthesized awakening of the fires of night in 'Don't You Know What the Night Can Do,' and the the ear-catching density of the organ embroidery in 'Hearts of Fire.' As nearly always, Winwood's music was stronger than his songs. An abler composer but less gifted musician, Dave Mason blamed this on Steve's knowing 'too much about music. He can't reconcile himself to working in the format of rock 'n' roll.'[8] With no axe to grind, Joe Cocker – who had a mere Great Voice – had been more positive: 'He's such a tasty musician. He just rolled along. Every take he played (on bass for Joe's version of Dylan's 'Dear Landlord') was different . . . but so good.'[9] Of no less import was an opinion proffered on a March morning in 1969 when Steve had been in a music shop buying another electric organ. 'I played a few things and a cleaning woman said "That sounds nice." She really dug it.'[10]

DISCOGRAPHY 1964–88

This discography contains reissues, cassette tape and compact disc releases only when they differ from the original vinyl records. An asterisk (*) indicates an alternative version to the previous recording. Unless otherwise stated, all recordings are UK releases; all Spencer Davis Group records were released on Fontana, and all Traffic and Steve Winwood solo recordings were released on Island.

The Spencer Davis Rhythm and Blues Quartet

COMPILATION ALBUMS

1972 *Rock Generation Volume Five* – includes 'Dimples' and 'Night Time Is the Right Time' in concert at Birmingham Town Hall in February 1964 (French BYG 529705)
1973 *The History of British Blues* – includes Decca demo of 'Mean Old 'Frisco' (USA Sire SAS-3701)

The Spencer Davis Group

SINGLES

August 1964 'Dimples'*/'Sittin' and Thinkin'' (TF 471)
October 1964 'I Can't Stand It'/'Midnight Train' (TF 499)
February 1965 'Every Little Bit Hurts'/'It Hurts Me So' (TF 530)
May 1965 'Strong Love'/'This Hammer' (TF 571)
November 1965 'Keep On Running'/'High Time Baby' (TF 632)

235

March 1966 'Somebody Help Me'/'Stevie's Blues' (TF 679)
September 1966 'When I Come Home'/'Trampoline' (TF 739)
November 1966 'Gimme Some Lovin' '/'Blues In F' (TF 762)
1966 'Det war in Schöneberg' – 'Mädel ruck-ruck-ruck' (medley)/
'Stevie's Groove' (German Fontana 269 344 TF)
January 1967 'I'm a Man'/'I Can't Get Enough of It' (TF 785)
August 1976 'Gimme Some Lovin' '/'Gimme Some Lovin' '*

EXTENDED PLAY

August 1965 'Every Little Bit Hurts'/'It Hurts Me So'/'I Can't
Stand it'/'Midnight Train' (TE 17450)
November 1966 'She Put the Hurt On Me'/'It's Getting Better'/'I'll
Drown in My Own Tears'/'Goodbye Stevie' (TE 17444)
June 1966 'Sittin' and Thinkin' '/'Dimples'/'Searchin' '/'Jump
Back'
May 1978 'Keep On Running'/'Somebody Help Me'/'Gimme
Some Lovin' '/'I'm a Man' (Island 1EP 10)

ALBUMS

July 1965 *Their First LP* – 'My Babe'/'Dimples'/'Searchin' '/'Every
Little Bit Hurts'/'I'm Blue' (Gong Gong song)/'Sittin' and Think-
in' '/'I Can't Stand It'/'Here Right Now'/'Jump Back'/'It's Gonna
Work Out Fine'/'Midnight Train'/'It Hurts Me So' (TL 5242)
February 1966 *Second Album* – 'Look Away'/'Keep On Running'/
'This Hammer'/'Georgia on My Mind'/'Please Do Something'/
'Let Me Down Easy'/'Strong Love'/'I Washed My Hands in
Muddy Water'/'Since I Met You Baby'/'You Must Believe Me'/
'Hey Darling'/'Watch Your Step' (TL 5295)
September 1966 *Autumn '66* – 'Together Till the End of Time'/
'Take This Hurt off Me'/'Nobody Loves You When You're Down
and Out'/'Midnight Special'/'When a Man Loves a Woman'/
'When I Come Home'/'Mean Woman Blues'/'Dust My Blues'/'On
the Green Light'/'Neighbour Neighbour'/'High Time Baby'/
'Somebody Help Me' (TL 5349)
1969 *The Best of the Spencer Davis Group* – 'I'm a Man'/'Gimme
Some Lovin' '*/'Every Little Bit Hurts'*/'This Hammer'/'Back
into My Life Again'/'Waltz for Lumumba'/'Together Till the End
of Time'/'Keep On Running'/'Trampoline'/'When I Come
Home'/'Strong Love'/'Somebody Help Me'/'She Put the Hurt on
Me'/'Goodbye Stevie'

ography*

COMPILATION ALBUMS

1967 *Here We Go Round the Mulberry Bush* – includes 'Waltz for Caroline' (United Artists SULP 1186)

Traffic

SINGLES

May 1967 'Paper Sun'/'Giving to You' (WIP 6002)
August 1967 'Hole in My Shoe'/'Smiling Phases' (WIP 6017)
November 1967 'Here We Go Round the Mulberry Bush'/ 'Coloured Rain' (WIP 6025)
February 1968 'No Face No Name No Number'/'Roamin' in the Gloamin'' (WIP 6030)
September 1968 'Feelin' Alright'/'Withering Tree' (WIP 6041)
December 1968 'Medicated Goo'/'Shanghai Noodle Factory' (WIP 6050)
October 1974 'Walking in the Wind'/'Walking in the Wind'* (WIP 6207)

ALBUMS

December 1967 *Mr Fantasy* – 'Dealer'/'Utterly Simple'/'Coloured Rain'/'Hope I Never Find Me There'/'Giving to You'*/'Heaven Is in Your Mind'/'Berkshire Poppies'/'House for Everyone'/'No Face No Name No Number'/'Dear Mr Fantasy' (ILP 961/ILPS 9061)
October 1968 *Traffic* – 'You Can All Join In'/'Pearly Queen'/'Don't Be Sad'/'Who Knows What Tomorrow May Bring'/'Feelin' Alright'/'Vagabond Virgin'/'Forty Thousand Headmen'/'Cryin' to Be Heard'/'No Time to Live'/'Means to an End' (ILP 981/ILPS 9081)
May 1969 *Last Exit* – 'Just for You'/'Shanghai Noodle Factory'/ 'Something's Got a Hold on My Toe'/'Withering Tree'/'Medicated Goo'/'Feelin' Good'/'Blind Man' (ILPS 9097)
October 1969 *The Best of Traffic* – 'Paper Sun'/'No Face No Name No Number'/'Coloured Rain'/'Smiling Phases'/'Hole in My Shoe'/'Medicated Goo'/'Forty Thousand Headmen'/'Feelin' Alright'/'Shanghai Noodle Factory'/'Dear Mr Fantasy' (ILPS 9112)

237

November 1970 *Traffic Live '70* (release cancelled)

July 1971 *John Barleycorn Must Die* – 'Glad'/'Freedom Rider'/ 'Empty Pages'/'Stranger to Himself'/'John Barleycorn'/'Every Mother's Son' (ILPS 9116)

September 1971 *Welcome to the Canteen* – 'Medicated Goo'*/'Sad and Deep as You'/'Forty Thousand Headmen'*/'Shouldn't Have Took More Than You Gave'/'Dear Mr Fantasy'*/'Gimme Some Lovin' '* (ILPS 9166)

November 1971 *Low Spark of High-heeled Boys* – 'Hidden Treasure'/ title track/'Light Up or Leave Me Alone'/'Rock and Roll Stew'/ 'Many a Mile to Freedom'/'Rainmaker' (ILPS 9180)

February 1973 *Shoot Out at the Fantasy Factory* – title track/'Roll Right Stones'/'Evening Blue'/'Tragic Magic'/'Uninspired' (ILPS 9224)

October 1973 *On the Road* – 'Glad'*/'Freedom Rider'*/'Tragic Magic'*/'Uninspired'*/'Shoot Out at the Fantasy Factory'*/'Light Up or Leave Me Alone'*/'Low Spark of High-heeled Boys'* (ISLD 2)

September 1974 *When the Eagle Flies* – 'Something New'/'Dream Gerrard'/'Graveyard People'/'Walkin' in the Wind'/'Memories of a Rock 'n' Rolla'/'Love'/title track (ILPS 9273)

COMPILATION ALBUM

1967 *Here We Go Round the Mulberry Bush* – includes 'Utterly Simple' and 'Am I What I Was or Was I What I Am?' (United Artists SULP 1186)

Blind Faith

ALBUMS

September 1967 *Blind Faith* – 'Had to Cry Today'/'Can't Find My Way Home'/'Well . . . All Right'/'Presence of the Lord'/'Sea of Joy'/'Do What You Like' (Polydor 583059)

COMPILATION ALBUM

April 1988 *Crossroads* (Eric Clapton) – includes 'Sleeping in the Ground,' composed by Sid Myers (Polydor ROAD 1)

COMPACT DISC

April 1986 *Blind Faith* includes 'Exchange and Mart' and 'Spending All My Days' (Polydor 825094-2)

Steve Winwood (solo)

SINGLES

July 1977 'Time Is Running Out'/'Penultimate Zone' (12 WIP 6394)
January 1981 'While You See a Chance'/'Vacant Chair' (WIP 6655)
April 1981 'Spanish Dancer'/'Hold On' (WIP 6680)
September 1981 'Night Train'/'Night Train'* (WIP 6710)
January 1982 'There's a River'/'Two Way Stretch' (WIP 6747)
April 1982 'Still in the Game'/'Dust' (WIP 6786)
September 1982 'Valerie'/'Slowdown Sundown' (WIP 6818)
June 1986 'Higher Love'/'And I Go' (IS 288)
August 1986 'Freedom Overspill'/'Spanish Dancer' (IS 294)
September 1987 'Valerie'*/'Talking Back to the Night'/'The Finer Things' (IS 336)
May 1988 'Roll With It'/'The Morning Side' (Virgin VS1085)

ALBUMS

July 1977 *Steve Winwood* – 'Hold On'/'Time Is Running Out'/ 'Midland Maniac'/'Vacant Chair'/'Luck's In'/'Let Me Make Something in Your Life' (ILPS 9494)
December 1980 *Arc of a Diver* – 'While You See a Chance'/title track/ 'Second-hand Woman'/'Slowdown Sundown'/'Spanish Dancer'/ 'Night Train'/'Dust' (ILPS 9576)
September 1982 *Talking Back to the Night* – 'Valerie'/'Big Girls Walk Away'/'And I Go'/title track/'Help Me Angel'/'It Was Happiness'/'Still in the Game'/'There's a River' (ILPS 9777)
July 1986 *Back in the High Life* – 'Higher Love'/'Take It as It Comes'/'Freedom Overspill'/'Back in the High Life Again'/'The Finer Things'/'Wake Me Up on Judgement Day'/'Split Decision'/ 'My Love's Leavin'' (ILPS 9844)
October 1987 *Chronicles* – 'Valerie'*/'Arc of a Diver'/'My Love's Leavin''/'While You See a Chance'*/'Spanish Dancer'/'Talking Back to the Night'*/'Help Me Angel'/'Vacant Chair'/'Wake Me Up on Judgement Day' (SSW1)

June 1988 *Roll With It* – title track/'Holding On'/'The Morning Side'/'Put On Your Dancing Shoes'/'Don't You Know What The Night Can Do'/'Hearts Of Fire'/'One More Morning'/'Shining Song' (Virgin V2532)

The Anglos

SINGLE

1966 'Incense'/'You're Fooling Me' (Fontana TF 589)

John Mayall and Steve Anglo (Steve Winwood)

COMPILATION ALBUM

1967 *Raw Blues* – includes 'Long Night' (Ace of Clubs SCL/ACL 1220)

The Powerhouse

COMPILATION ALBUM

1967 *What's Shakin'* – includes 'Crossroads,' 'Steppin' Out' and 'I Want to Know' (Elektra EUKS 7260)

Stomu Yamash'ta's Go

ALBUMS

June 1976 *Go* – includes 'Winner/Loser,' composed by Steve Winwood (Island ILPS 9387)
1977 *Go Live from Paris* (Island ISLD 10)

During his career, Steve Winwood has appeared as a session musician on many recordings by other artists. Most of these are mentioned in the text.

NOTES

In addition to my own correspondence and interviews, I have used the following sources which I would like to credit:

Prologue: 'Back in the High Life Again'

1. *New Musical Express,* 9 November 1967
2. Trevor Dann
3. *Record Collector,* August 1987
4. *Bob Marley,* Stephen Davis (Granada, 1984)
5. *Daily Mirror,* 26 October 1987
6. *Disc,* 16 April 1966
7. *Goldmine,* September 1981
8. *The Times,* 24 January 1981
9. *The Stage,* 3 December 1987
10. *The Stage,* 19 November 1987
11. BBC Breakfast Television, 29 November 1987

1:   'Jump Back'

1. *Goldmine,* September 1981
2. *The Anglo-Saxon Chronicle* (Ingram Text)
3. *Cassell's History of England,* vol. i (Cassell, 1894)
4. *Dictionary of National Biography*
5. *A History of Warwickshire,* vol. i, ed. W. Page (Constable, 1908)
6. *Stevie Winwood and Friends,* ed. H. Wise (Music Sales Corporation, 1970)
7. *Melody Maker,* 8 January 1966
8. *Singing Together* (BBC Publications, 1953)
9. *Midland Beat,* No. 1, October 1963

10. *Melody Maker*, 9 April 1966
11. *Beat Instrumental*, February 1966
12. *The Times*, 24 January 1981
13. *Stevie Winwood and Friends*
14. *Disc*, 16 April 1966
15. *Melody Maker*, 6 March 1966
16. *New Musical Express*, 8 January 1966
17. Island press release, November 1964
18. E.g. *Disc*, 16 April 1966
19. *Melody Maker*, 23 April 1977
20. *Rolling Stone*, 3 May 1969
21. *In the Groove*, T. Fox (St Martin's Press, 1988)
22. *Midland Beat*, No. 36, December 1966
23. *New Musical Express*, 12 February 1966
24. *Skiffle*, by B. Bird (Robert Hale, 1958)
25. *Rolling Stone*, 27 April 1968
26. *Melody Maker*, 10 April 1967

2: The Birmingham Backbeat

1. US segregationalist handbill
2. *The Times*, 24 January 1981
3. *Midland Beat*, No. 1
4. *Midland Beat*, No. 3, December 1963
5. Pete Frame
6. *Rock Explosion*, H. Bronson (Blandford Press, 1986)
7. *Midland Beat*, No. 8, May 1964
8. *Beat Instrumental*, September 1966
9. *Midland Beat*, No. 23, August 1965
10. *The Stage*, 19 November 1987
11. *Midland Beat*, No. 10, July 1963
12. *Slade*, G. Tremlett (Futura, 1975)

3: 'Night Time Is the Right Time'

1. *Midland Beat*, No. 1
2. *Sunday Times*, 16 January 1966
3. *Melody Maker*, 11 February 1967
4. *New Musical Express*, 12 February 1966
5. *Melody Maker*, 9 April 1966
6. *Birmingham Sunday Mercury*, 28 August 1966
7. Sleeve notes to *Best of the Spencer Davis Group* (Rhino RNLP 117)

8. *Beat Instrumental*, February 1966
9. EMI press release, January 1968
10. *Stevie Winwood and Friends*
11. Disc, 14 November 1964
12. *Melody Maker*, 26 March 1966
13. *Where Did You Go to, My Lovely*, F. Dellar (W. H. Allen, 1983)
14. *Midland Beat*, No. 11, August 1964
15. *Midland Beat*, No. 13, October 1964
16. *Midland Beat*, No. 28, January 1966
17. *Melody Maker*, 20 March 1965
18. *Midland Beat*, No. 7, April 1964
19. Advertisement in *Where to Go in London and Around*, 27 October 1966
20. *Beat Instrumental*, August 1968
21. *In the Groove*
22. *The Island Story* (Channel Four, 3 January 1988)
23. *Bob Marley*
24. *Melody Maker*, 12 June 1965

4: 'Pop Gear'

1. *Sounds of the Sixties* (Radio Two, 8 November 1986)
2. Press release, November 1964
3. *New Musical Express,* 8 January 1966
4. *Radio Luxembourg Record Stars Book No. 5* (Souvenir Press)
5. *Melody Maker*, 17 October 1964
6. *Melody Maker*, 9 April 1966
7. *Melody Maker*, 11 February 1967
8. *Melody Maker*, 1 August 1970
9. *Goldmine*, September 1981
10. Trevor Dann
11. *Disc*, 16 April 1966
12. *Melody Maker*, 17 September 1966
13. *Midland Beat*, No. 29, February 1966
14. *Midland Beat*, No. 15, December 1964
15. Not the Jamaican group of the same name
16. *In the Groove*
17. *Record Song Book*, December 1964
18. *Beat Instrumental*, February 1966
19. *Melody Maker*, 15 October 1966
20. Sleeve notes to *Autumn '66* (Fontana TL 5349)
21. *Melody Maker*, 17 October 1964
22. *Melody Maker*, 12 April 1965

23. *Midland Beat*, No. 29, February 1966
24. *Beat Instrumental*, September 1966. Reg, apparently, offered the ballad 'Cousin Jane', which the Troggs themselves recorded on *Troggolodynamite* (Page One POL 5003)

5: 'Tomorrow Never Comes'

1. *Midland Beat*, No. 1
2. *Trouser Press*, January 1978
3. *Melody Maker*, 12 June 1971
4. *Midland Beat*, No. 7, April 1964
5. *TV Times*, February 1965
6. Track 4, side two of *In Town* (Piccadilly)
7. *Midland Beat*, No. 27, October 1966

6: 'Gonna Mess Up a Good Thing'

1. *Melody Maker*, 26 November 1965
2. *Stevie Winwood and Friends*
3. *New Musical Express* 26 March 1965
4. *Midland Beat*, No. 25, October 1965
5. *Midland Beat*, No. 41, February 1967
6. *Melody Maker*, 15 January 1966
7. *Melody Maker*, 8 January 1966
8. Press release, November 1964
9. *Midland Beat,* No. 32, May 1966
10. *New Musical Express*, 16 April 1966 (Spencer Davis)
11. *Melody Maker*, 26 February 1966
12. Princess Margaret's reported remarks at the Wembley Pool show in aid of spastics in May 1966, starring the Spencer Davis Group, Cliff Richard, the Moody Blues and Pete Murray (*Midland Beat*, No. 32.)
13. *Birmingham Sunday Mercury*, 28 August 1966
14. *Beat Instrumental*, September 1966
15. *Melody Maker*, 17 September 1966
16. *Midland Beat*, No. 31, April 1966
17. *Melody Maker*, 29 October 1966
18. *Melody Maker*, 4 March 1967
19. *Disc*, 14 November 1964
20. *Midland Beat*, No. 26, November 1965
21. *Disc*, 16 April 1966
22. Sleeve notes to *Gorilla* by the Bonzo Dog Doo-Dah Band (Liberty)

23. *Zigzag*, vol. 4, no. 3
24. *Melody Maker*, 11 February 1967
25. *Beat Instrumental*, April 1968
26. *Best of the Spencer Davis Group*
27. *Melody Maker*, 10 June 1967

7:   'Berkshire Poppies'

1. *Melody Maker*, 4 March 1967
2. *Goldmine*, September 1981
3. *In the Groove*
4. *Sunday Times*, 29 December 1963
5. *Melody Maker*, 10 June 1967 and 8 June 1974
6. Trevor Dann
7. *Melody Maker*, 3 January 1981 (Steve Winwood)
8. *Disc*, 25 May 1968
9. *New Musical Express*, 23 March 1968
10. *Record Mirror*, 30 July 1970
11. *Zigzag*, 40, vol 4, no. 3
12. *Rolling Stone*, 27 April 1968
13. *Sounds of the Sixties*
14. *Beat Instrumental*, June 1968
15. *Rolling Stone*, 2 May 1969
16. *Neil's Book of the Dead*, N. Planer and T. Blacker (Pavilion, 1984)
17. *Beat Instrumental*, August 1968
18. *Disc*, 16 December 1967
19. *Stevie Winwood and Friends*
20. *Melody Maker*, 4 January 1969 (Steve Winwood)
21. *Melody Maker*, 10 June 1967
22. *Melody Maker*, 30 November 1967
23. *Trouser Press*, January 1978
24. Also known as 'Waltz for Caroline'
25. *Melody Maker*, 2 November 1967
26. *Melody Maker*, 6 January 1968
27. *Melody Maker*, 28 June 1968
28. *Wycombe Observer*, 31 January 1968
29. *Rolling Stone*, 27 August 1987
30. Also known as 'Roaming in the Gloaming with 40,000 Headmen'
31. *Jackie*, December 1968
32. *Beat Instrumental*, February 1969

8: 'Well . . . All Right'

1. *Melody Maker*, 7 December 1968
2. *Behind the Mask*, (Radio One, 1985)
3. *Beat Instrumental*, September 1966
4. *Goldmine*, September 1981
5. *Rolling Stone*, 15 October 1970
6. *Friendz*, 29 May 1970
7. Q, January 1987
8. *Melody Maker*, 15 February 1969
9. *Midland Beat*, No. 34, July 1966
10. *Melody Maker*, 19 April 1969
11. *Melody Maker*, 12 April 1969
12. *Melody Maker*, 14 May 1969
13. *Melody Maker*, October 1969
14. 21 June 1969
15. *Zigzag*, September 1969
16. *Zigzag*, 40, vol. 4, no. 3
17. To John Pidgeon
18. *Rolling Stone*, 18 May 1970
19. *Beat Instrumental*, September 1969
20. KRLA concert poster
21. Californian fanzine, autumn 1969
22. *Melody Maker*, 14 March 1970
23. Q, January 1988

9: 'On the Road'

1. *Disc*, 25 May 1968
2. *Melody Maker*, 30 July 1970
3. *Stevie Winwood and Friends*
4. *Melody Maker*, 24 August 1974
5. *International Times*, October 1968
6. *Melody Maker*, 3 January 1981
7. *Melody Maker*, 1 August 1970
8. Vivian Stanshall
9. *English Dance and Song*, spring 1970
10. *Rolling Stone*, 3 May 1969
11. *Melody Maker*, 30 July 1977
12. *Rolling Stone*, 15 October 1970
13. *Record Collector*, November 1984 (Jim Capaldi)
14. Hot Wacks 3 (Jim Capaldi)
15. *Melody Maker*, 12 June 1971

16. *Melody Maker*, 1 August 1970
17. *Melody Maker*, 20 June 1970
18. *Melody Maker*, 15 April 1972
19. *Zigzag*, 40, vol. 4, no. 3
20. *The Wit and Wisdom of Rock 'n' Roll*, M. Jakubowski (Unwin, 1983)
21. *Melody Maker* 17 March, 1973
22. *New Musical Express*, 12 January 1966
23. *Goldmine*, September 1981
24. *Behind the Mask*
25. *In the Groove*
26. *Melody Maker*, 23 July 1974
27. *Melody Maker*, 30 July 1977

10: 'Boy in Shadow'

1. *Melody Maker*, 8 November 1966
2. *Melody Maker*, 30 July 1981
3. *Behind the Mask*
4. *Zigzag*, April 1977
5. *Goldmine*, September 1981
6. *The Sun*, 9 May 1983
7. Trevor Dann
8. *Melody Maker*, 3 January 1981
9. Q, November 1987
10. *Midland Beat*, No. 14, November 1964
11. *The Guardian*, 28 June 1977
12. *Melody Maker*, 30 July 1977
13. *The Times*, 24 January 1981
14. Arista press biography, October 1977
15. *Melody Maker*, 28 April 1976
16. Notes to score of H. W. Henze's *The Tedious Way to the Place of Natasha Ungeheur*
17. *Melody Maker*, 24 April 1976
18. *Stevie Winwood and Friends*
19. *Beat Instrumental, April 1968*
20. *Evening Standard*, 10 June 1986
21. *In the Groove*
22. *Daily Mirror*, 19 October 1982

11: 'Without the Little Barleycorn'

1. *Trouser Press*, January 1978

2. *New Musical Express*, 23 March 1968
3. *Sounds*, 16 July 1977
4. 'The wish to be cured is itself a step towards health' (Seneca)
5. *The Musician*, December 1982
6. *Melody Maker*, 14 February 1970
7. *Melody Maker*, 5 August 1967
8. *Melody Maker*, 11 March 1967
9. *Midland Beat*, No. 44, May 1967
10. *Melody Maker*, 12 October 1968
11. *Beat Instrumental*, December 1970
12. *Where Did You Go to, My Lovely*, F. Dellar (W. H. Allen, 1983)

12:   'Still in the Game'

1. *Daily Mail*, September 1986
2. *Record Collector*, December 1987
3. *Melody Maker*, 30 April 1977
4. *Goldmine*, September 1981
5. *Daily Mirror*, 19 October 1982
6. *Melody Maker*, 3 January 1981
7. Trevor Dann
8. *Melody Maker*, 17 March 1973
9. *The Observer*, 22 June 1977
10. *The Guardian*, 28 June 1977
11. *The Times*, 24 January 1981
12. *Making Music*, December 1986
13. *Evening Standard*, 10 April 1986
14. *Melody Maker*, 23 April 1977
15. Trevor Dann.

Epilogue: Autumn '88

1. *Goldmine*, September 1981
2. *The Guardian*, 28 May 1988
3. *Melody Maker*, November 1966
4. Johnny Walker (Radio One), 11 June 1988
5. 'When you moralise keep it short'
6. *Melody Maker*, 30 July 1977
7. Q, July 1988
8. *Zigzag*, 40, vol. 4, no. 3
9. *Rolling Stone*, 11 June 1970
10. *Melody Maker*, 4 January 1969